1988

No More Teacher Traps—
Neither in the Name
of Holmes nor Carnegie

NO MORE
TEACHER TRAPS—

NEITHER IN THE
NAME OF HOLMES
NOR CARNEGIE

Six Letters to the
President of the U.S.A.
on Educational Reform

Julius G. Goldberg
The Ohio State University

VANTAGE PRESS

New York / Washington / Atlanta
Los Angeles / Chicago

This book was written in collaboration with Anelya E. Rugaleva and translated by Vladimir L. Talmy, to whom the author wishes to express his gratitude.

During 1982–84 twenty-five
copyrighted manuscript copies
of this book were sent to
educators associated with
universities, educational commissions,
study groups, and federal agencies.

Published by Vantage Press, Inc.
516 West 34th Street, New York, New York 10001

Manufactured in the United States of America
ISBN: 0-533-06550-X

Library of Congress Catalog Card No.: 85-90009

**To millions of our students and educators
who are in trouble**

Contents

NO MORE TEACHER TRAPS—
NEITHER IN THE NAME OF HOLMES
NOR CARNEGIE

LETTER ONE

INTRODUCTORY

We would have him [21st century man] be a man with a strong sense of himself and his own humanness, with awareness of his thoughts and feelings, with the capacity to feel and express love and joy and to recognize tragedy and feel grief. We would have him be a man who, with a strong and realistic sense of his own worth, is able to relate openly with others, to cooperate effectively with them toward common ends, and to view mankind as one while respecting diversity and difference. We would want him to be a being who, even while very young, somehow senses that he has it within himself to become more than he now is, that he has the capacity for lifelong spiritual and intellectual growth. We would want him to cherish that vision of the man he is capable of becoming and to cherish the development of the same potentiality in others.

—The 1970 White House Conference
on Children

By the year 2000, two out of three Americans could be illiterate.
Read that again, just to be sure you read it correctly.
Because, believe it or not, it's true.
Even today, about one American adult in three can't read adequately. And, each year that goes by, reading skills continue to decline while the standards for literacy keep rising. By the year 2000, Americans will need greater reading skills than ever before, but fewer Americans will have them. If these trends continue unchecked for two decades, U.S. News & World Report *envisions an America with a literacy rate of only 30 percent. Which means that the average person with three grandchildren could find that two of them are considered illiterate.*
Before that America comes to be, you can stop it by joining the fight against illiteracy today. It takes no special qualifications. If you can read, you can tutor or help us in countless other ways. You'll be trained to work in programs right in your own community, sharing the satisfaction of seeing people learning and growing. And you'll know that you're not just helping them but their children and grandchildren, too. Because you're stopping illiteracy before it reaches them . . .
—U.S. News & World Report, 30 September 1985

1

OSU
The Ohio State University
at Marion

February 21, 1984

Ronald Reagan
The President of the United States
The White House Office
1600 Pennsylvania Avenue NW
Washington, D.C. 20500

Mr. President:

Circumstances of the utmost importance have compelled us to address you. Our country does not have—never has had—an educational system. The nation does not know what it is. Teachers and students have been cruelly and unfairly forced into the role of the cause of the American educational tragedy, whereas in fact they are its victims.

No tests, projects, or innovations, which today substitute for an academic process, no parents or politicians are capable of improving what does not exist: the nation's educational system. We are lacking in educated teachers, we are lacking in students capable of studying, we are lacking in lessons capable of teaching the ones and the others. But we will acquire all this; we show how it can be achieved.

At issue is the nation's future. At issue is the development of an educational system having nothing in common with the naive and helpless structure currently claiming to fill that role.

Our educators devote too much time to elaborating on isolated problems. Those problems are posed and solved without any relationship to each other or to the general problems of contemporary mass education. Therefore, even though a solution is found to a particular problem, it does not bring about the desired effect. Meanwhile, the ways of solving the general problems have not yet been worked out, and these problems have not even been formulated.

We witness today the deepening troubles of our education. High schools turn out graduates who are poorly equipped for continuing their education at college level or for functioning in jobs. Universities enroll unprepared students and are unable to train future teachers for elementary and secondary school who would satisfy the desirable standards. This, in turn, results in the progressive weakening of the fresh supply of teachers filling our schools. As a consequence, the level of high school preparation is further declining, along with college and university training. It is not enough to say that our education is caught in a vicious circle: it is spiraling down.

"Education in science and math at elementary levels is still very poor or nonexistent."[1]

Our prospective elementary teachers are required to take 100–150 classroom hours of mathematics in college, while in other countries, our competitors, the requirement is 2,000 hours.

"U.S. elementary and secondary students [are] lagging behind students from other countries in achievement in mathematics."[2]

Our prospective secondary teachers are required to take 500–600 classroom hours of mathematics in college, while in other countries, our competitors, 2,000 hours are required.

"In 1975 . . . secondary-school students attacked 63,000 teachers. . . ."[3]

"Last year 110,000 teachers, 5% of the U.S. total, reported they were attacked by students, an increase of 57% over 1977–78."[4]

"282,000 students are attack victims each month. . . . New York City schools confiscated 2,000 weapons last year."[5]

Our nation has 1.5 million homeless youngsters.[6]

"Some [Los Angeles] area students attend classes only to see friends . . . 'We may even have a worse generation on the way'."[7]

". . . teachers feel unable to do enough that is constructive and rewarding in their classrooms."[4]

"In the past 15 years the number of teachers with 20 years or more experience has dropped by nearly half. Four out of ten claim they plan to quit before retirement."[4]

4

"From 1971 to 1980, the number of math teachers dropped 78% nationwide. Massachusetts universities produced only two graduates last June certified to teach chemistry on the high-school level and only two who could teach physics. Berkeley, the proud flagship of the California system, did not graduate a single one."[8]

". . . colleges do not involve new students in the learning process and keep them involved. 'Only half of those who enter college with the intention of receiving a bachelor's degree actually attain this goal.' "[9]

". . . we're turning out graduates who don't know anything! They've got diplomas but they can't read! They can't write! They can't think!"[10]

Our biology majors, chemistry majors, physics majors, and mathematics majors are required to take 100, 300, 350, and 600 classroom hours of mathematics respectively. Our competitors require of their prospective scientists and mathematicians to take 200, 600, 900, and 3,000 hours respectively.

" 'A Thanksgiving Day Statement' . . . pointed to rising rates of death by suicide and homicide. . . . Student drug and alcohol use also are persisting at distressing rates . . ."[11]

". . . the number of Ph.D.s awarded in the field [mathematics—J.G.] had dropped by more than 50% from 1968 to 1982."[12]

"In 1983, international students received 54% of U.S. engineering doctorates and more than a third of those awarded in mathematics and agriculture."[13]

"Suicides Per 100,000 Persons. Age 15–24. 1950—4.9;
                                            1965—8.1;
                                            1983—11.7 (est.)."[14]

Inadequately educated people—the predominant product of our educational system—are inundating the nation.

Business spends sixty billion dollars a year to upgrade or retrain the engineers supplied by our colleges.

At present, we have seventy engineers and scientists to every 10,000 of the population, while Japan, for example, has 400.

In college we offer future schoolteachers and engineers 2,000 classroom hours, while Russia, for example, gives 4,000 to 6,000.

In our schools we give 720 hours of regular math courses, and only to some pupils, while Russia gives 1,500 hours to all its children. Our schoolchildren—by no means all—get 180 hours of physics and 180 hours of chemistry. Russian children—every last one—get 670 hours of physics and 450 hours of chemistry in school.

Our country is experiencing an acute shortage of engineers in virtually all fields. We have a shortage of 2,500 faculty members in our engineering colleges. In forty-two states we are short of thousands of math and science teachers, and in eighteen states the situation is critical.

In the last ten years there has been a 77 percent drop in the number of college graduates intending to teach secondary-school math and a 66 percent decline in those planning to teach science.

Ignorant in math and science, our children shun math and science courses in college. Those high-school graduates who don't realize the depth of their ignorance and venture to take math and science in college soon also flee from the courses in horror, despite the steadily declining standards of those courses and their requirements. We have dropped to ninth place in the world in labor productivity.

Education is not the private affair of teachers and educational establishments. Let us look back and think calmly: What is the way out? Where lies salvation? To answer these questions is the purpose of our letters.

What is the nature and development of the machinery that will allow us to teach mathematics and science to children from grade 4 and up—on a nationwide scale—through teachers whose preparation is higher than that of math and science majors in our universities? How, in the preparation of elementary and secondary school teachers, do we avoid being guided primarily by the principle of applicability of knowledge in teaching, which inevitably leads to a virtual elimination of mathematics and science in schools?

What teaching methods should instructors employ in order to ensure constant consolidation of students' knowledge, to form sound, basic skills, and to prevent the destruction of knowledge?—crucial factors which determine the success of the nation's entire educational system.

How to carry out, nationwide, a suitable training in schools for students of Olympiad caliber? How to provide education in schools for gifted students that would be comparable with today's training in our universities? What teacher training is needed for such schools?

How to secure dissemination and implementation of effective means and methods of teaching? How to ensure permanent professional growth of teachers—both scholarly and pedagogical? In what ways should college and university departments influence schools? How to make this influence effective and constant? How to safeguard schools and colleges against using illiterate textbooks and self-styled pedagogical ideas and methods? What should be the role of leading scholars in shaping the quality of education in the country?

What can be done to ensure the validity of research in education and educational psychology?

How to guarantee a high standard of preparation for all students entering graduate schools, and a high quality of graduate research?

6

Our university is in a position to begin immediate and simultaneous work along several lines. The ultimate goal is to embrace all the aspects mentioned above and, within several years, to bring education in this country out of the critical situation in which it is today. Cooperation with other scholars and schools would be desirable, but not until we obtain tangible results pertaining not so much to the survey of the existing successful experience in mass education, but rather to the development of ways, means, and methods that could be used in this country.

To illustrate the paramount importance of this work for mass education, consider these two examples.

At the middle of this century it became evident to the whole world that some countries had indeed coped successfully with mass education. But few knew then that school training had been conducted in those countries with textbooks already in existence for over fifty years. If our educators had taken better notice of this fact they probably would not have devoted most of their efforts to the reform of the content of education. Then the American "revolution" in school education would not have led to catastrophe.

Another example. By the turn of the century a philosophy of education reigned in the world which was based on the assumption that students will unfailingly display creativity and initiative while solving great numbers of problems. It was also assumed that the necessary development of thought and the ability of logical reasoning would be promoted through examining model solutions and through independent search and substantiation of solutions. Worldwide teaching practice of over one hundred years disproved the hypothesis. Only a very few (gifted students) could solve problems independently, fathom the logical structure, and thus get the stimulus for the promotion of mental development and cognitive abilities. The majority of students, however, either had to discontinue their math and science courses or stop their education altogether. This was one of the main causes of the appearance, at the beginning of this century, of an international movement for the reform of school education, headed by Felix Klein. For some reason this approach is enthusiastically practiced in schools and colleges of this country today. In its "An Agenda for Action. Recommendations for School Mathematics of the 1980s," the National Council of Teachers of Mathematics listed in first place: "Problem-solving must be the focus of school mathematics in the 1980s." Moreover, the practice has become really destructive for our education, because it is dangerously simplified: model solutions are not always offered, and logical substantiations have long and hopelessly been forgotten.

Teaching mathematics and science is replaced by toying with symbols. What is especially dangerous is that both teachers and students are carried away with the game.

Education in the country is sliding downhill with increasing speed. From year to year departments of mathematics and science are forced to bring down the requirements on students' background and performance. This, in turn, leads to lower theoretical levels of the courses, on the one hand, and to inflated grades, on the other. Some years ago colleges got away with two courses of school mathematics preceding calculus; now they have to offer four or five, and still find them insufficient. Private universities, which have never before experienced such difficulties, now pounce frantically one after another on such remedial courses in order to be able to continue more or less normal work. Math and science departments discard good textbooks and use more primitive ones instead because the students are unable to keep up with the standards. It is now considered a merit of the text if theory is crammed into an appendix and typed in abbreviated form. More and more often the alluring "no prerequisite" is added to course offerings. Less and less becomes the number of college graduates who satisfy the requirements of graduate school.

The history of education has shown that leading universities of a nation represent the only force capable of reviving mass education. Our faculty have the expertise and the necessary experience to head the process of reversing today's decline of our education.

We would like to draw your attention to the fundamental differences between our letters and existing books and articles devoted to present-day American education. Namely, all those works speak only of certain shortcomings of the educational system, and they only list some of the faults that should be overcome and some of the new things to be done. In other words, they do not go beyond wishful thinking, which falls short of resolving the problem of building up a new educational system.

By contrast, in our work we discuss in detail how—by what specific ways, means, and methods—all the undesirable features of the educational system can be removed and all the positive features retained and how everything necessary for its successful functioning can be created. We suggest specific and realistic ways and means of building up a new, viable, workable, and self-reproducing system of education in this country; we justify the need to appoint a Presidential Educational Council with the purpose of developing an educational reform.

We are confident that after studying these letters, the President and his advisers will come to the conclusion that today The Ohio State University is in a position to be affiliated with the Presidential Council.

We consider the creation of the Council to be a matter of high priority. The very existence of such a council would create feelings of hope and gratification in our scientists, politicians, military and business leaders; in our educators and parents; in our children.

Millions of skilled specialists, educated and happy people, will join our society every year when the nation organizes a successful teaching-learning process in its schools and colleges instead of humiliating and destroying our children and their teachers; this will come to pass only when the nation finds the courage and the strength to stem the flood of ignorance currently engulfing our schools and colleges. The sources of human tragedies and breeding grounds of hopelessness, cruelty, and crime will be eliminated. Proud, honest, and happy eyes will sparkle in what are today grim, malevolent, and hateful educational establishments.

An incredible machine of fantastic strength and structure has been created and is successfully defending schools, colleges, and universities filled with cruelty and hopelessness and completely hidden from the eyes of society. Their purpose is to propagate fantastic ideas having nothing in common with a pedagogical process and create an appearance of active and useful activity to conceal our children's involvement in a terrible game which is proudly and falsely called universal education.

The problem of building up an effective educational system is so complex that without the involvement of the highest echelons of legislative and executive authority its resolution within the next decades is impossible.

Sincerely,
Julius G. Goldberg
Associate Professor, Department of Mathematics
Marion Regional Campus
Home address: 157 East Oakland Ave., Columbus, Ohio 43201

Notes

1. "Study Reveals Math, Science Inadequacies," the *Marion Star*, 21 October 1984, p. 3.

2. Charles Cable, "U.S. Students Rank Below Students from Other Countries in International Study," *Focus: The Newsletter of the Mathematical Association of America*, Vol. 4, No. 6 (November-December 1984), p. 1.

3. "High Schools Under Fire," *Time*, 14 November 1977, p. 63.

4. "Help! Teacher Can't Teach!", *Time*, 16 June 1980, p. 59.

5. "Tomorrow," *U.S. News and World Report*, 28 January 1985, p. 18.

6. " 'Runaways', 'Throwaways', 'Bad Kids'—An Army of Drifted Teens," *U.S. News and World Report*, 11 March 1985, p. 53.

7. Steeve L. Hawkins, " 'Rat Pack' Youth: Teenage Rebels in Suburbia," *U.S. News and World Report*, 11 March 1985, p. 54.

8. Ellie McGrath, "The Bold Quest for Quality," *Time*, 10 October 1983, p. 63.

9. Ezra Bowen, "Bringing Colleges Under Fire," *Time*, 29 October 1984, p. 78.

10. Lucia Solorzano, "Think! Now Schools Are Teaching How," *U.S. News and World Report*, 14 January 1985, p. 78.

11. Chris Eversole, "Group Cites Concern for Character in Education," *The Ohio State University on Campus*, 29 November 1984, p. 8.

12. "It Figures," *Focus: The Newsletter of the Mathematical Association of America*, Vol. 5, No. 2 (March-April 1985), p. 1.

13. Lucia Solorzano, "Colleges Turn Abroad For More Students," *U.S. News and World Report*, 11 March 1985, p. 72.

14. Michael Doan with Sarah Peterson, "As 'Cluster Suicides' Take Toll of Teenagers," *U.S. News and World Report*, 12 November 1984, p. 49.

9

10

NEW MEXICO
Pete V. Domenici
Jeff Bingaman

NEW YORK
Alfonse M. D'Amato
Daniel Patrick Moynihan

NORTH CAROLINA
John P. East
Jesse Helms

NORTH DAKOTA
Mark Andrews
Quentin N. Burdick

OHIO
John Glenn
Howard M. Metzenbaum

OKLAHOMA
Don Nickles
David L. Boren

OREGON
Mark O. Hatfield
Bob Packwood

PENNSYLVANIA
John Heinz
Arlen Specter

RHODE ISLAND
John H. Chafee
Claiborne Pell

SOUTH CAROLINA
Strom Thurmond
Ernest F. Hollings

SOUTH DAKOTA
James Abdnor
Larry Pressler

TENNESSEE
Albert Gore, Jr.
Jim Sasser

TEXAS
Phil Gramm
Lloyd Bentsen

UTAH
Jake Garn
Orrin G. Hatch

VERMONT
Robert T. Stafford
Patrick J. Leahy

VIRGINIA
Paul S. Trible, Jr.
John W. Warner

WASHINGTON
Daniel J. Evans
Slade Gorton

WEST VIRGINIA
Robert C. Byrd
John D. "Jay"
Rockefeller IV

WISCONSIN
Bob Kasten
William Proxmire

WYOMING
Alan K. Simpson
Malcolm Wallop

*Roman type signifies senator elected in 1984.

Congressmen of the United States*

ALABAMA
H.L. "Sonny" Callahan
William L. Dickinson
Bill Nichols
Tom Bevill
Ronnie G. Flippo
Ben Erdreich
Richard C. Shelby

ALASKA
AL Don Young

ARIZONA
John McCain
Morris K. Udall
Bob Stump
Eldon Rudd
Jim Kolbe

ARKANSAS
Bill Alexander
Tommy Robinson
John Paul Hammer-
schmidt
Beryl Anthony, Jr.

CALIFORNIA
Douglas H. Bosco
Gene Chappie
Robert T. Matsui
Vic Fazio
Sala Burton
Barbara Boxer
George Miller
Ronald V. Dellums
Fortney H. "Pete" Stark
Don Edwards
Tom Lantos
Ed Zschau
Norman Y. Mineta
Norman D. Shumway
Tony Coelho
Leon E. Panetta

Charles Pashayan, Jr.
Richard H. Lehman
Robert J. Lagomarsino
William M. Thomas
Bobbi Fiedler
Carlos J. Moorhead
Anthony C. Beilenson
Henry A. Waxman
Edward R. Roybal
Howard L. Berman
Mel Levine
Julian C. Dixon
Augustus F. Hawkins
Matthew G. Martinez
Mervyn M. Dymally
Glenn M. Anderson
David Dreier
Esteban Edward Torres
Jerry Lewis
George E. Brown, Jr.
Al McCandless
Robert K. Dornan
William E. Dannemeyer
Robert E. Badham
Bill Lowery
Dan Lungren
Ron Packard
Jim Bates
Duncan L. Hunter

COLORADO
Patricia Schroeder
Timothy E. Wirth
Michael L. Strang
Hank Brown
Ken Kramer
Daniel L. Schaeter

CONNECTICUT
Barbara B. Kennelly
Sam Gejdenson
Bruce A. Morrison

Stewart B. McKinney
John G. Rowland
Nancy L. Johnson

DELAWARE
AL Thomas R. Carper

FLORIDA
Earl Hutto
Don Fuqua
Charles E. Bennett
Bill Chappell, Jr.
Bill McCallum
Buddy MacKay
Sam Gibbons
C.W. Bill Young
Michael Bilirakis
Andy Ireland
Bill Nelson
Tom Lewis
Connie Mack
Daniel A. Mica
E. Clay Shaw, Jr.
Larry Smith
William Lehman
Claude Pepper
Dante B. Fascell

GEORGIA
Lindsay Thomas
Charles Hatcher
Richard Ray
Patrick L. Swindall
Wyche Fowler, Jr.
Newt Gingrich
George W. "Buddy"
Darden
J. Roy Rowland
Ed Jenkins
Doug Barnard, Jr.

HAWAII
Cecil Heftel
Daniel K. Akaka

IDAHO
Larry E. Craig
Richard Stallings

ILLINOIS
Charles A. Hayes
Gus Savage
Marty Russo
George M. O'Brien
William O. Lipinski
Henry J. Hyde
Cardiss Collins
Dan Rostenkowski
Sidney R. Yates
John Edward Porter
Frank Annunzio
Philip M. Crane
Harris W. Fawell
John E. Grotberg
Edward R. Madigan
Lynn Martin
Lane Evans
Robert H. Michel
Terry L. Bruce
Dick Durbin
Melvin Price
Kenneth J. Gray

INDIANA
Peter J. Visclosky
Philip R. Sharp
John Hiler
Dan Coats
Elwood Hillis
Dan Burton
John T. Myers
Frank McCloskey
Lee H. Hamilton
Andrew Jacobs, Jr.

IOWA
Jim Leach
Tom Tauke
Cooper Evans
Neal Smith
Jim Ross Lightfoot
Berkley Bedell

KANSAS
Pat Roberts
Jim Slattery
Jan Meyers
Dan Glickman
Bob Whittaker

KENTUCKY
Carroll Hubbard, Jr.
William H. Natcher
Romano L. Mazzoli
Gene Snyder
Harold Rogers
Larry J. Hopkins
Carl C. "Chris" Perkins

LOUISIANA
Bob Livingston
Lindy (Mrs. Hale) Boggs
W.J. "Billy" Tauzin
Buddy Roemer
Jerry Huckaby
Henson Moore
John B. Breaux
Gillis W. Long

MAINE
John R. McKernan, Jr.
Olympia J. Snowe

MARYLAND
Roy Dyson
Helen Delich Bentley
Barbara A. Mikulski
Marjorie S. Holt
Steny H. Hoyer
Beverly B. Byron
Parren J. Mitchell
Michael D. Barnes

MASSACHUSETTS
Silvio O. Conte
Edward P. Boland
Joseph D. Early
Barney Frank
Chester G. Atkins
Nicholas Mavroules

Edward J. Markey
Thomas P. O'Neill, Jr.
Joe Moakley
Gerry E. Studds
Brian J. Donnelly

MICHIGAN
John Conyers, Jr.
Carl D. Pursell
Howard Wolpe
Mark D. Siljander
Paul B. Henry
Bob Carr
Dale E. Kildee
Bob Traxler
Guy Vander Jagt
Bill Schuette
Robert W. Davis
David E. Bonior
George W. Crockett, Jr.
Dennis M. Hertel
William D. Ford
John D. Dingell
Sander M. Levin
William S. Broomfield

MINNESOTA
Timothy J. Penny
Vin Weber
Bill Frenzel
Bruce F. Vento
Martin Olav Sabo
Gerry Sikorski
Arlan Stangeland
James L. Oberstar

MISSISSIPPI
Jamie L. Whitten
Webb Franklin
G.V. "Sonny"
  Montgomery
Wayne Dowdy
Trent Lott

13

MISSOURI
William Clay
Robert A. Young
Richard A. Gephardt
Ike Skelton
Alan Wheat
E. Thomas Coleman
Gene Taylor
Bill Emerson
Harold L. Volkmer

MONTANA
Pat Williams
Ron Marlenee

NEBRASKA
Douglas K. Bereuter
Hal Daub
Virginia Smith

NEVADA
Harry Reid
Barbara F. Vucanovich

NEW HAMPSHIRE
Robert C. Smith
Judd Gregg

NEW JERSEY
James J. Florio
William J. Hughes
James J. Howard
Christopher H. Smith
Marge Roukema
Bernard J. Dwyer
Matthew J. Rinaldo
Robert A. Roe
Robert G. Torricelli
Peter W. Rodino, Jr.
Dean A. Gallo
Jim Courter
H. James Saxton
Frank J. Guarini

NEW MEXICO
Manuel Lujan, Jr.
Joe Skeen
Bill Richardson

NEW YORK
William Carney
Thomas J. Downey
Robert J. Mrazek
Norman F. Lent
Raymond J. McGrath
Joseph P. Addabbo
Gary L. Ackerman
James H. Scheuer
Thomas J. Manton
Charles E. Schumer
Edolphus Towns
Major R. Owens
Stephen J. Solarz
Guy V. Molinari
Bill Green
Charles B. Rangel
Ted Weiss
Robert Garcia
Mario Biaggi
Joseph D. DioGuardi
Hamilton Fish, Jr.
Benjamin A. Gilman
Samuel S. Stratton
Gerald B.H. Solomon
Sherwood L. Boehlert
David O'B. Martin
George C. Wortley
Matthew F. McHugh
Frank Horton
Fred J. Eckert
Jack F. Kemp
John J. LaFalce
Henry J. Nowak
Stanley N. Lundine

NORTH CAROLINA
Walter B. Jones
Tim Valentine, Jr.
Charles Whitley
William W. Cobey, Jr.
Stephen L. Neal
Howard Coble
Charlie Rose
W.G. "Bill" Hefner
J. Alex McMillan
James T. Broyhill

Bill Hendon

NORTH DAKOTA
AL Byron L. Dorgan

OHIO
Thomas A. Luken
Bill Gradison
Tony P. Hall
Mike Oxley
Delbert L. Latta
Bob McEwen
Michael DeWine
Thomas N. Kindness
Marcy Kaptur
Clarence E. Miller
Dennis E. Eckart
John R. Kasich
Don J. Pease
John F. Seiberling
Chalmers P. Wylie
Ralph Regula
James A. Traficant, Jr.
Douglas Applegate
Edward F. Feighan
Mary Rose Oakar
Louis Stokes

OKLAHOMA
James R. Jones
Mike Synar
Wes Watkins
Dave McCurdy
Mickey Edwards
Glenn English

OREGON
Les AuCoin
Bob Smith
Ron Wyden
James Weaver
Denny Smith

PENNSYLVANIA
Thomas M. Foglietta
William H. Gray III
Robert A. Borski
Joe Kolter

Richard T. Schulze
Gus Yatron
Bob Edgar
Peter H. Kostmayer
Bud Shuster
Joseph M. McDade
Paul E. Kanjorski
John P. Murtha
Lawrence Coughlin
William J. Coyne
Don Ritter
Robert S. Walker
George W. Gekas
Doug Walgren
Bill Goodling
Joseph M. Gaydos
Tom Ridge
Austin J. Murphy
William F. Clinger, Jr.

RHODE ISLAND
Fernand J. St Germain
Claudine Schneider

SOUTH CAROLINA
Thomas F. Hartnett
Floyd Spence
Butler Derrick
Carroll A. Campbell, Jr.
John M. Spratt, Jr.
Robert Tallon

SOUTH DAKOTA
AL Thomas A. Daschle

TENNESSEE
James H. Quillen
John J. Duncan
Marilyn Lloyd
Jim Cooper
Bill Boner
Bart Gordon
Don Sundquist
Ed Jones
Harold E. Ford

TEXAS
Sam B. Hall, Jr.
Charles Wilson

Steve Bartlett
Ralph M. Hall
John Bryant
Joe Barton
Bill Archer
Jack Fields
Jack Brooks
J.J. Pickle
Marvin Leath
Jim Wright
Beau Boulter
Mac Sweeny
E. "Kika" de la Garza
Ronald Coleman
Charles W. Stenholm
Mickey Leland
Larry Combest
Henry B. Gonzalez
Tom Loeffler
Tom DeLay
Albert G. Bustamante
Martin Frost
Michael A. Andrews
Richard Armey
Solomon P. Ortiz

UTAH
James V. Hansen
David S. Monson
Howard C. Nielson

VERMONT
AL James M. Jeffords

VIRGINIA
Herbert H. Bateman
G. William Whitehurst
Thomas J. Bliley, Jr.
Norman Sisisky
Dan Daniel
James R. Olin
D. French Slaughter
Stan Parris
Frederick C. Boucher
Frank R. Wolf

WASHINGTON
John Miller
Al Swift
Don Bonker
Sid Morrison
Thomas S. Foley
Norman D. Dicks
Mike Lowry
Rod Chandler

WEST VIRGINIA
Alan B. Mollohan
Harley O. Staggers, Jr.
Bob Wise
Nick J. Rahall II

WISCONSIN
Les Aspin
Robert W. Kastenmeier
Steve Gunderson
Gerald D. Kleczka
Jim Moody
Thomas E. Petri
David R. Obey
Toby Roth
F. James Sensen-
  brenner,

WYOMING
AL Dick Cheney Jr.

15

LETTER TWO

SOME ASPECTS OF AN EDUCATIONAL REFORM FOR THE UNITED STATES OF AMERICA

Suffrage without schooling produces mobocracy, not democracy—not rule of law, not constitutional government by the people as well as for them.
> —Mortimer J. Adler, *The Paideia Proposal*, Macmillan Publishing Co.: New York, 1982, p. 3.

American schools are in trouble. . . . It is possible that our entire public educational system is nearing collapse.
> —John I. Goodlad, *A Place Called School*, McGraw-Hill Book Co.: New York, 1984, p. 1.

Our educational system has, in many cases, suffered from shocking past neglect, misdirection, and deeply entrenched practices that are difficult to alter. Inertia, as well as often sincere opposition to many needed reforms, must also be overcome. Great change is required.
> —The National Science Board Commission on Precollege Education in Mathematics, Science, and Technology, *Educating Americans for the 21st Century*, Washington, D.C., 1983, p. 6.

2.1. OUR COUNTRY HAS NO EDUCATIONAL SYSTEM. THERE ARE NEITHER PROFESSIONAL TEACHERS NOR STUDENTS. A FREE SOCIETY MUST AND CAN HAVE AN EDUCATIONAL SYSTEM WORTHY OF IT

2.1.1. Whenever the topic turns to the low standards of knowledges* of our teachers and students or to the shortcomings in the work of our schools, colleges, and universities, it is sufficient to remark either that this is due to social causes or that it is an international problem for everyone to feel relieved and try to move away from the topic.

We will try to do differently. We will not be intimidated by the abundance of tragic occurrences in our mass education or their social causes, which are so frequently cited out of context—just because it is fashionable—or out of fear, or to frighten others. We will reveal, as far as possible, all the drawbacks of our so-called educational system and indicate ways of overcoming them.

2.1.2. A free society should and can have an educational system for its children that is worthy of it: effective, humanitarian, free from violence. Our purpose is to do away with, and prevent the recurrence of, all that prevents the establishment of an effective system of genuine mass education in this country. It should be an education offering the joy of cognition and the happiness of creative endeavor for the millions of our children and their teachers. At present, both are helpless, deeply and hopelessly unhappy, and embittered; they vainly try to drown their pain in a mutual, bitter struggle against each other. This struggle is waged to the end, to complete victory and the subordination of one party to the victors, who are usually the students.

2.1.3. To develop an effective system of mass education and find effective ways of maintaining and constantly upgrading it is more difficult than to state facts or criticize teachers and students, both of whom are portrayed as the cause of all the troubles within our educational system. No good can be gained from the naive, half-hearted attempts

*The term "knowledges" is used to indicate knowledge in several discrete fields.

to improve the process which everyone accepts to be an academic process, or the system which is taken for a mass education system, for in actual fact both are nonexistent. We will show why they are nonexistent.

2.1.4. The proof of a system of mass education is not in the number of schools, colleges, and universities, but in mass, positive results.

Schools must turn out people possessing study habits, who are knowledgeable, and who have the skills and capabilities enabling them to operate with the basic concepts, ideas, and methods of the classical and modern sciences. School graduates must possess a level of intellectual, creative, and cognitive abilities sufficient for spiritual growth and for continuing education. They must be capable of seeing and enjoying the beautiful in life, literature, and art, and, to the best of their abilities, of creating it.

If colleges set as their objective the training of specialists in relatively narrow fields of learning, their knowledges must be adequate for professional activity in conditions of continued, uninterrupted improvement. Such improvement should take place under the impact of scientific and technological development and under the guidance of experienced specialists in command of the process and the results of that development, who must also be capable of freely communicating and effectively collaborating with others.

Our schools and colleges fail to meet any one of these minimal requirements. This country has never had a system of mass education or a mass educational process. All we have had are local administrative educational agencies and institutions striving to isolate themselves from each other. In these letters we will show how the educational administrative bodies and schools can be made viable and effective.

2.1.5. It is much easier never to have an educational system or to dismantle an existing one rather than to set up a new one and create opportunities for its development and reproduction. This is not only because it's so much simpler to criticize and destroy than to build and create, but also because there are so many more ways and means of preventing mass education than of creating and preserving it. The tragedy is that every means of preventing the development of an effective teaching-learning process is so pervasive. Just one is sufficient to reduce to naught the heroic efforts of teachers and researchers aimed at creating a viable national educational system. It can even prove sufficient to destroy a well-functioning educational system. Although this is not yet a matter of concern, we will speak of it in detail so as to remove the threat of destroying, in the future, that which will take so much time and effort to build up.

2.1.6. The absence of any exchange of available educational experience among school and college instructors who, moreover, have never been taught or told how to work with their colleagues has been and continues to be a major obstacle to the creation of a national educational system. We are not speaking of lectures, teacher conferences, or books and articles on educational topics. We are speaking of active,

20

practical, and systematic training of teachers in pedagogical skills in the schools where they are working. This training should be pursued in the form of mini-researches, which should include as follows: joint preparation of some lessons by a group of educators; video-taping and/or attendance of these lessons by teachers and administrators; detailed discussion of the course and results of lessons or a series of lessons after they have been conducted; evaluation of the merits and demerits of the lessons; recommendations, suggestions, and advice for the teacher who conducted the lessons aimed at improving them; practical verification of these recommendations and suggestions in the course of subsequent lessons, and if possible, their subsequent verification by other teachers and educational establishments; formulation of the ultimate results of such a teaching-learning process; dissemination of its results within the school where it was organized and conducted; and, if possible, their introduction in the teaching practices of other schools. That is what we mean by mini-researches. They are one of the essential prerequisites of the successful operation of the country's educational system. They will be examined and described in thorough detail in our letters.

2.1.7. The situation of education in our country is much more serious and tragic than many imagine, or pretend to imagine. Instructors in schools and colleges are teaching our children less and less, because all attempts to set up a satisfactory teaching-learning process are almost universally failing. We will try to pinpoint all the reasons for this and outline the ways and means of eliminating them.

To begin with, let us note that for a successful academic process there must be a group of students capable of reacting to the teacher's efforts in such a way as to make the lesson meaningful. The lesson must be meaningful from the point of view of the students' acquisition of knowledge, skills, and habits. A succession of such lessons must be developed to create a course.

If a teacher attempts repeatedly to organize the teaching-learning process but, in response, encounters the total indifference of students who have never been involved in an educational process, or if a class is incapable of appreciating and supporting the teacher's efforts, that teacher will find the ground slipping out from under his feet. There will be no teaching-learning process, and none in the offing. The students will be basically incapable of mastering the course. The academic process is impossible because of the absence of one of its main components—professional, competent students.

The teacher is engulfed by horror and despair, which gradually evolve into apathy and depression, and maintaining only the appearance of work. Today nothing else is possible: empty tests, sample tests, jokes, anecdotes, reciprocal flirting with the class. The process of final disintegration of what is called the educational system continues.

Today this is the rule, the law of our schools and colleges. It is a deep chasm, a national tragedy. This has to be realized; it has to be clearly and vocally stated.

21

2.1.8. Declarations alone are not enough. The time has come to stop seeking refuge behind platitudes, behind new and eternally revised and refurbished programs, curricula, and innovations. The time has come for competent and effective action: we will show how to go about it.

We would like to note from the outset that the country's educational system cannot be created by setting goals for teachers in different subjects for the next few and subsequent years, nor by analyzing college training and retraining of teachers for a nonexistent school system, nor by studying the results of the latest factographic tests, nor by the semblance of supervision of a nonexistent teaching-learning process.

2.1.9. Our children and parents, our esteemed educators should muster their courage and patience. It will take time and effort to overcome the legacy of the fifty or sixty million people whom we now call students, but who are at present incapable of responding to instruction. It will take years of hard work to create a student—and we need tens of millions of them. We also need five million teachers capable of teaching effectively.

Matters are much more tragic and complicated with the fifty or sixty million professional trainees than with those who would train them—although one could argue about this. We are deliberately avoiding such an argument for the time being, but we will get back to it—with an answer.

2.1.10. Words like "tragic" and "difficult" don't even begin to describe the real tragedy, horror, and complexity of the situation the nation finds itself in today. What are we to do with the fifty or sixty million of our children who just sit behind their desks, which is all they are capable of doing? They listen but don't hear; they look but don't see; they read but can't understand. They are incapable of learning—they don't know how because no one has ever taught them how to learn. Where are we to get the fifty or sixty million students with whom our educators could launch the teaching-learning process? On the other hand, who will present us with the five million educators to conduct the academic process with students capable of participating in it? What should we do with the millions of educators currently incapable of conducting an academic process with anyone? There are answers to all these questions. We will set them forth in thorough detail.

2.1.11. If a semblance of a normal academic process is still maintained in some classrooms, that is purely accidental. Where there happens to be several independently working students in the hands of a capable teacher, there is peace and calm. The unknown factor is whether the students possess the level of knowledges, skills, habits, and intellectual, creative, and cognitive abilities they should at the given stage in their education. Who in the whole country can answer this question today? The same question arises in the few schools and colleges enjoying an excellent reputation. Superficial calm and equilibrium are necessary aspects of a scientifically organized academic process, but they are not enough. The absence of apparent evil doesn't necessarily imply the triumph of good. At what level is the teaching and learning process in those few schools and colleges? What is the level of the knowledges, skills, and habits and intellectual, creative, and cognitive abilities of every single student in them? No one knows this, and no one is even trying to measure or evaluate that level. No one—in a great land of modern civilization, in which the spread of ignorance is reaching alarming dimensions, causing depression, cruelty, and crime, as well as the collapse of morality, the economy, and military strength.

2.1.12. Our educational system is a still-born child. It is a corpse which people are attempting to resuscitate with flattery, threats, beatings, lavish entertainment, parades, or billions of dollars. Some of us have realized that the baby is dead and it is useless and dangerous to expect it to come back to life. Others try to convince themselves that it's alive and healthy, that it's not a baby at all but a mature, adult being. As for its shortcomings—who is without them? After all, nothing is perfect.

Indeed, nothing is perfect. It is necessary to set up an educational system in which competent professionals would be in control and bear full responsibility for their professional activities and their results. That is how it has always been and always will be, in all spheres of professional activity. As for our educational system—these are standards it never had, doesn't have, but will have. Have the courage and patience to attentively read through these letters to the end.

2.2 WE NEED AN ALLIANCE OF THE SCHOOL AND THE FAMILY. A PEDAGOGICAL VACUUM

2.2.1. All educational establishments are most directly and actively involved in the social education of our children and teachers. Whether we like it or not is immaterial: this has always been and will always be beyond our wills and desires. Moreover, the family should not even attempt to deny the school this right, for the simple reason that it is more than a right: it is an objective fact. Its absence indicates the absence of an educational institution. Any sincere cries about the inadmissibility of educational institutions actively influencing their students are due to the extremely low quality of educational work in them.

Low teaching standards invariably lead to ignorance and duplicity on the part of the students and foster other consequent negative traits. This process can be halted in only one of two ways: either by removing children from all forms of education, or by eliminating ignorance and duplicity from all educational institutions. The latter must be accompanied by a gradual but continuous drawing together of educational establishments and institutions and the family. This should be a businesslike rapprochement, without competition or confrontation for spheres of influence over the children. It should be based on common objectives, sincerity, and the mutual help of the family and the school in bringing up and educating our children. There is no place for confrontation between these two most important institutions of modern society. At the same time, it is inevitable that in each specific case one of these institutions will have a greater influence over the children at the expense of the other. Again, this is independent of anyone's will and depends on the specific situation.

The atmosphere in the family can destroy or consolidate whatever good the child brings home from school. The same must be borne in mind when we speak of the school's influence on children as opposed to, or in community with, the influence exerted by the family. Nor should any attempts be made to separate the school from the family. This would be unrealistic.

2.2.2. If an educational establishment is not staffed with people who are professional educators capable of both teaching and learning, it ceases to function as a school. The teaching-learning process—the basic source of positively influencing both teachers and students—dies, if it ever existed. This at the same time spells the demise of the people who create, inspire, and carry on the teaching-learning process—the teachers. The first to disappear are the teachers in those subjects which require especially thorough, competent, long-term guidance of student work; that is, math and science teachers. In our letters we will show how to halt and reverse this tragic process.

2.2.3. In spite of all their efforts, no one in the schools has been able to offer any alternative to the teaching-learning and character-building process, which is hardly surprising. Educators with nothing at their disposal to substitute for the teaching-learning process find themselves all alone vis-à-vis their classes. The vacuum in the classroom—that is, the absence of any educational process—is filled in different ways in different schools: sometimes with the total inaction of both teacher and students, more often with an appearance of study activity on both sides. That is all that schools and colleges are capable of today.

2.2.4. Simulated teaching and learning activity, with pedagogical helplessness and the absence of any interest on the part of the students, leads to boredom, which erupts into protests against the school and the teacher. This protest takes a variety of forms, such as permanent irritation, back-talking, disobedience, rage, insults directed at the teacher and at each other, and crime. The qualities with which our schools endow our children are aggravated by the children's total ignorance.

2.2.5. The educational vacuum in colleges is as fiercely defended as in the schools, though by other means. The qualities acquired by students in high school are perfected there and mature together with the disintegration of the teaching-learning and character-building process. To halt this disintegration is one of the purposes of our letters.

2.2.6. The schools are inundated with a steady influx of underqualified teachers. They are governed by underqualified administrators. The educational process is dead. Millions of new students flock to the colleges, but the educational process is dead there, too.

24

How can we breach this vicious circle? Our letters give the answer to this question.

2.3. THE NATION WILL BUILD UP THE NATION'S EDUCATIONAL SYSTEM. EDUCATION IS NOT THE PRIVATE AFFAIR OF TEACHERS AND EDUCATIONAL ESTABLISHMENTS

2.3.1. It will take more than amateurs and dilettantes for the nation to build up a viable educational system; it will require more than closing down some courses and opening others, more than throwing out some curricula and revising others, more than dismissing teachers from some schools and seeing them move with all their shortcomings to others. The latter can be done, but only after the initial school has proved incapable of helping the teacher to become a competent expert, while the other school is able to do this.

How many schools and colleges are good today, not only for their students, but also for the teachers working in them? We have no such schools or colleges, but we will have them. We will speak of the ways and means of creating them and assuring their successful operation.

2.3.2. The process of building up our educational system will develop in two directions: from the bottom up—from the educational institutions to authorities for the scientific supervision of education; then, in a new capacity, from the top to the bottom—from the authorities for the scientific supervision of the country's educational system to the educational establishments. This two-way process will be based not on subjective authority and a bureaucratic machinery, which many continue to hope for to this day. The source of its strength and activity will be the objective authority of a mass teaching, learning, and educating process. We will show in these letters what this means and how it can be achieved in practice.

2.3.3. Comparisons prove nothing. They are only a means of expressing an idea more clearly. The possibility of comparing the teaching process with a performance or concert provided the justification for numerous opponents of universal education to declare teaching an art.

Like every art, the art of teaching has been declared a profoundly personal thing. In our case it has been declared the personal concern of the teacher, however ignorant, inexperienced, naive, or cruel he might be. It is therefore claimed that influencing the teaching process in any way can only have negative results.

A consequence of such exploitation of the nation's pedagogical ignorance by people who are pedagogically ignorant, naive, or hostile to the idea of universal education is the perpetuation of the nation's intellectual and moral devastation and its deliberate degradation.

To be sure, a performance is a joint product of actors and audience; it is sometimes a work of art, sometimes a shoddy piece of rubbish. To

25

be sure, a lesson is a joint product of a teacher and his students—sometimes reminiscent of a work of art, sometimes a shoddy piece of rubbish. To be sure, a concert is a joint product of musicians and their audience—sometimes it is a work of art, sometimes a shoddy piece of rubbish. Yet absolutely nothing follows from this, just as nothing follows logically from any comparison.

The lesson is the basic source for the development of the knowledges, skills, and habits and the intellectual, creative, and cognitive abilities of teachers and students. A special letter is devoted specifically to the theory and practice of conducting a modern lesson.

2.4. THE LESSON AS A PLEASURE, THE LESSON AS A HOLIDAY. ONE OF THE CRITERIA FOR EVALUATING A TEACHER'S WORK SHOULD BE THE TIME A STUDENT DEVOTES TO HOMEWORK

2.4.1. The cause of adolescent inaction—both in and outside the school—lies where we educators refuse to see it: in the quality of the lesson, in the quality of our education. Poorly-trained teachers working in the system of one-year courses give nothing to our children. They are unhappy and sick at heart in the inner realization of their total pedagogical helplessness and the total hopelessness of the situation in which they and their students find themselves. The absence of the professionalism and time needed for a teacher to be able to prepare high-quality lessons; the absence of any assistance for educators, except for a stick to beat the children; the absence of a correct understanding of the teacher's duties and childish notions of their profession; meaningless lessons filled with mediocrity, boredom, and the absence of thought or activity—all this drives teachers and students to a state of mutual loathing, contempt, and despair. Nothing is left for serious lessons or homework, nor for mutual attachment and respect of teachers and students. Instead there is animosity and hatred, the stick and the lock.

We must carefully and gradually reduce for some students and increase for others the time of daily mandatory presence in the school, while at the same time improving the quality of the lesson and the quality of preparation of home assignments by the students. This process of strategic importance, which will initially come as a consequence of improvements in the academic process and mini-researches, will subsequently contribute to the continuous upgrading of their quality. We will speak a lot in these letters about the creation and maintenance of this process.

2.4.2. The nation's educational system will be so structured as to give teachers the opportunity of preparing and giving good, instructive lessons—today, tomorrow, and every day. Each lesson should be a holiday, a pleasure for the teacher and all the students, from the strongest to the weakest. We will show in our letters how to assure that students of all ages do their assignments daily and of their own free will. These assignments, together with the reduction of the time the better students have to spend in school and the prolongation of school hours for the slower ones, will thus become the most effective form of individualization of education. This individualization will be promoted according to the students' capabilities, interests, and inclinations. It will be one of the most effective means for the fullest development of the individual.

2.4.3. The quality of work of the teacher and the school as a whole will in large measure be determined by the amount of time the students sit at home over their home assignments, and on the success of that effort. The students will work voluntarily, without the threat of locks or sticks, but under the direct influence of the quality of work of the teacher who gave the assignment, making sure that it is within the students' power and is capable of arousing their interest. We will show how such a teacher will be created.

The teacher will involve the student in the follow-up work on the assignment in class at the next joyful lesson.

Differentiation of the time teachers and students have to spend in the school will leave much more time for the teachers and administrators to prepare for classes, discuss jointly-prepared lessons, and attend each other's classes to share experience. Only teacher freedom, like student freedom—of course, within the limits of the law—will lead to a creative, happy school. At present, however, the laws which pervade the whole life of students and teachers turn them into slaves and robots and lead to the total degradation of the school—its administrators, educators, and students.

2.4.4. As soon as a pupil leaves school and lands in college he is wisely offered only two or three hours of class a day, rarely more. But the student can't work on his own because no one ever taught him how in school.

Classes at college are of about the same quality as at school, and often worse, especially when the work is farmed out to an army of picturesque, fearless, cheerful TAs (Teaching Assistants). It is, of course, assumed that the student will devote all the time he isn't under the supervision of an instructor to independent work and that he will attend consultations and fire questions at the professors and their assistants; in short, he will undergo a complete change. The obvious assumption is that a miracle will take place during the few months between the end of school and beginning of college. But miracles don't happen. Students stop attending courses, they drop out of colleges, and reach out for the tried and tested ways of escaping from the terrible trap so skillfully set up for them: drugs, alcohol, and violence.

2.5. INVESTMENTS DON'T ALWAYS YIELD RETURNS. ONE CANNOT IMPROVE WHAT DOESN'T EXIST: THE EDUCATIONAL SYSTEM. A NEW EDUCATIONAL SYSTEM WILL BE BUILT, TOGETHER WITH A SYSTEM FOR ITS REPRODUCTION AND SELF-IMPROVEMENT

2.5.1. One cannot invest billions in an enterprise if one has no idea whether it can survive, whether it has skilled personnel, forces, successful experience, or whether it is at least a viable experiment. It is incredibly irresponsible to hope that it's all just a question of time.

Billions of dollars work automatically in fields entrusted to qualified people. These people must have successful experience. They should be capable of making the best use of the money. Our educational system, however, is as far from successful activity as from activity in general. Neither concept can be applied to it. We simply postulate that it exists.

Unfortunately, that isn't enough. Before investing dollars in improving a thing, that thing must be created—like television, nuclear reactors, or computers. In other words, the question is not of improving, perfecting, or developing the educational system, but of creating one—the topic to which these letters are devoted. The question is not of the relative qualities of different programs, but whether there exists any realistic possibility of applying any programs at all to provide an education for fifty or sixty million people who have never been taught anything, with the help of teachers who have never taught anyone successfully. Besides, and more tragically, these teachers haven't the slightest idea of what successful teaching is: not only the transfer of knowledge, skills, and habits, but also the development of intellectual, creative, and cognitive abilities, as well as developing a sense of social responsibility in the students and in themselves.

In other words, any new appropriations can be useful for the educational system only if they get into the hands of people capable of properly organizing, directing, and implementing the teaching-learning process. Then they would indeed contribute to the improvement of the process rather than to the consolidation of forces inimicable to the creation and operation of a system of effective mass education.

When appropriations for education are used inefficiently, without any scientific justification, on fantastic projects, innovations, courses, and programs—which have replaced the teaching-learning process—they can only increase the rate and scope of the disintegration of what we call the educational system.

Increasing the salaries of teachers, managers of school systems, and college faculties, and the creation and expansion of libraries and physics, chemistry, and biology rooms is all very fine, provided one doesn't hope that this by itself is enough to create or appreciably improve the country's educational system, which so far exists only in the imagination of some people.

2.5.2. We lack the key element: the self-improvement of the lesson, the teacher, and the student, and a system for their self-improvement and expanded reproduction. But we will build up—and we will show how—a real-life mechanism, a functioning scientific research structure, and an educational system possessing the means of management and reproduction, as well as a highly-qualified personnel. We are speaking of personnel in control of those means, capable of using them in such a way as to ensure improvement of the educational system at all levels. This activity will self-rejuvenate and self-improve in all its elements and at all times if, for some reason or other, it is hampered or ceases to be effective.

This educational system will be capable of seeing, understanding, and either carefully encouraging or resolutely nipping in the bud any trends in its development. This will involve every student, teacher, and lesson; every class and textbook; every program, course, school, and school system; every college, department, and university.

2.6. EVERYONE TRIES TO TEACH OUR CHILDREN, WHICH IS WHY WE HAVE NO EDUCATION. DIDACTIC KINDNESS. AN EDUCATIONAL SYSTEM WILL BE BUILT

2.6.1. If an airplane is unreliable in flight no airline will take it; if a car has a fault it is recalled; if a drug is harmful it is removed from the shelves. Nothing of the sort happens in the educational system.

Soldiers who can't shoot are put through rigorous training; officers and generals teach their subordinates and keep studying themselves; general practitioners don't do open-heart surgery; a painter doesn't go ballet dancing; a musician doesn't try tightrope walking. Yet everyone rushes in to teach our children, though no one really does, which is hardly surprising.

Students demand that we, their teachers, pay them for their work and studies. Moreover, they require payment in gold, pure gold, and only "in advance." But we keep dodging: we pay less than we could and keep penny-pinching. We either hurriedly shove them counterfeit money or don't pay at all, because we have nothing to offer. If we are incapable of paying our students—whether they are six or thirty-six years old—with sincere, competent work, sincere affection, devotion, and all our strength and efforts, we should not, and have no right to, demand anything from them. When we do make demands, we quite naturally get in response coldness, indifference, acute hatred, contempt, and cru-

29

elty. The children are repaying us for the humiliation to which we subject them by demanding the impossible, by demanding things they never knew and couldn't know, because no one ever gave them anything.

Children have never been taught—neither in kindergarten nor in school—how to read, write, listen, or how to work with a book or with the teacher. It isn't fair to blame the family for all this. It is our duty as teachers. This is our profession: to patiently teach children to read, write, and understand what is written; to understand questions and formulate answers; to defend their own answers and judge the answers of others; and many other things which every child needs and enjoys, and which we will speak of at length and in detail in these letters.

2.6.2 Didactic kindness in an educational establishment—that is, a highly professional and humane teaching-learning process involving surmountable difficulties—is as essential for a child as kindness at home. It gives the child the ability to feel and express love and joy. It is one of the prime movers of the teaching and learning process.

Note that we are speaking not of a kind teacher but of a kind, and probably very difficult, teaching and learning process. We are speaking of either a kind or a cruel lesson, textbook, course, assignment, or question.

2.6.3. Professional impotence and the realization of one's total helplessness in the classroom creates psychological problems in teachers, breeding persecution and inferiority complexes, as well as plain fear. Our teachers are in mortal fear of this group of people whom they have to teach, involve, and imbue with habits of study work. They are overwhelmed by fear of the children whom they must supervise while overseeing their study activity. There is no other way. But this is just what our teachers can't do. They were never taught it in college. Even worse, no one in the school—where they intend to spend the rest of their lives, enjoying happiness and giving joy and happiness to others—even attempts, with didactic kindness, to teach them this. Their professional impotence and rapidly developing depression and apathy breed meaningless lessons which are quickly filled with mischief, unrestrained merriment, and pranks, followed by fights, rowdiness, defiance, and the humiliation of helpless teachers.

2.6.4. Some teachers don't even try to intervene in the desperate tragedy that is turning our children into cruel tyrants. Others reach for the stick. They clobber our beloved children with cold-blooded sadism and then go on to declare in the pages of scholarly journals that corporal punishment improves discipline in school; that it reduces the number of attacks against teachers; that potential juvenile muggers refrain from carrying out their plans in the knowledge that they will be made to pay dearly; that punishment is meted out to boys and girls as a warning to others not to disturb the peace and tranquility of the so-called school and its pitiful, pitiless, and increasingly embittered teachers, united by the common desire to survive and to keep our children in fear and obedience by whatever means. All means are good except for the only right one: a competently conducted, humane, teaching-learning process nurtured by didactic kindness.

2.6.5. The academic process requires an educator's total devotion, all his strength, sincerity, and love of his students. It requires dedication to them, constant upgrading of the knowledges and creative and cognitive abilities of all students, both the good and not-so-good. It certainly requires the continuous, ongoing upgrading of the pedagogical knowledges, skills, and habits of teachers of all ranks and levels.

Children, the teachers, and all those who lay claim to the role of teacher of teachers and manager of teachers—they all have to be taught, with didactic kindness, not for a year or two, but all their lives. And we will show, in thorough detail, how this can be accomplished, as well as who can set up, maintain, and improve a teaching, educating, academic process. It will give knowledge, joy, happiness, and satisfaction with life and society—instead of cruelty, hostility, and crime—to tens of millions of our children and millions of our teachers.

2.6.6. No educational system is capable of preventing all tragedies and evils; it can, however, expand and refine them with tragic success. This is achieved both by the very fact of coldness and indifference to children and the absence of attention, love, and concern for them, and through the inability to establish and continuously maintain a didactically kind academic process. We are speaking of a process offering knowledge and developing the intellectual, creative, and cognitive abilities of every teacher and every student in full accord with their abilities, inclinations, and talents. This process must be conducted in equal measure, lovingly and competently with respect to all children, by all those people who have opted for the noble but very difficult task of teaching and bringing up children.

2.6.7. We should avoid people who try to convince themselves and others that whoever really wants to will acquire knowledge. Such people tend to forget that this is only true in the case of brilliant individuals. Those who don't want to, the opponents of mass education claim, shouldn't be taught, because they can't be forced to study.

We certainly have no intention of forcing anyone to study. But before one can desire something, including knowledge and a sense of self-development, one has to see, feel, and understand it. We can't expect a child to scream with delight at the prospect of being taught subtraction of common fractions. However, instruction in even such an uninteresting subject can and should be so organized for the child to derive satisfaction from it. We will show how this can be done.

2.6.8. Educational activity must be launched on a stupendous scale, involving, as far as possible, all students and teachers in all the nation's educational establishments at once. We will discuss its forms and content at great length and in great detail. We cannot hope for its unconditional effectiveness from the very outset. But in twenty years or so we will have a totally new, effective, self-improving educational system.

The main thing in the whole of this twenty-year undertaking—during which period the whole student body, from primary to graduate school, will be replaced—is not to expect all of the good and positive things for our teachers and students to come of their own accord or through some single, even very useful action:

All we need is to give teachers a good education in pedagogical subjects and in the field of their choice, and all the troubles of our education will vanish.

All we have to do is rid universities of their as yet helpless TAs.

All we have to do is organize a series of lectures and seminars for school and college teachers.

All we have to do is start teaching foreign languages in kindergarten instead of in junior high school.

All we have to do is create a system of specialized schools with higher standards of instruction in, say, physics, chemistry, or mathematics, or in history or foreign languages.

All we have to do for the development of oral and written speech is to regularly have students memorize poems and prose extracts in all grades from K to 12, and in foreign languages as well.

All we have to do is organize collective preparation of lessons by teachers in schools and colleges, with collective attendance and discussion of those lessons.

All we have to do is to ensure that all schools contain all grades—from K to 12.

All we have to do is give administrators of all levels instruction in education and oblige them to attend classes, and ensure the advanced training of every teacher.

All we have to do is train supervisors in all the subjects taught in school and college, either by inviting teachers and college professors with the best instruction skills for this purpose, or by organizing the training of supervisors in the graduate school system and enrolling only people with outstanding teaching records.

All we have to do is have college and university departments sponsor the study and dissemination of the experience of the best teachers of the country, including the use of M.A. papers and Ph.D. dissertations written on this topic.

All we have to do is reduce the size of classes in all schools and colleges.

All we have to do is develop a curriculum guide for elementary and secondary school.

All we have to do is make the academic year longer.

All we have to do is have all schools differentiate—very carefully and tactfully—the number of hours teachers and students must spend each day in school.

All we have to do is raise the salaries of teachers and college professors.

All we have to do is devote not one, but three to five school years to physics, chemistry, biology, geometry, trigonometry, algebra, and calculus, increasing the number of periods devoted to each of these subjects several times over.

All we have to do is set down goals and objectives for each grade.

All we have to do is increase the total undergraduate contact hours from 2,000 to 3,000–4,000.

All we have to do is entrust the teaching of remedial courses in colleges and universities only to qualified educators.

All we have to do is publish beautiful textbooks and study aids for all students and teachers and organize a streamlined, effective system of evaluating the quality of textbooks and the educational effectiveness of all types of study aids.

And, presto, the nation's educational system will become viable and effective, humane and filled with the joy of creative work.

Nothing of the sort will happen.

All this has to be done: give teachers a fine education; rid universities of today's TAs; open very many special schools with enhanced levels of instruction in certain subjects—and at the same time do many other things of which we have spoken and which we will discuss at length later on.

All these transformations in the educational system are stupendous, considered separately or all together; in scale as well as in the difficulty of implementing them in a country where tens of millions of people are illiterate in the very conventional sense of the word; in a country with 16,000 school systems and 18,000 decision-making organizations in the educational field; in a country with millions of helpless students and helpless teachers; in a country where every innovation in education is hailed only because it is new.

2.6.9. Let us get back to the question: What are we to do with all of today's students and teachers?

We have no intention of dealing only with those coming to school for the first time, and then year by year building up the quality of only their education and the level of only their knowledges, skills, and habits and intellectual, creative, and cognitive abilities. We have no intention of waiting—patiently and cruelly—until all schools and colleges throughout the country will thus fill with trained and highly qualified students and teachers.

The general, all-American fight for the future and happiness of our children, for the future of America, must be started now, without waiting another year, another month. It must be conducted in all schools, colleges and universities, in all states and all school systems, and, as far as possible, in all directions at once. It must be carried on continuously, tirelessly, courageously. And we will show in detail how to do this.

We say "as far as possible" because we fully realize how much work and time will be required in this titanic effort on the part of students and their parents, on the part of educators, and on the part of the administrators and managers of the country's so-called educational system to create an effective educational system.

33

2.7. WE WILL CREATE A NEW TYPE OF TEACHER FOR THE NEW EDUCATIONAL SYSTEM

2.7.1. We will be returning repeatedly to the question, "Where do we begin building up a genuine teaching and educating process?" We should start, however, by declaring that it will take many years before we can guarantee that good will triumph over evil.

During the time it will take to renovate the whole student body throughout the nation and for all teachers to get a real education, the reversal of the current downward spiraling motion will take different forms in different schools, colleges, and universities. In some educational establishments a stable academic process may be installed in three or four years, in some it may take five to eight years, in others, all of twenty years. It will all depend on the current makeup and possibilities of the student body and the faculty.

2.7.2. Schools should always strive for a stable student body working with the same teacher for as long as possible. For that they need courses spanning several years. Without many-year courses no changes in teacher training or work with teachers in school will be of any avail. The necessary foundation of a successful academic process is created by the teacher's knowledge of his students and by many years of work with them.

Moreover, and more important, the development of scientific concepts and ideas in the conditions of many-year math and science courses will promote the gradual and natural many-year development of the students' intellectual, creative, and cognitive abilities. This in turn will enable our children to gradually and successfully master more and more complex and abstract concepts, ideas, and methods in the studied sciences. The total catastrophe with the teaching and teachers of mathematics and science in all our schools and many of our colleges is only natural. Without many-year courses, taught and studied in conditions of mini-researches, it is impossible to save the nation from a downhill path.

Mastering a course, correcting mistakes made by teacher and students during the teaching-learning process, and realizing of the whole measure of the responsibility of every student and every teacher during the teaching and learning of a course requires much time: it requires years. Nothing like this can be achieved within a single year. In addition, with courses spanning several years the pace of development of the students' cognitive abilities will enable them to keep abreast of the internal logical progression of the ideas and concepts in the given subject. Therefore, while teaching these subjects the teacher will be able to lead the children on by the force of the knowledges, skills, and habits and intellectual, creative, and cognitive abilities he has fostered in the same students over a period of several years. Only in conditions of many-year courses can he teach children sincerely, benevolently, lovingly, and pa-

34

tiently. He will work without haste or fuss in conditions of ongoing development of the students' abilities, never losing sight of a single one of his students. Such pedagogical passion, unswerving and competent desire, ability and real possibility for the educator to teach all his students is very soon appreciated by them. It is the most powerful, reliable tool of civilized society in the fight against ignorance.

2.7.3. With the help of mini-researches we will teach all teachers the skill of giving children didactic kindness. We will teach them how to organize every lesson in such a way that the students will derive satisfaction from successful work and gradually acquire a feeling of joy and pride in themselves. Such an academic process will take place, from the very first years of schooling until the last, in all classes, in all schools, and in all colleges of the country—and we will show how to organize it.

2.7.4. With the graduation from the school of each class—which is at present mostly made up of illiterate, helpless people antagonistic towards the society—a new class of six-year-olds will enter the school. They will have an entirely different school life in store. Their teachers will receive the attention and care of the best, experienced teachers of the school and the school system. They will prepare for lessons together with other teachers; attend the lessons of other teachers and college and university professors who are good educators in their own right; analyze and discuss the lessons they attend and give themselves.

Given many-year courses, teachers working in collaboration with one another, administrators, supervisors, and college and university professors will inevitably become more qualified. They will be more experienced, self-confident, and confident in their colleagues who helped them or whom they helped.

They will steadfastly, but didactically and kindly, require the students to work to the best of their abilities. They will require initially elementary and simple knowledges and skills, gradually increasing their complexity and difficulty, along with increasing their students' cognitive abilities. They will teach more and more effectively with each passing year. Thus, year after year, we will fill the schools with qualified, viable learning and teaching students and teachers. This process is set forth in thorough detail in our letters.

2.7.5. Something along these lines will occur in all colleges of the country: we will show how. The graduate school will become simultaneously a scientific research institute and an educational establishment that graduates mature researchers. It will get rid of the helpless people which now fill it and are trying to learn something, because in college they were unable to learn anything.

2.7.6. For victory we need not meaningless experiments to study children's behavior in a school cafeteria or the specific features of teaching art in city schools as compared with rural schools. We need years of intense, devoted, selfless effort by students, educators, scientists, politicians, administrators, parents, publishers, and the authors of textbooks and study aids. In these letters we will show how such efforts should be organized.

2.7.7. The training of our elementary teachers is at present so unsatisfactory that they should teach only in primary school, never higher. To be able to teach in upper elementary and secondary school, teachers' training should be higher than what our best universities now give majors in the respective fields.

To be able to supervise an active teaching-learning process a teacher must be capable of easily and quickly adjusting to the conditions of a debate in a class of thirty or forty students. He must be its initiator, supervisor, participant, and referee. In addition, he must professionally and knowledgeably organize and continually supervise the process of systematization, structuralization, enrichment, and consolidation of the students' knowledges, skills, and habits and the development of their intellectual, creative, and cognitive abilities. He must be capable of conducting this work through all stages of education on the basis of the development of the scientific ideas and concepts represented in school curricula. From the point of view of the pedagogically expedient development of these ideas and concepts, he must take part in the discussion of lessons in all classes of the school. A teacher cannot work in a school if he is unable to participate in reciprocal teaching and learning among its teachers. Such reciprocal teaching and learning will be his primary obligation, to himself and the other teachers. We must prepare the teacher—every teacher—for such work, and we will show how this can be done.

At present, with rare exceptions, we have no such teachers, and they will not come as a gift. We will create them—knowledgeable and capable of organizing an active academic process at all stages of education, capable of developing potential abilities and talents—their own, their colleagues', their students'. We will create them—educated, self-confident, calm, qualified, and happy, loving children and loved by them, giving them the joy and happiness of cognition.

The best educators, administrators, and researchers in all educational establishments will lead all the educators of the nation. They will do this in conditions of many-year courses and mini-researches.

Society's unswerving, competent efforts to give knowledge and the maximum level of development of the intellectual, creative, and cognitive abilities of every teacher and every student will be our gradually more and more effective weapon in the fight against ignorance and crime. In these letters we will show, step by step, the content and whole diversity of forms and methods that our society should use to create the Professional Teacher simultaneously with, and by means of, creating the Professional Student. On the other hand, the creation of the Professional

Student will take place not in parallel, but with the help and by means of the creation of the Professional Teacher.

2.7.8. We have said nothing of the victims of the process of creating the new educational system, and with good reason. There should be no victims in this stupendous movement. At least no deliberate victims. If we embark on the road of cruelty in this humane process we may come up with an operable educational system, but it will also be cruel.

2.7.9. We will build up an educational system the structure and work methods of which will include the continuous mutual upgrading of the knowledges, skills, habits, and intellectual, creative, and cognitive abilities of all students, teachers, and administrators. None of millions of students and teachers should be subjected to any pressure, persecution, or anything of that nature. Overly energetic people can resort to this just like that, just to start doing something. They don't realize that the educational system should improve itself continuously by virtue of its inner qualities, features, and possibilities inherent in its very structure, by virtue of its inherent nature.

2.7.10. We would not like to try to determine who is or is not to blame for the fact that we have no educational system. In the present situation no good can be gained from either punishing or thanking anyone: the bundle of mutual recriminations will grow like a snowball, inevitably engulfing—or at least significantly retarding—the process of developing and launching an operable mass educational system.

A comparative analysis of teaching in different schools, colleges, and universities by different teachers is a necessary and natural thing in the process of creating and operating an educational system. But the sole purpose of such a comparative analysis should be to identify those features in the work of schools, colleges, and universities that deserve close attention and comprehensive study, together with an analysis of the sources that generated them. This is necessary so as to be able to tell educational establishments how to get rid of some of those features and acquire others. After a while an even more thorough study of the results caused by changes in the operation of those educational establishments will make it possible to draw definite conclusions regarding the worth or questionability of the advanced hypotheses.

In this difficult process, which must be based on didactic humaneness and didactic kindness with respect to all our teachers and students, we must prevent—we repeat it again and again—any recriminations and punishments. Recriminations and punishments—such as testing teachers, for example—will not only be of no help in building up an effectively operating educational system, but will substitute one question with another, which may, unfortunately, be their true purpose.

2.8. HOW WELL DO STUDENTS COMPREHEND AND ASSIMILATE NEW INFORMATION? ACTIVITY IN CLASS AND ACTIVE ASSIMILATION OF KNOWLEDGE

2.8.1. Virtually all our educational establishments have for one reason or other mercilessly, irresponsibly, and uselessly placed the whole burden of study work on the students' shoulders. This is one of the main reasons for the final disintegration of our educational system.

It is hard to find a teacher who would conclude his presentation of new information by attempting to determine how well his pupils have really grasped the new concepts, operations, and ideas. Even fewer educators in our country bother to achieve what is a fundamental element of pedagogical work aimed at ensuring the students' knowledges, skills, and habits and is one of the manifestations of didactic kindness: the long and complex process of assimilation and consolidation of new knowledge, which must be correctly understood and digested. In these letters we will show how the comprehension, perception, assimilation, and consolidation of knowledge is effected in the academic process.

2.8.2. The process of consolidating knowledge should commence only after the teacher has made sure that the material has been correctly understood and assimilated. Otherwise the consolidation will affect misunderstood or partially understood and wrongly assimilated knowledge—a very widespread process that is hard to reverse. This is to say that the process of verifying the correctness of the students' comprehension and assimilation of new information and the process of consolidating their knowledge are not one and the same thing. The question of distinguishing between these two processes is especially acute in our country because passive forms of instruction prevail in all educational establishments—if any forms remain at all.

2.8.3. Suppose a teacher is explaining new material or giving a lecture, perhaps even repeating the same things several times. Or suppose the students are independently studying new material at the same lesson. In all such cases, the most dangerous thing is for the students from the outset, from the very first minutes of the lesson, to assimilate misunderstood material. If such assimilation is not prevented it gives rise to didactic cruelties. What will happen is the consolidation of mistakes when doing exercises, because they will involve distorted concepts, misunderstood ideas, or wrongly assimilated operations. In such cases ignorance acquires militancy, because a person has acquired, assimilated, consolidated, and systematized erroneous, distorted knowledge, skills, and habits. He angrily, desperately, and aggressively insists that he is right. He defends his point of view stubbornly and with a sense of outrage. He listens distrustfully, looking around helplessly, feeling himself at bay. Then, if he can finally be convinced that he is wrong, his anger and despair either erupt into rage or fizzle out in hopeless depression. He feels that he was taught wrongly, cruelly misled, set on the wrong track, and given harmful information at variance with the truth.

2.8.4. One of the simplest and most essential forms of verifying the correctness of initial comprehension and assimilation of knowledge and skills is a well-thought-out discussion that the teacher conducts with the class, either before or after introducing the new material. Teachers should be universally taught the skills of conducting such discussions: we will show how. We insist on the need for such discussions. Failure to conduct such discussions—especially in the senior grades of high school and in college—out of fear of unintentionally hurting the students' self-esteem or violating the inviolability of the individual has resulted in oblivion of the individual. It has resulted in the school's indifference toward the fate of our children and their development, and toward the level of their knowledges, skills, and habits and intellectual, creative, and cognitive abilities.

It has become an expression of supreme pedagogical tact to listen to the responses of only those students who volunteer them. Virtually all the students are left with erroneously perceived knowledges—without speech, without thoughts, without the clarification, development, and upgrading of knowledge. Some students avoid working in class because they don't understand its importance and necessity. Many fail to take part in the work out of modesty, wrongly imagining that they know everything and not venturing to show off their knowledge. Such students constitute a huge inert mass which gradually grows with the years. Moreover, as time passes their inertia and illusions of knowledge increase together with ignorance. One of the objectives of our letters is to put an end to this process, which is destroying our schools and colleges.

2.8.5. A teacher's influence and strength do not imply shielding children from difficulties. This tendency of our education is indubitable and harmful. We give primitive problems, we offer short, primitive courses so as to do away with them as quickly as possible, and we avoid creative and problem-oriented exercises. Inflation of grades is common, and there are no demanding daily discussions. All this is a consequence of pseudohumanism, which has evolved into cruelty and the alienation of children and teachers from the academic process.

2.8.6. A teacher must be taught—and we will show how—to come to the student's aid so as to prevent his difficulties from expanding into insurmountable barriers, to prevent his errors and misunderstandings from becoming a part of his way of thinking, a trait of his character. We find whole classes that are incapable of distinguishing between comprehension and incomprehension. Students don't understand what understanding means. That is why the idea of clearing up a misunderstood point is beyond them. To them everything is either clear or suspicious. They either believe nothing or instantaneously accept any statement—to such a degree are their minds dulled and their knowledges distorted by deformed education.

2.8.7. Written tests are not enough to check correct understanding or the initial assimilation of knowledges and skills. This can be effectively verified only in a free discussion. Tests, even daily, cannot replace the exchange of ideas, arguments, proofs, debates, or refutations. They cannot replace a discussion which improves initially assimilated knowledge and at the same time fosters the development of a thinking, intelligent person, confident in his knowledges, capable of making himself understood, with a sober logic and bold ideas.

2.8.8. Just as written testing cannot substitute for discussion, so discussion should not have the purpose of substituting for written assignments. Children should be able to concentrate on one question, try to answer it without outside help, and set the answer forth meaningfully in written form. They can then return to the question on their own, independently verify the answers to it, or improve the form in which it is presented. Or they may see that the answers are wrong, reject them, and offer new ones. They should be able to do all this quite independently: alone with themselves, with their knowledges, skills and habits; alone with their creative abilities and level of thinking. They should do this both in class and at home, and we will show how to teach them.

2.8.9. An issue of critical importance to the whole educational system is that of active lessons, of questions and answers, of discussions, arguments, proofs, and refutations at every lesson. The educator is duty bound to conduct active lessons at all stages of understanding, assimilation, consolidation, and improvement of the students' knowledge, at all stages of instruction. He must also demand precise answers to questions from all students, not just the boldest. This is one of the manifestations of didactic humaneness and didactic kindness.

It is the educator's duty to organize the academic process in such a way that questions will not frighten children or set out the good students from the weak. The ideal situation will come after many years, when we learn to gradually accustom children to questions, arguments, discussions, debates, proofs, and refutations and continue this work up to graduation from college. Some teachers already do this in junior classes—but when the study material gets more difficult the teachers gradually abandon active work, some earlier, some later. They are unable to debate a topic which they don't know. This is terrible; it is one of the main reasons for the decay of the school and college. We will show how this can be overcome.

2.8.10. After a class has been passive for many years some energetic teacher, knowledgeable in his subject, may occasionally try to revitalize the pupils, but it's too late. They are tongue-tied, they have forgotten how to take part in discussions, and don't want to, because it's much simpler that way. Besides, there are fewer and fewer teachers eager to combat ignorance and win. The teachers coming out of college are increasingly incapable of debate because of their ignorance. Sometimes a new teacher may do nothing more than copy a few passages from a textbook on the blackboard, while the class looks passively on.

Pedagogical helplessness is another reason why teachers are incapable of leading discussions in class. Some of our children have never participated in a discussion, sitting in silence through all those years in the presence of a silent or entertaining mentor.

2.8.11. Who, on the scale of the country as a whole, can assure the continuity of an active school which can so easily, naturally, and simply be active through the child's first few years in school? Only supervisors, the best teachers, principals, and vice-principals willing to learn and to teach their teachers, are capable of assuring an active lesson, an active school, the blossoming of didactic humaneness and didactic kindness. But this can happen only when they work in the same school for many years, organizing and supervising mini-researches.

All kinds of transfers of teachers and administrators, students jumping from school to school, courses lasting only a year or even six months—all this denies our educators both the practical opportunity of meaningful teaching and responsibility to the children, their parents, and themselves. It kills the academic process. In school everything must be stable to be meaningful.

2.8.12. Teachers must be especially carefully taught that one of the prime obligations of an educator is to encourage and maintain the children's activity, as well as fostering their ability, habit, and need to take part in discussions and to answer questions and ask themselves, their classmates, and their teacher questions.

Principals and vice-principals should continue instructive work with teachers all through their tenure. This work should take a wide variety of forms: attendance of lessons by administrators, mini-researches, seminars for teachers, courses in neighboring universities or colleges, reciprocal attendance of lessons by teachers of the school, and open lessons. The school management should use all this to teach teachers, among other things, the art of preserving child activity all through school.

Active lessons are very difficult for both the teacher and the children. Daily active work in class requires thorough daily preparation for the lessons by both teacher and pupils; we will show how this can be achieved. The decline of the active school legitimizes inaction and secures the right to inaction by teachers, children, administrators, and the whole educational system.

2.8.13. Children who are used to being active in class from the first grade see it as a natural state. They are not unhappy. They are not offended by questions or by their own mistaken answers. It is not a competition among pupils, but joint work with the teacher and with each other. It all depends on the teacher's tact, his love of the children, his

41

devotion to them, his education, his desire to win, and his honesty and sincerity. The same holds true for administrators.

When discussion lessons are held regularly children don't mind when they get in trouble with a question they ask or are asked. When a class is active, this happens all the time. Even a teacher can make mistakes. Mistakes are part of man's nature.

The teacher must encourage students not to be afraid of asking any questions they want, or of answering any question as best they can. He should know when to praise and support a student and when to ask a question the student can surely answer. He must require knowledge of facts, definitions of concepts, the formulation of axiomatic and provable propositions, and the memorization of all that is understandable and understood. Furthermore, he must continuously raise the difficulty of questions and the complexity of problems and problem situations. Thus, students will progress forward and upward, day after day, year after year; didactic humanism and didactic kindness will come to dominate the educational system.

2.8.14. Discussions in class can have different objectives: to introduce new knowledge; to verify the comprehension and assimilation of that knowledge; to consolidate new knowledge; to review old material; to check home assignments. They all differ in content, objectives, and form—but they also have several things in common: They provide a forum for an exchange of ideas between the teacher and the class, between the teacher and every student, and among the students themselves for debate and argument; they tackle obstacles and overcome them by analyzing propositions, proofs, refutations, examples, and counter-examples presented by the teacher and the students; they provide a forum for the free flow of ideas, and for free expression and statements—whether they be comprehensive or fragmented, true or false, precise or vague; they tackle a vareity of questions of the type, "Why do we do this?" "What if we remove this condition?" "What if we add this requirement?"; they study and discuss problem situations; they use newly introduced concepts, ideas, and operations in problem solutions which had previously been unsolvable or only partially solvable; they help to correct wrong answers and clarify imprecise or incomplete answers; they facilitate the structuralization, systematization, and generalization of knowledge.

2.8.15. The purpose, course, and content of a discussion; the age of the pupils; the level of their knowledges, skills, and habits and intellectual, creative, and cognitive abilities; the training and pedagogical skill of the teacher—all these determine its educational value in a specific class, working with specific material, with a specific teacher. This makes it possible for us to teach both pupil and teacher the art of conducting a discussion and to professionally analyze and evaluate its quality and results. We will show how this should be done in a special letter devoted to the lesson.

Here we will indicate but a few features of the discussion and its results: (1) active participation of all pupils; (2) the guiding role of the teacher in tackling and overcoming obstacles; (3) the teacher's knowledge of the class as the basis for distributing questions according to the pupils' ability to answer them; (4) tactful reaction by the teacher to good and bad questions and answers by the pupils—in accordance with the degree of development and level of knowledge of each of them; (5) problem orientation, i.e., the investigation of problem situations in the course of the discussion; (6) high degree of assimilation of knowledge; (7) active development of the pupils' speaking, intellectual, creative, and cognitive abilities.

2.9. A CRUEL EDUCATIONAL SYSTEM CAN DESTROY A FREE SOCIETY

2.9.1. We do not want to say that teacher training in college is a secondary matter, or that the main thing is who teaches the teacher in the course of his independent work in the school, and for how long. But we wish to draw the attention of the educators and lay people holding the reins of educational administration in their hands that it is impossible to say whether a person will develop into a knowledgeable, capable teacher—offering himself and others knowledge and joys of cognition and creativity—before that person has worked as a teacher in school or college and diligently devoted himself to ongoing education there. Schools and colleges are designed to teach not only their students, but their teachers as well, if not more so.

2.9.2. The administration of tests for young teachers prior to employment can be explained—but not justified—only by the absence of pedagogical creativity and collaboration among teachers and administrators in schools and colleges. At best, such tests are misconceived. They display a lack of comprehension of the structure and nature of mass education, a desire to achieve a quick and easy good showing—something our profession cannot and never will produce.

Teachers' knowledge can't be improved by tests. Testing is a humiliating, naive, and cruel experience for both the teachers and the schools that stage punishing examinations of young teachers. Let us rejoice that not all of them are so victimized. Let us rejoice that the teachers entering the testing zone can escape and pass into another, less inhumane, thoughtless, and naive one. There is nothing else to rejoice over. What is revealed here is the whole inhuman cruelty—unprecedented in the modern world—and the total collapse of what is called the educational system of our country—the most humane great power in world history. To give students and teachers nothing, yet impose greater or lesser demands on them—that is the savage law which has destroyed the lives of millions of our children and teachers.

43

Teachers, nonteachers, politicians, and educators punish innocent people instead of teaching them. They resort to the former only because it is so simple, doesn't take much time, and is so available to them. The latter—that is, the teaching of teachers—possesses none of these qualities. They don't even stop to think—or they fail to understand—that they are also punishing themselves. They have set themselves the hopeless task of educating the nation by punishing rather than teaching teachers. They hope that the teacher they rejected will immediately reach out for a book and quickly become knowledgeable. He cannot do this outside the school. Placing hopes in the effective intimidation of prospective teachers with these tests is also futile. These would-be teachers are filled with fear even without such tests. They need knowledge, which we don't give them. We bar from the schools people who may be very talented and love their profession and children, but whom we ourselves have taught nothing or almost nothing. We are placing the country's educational system in an even graver situation than it is today. We must teach teachers—always, everywhere, and everything. This is difficult, very difficult. But there is no other way.

We will show in these letters, in as comprehensive detail as possible, how to organize universal, ongoing training and reciprocal training of teachers in the course of their pedagogical work in school and college.

2.9.3. An educational system based on cruelty, coercion, and unjustified, unprofessional demands cannot survive. The appearance of education put together by cruel methods in some states will prove short-lived. Violence and terror are inimical to any educational system. They are not the means of building up an educational system but a consequence of its disintegration. The testing of teachers—monstrous in its cruelty, irrationality, and pedagogical and political blindness—is simply a natural and logical consequence—even more monstrous in scope and tragic in consequences—of the universal testing of our children instead of teaching them.

We shall never tire of repeating the following: A system of education, however perfect and humane, is not omnipotent. By itself, relying only on its inherent forces, it is incapable of overcoming all the shortcomings of society, however free, open, and democratic—or despotic—that society might be. However, an educational system which is mass only in form and deceptive, fallacious, and cruel in content, can by itself, with only its inherent forces, corrupt and destroy any society, turn it into a camp of criminals, and breed and rear a mob of multimillions.

2.10. MINI-RESEARCHES

2.10.1. Organization of the process of initial reception of new information by the students;

Verification of the effectiveness of the process;

Acquisition and upgrading of the students' knowledges, skills, and habits;

Prevention of their deterioration;

Development of the students' intellectual, creative, and cognitive abilities with the help of ongoing debates, by increasing the difficulty and complexity of the study material, its problem orientation, student independence, and the volume of material studied and assimilated in unit time;

Establishing the connections between newly and previously studied and assimilated questions and topics;

Structuralization and systematization of previously acquired knowledge from new, more general and fruitful positions;

Preliminary familiarization of students with the fundamental ideas, concepts, and structures of science they will encounter in future;

Implementation of all of the foregoing in the unity of the lesson and extramural studies.

The above is far from the complete scheme of a teaching and learning academic process that is didactically humane and kind with respect to teachers and students. Such a process can be realized with the help of mini-researches, i.e., researches where the topic of each research is one lesson. We will sometimes call this lesson a mini-research as well.

Mini-researches naturally expand into conferences organized within one school or encompassing several schools, several schools and colleges, several colleges, several school systems, and several cities, states, or nations.

To avoid any possible misunderstanding of the content and purpose of this discourse, we would like to state clearly and at once the following: All these mini- and maxi-researches and conferences, the whole process of training teachers in colleges of education and subsequently in the educational establishments where they are working, all the types of supplementary classes with the students, all the forms of advanced teacher training—all this is for the lesson—for the continuous development and upgrading of the knowledges, skills, and habits and intellectual, creative, and cognitive abilities of teachers and students—mainly and necessarily during the lesson, coupled with important extramural work subordinated to the lesson.

Only a very few children endowed by God with tremendous talent will pass through the lessons, perhaps not even noticing them. They may even pass not through but by them. This, however, in no way detracts from the power and glory of the lesson, just as it does not detract from the unity and connection of the lesson with extramural activities. We are devoting a special letter to the lesson.

2.10.2. We can talk about education or write dissertations, papers, and books without end for the next 200 years in our nation's life. But nothing, absolutely nothing, will change in the practical activity of our teachers, schools, colleges, and universities until we start to conduct universal and continuous on-the-job instruction for all our country's educators in the organization and supervision of the academic process.

45

No college of education in the whole world can hope to cope with this task, nor should they try.

The training of educators requires years of mini-researches involving the continuous collective preparation of lessons by the teachers with the participation of administrators of educational establishments and school systems. This work must be accompanied by collective attendance and/or video-taping of as many as possible of the lessons conducted by the trainee teachers. The taped lessons must then be thoroughly discussed and analyzed by the educators with the purpose of seeking ways of improving them. This means discussion of the merits and demerits of every attended and/or taped lesson; collective preparation and attendance of the next lesson; discussion of all the positive results the teacher was able to achieve at that lesson as compared with the preceding one, as well as all the shortcomings he was unable to overcome. This also means discussion of all new elements—both positive and negative—not revealed at the preceding lesson, but which are very important for the academic process.

Thus, day after day, month after month, and year after year, such work will be conducted with every educator in turn and with several simultaneously. It may or may not involve publication of papers in journals, it may or may not involve conferences and meetings at the school, city, state, or national level. This work will be accompanied by the gradual but inevitable transformation of every department, school, college, university, school system, and state educational system into research laboratories and institutes.

Even more gradually, but as inevitably, mini-researches will help transform the country's educational system into a gigantic scientific research institute. The people working, studying, and thereby conducting ongoing research in the educational field will be school teachers, college professors, administrators of all levels, the authors of textbooks and study aids, supervisors, students of teacher education colleges, and TAs.

2.10.3. Every lesson is a study, regardless of whether it is being prepared by the teacher alone or with somebody's help, whether it is attended or viewed on the tape by other educators, or whether they discuss it after it is held.

Every sequence of lessons is also a full-blooded educational study. Both a lesson and a sequence of lessons contain a scientific hypothesis: What will the students get from the lesson? What knowledges, skills, and habits will they acquire? Before conducting a lesson or sequence of lessons the teacher must consider what means to use to encourage active acquisition of knowledge by the students. He should plan how to review theoretical questions and reactivate previously acquired skills and habits needed for the students to assimilate the content of the forthcoming lesson or lessons. The teacher must make sure what study material should be reviewed, systematized, and structuralized so as to organize the previously and newly acquired knowledges, skills, and habits. He must also study the ways and means of establishing the unity of all the students'

46

knowledges, skills, and habits with the knowledges, skills, and habits they are still to acquire in the course of the coming lessons. A scientific hypothesis includes the ways and means of stimulating and consistently developing the students' intellectual, creative, and cognitive abilities during the lessons, the connections between home assignments and class work, and many, many other things (which we will discuss in great detail in the letter specially devoted to the lesson).

2.10.4. The teacher must enunciate his scientific hypothesis, which should be discussed by all the members of the research team working with him. They must put forward their own propositions and endorse or reject the propositions and hypotheses set forth by the author of the lesson. The discussion can be protracted, covering several sessions. For that reason preparations for lessons should start long before they are to be held; we will show how.

2.10.5. The members of the study group can put forward any number of propositions in preparation for the mini-research, but the final word, as well as full responsibility for the lessons, rests with the teacher conducting them. No one can bring pressure to bear on the teacher in any form whatsoever, still less in administrative form. This should be one of the manifestations of academic freedom.

No one, under any circumstances, can interfere with the teacher's work during a lesson—that is the second manifestation of academic freedom.

Every lesson, preferably video-taped, must be followed by a thorough discussion: a small, unpretentious, scientific conference. The opening and concluding remarks at every such discussion are given by the teacher who conducted the lesson—that is the third manifestation of academic freedom.

The time between the teacher's opening and concluding remarks is filled with analyses and evaluations of the lesson and suggestions for the future contributed by all members of the working party—anywhere from one to ten people, rarely more. Especially welcome are contributions from students who may be taking teacher training at the school, new teachers, and recognized authorities—if there are any.

The discussion of lessons should take the form of a free debate. All participants are equal, irrespective of their job position. How lessons should be discussed before and after they are held will be set forth in great detail in these letters.

2.10.6. But how, and from where, will mini-researches acquire the ways and means of building up a successful teaching and learning process? What can be done if no one among the department faculty can answer a question that has arisen in the course of the academic process? What should be done if no one among the faculty is capable of developing a sequence of viable lessons, organizing regular revision of previously taught material, and so on? Of strategic importance for the whole educational system of the nation, the states, the school systems, and individual schools and colleges are the following (1) to universally locate the best teachers who are already today capable of giving the students good lessons and high standards of knowledges, skills, habits, and intellectual, creative, and cognitive abilities. They can do this thanks not only to innate pedagogical talents, but also due to effective work in spite of our morbid, so-called educational system; (2) to thoroughly study and scientifically summarize the experience of such teachers with the help of supervisors in all subjects, school and college administrators having a pedagogical education, and Ph.D. dissertations and master's papers; (3) to universally disseminate the studied and scientifically substantiated experience of such teachers with the help of mini-researches in the schools and colleges where they work, as well as with the help of articles, booklets, videotapes, lectures, papers, seminars, and other means of mass information, with the purpose of making mini-researches universally effective and capable of serving as the basic means of building up and operating a national educational system.

2.10.7. The national educational research institute and state educational research institutes should be staffed with professional education supervisors. Together with colleges and universities, the research institutes will organize seminars, conferences, workshops, and other activities for the faculties of the educational establishments—i.e., research institutes—subordinate to them.

School systems, schools, colleges, and universities, while operating as independent research institutes, need not have a single more staff employee than they have today. Some of the current supervisors of school systems can be retained as directors of the research institutes of those systems. If we reduce the number of school systems drastically we can save billions of dollars. Over the last half-century the number of school systems has declined from 100,000 to 16,000 but even that is much too much. With the help of large research institutes spanning several counties and several cities we can build a modern, efficient educational system.

In schools, the director of the research institute is the principal; in colleges it is the president or dean; in universities it is the university president.

2.10.8. There is also another way.

For every subject taught in the country's schools and colleges, a Head Department should be set up in one of the universities. It must be recognized as the best department in the respective field in the country. It will supervise the teaching of courses in this field in all fifty states. Of course, the staff of this department will have to be considerably larger in comparison with departments whose duties do not go beyond the university. Such a department could move from one university to another in connection with changes in its staff and the quality of its educational research, as well as in connection with changes in the quality of educational researches and the educational process organized by it in other educational establishments. These departments would be supervised by the university administration in the same way as all the other departments. The heads of such departments would have titles such as, for example, Chairman of the U.S. Department of Math Education, Chairman of the U.S. Department of Foreign Language Education, et cetera.

Similar duties would be assigned to many other college and university departments across the country. They would supervise the educational process in all the school systems and colleges of their respective states, each department in its field. These departments would be headed, for example, by the Chairman of the Ohio State Department of Math Education, Chairman of the Ohio State Department of Foreign Language Education, and so on. They would be accountable for their work to the university administration and the national head department in the respective spheres of learning and be staffed with extra faculty and personnel.

2.10.9. If we merge groups of neighboring small colleges and universities that are for some reason in jeopardy of closing down, we will obtain the same tremendous advantages as from the merger of school systems. This could produce a huge saving of money that is currently being squandered by the nation for administrative and technical personnel. We envisage a sharp upsurge in educational and scientific work throughout the country generated by the high concentration of pedagogical wisdom and scientific schools, and the free and natural exchange of views and work experience among them.

2.11. CONTRADICTION TO THE THEORIES OF J. PIAGET. ON THE RELATIONS BETWEEN TEACHER AND STUDENTS

2.11.1. In contradiction to the view of J. Piaget, on the basis of international teaching experience spanning the last fifty years, we can justifiably claim that the sequence and the nature of the stages in the student's cognitive development can be altered (1) by the nature of teaching strategies, as well as (2) by the content of the studied theoretical material, and (3) by the nature and difficulty of the problems solved by the students.

Problems and problem situations involving levels of difficulty beyond the current cognitive and creative capabilities of the class should not be kept waiting until the students rise up to them. Students should not be kept at a level of exercises and theoretical material they can handle freely and easily. This slows down the development of their cognitive and creative abilities.

The difference between learning with a teacher and self-learning is, among other things, that a knowledgeable and trainable teacher is capable of holding the class in a state of constant but humane strain and actively supervising the energetic development of the students' cognitive and creative abilities.

In these letters we will show how such supervision can be effected in the course of a mass academic process.

2.11.2. A class should not feel impatience or displeasure at the lesson. They generate apathy, indifference to lessons, and boredom. They also generate rudeness, disobedience, and misbehavior.

Such things are an indication that the class is bored and impatient. The class can get out of touch with the teacher and the studied material not only when the material is worked over for too long with no apparent progress. The class may also rebel if the following situations apply: the material is too difficult or if there is too much of it; the class is unprepared and the teacher has failed to spot this; the class is entrenched in its passive role in the teaching-learning process; there is a combination of all these reasons, which is common enough in the nation's current pedagogical tragedy.

2.11.3. Alienation of the class from the subject and the teacher is equally dangerous for the teacher and the students. Mini-researches must include the following among their prime objectives: (1) analysis of the teacher's relations with the class; (2) analysis of the students' relations with the lesson, the teaching-learning process, and the textbook; and (3) determination of the ways and means of preserving and consolidating all of the best there is in the teacher's work with the students and removing all that prevents the organization, consolidation, and preservation of an efficient teaching and learning academic process. (We will discuss this at length in our letters.)

2.11.4. The solution of problems and investigation of problem situations at higher levels of difficulty by means of an active lesson and active involvement of the students is a formidable weapon in our fight against ignorance and student disrespect for the school and the teacher. However, if the class has grown used to an easy life, if it is accustomed to but a passive presence during the lesson, if before it encountered a qualified teacher it received only assignments requiring technical operations without their logical substantiation and without serious, active learning of theoretical questions—don't be in too great a hurry to set the children right, and arm yourself with patience. Be extremely careful with creative assignments, especially the more difficult ones. Because of its ignorance the class will simply laugh at you and your assignments.

If fate has thrown you in with such a class, don't pressure the students too hard. Introduce them to your subject persistently and consistently, but cautiously, without getting into a fight. For a while you should try to avoid sudden changes of any kind in the fulfillment of home assignments, in the students' ability to work in class, listen to the teacher, hear the teacher, understand questions, ask questions, distinguish the true statement from the absurd, follow the presentation of material by the teacher or other students, and so on and so forth.

The first thing to do is to make every one of your pupils a Professional Student (later on we will speak of this at length in the letter devoted to the student). Gradually, but with growing frequency, give the class harder and harder exercises. Help the students cope with them in class by asking questions, the answers to which lead to the solution, or divide a creative assignment into parts, each of which can be tackled by the students without any questions on your part. Gradually but inexorably increase the difficulty of assignments and the activity of the students.

Do this in class. Do this also with creative home assignments. That is, in class set forth the plan for carrying them out with the help of well-considered questions. Initially, let the class write them down—the questions, that is, but not the answers to them. At the next lesson analyze the home assignment thoroughly. Repeat this strategy from one lesson to another.

The class will gradually develop confidence in its abilities. One by one the children will join you in your efforts to give them knowledge and the abilities to think, cognize, and create. Gradually and consistently continue to increase the students' degree of independence by asking more and more general questions and requiring more and more detailed and substantiated answers. This way in a year or two you can turn thirty or forty victims of the national calamity, known as the educational system, into thirty or forty professional working students. Don't pass them on to anyone else. Lead them yourself through their next year, and the next, and next, until they finish school.

Success will come only if we establish many-year courses in place of the present one-year ones. If the educational system seriously intends to teach children instead of misleading and destroying the nation, the process of setting up many-year courses is inevitable.

2.11.5. The current upper elementary and middle school grades cannot be left as they are today. They are one of the breeders of all the epidemics in which our educational system abounds. They should not be left in the hands of elementary teachers incapable of teaching them because of their ignorance. They must be placed in the hands of educators capable of providing many years of qualified education, who are specialists in narrow fields of learning: mathematics, physics, chemistry, biology, history, literature. We will return again and again to the idea of giving courses in math and science lasting not one year but three to five or more years each, with two or three lessons a week for each subject, in schools each of which has all the grades from K to 12. We will thoroughly justify the replacement of one-year math and science courses with many-year courses, which will result in a radical improvement of student-teacher relations and academic efficiency in school and in college.

2.11.6. Another important contribution to the creation of the new humane school and the new college will be the establishment of a grade or two preceding kindergarten for children who need this. Such classes are essential for children for whom English is not their native tongue, children from destroyed families, and, in general, for children from families which cannot prepare them for kindergarten. Instead of the desperate 12-year war between such children and their teachers that we have today, we will be able to establish a humane and effective academic process in all grades, because all the children will have the preparation needed for them to start the first grade.

2.11.7. Today's lazy, idle, cruel, futile, and ignorant school has become hateful to our children and teachers. This school is at present either a vacuum, which corrupts our children and teachers, or it is filled with ignorant teaching, which corrupts them even more, arousing mutual hostility in them. As we have just said, it should be filled with many-year courses in math and science, accessible to both teachers and students. Each of these courses will be conducted by one teacher over a period of three to five years or more, in collaboration with the students, who will be prompted by the duration, accessibility, and high exactingness of those courses. We will show—and this is one of the basic tasks of our letters—how to create both a professional teacher capable of developing a many-year effective and humane teaching-learning process, and students capable of successfully participating in it. We will also show how to use those many-year courses to naturally blend lessons with home assignments, which will keep our children busy working on those assignments rather than spending time in the company of drug addicts and criminals.

2.11.8. No affinity between teachers and students is possible as long as teachers are placed in difficult conditions. All the nation's efforts should be directed at the most important thing for the teacher: the universal functioning, wherever possible, only of schools spanning all grades from K to 12; ongoing training and mutual training in such schools of teachers of different qualifications and administrators with the help of mini-researches and special courses in colleges and universities; reduction of the teacher's working week; reduction of the number of every teacher's daily lessons; raising teacher salaries; increasing financial assistance for future math and science teachers; retraining of today's elementary teachers, as well as former engineers and military personnel to teach math and science; offering part-time positions to engineers and military people; especially higher salaries for former math and science teachers if they return to school, including retired teachers who can and want to teach.

2.11.9. Elementary teachers should only teach in pre-kindergarten classes; that is, in K–1 and K–2, and in kindergarten—i.e., K–3, and in grades 1 to 3. Giving them children higher than the third grade is cruel with respect to both teachers and students. They cannot give the students knowledge, and in the senior grades this turns into ineradicable hostility between teachers and students.

As half a century of experience in mass education shows, grades 4 to 12 should gradually be filled with teachers whose training in the subjects they teach is superior to the training of majors in the respective fields.

2.11.10. Let us consider in greater detail schools spanning all grades from K to 12.

Every school should have both teachers and students of all ages. The concentration of classes in such a school is not horizontal but vertical, from K to 12.

Only in such schools is it possible to require one teacher to teach the same group of students for many years. The question of discipline among the senior students is much easier to solve, because there are much fewer of them than in today's high schools; moreover, the teachers of the junior grades remain in touch with their former students, keep track of their achievements and take pride in them, and the very presence of small children makes the school more childlike, tender, less official, and more manageable.

In such a school, the teachers of the junior grades gradually get to see, with the help of mini-researches, what they should prepare their pupils for, and what demands they will be facing in the senior grades. In the course of mini-researches the teachers of the senior grades will learn to be more careful in building up the difficulty of theoretical material and problems; they will learn to be more thorough in the teaching of each student and to pay more attention to home assignments, and many other things. Furthermore, they will get to understand how and at what level their future pupils in the junior grades are being trained and can be trained. They will be able to actively influence that level and the whole academic process of the junior classes. Such knowledgeability of the teachers of both junior and senior classes is an essential prerequisite of a successful academic process and sincere relations of good will among teachers and students.

In other words, in the process of mini-researches the teachers of both the junior and senior grades will be sure to find that they have things to learn from each other. They will stop stewing in their own juice. They will subconsciously be raising their qualifications through the very act of joint preparation, attendance, and discussion of lessons in all the school's classes, with the participation of students of all ages and teachers of different ages and experience.

The current isolation of teachers of junior grades from the more educated teachers of senior grades is one of the causes of the degradation of elementary teachers and the elementary school and, hence, of the nation's whole educational system.

2.11.11. In schools having grades K through 12, senior students can be used as tutors for pupils in the junior grades. Such tutorship will do much good to both the teaching and the taught students, bringing them closer together, and to the teachers supervising such tutorship.

Children can have a much greater influence on each other than their teacher: we all know this. They are closer in age and position. It depends on us what that influence is like and who sets the pace in the school: the students who value and respect the school and their teachers; or the children whose respect and affection we have failed to earn.

2.11.12. Small schools can do us no good, but they can be extremely harmful. This is inevitable, whatever their structure, and here is why:

They offer no opportunity for the reciprocal education of teachers, because every department consists of only one or two teachers. Teachers and students of the junior grades will continue to be isolated from the teachers and students in the senior grades. Many-year courses conducted by the same teacher are impossible in such schools. Students will vacillate from one school to another and from one teacher to another even more than they do now, which will make it even less possible to assure them a good education.

Furthermore, no supervisor, even one with a Ph.D. degree, can organize a successful academic process in all the subjects studied in a school. He can't be an expert in all spheres of learning. Besides, the cost of such schools will be needlessly high: compare, for instance, the cost of five schools with 300 students each with that of one with 1,500 students.

Only large school departments which are also research laboratories will be able to breathe new life into our schools, each of which will span all grades, from K to 12. These departments will gain strength and wisdom from the best teachers of the school, the school system, the state, and the Nation. Such words and concepts as Primary School, Elementary School, Secondary School, and Junior and Senior High School will partially vanish from our vocabulary and partially remain. But they will remain not as designations of different schools but as designations of different groups of classes in the only possible school, spanning all grades from K to 12, capable of teaching both teachers and students.

2.12. EDUCATIONAL RESEARCH INSTITUTES AND LABORATORIES

2.12.1. As we have said before, as each school, college, and university gets involved with mini-researches it will gradually turn into an educational research institute. Every school department will be an educational research laboratory, and every college and university department will become, or include, an educational research laboratory.

Specialization of the members of every educational research institute and laboratory is essential; otherwise, none of the educators will know anything. They will be submerged in a torrent of new pedagogical information or they will remain untouched by it, as the case is today.

The specialization of the members of the educational research laboratory should be along the lines of specialization of the faculty of university departments. For example, the mathematics department has specialists in topology, probability, geometry, functional analysis, number theory, and so on. In an educational research laboratory one educator will be studying the question of teaching the stages in the development of the concept of number, one will study the teaching of transcendental functions, one will be involved with developing the concept of exponent, one will deal with the concept of limit of a function, one with applications of the derivative, another with the application of integrals, and still another with the teaching of differential equations, number theory, vector analysis, linear algebra, algebraic and transcendental equations, inequalities and their systems, algebraic structures, et cetera, et cetera. In other words, each member of the educational research laboratory will engage in the comprehensive and in-depth study of at least one pedagogical problem and study it for many years. The educator will organize these studies in his own class as well as in the system of mini-researches within the group of educators studying each other's lessons. He will be a specialist, an unchallenged authority in the problem of his choice.

Whoever the members of the educational research laboratory are—school or college administrators, professors, or teachers—publication of papers is advisable, though not necessary, because their research consists in their daily successful work in the research laboratory.

2.12.2. The specialists working in the educational research laboratory should not feel guilty for carrying out studies in the field of education and not nuclear physics—and vice versa. Every person does his job.

Thus, every college and university department should, as a rule, have two laboratories. The only exceptions are departments consisting of two or three people. One of these laboratories will deal with educational research, the other with noneducational topics. Both must be totally independent of each other in questions pertaining to their investigations and the discussion of results, questions of hiring or dismissing personnel, salaries, professional advance, et cetera.

2.12.3. For a scientifically justified educational system to get launched and function successfully, the top administrators—the No. 1 officials of departments, schools, colleges, universities, and the city and state educational departments—must be scholars and researchers in the educational field. Their basic specialty and duty should be the launching and maintenance of a successful educational process, i.e., educational re-

55

search. There should be no apprehensions that the business, financial, or administrative aspects of the operation of educational establishments and agencies will suffer. These spheres will be supervised by professional specialists holding the No. 2 or No. 3 position in the school or education agency.

There need be no apprehension that the scientific work of our researchers in noneducational fields will suffer from this in any way. These researchers are in no need of help today, and they will not require any in future. They carry out their research in relatively narrow spheres of learning, capable of being judged by only a small group of people. For that reason the results of those researches can be accepted or rejected fairly quickly, without any outside pressure. The research process organized by them usually prevents any interference by lay people. It is much more individual, independent, and intimate—even when a large team is involved—than in the educational sphere.

Dozens and subsequently hundreds of people—participants, supporters, and opponents—get involved in educational research. The skilled hand of a powerful administrator is absolutely essential. It is necessary if only to protect educational research from lay people.

2.12.4. Researchers in noneducational sciences strive consistently, naturally, purposefully, and selflessly for the success and advance of their particular science. Why then is there no place in our country also for educational research and its basic component—the lesson? Need it be argued that noneducational and educational research cannot survive in isolation, and that society cannot survive either? Don't we see that our schools, colleges, and graduate schools are turning out people whose educational standards are declining from year to year? Don't we understand that those very people who are so cruelly and mercilessly alienated by the nation and by science are the ones who are called upon to serve them?

If we don't officially legitimize the right of researchers in the educational sphere to work in all colleges and universities, regardless of whether they publish the results of their researches or not, we will never have any learning or education in undergraduate school. Our country will never have an educational system, because researchers will not be devoting all their efforts to the continuous perfection of the educational process, despite the fact that it is research work by its very nature. Those efforts will be directed solely at publishing more papers—including papers on the educational process—at the cost of the total denigration and oblivion of the process.

2.12.5. Instructors teaching graduate courses have an obligation to be members of noneducational laboratories. In a noneducational laboratory some members need not engage in teaching at all. Professors conducting both undergraduate and graduate courses should belong to both laboratories. In the educational laboratory they will engage in research along with all the other members of the laboratory, i.e., they will attend classes conducted by other professors and discuss them before and after they are held. All administrative questions pertaining to such educators are handled by each laboratory independently. The final decision is made, on the recommendation of the heads of both laboratories, by the chairman of the department who, as mentioned before, is also a member of the educational laboratory.

Undergraduate courses should, as a rule, be conducted by members of the educational laboratory. Their research work can be restricted to mini-research, though if they wish they can broaden their scope. There is no obligation for members of the educational laboratory to publish the results of their studies, just as there is no such obligation for the faculty of the departments of art, theater, music, dance, and so on.

2.12.6. We are confident that our leading universities enjoying well-deserved fame and prestige both inside and outside the country will not be afraid of taking a bold, natural step along the road of building up an effective system of universal education. They will be able to carry out a natural redistribution of the faculty and TAs among the departments engaged solely in educational research and the departments engaged in noneducational research.

Let us explain this.

Let the department of chemistry of one of our universities have fifty regular faculty members teaching in undergraduate and graduate school. Let thirty-five of them be engaged in chemical research in the department, with the remaining fifteen not taking part in such research.

The faculty members not engaged in chemical research are in a false and very difficult position in the department. They have decided to dedicate themselves to pedagogical studies, that is, to educational work. Some of these researchers publish the results of their studies, others don't, justly considering that success in the teaching-learning process, its course and results—there for all to see, assess, and evaluate—speaks for itself.

Let the department of chemical education of that same university have ten regular faculty members. All of them will, as a rule, be carrying out research in the field of chemical education. If to this department are added all the fifteen people from the department of chemistry not engaged in chemical research, plus another forty TA instructors from the department, we can create real opportunities for both departments, chemistry and chemical education, to thrive.

The members of the chemical department will be relieved of the necessity—though not the opportunity—of getting involved in the burdensome duty of teaching elementary courses. They can teach such courses if they choose, or they can opt not to teach at all, either in graduate or in undergraduate school. The researchers in chemical education will engage in pedagogical research. That is, they will teach, and this teaching can include graduate school, provided they have the ability and the desire.

57

TAs of the chemistry department must belong to two departments: chemistry and chemistry education. By participating in mini-researches of the department of chemistry education, they will learn to conduct classes and at the same time rid their science supervisors from the chemistry department of the very burdensome need to monitor their teaching activities. Furthermore, within three or four years our colleges and universities would start to get young professors with a qualified pedagogical education obtained in graduate school.

In other words, mass education in the country will produce a mass profession: professor-educator. Attempts to get along without a professor-educator and substitute instead graduate students, undergraduate students, or a professor engaged in research in noneducational fields are not serious but utopian. They have led to the catastrophe in undergraduate education. This catastrophe is natural: no nation but ours has ever even attempted to find hundreds of thousands of professors having two callings and two professions at once, capable of carrying out successful research in two fields simultaneously. We cannot make use of the experience of modern Western countries because (1) these countries do not have a mass education, and (2) the standards of the people graduating from their schools are sufficient for them to continue to study successfully in universities.

With the creation of the new profession of professor-educator, the current unending spiral, which education in our country is rapidly sliding down, will be halted at the undergraduate school stage. Schools will start getting knowledgeable teachers prepared for successful work in the system of mini-researches. The number of students going into the engineering professions and colleges of education will increase sharply because, thanks to many-year courses and knowledgeable teachers working in the system of mini-researches, schoolchildren will be well prepared in math and science. Furthermore, they will cease to be cowed by the prospect of being turned into the helpless, miserable, and embittered teachers who now fill our schools, because there will no longer be such teachers—especially math and science teachers. The nation will no longer have to spend tens of billions of dollars every year to upgrade and retrain engineers graduated by our colleges. Most of that money can be used to raise the salaries of schoolteachers and reduce the cost of products manufactured by our industry. Finally, the decline and disintegration of our colleges and universities as institutes of higher education will be slowed down and then halted.

2.12.7. At present, researchers in noneducational fields are facing rapidly growing demands. Every researcher naturally seeks to publish more and more papers to assure the future of his department and college in conditions of financial upheavals. The new professors hired in these conditions are naturally chosen by colleges and universities solely according to the criterion of their value as researchers in noneducational spheres. With each passing year, this principle is becoming more and more cruel with respect to our children. This process is expanding and will continue to expand in our education with mounting intensity, fueled by the equally rapid disintegration of the educational process, if we do not create and preserve the mass profession of professor-educator.

2.12.8. The process of establishing Educational Research Institutes (EdRI) and Educational Research Laboratories (EdRL) will take place not as a series of administrative operations but as a natural development of the system of mini-researches in departments and educational establishments. As we have said before, every school, college, and university will operate as an EdRI with departments that either function as EdRLs or have EdRLs of their own.

All EdRL staff will conduct lessons that are mini-researches. They will teach others and learn themselves; and thus will every EdRL associate teach and learn all his life. His mini-research lessons and his self-learning activity will merge into one. Sooner or later it will yield positive results. It will bring knowledge to his pupils and develop their intellectual, creative, and cognitive abilities. Other EdRI and RL associates will help him and guide his research activity whenever necessary; they will also get advice and help from him in those fields and spheres of research in which he has achieved positive results.

In other words, the work of every teacher will be continuously analyzed in the course of mini-researches, i.e., in the course of continuous collective discussions of lessons while they are being prepared, attendance of those lessons and their subsequent discussion, and during repeat attendance of lessons or perhaps of a series of lessons covering a whole topic. The teachers will thus get advice and help in those aspects of their work in which they seem to be failing. At the same time, their achievements and the achievements of their pupils will be noted and reinforced whenever they are apparent. The causes of successes and reasons for failures will be determined, and the ways and means of preserving and expanding the achievements and gradually weeding out and eliminating all the negative aspects of the academic process will be devised.

2.12.9. In the course of their pedagogical research some of our educators, including administrators, as well as researchers in noneducational fields, will realize how mini-researches benefit them, the students, and other members of the EdRI. They will gain an appreciation of this work and the profession of educator. To many of them the profession will be virtually new, with new variations that they had formerly only dreamed of or never even suspected. It will give them the skills and habits of educational work, confidence in their forces, and the desire to study independently so as to rise above the level of pedagogical knowledge, skills, and habits they have already achieved. Some of them may even go on to study at special courses and seminars for teachers and administrators, which will be set up in colleges and universities all over the country, both in the subjects they teach and in educational subjects. From these people we will create millions of fine teachers, supervisors, and administrators. As they learn and teach others in the system of mini-researches, they will, with the help of instructive lessons and an efficient teaching-learning process that is didactically humane and kind with respect to both students and teachers, create the student and our educational system.

Other people engaged and preoccupied in noneducational fields may feel unhappy under the conditions of creative educational work, with lessons that are mini-researches. Perhaps these mini-researches will keep them from following their calling and prevent their talents from blossoming. They will abandon the Educational RL and devote themselves fully to their favorite work. Still others will gladly carry out research in both education and in fields having no bearing on the academic process.

2.12.10. The publishing business must cease being the extremely dangerous hazard it has become to the nation as an effective means of destroying education in our country.

We should set up a Scientific-Editorial Center, made up of the nation's best educators and scientists elected to it for terms of three to five years. This center would recommend lists of textbooks in every subject for schools and undergraduate schools. It would offer expert opinion on manuscripts of new textbooks. The manuscripts would be coded so as not to reveal the names of the authors. The costs of reviewing the manuscripts would be borne by the authors and, perhaps, the publishers.

This procedure would in no way interfere with the publication of all and any books by any publisher and any author. But it would be for us to decide whether to accept them as textbooks or not. A law should be promulgated on this, similar to the laws banning trafficking in drugs and pornography. It would, in much the same way, safeguard our education from its organized destruction.

We have no intention of denying authors and publishers full freedom to endeavor, by every means at their disposal, to get our schools and institutes of higher education to use their very good or bad textbooks. It is not for us to judge their efforts. But what we can and must do is prevent any textbook published without the endorsement of highly qualified reviewers from ever being used in any educational establishment. The reviewers, as we have said, should be selected by the Scientific-Editorial Center from among the best experts in the country.

Initially, the names of the reviewers and authors will not be disclosed to anyone. If the reviewers conclude that a given code-named book deserves to be published as a possible future textbook, the Scientific-Editorial Center will endorse its publication.

Once again, we repeat the following: Let authors write whatever they want, and let publishers publish whatever they want. But it would be the law that without the endorsement of the Scientific-Editorial Center, no book would ever be used as a textbook in any educational institution; moreover, it would be barred from being entered in the forthcoming contest designed to select several books among those claiming the title of "textbook."

The prospective textbooks will be distributed under their code

60

names, without indicating their authors, to schools in different parts of the country, to be tried out by instructors and professors for two or three years. The best will be adopted as textbooks. At that time the authors' names will be revealed and all the reviews written during all the stages of study and evaluation will be published. At that point, too, the authors of the reviews will be made known. Thus, and only thus, can we assure that the reviews are objective, qualified, and are not harmful, but instead useful, to our country.

Thus, only *after* the unnamed prospective textbooks have been tried out in practice by several educational establishments—and been positively reviewed by them—will the Scientific-Editorial Center sign contracts with the publishers. Each textbook will be provided with a blurb stating that it has passed all the official stages of evaluation; it will also have the author's name. All the official reviews written during all the stages of its study and practical testing in schools, colleges, and universities will be published, either at the beginning of the book or in a journal for educators in the respective field. On the one hand, these reviews at the beginning of the textbook or in the journals will help educators see what they cannot see for themselves. On the other, we acquire an excellent opportunity for master's and Ph.D. research. The test of each new textbook is an investigation which can be carried out as master's or Ph.D. work.

The proposed system of publishing textbooks in conditions of mass education is absolutely essential. It is especially important during the first stages of building up a mass education.

Years will pass, and with time every school and every college will have teachers who take an active part in compiling and reviewing textbooks and study aids for all our educational institutions. As yet, however, we still lack the conditions in which every teacher can create his own textbook or select one from the mass of textbooks and study aids in print, many of them illiterate and totally disastrous for the cause of education.

Thus, let authors write textbooks and create study aids as they do today. Let publishers and companies publish books and produce study aids as they do now. But if the authors, the publishers, and the companies hope and want us educators to use those textbooks and study aids, let us strike a deal. It is for you to write, invent, publish, create. It is for us to like or dislike the products you create. We are developing a procedure, which you can avoid. But in that case, no educational establishment can consider your textbooks and study aids to be their textbooks and study aids.

2.13. ON TEACHING MATH AND SCIENCE

2.13.1. All school and undergraduate math and science courses in our country are doomed. The vast conglomeration of material that is to

61

be studied during a one-year course is one of the causes of the all-American educational tragedy. It is impossible to professionally conceive and ably realize a single lesson: this requires time, which we don't have.

Furthermore, and much more importantly, during a one-year course, with daily lessons, the abstract nature and complexity of concepts, ideas, and structures increases faster than the child's intellectual and cognitive abilities. Or to put it differently, the cognitive abilities of school-children develop at a much slower pace during our one-year math and science courses than the ideas, concepts, and structures of those sciences. That is to say that in our country's schools and colleges it is basically impossible to successfully master mathematics and science. Individual lessons may be successful—when they present primitive material—at the cost of the total collapse of the other lessons. This collapse leads to (1) the absence of active teaching-learning methods in our schools and colleges, because their application requires more time than is provided for by the rapid monologue of the teacher or the requirement that students work independently and pass their examinations; (2) the basic impossibility of pedagogical creativity; (3) the inflation of grades; (4) the steady increase of mental disorders among teachers and students; (5) mutual hostility of students and teachers to the extent of mutual physical confrontations; (6) the mass flight of students and math and science teachers from the schools; and (7) a catastrophic nationwide shortage of not only math and science teachers, but of engineers as well, because it is quite impossible to study math or science either in school or in college.

As we have said before, a single obstacle is sufficient to prevent building up the nation's educational system. Given the current duration of math and science courses and the number of hours devoted to them in our schools and colleges, they represent just one such obstacle.

2.13.2. Our children begin to take regular courses in physics, chemistry, biology, algebra, geometry, trigonometry, and calculus only in the senior grades. By that time they have been transformed into creatures whose mental capacities have been forcibly retarded by incredibly stupifying courses in so-called general science and general mathematics. These courses represent an aggregate of teacher ignorance and naive, primitive study material, which is extremely dangerous to a normal child. They have been turned into a stupifying routine of students working with textbooks doubling as handbooks. These courses have emasculated instruction of thought, scientific content, and the development of ideas, concepts, and structures.

Students can assimilate scientific concepts, ideas, and structures only as a result of mental activity, not memorization. To repeat once again: in the course of one-year presentations of courses in math and science, the complexity and abstract nature of concepts, ideas, and structure increases faster than the students' mental and cognitive aptitudes. That is why we see that students are totally incapable of learning one-year courses and teachers are totally incapable of teaching them. That is why there is no one to teach math and science in our country. That is why we are forced to resort to remedial courses creating an appearance of useful activity.

2.13.3. The introduction of many-year courses in math and science, a sharp increase in the number of hours devoted to them, and their presentation by trained teacher-specialists—this is what will make the school not only serious, academic, and exacting, but also accessible and understandable to teachers and students, thereby winning their respect. To these characteristic features of the new school we should add high scientific standards of the study material, mastery of which will require continuous, many-year efforts and foster the development of the students' intellectual abilities and creativity.

Many-year courses and lessons that are mini-researches, whether they are observed and discussed by others or not, will ensure that the teaching and learning processes are commensurate with the students' capacity to assimilate the material, and that both students and teachers can daily appreciate the results achieved and enjoy the happiness of creative effort permeated with thought and didactic humanism and kindness.

2.13.4. There should be one teacher for each of the courses in physics and chemistry. He must be a specialist in one of these subjects. Colleges of education shouldn't even try to train teachers capable of teaching both these subjects. Classes in biology and geography can be assigned to one teacher.

All our efforts should be directed at having one and the same teacher conducting all math courses with the same group of students from the 4th to the 10th grade, or even up to graduation. The same is true for science teachers.

Courses in general mathematics and general science should be forgotten once and for all.

2.13.5. Specialists in different fields of learning are bound to fight over the number of lessons to be devoted to studying each school subject in different grades.

Many years of experience in teaching many-year math and science courses indicate that under the conditions of mass education, five or six hours of math and five or six hours of science a week in all grades is adequate. A possible breakdown of math and science courses by grades is presented in Table 1.

We can already hear the peremptory challenge: How do you expect to provide enough teachers for your many-year math and science courses when we don't have enough even for one-year courses?

The fact of the matter is that one-year courses are the main reason why we are short in math and science teachers. Upon leaving school, our children are so discouraged by the school courses that they avoid ever coming to grips with math and science again. What we want to say is that the only way we can provide the nation with math and science

Table 1
Each Academic Year Has 200 Working Days

1-3	4	5	6	7	8	9	10	11	12
Arithmetic with elements of algebra and geometry 600 hours	Arithmetic with elements of geometry 3 hours a week 120 hours								
		Algebra 1 3 hours a week 360 hours	Geometry 2 hours a week 240 hours	Algebra 2 3 hours a week 120 hours	Trigonometry and Analytical Geometry 1 2 hours a week 240 hours			Analytical Geometry and Trigonometry 2 2 hours a week 160 hours	
					Algebra 2 2 hrs-week, 240 hours · Calculus 1 2 hours a week 240 hours			Calculus 2 3 hours a week 240 hours	
		Geography 2 hours a week 240 hours		Physics 1 2 hours a week 320 hours				Physics 2 3 hours a week 240 hours	
			Biology 1 3 hours a week 240 hours		Biology 2 2 hours a week 240 hours		Chemistry 1 2 hours a week 240 hours	Chemistry 2 3 hours a week 240 hours	

teachers, as well as with engineers and scientists, is to introduce many-year courses. For the first few years we will enroll teachers from among retirees, engineers, elementary teachers, and graduate students. It wouldn't be a bad idea to recruit some from other countries by offering them high salaries.

Many-year courses in math and science will work miracles within the school. They will make it humane, disciplined, and responsible, because every student and teacher will be doing work for which they are responsible over a number of years. Many-year math and science courses can be made attractive to tens of millions of children and teachers who are today engaged in hopeless combat with them or judiciously avoid them altogether. A one-year course cannot be made understandable, scientific, or interesting.

2.13.6. The training of teachers, engineers, and scientists in our country will be guaranteed by many-year, highly scientific courses both in school and in college. The college courses will differ radically from today's undergraduate courses. They will be built on the firm foundation of secondary schooling and mini-researches creating and accompanying the teaching-learning process both in school and in college.

The graduate school will change, too. Its students will engage in research, not in filling in the gaps of undergraduate education.

2.13.7. It is time for the nation to seriously consider the need for expanding four-year colleges with 2,000 hours to 3,000 or 4,000 hours. Nowadays there are quite a few colleges in other countries with 4,000–6,000 hours of class over four to six years.

Many-year school and college courses developed in the course of mini-researches can be highly scientific and at the same time understandable to all students—this is both the prerequisite and consequence of the creation and continuous improvement of a modern nation's system of effective mass education. These courses, of course, will not appear out of thin air.

We need millions of educated and continuously learning teachers capable of creating instructive lessons and an instructive teaching-learning process. Letter Three is devoted to the creation and training of such teachers.

We need lessons that constitute a teaching-learning process and offer both students and teachers knowledges, skills, and habits and develop their intellectual, creative, and cognitive abilities. Letter Four is devoted to the development of such lessons.

We need students capable of learning both in and out of class. Letter Five is devoted to the creation of such students.

We need a teaching-learning process constructed by the teacher with the help of instructive lessons. We talk about the creation of such a process throughout the book.

As schools, colleges, universities, and departments gradually acquire (1) knowledgeable teachers continuously upgrading their knowledges with the help of mini-researches; (2) active and instructive lessons constituting a teaching-learning process; (3) many-year, highly scientific courses that are within reach of the students; and (4) professional students eager to be taught and to learn, they will gradually and inevitably turn into Educational Research Institutes and Educational Research Laboratories. They will gradually put forward from their midst the best educators capable of creating and administering the new educational system, the system of Educational Research Institutes and Educational Research Laboratories.

*　*　*

The question is of creating and effectively operating a new educational system for our country, an educational system having nothing in common with the currently existing one. The question is whether we will give our children an education—and if yes, then how—or whether we will continue to leave it up to them.

It is easy and even gratifying to criticize and express noble wrath and indignation. The perpetrators of evil are thrown off their pedestals, evil is disgraced, and good triumphs. Good hasn't yet triumphed in our field, but it will, provided we don't resign ourselves to the idea of turning our country into a helpless camp filled with growing numbers of ignoramuses and criminals to whom the powerful nations of all continents will dictate their will.

LETTER THREE

HOW TO CREATE A NEW TEACHER*

In the past four years, students and teachers in mathematics classrooms across the U.S. joined their counterparts in over twenty countries around the world in a comprehensive study of school mathematics [Second International Mathematics Study]. This study was designed to provide detailed information for each country about the content of the mathematics curriculum, how mathematics is taught, and how much mathematics students learn. . . . In no case did the U.S. mean fall in the top half of the means for the participating countries. . . . overall [eighth-grade], students' achievement declined modestly from 1964 to 1982. . . . much of the decline was on the more difficult comprehension and application items rather than just on the computational items. . . . The teachers instructing these students were experienced and well trained. . . .

What patterns of instruction are effective in increasing students' achievement? What might be done to improve the performance of U.S. students in the future? Interested persons might like . . . to join in the effort to understand the significance of those results for mathematics education in the U.S.
—Arithmetic Teacher, Volume 32, Number 8, April 1985

. . . The teachers instructing these [twelfth-grade] students were experienced and well trained. . . . The subsample of calculus classes performed at least at or above the international median in all content areas, whereas the precalculus classes consistently performed below that median. . . . The portion of U.S. students in calculus classes was less than that for most other developed countries participating in the SIMS. . . . Interested persons might like . . . to join in the effort to understand the significance of those results for mathematics education in the U.S.
—Mathematics Teacher, Volume 78, Number 4, April 1985

*The reader can omit the examples from mathematics cited in these letters without detriment to the discourse.

3.1. TEACHING AS A PURELY TECHNICAL PROCESS. LIKE IT OR NOT—SCHOOLING PRODUCES EITHER FRIENDS OR FOES OF SOCIETY. THE TEACHER AND THE LESSON

3.1.1. The view of the teaching-learning process as a process involving the purely technical transmission of knowledge, skills, and habits to students is detrimental to the nation's education. It assumes that if the teacher talks, the students necessarily listen, absorb, and memorize what they hear; if not—that's their fault. If the teacher gives assignments, the students carry them out; if they don't for some reason, that's their fault. When students don't understand something, they naturally ask questions. The absence of questions means the teaching-learning process is progressing nicely.

This comfortable, naive, and dangerous view of education prevails in most of our educational institutions. It is actively promoted by our educators, both the conscientiously misled and those who would mislead others.

3.1.2. Mass education requires that we constantly impress upon our educators that insofar as we are speaking of teaching, and not of students independently studying school or undergraduate courses, the role of mentor and supervisor belongs to the educator. We must continuously teach our educators this supervisory role. We must also imbue them with faith in themselves and their pupils, with confidence that, given competent guidance, every student in good health can and should digest the minimum of knowledge, skills, and habits needed for a school and undergraduate education and acquire the standards needed to continue his education. We must and will continuously teach our present and future educators how to apply active teaching and learning processes to gradually develop the students' memory, speech, and intellectual and creative abilities, as well as the motivation for self-education and ability to acquire knowledge independently.

3.1.3. For the purposes of mass education it is a tragic mistake to

69

set apart teaching and learning. Teaching and learning are objectively closely intertwined and interdependent. We are *not* responsible for this interdependence; we *are* responsible for its extent and character. Teaching plays a leading, guiding role in the process of mass, nonelitist education. The leading role of teaching is a characteristic feature of mass education, which distinguishes it from elitist education. Pedagogical experience, especially the experience of the last hundred years, confirms that students' attitudes towards a study subject, their interest in learning, their successes, the level of acquired knowledge and development, the quality of acquired skills and habits, their speech, and their ability to work, acquire knowledge independently, rationalize, defend their views, prove a point, critically evaluate the statements of others, and investigate problem situations—that all this is determined not only by the students' capabilities but also by the quality of instruction. All this depends on who supervises the academic process, the teaching methods and devices, the organization of the teaching-learning process, and how the teaching of both learners and teachers is supervised.

3.1.4. Our schoolteachers and undergraduate instructors, our educators of all ranks and levels, should understand that, being the ones who give students knowledge, teach them, and supervise their studies, they have a tremendous educational impact on them. They offer their students examples—good or bad—of attitudes towards work. They foster in them willpower or the lack of it, honesty or dishonesty, truthfulness or deceit, confidence in themselves, expectations of success, or despair. They foster and encourage their curiosity, ability to think, and capacity for creative action—or they actively suppress all these qualities. It all depends on the teacher: his attitude towards his work; his erudition; on his love of, or indifference towards, children; his devotion to his profession; and on his sincere desire or unwillingness, ability or inability, to give his students knowledge and the skills of learning, creating, thinking, reasoning, proving, and standing up for their convictions. All of this is in the hands of the teacher, and virtually no one else.

Teaching and learning are necessarily educational—regardless of our desires or beliefs. Mastery of the structure and method of science in the course of an active teaching-learning process supervised by an educated and capable educator, in an atmosphere of didactic kindness, brings all students a sense of great emotional gratification, achievement, and inspiration. It fills them with respect for truth and demonstrable reasoning. It fosters feelings of gratitude and respect for the teachers, the school, and the society that gave them the joy and happiness of cognition and faith in themselves and in their powers, as well as in a happy and worthy future. But this can happen only when the educator himself possesses a profound and conscious knowledge of science, when he loves his science and sincerely and humanely strives for the students to master it, when he is in possession of effective methods of teaching, and has the opportunities for improving them.

An educator with an inadequate knowledge of the subject he is teaching, ignorant of the structure and method of his science or the methods of teaching it, steadily and consistently arouses in his students feelings of hostility towards the subject and its learning, and disdain for the truth and those who uphold it. Such a teacher turns scientific knowledge into an array of arbitrary, unconnected, and often contradictory facts on the surface of science. Scientific knowledge and the logic of science is replaced by bellicose ignorance. Students, even the most capable, are denied the opportunities for studying successfully. Their mental processes and cognitive abilities are deadened; they are helpless and unhappy. They despise the school, the teachers, and the society for the humiliating, helpless, and hopeless state to which the school, the teachers, and the society confines them.

Children are spiritually devastated. They are corrupted by imposed dishonesty, deliberate or involuntary cruelty, inadequate educational standards of teachers, teacher helplessness, sham optimism, or depression. Children seek escape from the school and from adults; they become either depressed, spineless and helpless lackeys, or desperate foes of society.

3.1.5. The effects of teaching cannot be reduced to a sum of particular educational devices, however appropriate they might seem. If a cruel or ignorant teacher requires students to do their tests and home assignments without first giving them the necessary knowledge, skills, and habits, this is also a form of education, but one which fosters fear, carelessness, lack of self-confidence, aversion to studies, and hostility towards a cruel school and a cruel society.

When students have to use ignorant textbooks; if they are required to solve problems they couldn't have learned in the time allocated by the curriculum; when integration with the help of partial fractions requires the solution of systems of equations in four or five unknowns, while the preparatory course covered only two; when a teacher introduces integration by parts, Taylor's formula, and convergence of series with only one or two examples, which is both cruel and totally useless for 90 or 95 percent of the students; when integration using trigonometric, inverse trigonometric, hyperbolic, and inverse hyperbolic functions is required of students who were never given the requisite knowledge or habits of operating with such functions; when geometric applications of multiple integrals and the application of differential equations to physics is required of students who were never taught geometry, integration techniques, mechanics, or electricity, nor the solution of equations—the result is an academic process with a 40 to 50 percent dropout rate. This process is cruel on the students, forcing them to cheat, explain the inexplicable, and prove the unprovable, and breeds a sense of enormous injustice, frustration, or bitter resentment.

3.1.6. The educational impact of schooling on students is inseparable from the educational impact of the quality of the teaching-learning process. Knowledge can have a positive impact on the molding of lofty personal traits when the teaching-learning process is pervaded with di-

71

dactic kindness; when it is humane; when it brings the joy of cognition—clear understanding of studied phenomena, propositions, and structures in their natural interrelationships and necessary interdependence; and when it helps the students understand the method of science and gives them the joy of attainable independent creativity. Only gifted, talented children can acquire all this independently, despite the low level of teachers and teaching, because they are above that level. It can't harm them or stifle their natural talents and aptitudes, or their natural thirst for knowledge and ability to acquire it independently. They are the ones who, in spite of our education, win awards in scholastic contests and tournaments and eventually get into graduate school in this country or in Europe. Some become celebrated scholars or brilliant professionals, thereby creating the illusion in the eyes of some people that all is well in the nation's educational system.

3.1.7. A nation that wishes to see its children educated, honest, and happy must have an educational system that: can and should produce comprehensively and profoundly knowledgeable professional educators for its schools and colleges; continually, throughout their whole educational careers, upgrades their knowledge, scholastic standards, and academic skill with the help of mini-researches or research lessons; evaluates the quality of their work solely in terms of the quality of the teaching and learning process conducted under their guidance and supervision; ensures that their work is supervised only by qualified supervisors and administrators, who are themselves educators and who, in turn, continuously upgrade and refine their pedagogical skills in a system of teacher training and specialized training for top-grade administrators and educators.

3.1.8. The acquisition of knowledge is hard work. When it is within the students' capabilities and, more importantly, is creative, it fosters the ability to overcome difficulties, the ability to judge the difficulty of problems and problem situations, and to find the best ways of resolving them. Thanks to the professional guidance of the teacher, the acquisition of knowledge gradually intensifies the students' spiritual forces, breeding initiative, persistence, and the ability to concentrate on the subject matters. It also instills work habits in general, and fosters energetic, active, and enterprising people. To such people, work and creativity, not violence and cruelty, are sources of joy and satisfaction.

3.1.9. Children imitate adults, especially those they respect. Every teacher—whether knowledgeable and conscientious, or lacking such qualities; whether kind and fair, or cruel and vengeful—has a tremendous influence on children, often greater than that of the family and the milieu, like it or not, accept it or not. This influence extends beyond students' attitudes to the study subject to learning in general, to the school and to adults. It is an active factor in shaping the personality which contributes to the upbringing of either educated, upright, fair, industrious, and conscientious people, or people devoid of these qualities.

72

A teacher who doesn't carry authority with his students, who has not earned their respect by his erudition, love of his profession, and a sincere desire to give his pupils profound knowledge and the joy of creative endeavor, is incapable of conducting a successful academic process. His efforts, his contact with our children, brings them no good, only indelible harm. Deceiving himself and the students, but refusing to acknowledge it even to himself, he tries to create an illusion of authority among the children by resorting to entertainment and prompting instead of instruction, by currying favor rather than being strict and exacting. He falls back on sample tests and is generous with high grades. Some teachers go to the other extreme and are unjustifiably harsh and demanding. In either case, the students develop attitudes of distrust, disrespect, and hostility towards their elders. Given the students' ability to adapt, the stability and variability of the hypocritical process, and the cruelty of our educational establishments, all this soon becomes a norm of behavior, an established habit, a character trait.

3.1.10. In conditions of mass education, the school teacher and the undergraduate professor must constantly supervise student learning. The absence of such competent supervision in conditions of didactic humanism and kindness discredits the idea of mass education. A teacher not only supervises his students' intellectual and practical activities in class. He also supervises them outside the class through a system of independent work closely linked with their work in class.

The purpose of the teacher's work is to give the required volume of knowledges and skills to all students, develop their thinking, teach them to work and acquire knowledge independently, competently prepare them to overcome difficulties, and, whenever necessary, assist them in their efforts. To place the whole burden of the learning effort on the students' shoulders, even with the help of good study aids and instructional media, is cruel and utterly useless for the overwhelming majority of our children. This is a fact which our so-called educational system refuses to face.

3.1.11. It is impossible for a teacher to successfully supervise the education of independently thinking people in the atmosphere of cold, formal relations between the teachers and the taught. This atmosphere prevails in virtually all of our nation's educational establishments because it makes things so much simpler and easier for both parties. Without educators who are sincerely concerned with our children's achievements and fortunes, without possessing authority in the eyes of their students, without mutual respect between students and teachers, and mutual exactingness and sincere confidence in each other—without all this a successful educational process is impossible. However, none of this can be achieved if educators and administrators at all levels do not constantly help each other, if they do not continuously train to upgrade their pedagogical skills.

3.1.12. Our educators don't understand that their students must do more than just memorize textbook passages. They don't understand that assimilation of new knowledge must be organized in such a way as to embed it in the students' minds. For this, every element of the new knowledge and every new idea should be an element of the students' personal mental or practical experience. That is why the teaching-learning process cannot be reduced to independent studies for nonbrilliant students. Only a competent and knowledgeable teacher can organize and encourage the active, purposeful work of such students—both mental and practical—in the course and as a result of which every new element of new knowledge becomes an inalienable part of the child's personal experience; that is, primary assimilation of knowledge occurs. Subsequent application and utilization of the assimilated knowledge constantly upgrades it. There is a continuous advance from incomplete and inaccurate to more complete and more accurate knowledge.

Moreover, as a result of competent, active teaching, the knowledge assimilated by the student becomes a tool of independent thinking and creative activity. There is more to such knowledge than a student's ability to reproduce it more or less successfully. Reproduction can be achieved by the mechanical rendition of recorded information from a book, program aid, study film, magnetic tape, et cetera. Consciously and actively assimilated knowledge is flexible and always on tap; that is, students are able to apply it independently in new situations, whether similar to previously encountered ones or entirely new. This is the supreme triumph of didactic kindness.

3.2. STUDYING THE STUDENTS. MUTUAL HOSTILITY OF STUDENTS AND TEACHERS. THE SCHOOL AND COLLEGE GAME. THE TEACHER MUST FIGHT FOR THE KNOWLEDGE OF EVERY STUDENT. MOVEMENT FOR THE SAKE OF MOVEMENT

3.2.1. For a teacher to provide genuine education he must start with studying his students—every student and every class as an instruction unit. The exploration and analysis of the class and each and every student in class—their abilities, interests, inclinations, and aspirations—must start at the very first minute of the very first lesson and be pursued continuously by duly organizing and implementing the academic process.

Success in teaching and learning, as well as in upgrading the knowledges, skills, and habits, intellectual, creative, and cognitive abilities of all students, is generated by continuously studying every student and every class in the course and as a consequence of the academic process.

3.2.2. A teacher's inability to structurize lessons and classes for different purposes and in a way capable of making form, content, and results appealing to the children, as well as inability to guide the continuous, active development of the knowledges and cognitive abilities of all students, starts to breed feelings of protest already in the primary school. We prefer to notice this gradually accumulated protest only in the middle or senior grades, when it acquires explosive forms and we are no longer able to deal with it.

Children of all ages feel when a teacher is indifferent to them, when he doesn't like them and doesn't—or can't—teach them. He may or may not realize this, but teaching is abhorrent to him. Irritation and dislike for the students soon pervades his whole system. He tyrannizes them with his indifference, which is rooted in pedagogical helplessness. The children are quick to reciprocate in kind. Very soon the life of both teacher and students turns into an implacable struggle and mutual hate, which our children and teachers carry bitterly all through school, and often through all their life.

Take the middle and senior grade teacher—helpless, inadequately schooled, and burdened with one or two hundred of our unfortunate children—hostile, embittered, believing in neither school, teachers, nor, for good measure, parents. Parents have nothing to offer except meaningless words about the good of education and the banes of ignorance. They, too, arouse the hostility of children with their contempt and totally impenetrable indifference. Children are possessed by apathy, hopelessness, futility, and a desire to withdraw from adults.

Take the college instructor who has to commence the course with a hundred such creatures: tormented, harassed, ignorant, with no skills or faith in anything or anyone. For twelve long years they were tormented by people who involuntarily became enemies even more tormented and harassed by their helplessness. Both students and teachers were placed in situations requiring the impossible. This inevitably and inexorably produced torrents of lies, carelessness, and derision of both teachers and children.

Originally, the children had looked forward to the future—to joy, the happiness of a trade or profession that had excited their imagination for many years, and to the growth of respect for themselves and others. But they came out of school unable to read, write, count, solve problems, or understand what they read.

3.2.3. The college instructor's mind is busy with his research; the TA worries about the exams he has to take. Both are preoccupied. The administrators keep demanding the results of research. These results determine one's place in the scientific community and society. The examination results are as important to the TA as the research results are to the professor. But academic results and the process itself are of interest to no one—in the school, in college, or anywhere. Who cares for our children? For twelve years they were involved with adults in a terrible game called school, spouting bombastic words about morality, good and evil, honesty, integrity, and the need for education. They continue the same game in college.

3.2.4. Education, the active process of acquiring knowledges, skills,

75

and habits and developing intellectual, creative, and cognitive abilities under the guidance of professional educators, creates the human personality. Educators are duty bound to strive for the maximum attainable level of knowledges and abilities of every person. They must do this as courageously and selflessly as doctors who fight for the health of every person, regardless of whether he is to become a footballer, plumber, or physician, like researchers who strive to achieve new, hitherto unknown, results.

3.2.5. Work on the curricula must be continued along with developing and improving the quality of work of schools, colleges, and universities, and it must continue to yield new results. It will always depend on the quality of training of practicing professionals, on the trends prevailing in modern science, as well as on the work of schools, teachers, colleges, and universities. However, the nation's educational system cannot be subjected to endless movement for the purpose of movement, as is the case today, nor to senseless juggling of courses and educationally harebrained innovations without cause or justification. Any efficiently operating system must be basically stable.

3.3. SCHOOLS AND COLLEGES TRY NOT TO HAVE A SINGLE GOOD TEACHER

The present academic system in the country is not self-reproductive; rather, it is self-destructive. Schools are sometimes unable to have even a single good educator: he may be hounded by all the other educators and the administrators so as not to serve as an example of what every educator should be like.

In other words, as soon as the students begin to identify an excellent educator, he immediately becomes the target—perhaps unintentionally—of the righteous indignation of the whole faculty, because the academic system is so wisely structured that it is impossible for educators to learn from the best among them. No one can or cares to. So the best educator is either quickly transferred to a job not directly involving the academic process or just eased out of the school or college.

It is most important to note in this connection that the best educator gets his walking papers not because the others don't like him, but because the academic system doesn't offer the other educators any real prospects of becoming as good as the one who has the misfortune of being better.

There is one exception. In the worst schools no one—neither students, nor teachers, nor administrators—has the slightest interest in, or concern for, the quality of instruction or the reaction of the instructed to it. It is each for himself, and the devil take the hindmost. Such schools can prove to be a haven for several outstanding teachers, who can unobtrusively teach a really fine course without arousing anyone's concern.

76

3.4. CHANGING TEACHER TRAINING ALONE WILL NOT HELP. TAs IN TEACHER TRAINING ARE EVEN WORSE THAN IN OTHER APPLICATIONS

3.4.1. The colleges that undertake to train teachers should always bear in mind the historically evolved mission of the teacher: to renovate and invigorate the teaching-learning process in the schools they come to work in with new ideas and fresh knowledge. Other teachers in the school may have graduated from the same or equivalent colleges many years ago, and the administrators should treat young teachers' knowledge and ideas with respect and confidence. They should also spare no effort within their means to make yesterday's college student a teacher: a professional, a master teacher in love with his profession and with children, a sincere and devoted specialist.

The young teacher, for his part, must be capable of bringing into the school a fresh, modern view of education acquired from erudite college professors who engage in educational research and have a good knowledge of the current theories and practices of teaching. The young educator must display talent or fresh ideas and knowledge, or both. Other teachers, who have been at the school for perhaps even dozens of years, will spontaneously and gratefully learn from him. The new teacher—almost always rather naive because of inexperience, forever overestimating his forces and pedagogical capabilities, forever underestimating the complexity and difficulty of the academic process—will, for his part, find very much to learn from his new friends, the teachers of his and other departments, and administrators.

If a country's educational system is not replenished each year with young specialists whose training is immeasurably higher than that of currently teaching educators—those who came to the school several years earlier—that system is dying.

3.4.2. We are afraid of being misunderstood. We are afraid that the reader will independently draw the wrong conclusion, fallacious from beginning to end. Unfortunately, it is extremely popular among us—the teachers—and extremely dangerous. What we wish to say is that, by themselves, improvements in teacher training, which is but one component of the multifaceted and multidimensional social structure we call the national educational system, however radical and progressive they might be, will change virtually nothing as long as the other components remain unchanged.

However successful we might be in improving teacher training in colleges, even if this is done in all states of the Union at once, it won't be enough. Nothing will change for the better without building up a new educational system capable of ensuring not only a high level of teacher training in the country's colleges, but also an incomparably higher level of performance of every working educator, in all the country's educational establishments without exception, mainly with the help of mini-researches.

3.4.3. In universities, TAs often get graduate-school specialization having nothing in common with their specialization obtained in undergraduate school. Moreover, they are physically incapable of conducting a successful academic process because of the time they must devote to their graduate studies. All this has a destructive effect on college students and the whole educational system. If the present status of TAs is retained, the nation's educational system will never be created, because every year millions of our children will be subjected to an irreversible process of pedagogical torture instead of education and instruction. This has an especially catastrophic effect on college students planning to be teachers. They will graduate from college pedagogically humiliated, with no faith in teaching, devasted by the lack of instruction, and fully embittered against society and its members.

The road for this great nation lies through a reversal of the disintegration of the academic system, through refusal to forget and repeat the errors of the past, but without wallowing in our present pain and helplessness, without self-flagellation and reciprocal flagellation, but carrying forward joy, happiness, enlightenment, and education for all its children.

3.5. THE ACADEMIC PROCESS WILL BE BASED ON THE REAL, NOT IMAGINED, LEVELS OF DEVELOPMENT OF STUDENTS AND TEACHERS

3.5.1. No instructor in the world would start a lesson without first making sure that his students have correctly understood and assimilated whatever they were taught at the previous lesson.

But not in our country.

Any teacher in any country would try to make sure that his pupils have understood his instructions and can recapitulate and repeat all the information in their memory without which the current lesson cannot be understood.

But not in our country.

One of the essential elements of teaching—and we mean teaching, not impassively watching children helplessly attempting to garner crumbs of knowledge on their own—is the teacher's gathering of information on the level of the knowledges, skills, and habits actually attained by the students—and we mean attained, not what they should have attained according to hypothetical fantasies in direct proportion to the naivete or cruelty of the instructor.

It seems incredible that most of our educators are guided in their actions not by what the children know, nor by what they can do, understand, and assimilate, but by what they should know, what they should be able to do, and what they should understand and assimilate. These expectations, moreover, are in direct proportion to the instructor's in-

78

competence. What could be more senseless, useless, and cruel in an educational system? Only the hope that it can function and improve based not on what the educators know, what they are capable of, and what they themselves can do, but on what they should know, what they should be capable of, and what they should be able to do. It is hardly surprising that we give the graduates of schools and colleges hardly any education. The surprising thing is that some students actually acquire knowledge. Fortunately, that is beyond our control.

To supervise an academic process one must know what to supervise. It must be studied. It is necessary constantly, every moment and at every lesson, to study what the students, at that moment and at that lesson, know, are capable of, and can do. That is the only basis for deciding what new information the students can digest the next moment or at the next lesson and what is still beyond them, and determining what they can learn to do and what they are still unprepared for. That should be the rule every day, at every lesson, during every minute of the lesson, every month and year, in all the country's schools and colleges. The new academic system, the system of research institutes, will provide the opportunities for this kind of activity.

In addition, the new educational system will provide for the continued, daily study of the level of knowledges, skills, and habits and intellectual, creative, and cognitive abilities of every teacher. On this basis, it will provide the opportunity for the more experienced and skilled educators, supervisors, and administrators to assign ever more serious and difficult pedagogical tasks to the educators receiving instruction. It will make it possible to impose ever higher demands on educators, but demands in keeping with their current levels of knowledge, skills, and habits and intellectual, creative, and cognitive abilities. This way it will be able to encourage every educator to become a master of the academic process, its inspirer and protector, a fighter against ignorance and crime, for our children's future.

3.5.2. As the teacher introduces new concepts and teaches how to perform new operations, he must constantly monitor the students' attention. This is difficult, very difficult, but it has to be taught. There is no sense in going on with the work until the teacher has gained the students' attention, perhaps by firing questions at them. The teacher is duty bound to see how correctly and successfully the students assimilate new concepts and operations. This is achieved by the teacher asking questions which are aimed at generating more questions from the students.

The teacher must know how well the assimilated information is retained in the students' memories and reflected in their skills—in the course of the lesson, in the course of the teaching and learning process, and as a consequence of the lesson. This is necessary for the students to cope with the next assignment and be ready to continue their study work at the next lesson.

The next lesson should, as a rule, include time for establishing how

79

ready the students are to absorb new information and acquire new knowledges and skills. If they are for some reason or other not ready, there is no sense introducing new information or trying to offer new knowledges and skills, however good the teacher might be, and however good his students. This stage may take a variety of forms, but they must all be humane, instructive, and didactically kind.

3.5.3. For an educational process to go beyond just talk and be instructive as well, it must be continuous. That means that the teacher should introduce new knowledges, generalizations, and operations only after the students have been prepared for them by all they have learned before. They must be introduced in a didactically humane and kind fashion; that is, (1) when every student possesses the necessary reserve of earlier acquired knowledge on which the new knowledge can be built; (2) when the generalizations cover what the students really know, not what they should or could know; (3) when the new operations are an expansion and development of known operations, which the students know how to perform. If the new operations are not associated with those formerly in use, their application algorithm must be clear and understandable.

A continuous, humane, and kind academic process in practice requires continuous, constant teacher concern and actions aimed at these goals:

1. Keeping the students from falling behind the pace of the academic process
2. Precluding inadequate understanding or misunderstanding of new information
3. Precluding an inadequate level of knowledges, skills, and habits
4. Timely supplementation of discovered shortfalls in knowledges, skills, and habits

3.5.4. The teacher must constantly pay attention—not to the formal aspect of student responses, oral or written, and not to whether a student's knowledge, level of skills, and habits can be formally considered satisfactory or unsatisfactory. The educator's fundamental professional duty is something we have never had, but which the new academic system will inevitably have; namely, continuous, never-ending concern for the following:

1. The completeness and comprehension of student responses
2. The provability of their assertions
3. The conviction of students regarding the correctness of their assertions
4. Their ability to defend their position
5. The correctness and clarity of oral and written speech
6. Comprehension in doing exercises
7. Firmness of habits

80

Without all this there can be no educational system. This is not something that the students can judge for themselves; demagoguery on this score costs the nation too much. This can be judged only by a competent educator who studies the great art of teaching all his life; who involves students in talks and discussions, allowing them to present examples and counterexamples of their own; cites his own examples; requires justification of the correctness of assertions, their logic, and comprehensiveness; and who strives for meaningful, purposeful operations, for their brevity and justification. He must teach his students not only how to analyze, generalize, and correct their mistakes, but how to overcome them and keep from making other such mistakes, and so on, and so forth.

3.5.5. Good, knowledgeable self-taught educators are rare. Teachers can and should be taught the great art of pedagogy continuously, everywhere, in all schools, colleges, and universities. That is the principle on which we propose to base our educational system, our system of mini-researches and scientific research institutes and laboratories. Useless, cruel one-year courses in math and science will rapidly disappear from schools and colleges, because it will be obvious to one and all that they are, by definition, doomed. We will stop humiliating children with remedial courses, as well as with courses in calculus, differential equations, real and complex variables, linear algebra, et cetera, which they can't digest in the allotted time. There will be no place for humiliating tests with hundreds of questions which can only deprive students of the ability to think and turn textbooks and students into handbooks. Before each lesson the teacher will set for the class and himself only such tasks that can be realistically and successfully performed.

3.5.6. Cruelty and hopelessness, demagoguery, ignorance, and crime will not vanish from our schools and colleges all at once—there should be no illusions on this score. But continuously and universally taught teachers, administrators, and supervisors who will teach others what they are taught and pool their efforts to create a controllable, active teaching and learning process, will inevitably make the educational system humane, effective, instructive, perceptive, controllable, respected by children, teachers and parents alike, and will bring the joy of mental awareness and creativity to millions of educators and tens of millions of students.

One can accept the view that it is the right of every student to devote more or less time to studies, to study better or worse. But it is the duty of every educator and the educational system as a whole to offer every student, at every lesson, in all educational establishments, a pedagogically realistic, not just proclaimed, opportunity to acquire knowledge, develop his mental and creative abilities, and acquire skills and habits, including skills of independent creative work. Putting sixty million people in classrooms and saying, "Study, while we see how you fare," is not the best means of achieving this great goal.

3.5.7. When students are exposed to abstract structures, concepts and ideas—both of classical and modern science—their intuition can no longer serve them. Not to deprive them of a possibility to continue education, the entire pedagogical system must ensure the following from the very first years of schooling: (1) the students are acquainted, gradually and carefully, with the method of science; and (2) the ideas of classical and modern science are cultivated, as well as the necessity for logical substantiation. This can be done only if both elementary and secondary school teachers receive thorough and sophisticated preservice and inservice training themselves.

3.6. THE NEW EDUCATIONAL SYSTEM WILL REQUIRE NEW TEACHER TRAINING COLLEGES

3.6.1. Whatever the quality of the body of educational knowledge with which the new teacher comes to his first school, he can become, he must be made into, a good educator: It is all in our hands.

This idea in no way contradicts what we said before and will repeat over and over again. We venture to state it here again: The system of training future teachers in our colleges must be radically changed—gradually, unhurriedly, and calmly, without accumulating mistakes. We must increase the total number of contact hours for prospective teachers by 50 percent if we don't want to force our children to go to other countries to advance their education; teacher-education colleges should not offer blanket courses for future teachers, housewives, veterinarians, plumbing engineers, and so on; incentives should be generated, including good pay, to staff teacher-education colleges with only the best educators and erudite scholars, and, if possible, researchers in fields associated with the educational and teaching sciences. One reason why this is so important is that the academic process in teacher-education colleges is, independently of our will, a prototype of the teaching-learning process their graduates will conduct in the schools; therefore, it should be a must for all professors of teacher-education colleges to get involved in one way or another in student teaching—not necessarily frequently, but regularly. Student teaching should be supervised by a professor with a Ph.D. in education, a teaching record of not less than five years, and/or by an educator who continues to work as a part-time teacher in a school. It should be a school devoted to research, where five or ten student teachers take their teaching practice under the professor's supervision. During the initial phase of their teaching practice, the student teachers should, as a rule, be required to prepare for their lessons and conduct them only under the supervision of the professor. Every lesson conducted by a student teacher should be organized as a mini-research, preferably video-taped, involving five or six students, the teacher of the class, other teachers of the school, and university professors.

The last few teaching practice lessons can be prepared by the student teachers independently, without any assistance, provided that by then they are sufficiently prepared to give independent, instructive lessons abreast of the best modern standards, in a class that they by then know well.

3.6.2. What are we hoping for when we annually throw helpless teachers into overcrowded classes, telling them to teach and educate our poor, unfortunate children, to foster thinking, creativity, independence, activity, self-control, self-appreciation, and respect for truth and goodness? What do we expect, after having failed to give those unfortunate creatures, whom we call teachers, any knowledge in the subject or any educational skills in even the most rudimentary forms? We have failed to give teachers any habits of evaluating educational work. How can they give our children anything useful, how can they intelligently conduct a class, if they have never been taught how to distinguish the useful from the useless and the harmful, the intelligent from the inane? We know only too well that no one even attempts to teach them this, either in college or, later, in the school. They are not taught this in the first year, or in the second—not ever, or anywhere, or in any form. Yet it is our duty, both in college with future teachers, and in all educational establishments with working teachers, to impart to them this knowledge.

3.6.3. We organize teaching practice for future teachers with unimaginable cruelty with respect to them and to the pupils who have the misfortune of becoming our utterly helpless victims. We have ignorant older children trying to teach something to ignorant younger children. The older ones were denied any serious guidance, instruction, or competent evaluation of the positive and negative aspects of their confrontation with that complex, demanding, good-natured entity called a class, which can so easily be alienated and become embittered, vengeful, and often cruel.

Instead of having several highly qualified people—representatives of departments of psychology, general pedagogy, and teaching methods—helping him prepare for the lesson, the student teacher does almost everything himself, with no help to speak of. The instructor's assistance is formal, aloof, and restricted to answering questions, while the poor student doesn't even know what to ask.

Students must be taught how to write lesson plans—models of lessons—very thoroughly and as much as a year in advance of the student teaching. These model plans should be thoroughly studied and discussed with qualified representatives of several departments. All the departments in which the student studies the subjects for the field he has opted to teach at school must take part in this work. And all the consultants must have many years of experience of successful work in schools; otherwise, the consultations will be of no appreciable use to the student.

An expert in, say, algebra, will see the merits and demerits of the plan from the purely mathematical point of view, as well as from the point of view of the understandability and consistency of the presented

83

material, the logic of the planned lesson, and its connection with the fundamental mathematical ideas and structures represented in school mathematics—those that precede the lesson, are covered in it, and will follow it later. He answers the student's questions, asks him questions, and evaluates his answers. Representatives of the departments of psychology, general education, and teaching methods each discuss the future lesson from their respective positions; they set requirements from the point of view of their own fields; they listen to, evaluate, and answer the student's questions and ask questions of their own.

Representatives of several departments should get involved in discussing lesson notes and plans long before and throughout the student teaching with the discussions conducted during scheduled hours.

The topics of the lessons to be discussed are usually irrelevant to the materials of the forthcoming student teaching, since it is impossible to anticipate at what point of the course a school will be in several months; moreover, it's not all that important. They can be selected by the students independently, or they can be suggested by the college instructor. They may be the same for several members of the study group, notably for those whose student teaching is scheduled for the same school.

The first two or three lesson plans should have the same topic for all students of the group. This is advisable for several reasons:

(a) The compilation of comprehensive, well-written lesson notes meeting present-day standards of the subject in specialization, pedagogy, psychology, and teaching methods is a real piece of research for inexperienced starters. If one student can't cope with this, even with the help of excellent professors, it is necessary to have all the students discuss the draft.

(b) If a study group consists of twenty or thirty people, each with a different topic, the consulting professors will be unable to cope with the torrent of work, and it will be discredited from the outset.

(c) Even two or three lesson topics can create impossible conditions within a group when the time comes for jointly discussing the notes prepared by all the students. These difficulties can make it hard to attain the main objective of compiling lesson notes, which is to foster in future teachers the skills and habits necessary for competently and creatively compiling, evaluating, and self-evaluating lesson plans or models.

(d) Every department should, if possible, assign more than one professor to act as an assistant and consultant to a group of twenty or thirty students. One professor will have too many students on his hands, making it impossible to conduct interesting discussions of the lesson notes and plans. This is especially true if a group consists of weak students.

Initially, despite the availability of professional journals, textbooks, and lectures, the weaker students will usually tend to unswervingly follow the advice of their professors. As a result, all twenty or thirty students may come up with almost identical notes without even having discussed them. That is why the professors, regardless of the number of students, their abilities, or degree of independence, should offer different variants of notes, with fundamentally differing pedagogical philosophies and special methods. In this, emphasis must be placed on instruction, not on forcing the student to do something. It is also bad policy to reject all student suggestions, even if they are debatable or doubtful, but not totally misconceived. The students' mistakes must always be proved and patiently explained.

3.6.4. The best teacher-education colleges will supplement the compilation of prototype lesson notes with collective attendance and videotaping of lessons at the best schools, conducted by the best teachers. The lesson topics may be quite irrelevant to the topics of the notes, though it is better to organize such visits in the schools where the students will be doing their teaching and with the teachers who will be involved with them: two to four students per teacher, one or two students per class. If a school has two or three knowledgeable, conscientious teachers, the number of students assigned to them for student teaching can be increased to ten or twelve, but not more.

Students of teacher-education colleges should have a special course devoted to the study of schools and teachers. The course should start in the freshman year, both with and without preparation of lesson notes and plans, and continue all through college. During this course the students must attend and then study video-taped lessons conducted by teachers of the given school, as well as model lessons conducted by college and university professors, followed by discussions of those lessons.

This course pursues several extremely important objectives which are unattainable by any other means:

(a) Our students will see school life with all its excitement and frustrations. They will involuntarily and inevitably imagine themselves in the role of supervisors, organizers, and responsible doers of all the good things they see. They will also see all the unpleasant and unhappy things they will have to courageously combat. This will cause some students to acquire an even deeper affection for the school, the children, and their future profession. Others will drop this profession as quickly as possible. Both developments are most welcome.

(b) Work on lesson notes, which should continue along with visits to schools and attendance of lessons, advances from the purely academic to the semipractical aspect. The purely practical aspect will come during student teaching and work in the school.

In the school, observation and discussion of lessons, as well as the possibility of consulting schoolteachers, will provide better opportunities for overcoming difficulties encountered when compiling lesson notes. On the other hand, new aspects of lessons will arise, which the students will reflect in their plans. These are aspects the students had never been aware of. They had failed to see or detect them in lectures, books, or in the lessons of their former schoolteachers. But they will see and note them now, when they reflect on every word of their plans—plans of imaginary lessons, but lessons all their own. It is necessary for them to develop these lessons independently, identifying them as closely as possible with imaginary classes. These classes will invariably mirror the composition, qualities, difficulties, and good and bad features of all the classes the students ever saw or observed before, especially over the last few months. These imaginary classes will represent syntheses of those classes and therefore provide a realistic basis for planning and conducting lessons with them.

(c) Work on lesson notes and concomitant attendance and discussion of lessons conducted by teachers is the first step towards the implementation of the prime objective of a teacher's pedagogical education: the preparation of a creatively and critically thinking doer of things, a creative educator, a master educator capable of seeing and sensing the class and each student individually. We need educators capable of perceiving the prime purpose of the lesson, the ways of achieving it, the merits and demerits of the lessons given by them and by other teachers, their causes, and the ways of overcoming the demerits and expanding, consolidating, and improving the merits. We are speaking of both individual lessons and series of lessons covering whole topics, when each lesson prepares the next one or a series of new lessons. A whole topic is also prepared in advance by the lessons covering preceding topics, and, in turn, provides the basis and prerequisites for successfully studying the subsequent topics of the course.

To achieve these objectives of rearing creative teachers it is necessary, among other things, to:

1. Analyze the teachers' lessons before they are held, discussing them with a group of students, teachers, college professors, and administrators to whom the teacher-author of the lesson submits his report.

2. Study and carefully pinpoint all aspects of the lessons while they are being conducted.

3. Compare other lessons with the one on which the student is working.

4. Ensure conscious self-training of the student in self-evaluation of his pedagogical views, as well as of the merits and demerits of the lessons he compiled and created independently, but which he is now capable of self-evaluating and comparing with the lessons conducted by teachers and with model lessons conducted by professors.

5. Discuss the lessons given by the teacher or professor within the group of students, teachers, professors, and administrators, and compare them with the student's lessons. This time, however, the student will have a fuller and more objective picture of a knowledgeably conceived lesson. His views, doubts, evaluations, self-evaluation, and control should be debated by a whole group of qualified specialists. Each student listens to them and compares their observations with his own evaluations, suggestions, and scenarios of the lesson. He submits these suggestions and scenarios for discussion by the whole group and takes part in discussing, analyzing, evaluating, endorsing, supplementing, abridging, or updating them. All this must be done in a reasoned, thorough, scientific, and professional manner, in the course of a lively debate which can evoke an abundance of fresh, unusual ideas, views, and approaches, because the group consists of young, energetic, and inquisitive students who are not afraid of questions or bold ideas, as well as of specialists grown wise with experience, education, erudition, profound knowledge of their work, and high professionalism.

86

Prior acquaintance of college students with teachers of the school where they are to do their student teaching facilitates the whole process of student teaching and makes it more effective for both the student and the school.

Group work is one of the important forms of training both working and student teachers and of fostering the art of self-evaluation and self-control in them. This can be achieved by continuously comparing the opinions of the members of the group: students, teachers of the school, administrators, and professors of the teacher-education college. The educators can thus clearly formulate the merits and demerits of every opinion as applied to the specific class. The subsequent lessons and discussions of them bring out the truth with ever greater clarity. Gradually, month after month and year after year, the future teacher and the schoolteachers will acquire comprehensive knowledge of the teaching-learning process in general, as applicable to a class with known qualities. We are speaking of comprehensive knowledge in the sense that the teacher gets the opportunity to independently adopt the teaching scenarios and methods for his class, to evaluate and control the results of the scenario he chooses for himself.

3.6.5. An educational system that claims to be effective must constantly nurture and expand the abilities acquired by teachers to rationally design and evaluate lessons through the medium of mini-research. This is essential, because with time all the parameters change: the teacher's age, his habits, his interests, the student body, the moods and behavior of the young people he teaches, their attitudes towards work in general, and study work, in particular. Programs and textbooks change, as do the scientific data acquired by the educational sciences: pedagogy, psychology, and teaching methods. Also subject to change and improvement are the results of the generalized experience of schools and educational research institutes within the school district, the state, the nation, and other countries of the world. New trends appear in educational sciences. All things change with time, and all one's life one must keep up; one must keep abreast of things. No single teacher can cope with this. Life forges ahead, young people head this movement, and the teacher who keeps to himself perishes—or is never even born. If there is no research institution every member of which has a field in which he specializes and of which he regularly informs others at conferences of the educational research institute or laboratory, with analyses of lessons being prepared or attended, the educational process cannot exist.

3.7. THE PROFESSION OF BEING A STUDENT

3.7.1. Let us discuss something we should probably have started out with: The profession of being a student or pupil.

More and more new programs are being drawn up, pedagogical theories are enunciated or rejected, conferences, symposiums, and dinners are sponsored, and projects are launched—all in the name of education, all in the name of mass education, of education for all. Our education has, indeed, everything—except for teachers, students, and lessons.

Before anyone can hope to ever master any profession, he must start out early in life to master the profession of being a student, regardless of his eventual profession or whether he will have more than one profession. Furthermore, success in all his future endeavors will depend directly on his capabilities as a student, and on the habits of education and self-education he has acquired—not in some narrow field, but in education and self-education in general.

Unfortunately, in our country we manage to turn out specialists in different fields—most of all professional educators—who have never had the benefit of being professional students. Our elementary schools especially are filled with teachers who have never mastered the profession of being a student.

We would like to draw attention to one of the many scenarios of the vicious circle in which we are trapped. Colleges and universities enroll millions of people who are classified as students but who haven't the slightest idea of what being a student professionally is all about. All of them, including future teachers, come out of their colleges and universities without any knowledge of the student's profession, because no one has ever taught it to them. The schools are again filled with teachers with no idea of the profession of student, who then go on to train future college and university students.

3.7.2. It is extremely difficult to establish a lasting, mass, multi-million-strong body of professional students on the scale of the country as a whole, especially when the schools are continuously replenished with unprofessional teachers. This can be achieved in school-research institutes and college-research institutes, and only through analysis and improvement of not only what students know, what they are capable of doing, and what their basic skills are, but also of (1) the level of their intellectual and creative abilities; (2) the level of their cognitive abilities—their ability to acquire knowledge with the help of the teacher, the textbook, their fellow students, and audiovisual aids; (3) how self-critical they are, and to what degree they understand the extent of their knowledges, skills, and habits at a given time and in a given field.

All of the foregoing are not isolated questions or admonitions, but a question of the viability and rationality of an educational system.

Teachers of all levels and all subjects, of all educational establishments in all countries, should share the common task of daily and hourly, at every lesson, continuously creating and perfecting that universal, eternal, international profession—student. It is sad and painful to see our 16,000 helpless school systems engaged in everything except the making of students.

3.7.3. The profession "Student" has one extremely important requirement: every student must also be a teacher. When doing his homework and other independent assignments, he must teach himself. He must be able to each day devise five, six, or more home lessons for himself; conduct those lessons as a teacher; and study well at those lessons and acquire knowledges, skills, and habits in unity with the knowledges, skills, and habits acquired during school classes.

When professional teachers work on their mini-researches they must never lose sight of an extremely important aspect of their professional activity: the ongoing training and upgrading of the student-teacher, on whom it is incumbent not only to organize an effective lesson for himself at home, but also a sequence of interrelated home lessons and classroom lessons.

Training of the self-teaching student should include student teaching; that is, practice in training a teacher. In this sense, all forms of partially independent and completely independent student activity in class should be justified: first with the active, but restricted, participation of the teacher, then with his increasingly passive and gradually tapering off of guidance and participation. The foregoing has nothing in common with the widespread form of so-called teaching in all our educational establishments, when the students are mercilessly committed to an *a priori* unequal battle with school and undergraduate courses in the hope that some of them will survive.

3.7.4. The complex teaching and learning process in school and college, supervised and guided by the faculty of educators and administrators aided by mini-researches, should and can give children knowledges, skills, and habits of self-instruction, self-teaching, and self-learning. It can and should foster the students' creative and cognitive abilities as applied to the cognition of self-teaching and self-learning, as well as to creativity in self-teaching and self-learning. This, however, can only be achieved through special training of all educators and all students, a brief description of which follows. A detailed analysis of this work is given in the letter devoted to the student.

Homilies about the need to do home assignments must be replaced by thorough instruction in how to do them. To this end the teacher must regularly, during class hours, give the students independent assignments within their capabilities, lasting fifteen or twenty minutes, with preliminary and subsequent discussion of how they are done. A guideline for doing the assignment is drawn up. At the teacher's request, the students make their own suggestions for each step of the assignment. These suggestions are discussed and the best one is selected. Then the next step or stage is discussed, and thus until the exercise is done.

The specific features of such work, as distinct from conventional work with the class as a whole, are that the teacher devotes prime attention not only (1) to the result of each stage, nor even, (2) to the process of carrying it out, but also to (3) the student's explanation of why he took this path and not another; what suggested such a beginning for doing the exercises and not another; what are the advantages and short-comings of each; what thoughts guided him when going on to the next stage; does he see the merits or demerits of the planned subsequent steps in carrying out the assignment; and so on. In short, when endeavoring to teach students how to do their home assignments, the importance of (3) increases as compared with (1) and (2): we accentuate not (1), the result, nor even (2), the process of carrying out the different stages of the assignment, but (3), the reasons that originated the process.

In preparing each new home assignment, the teacher must identify the most difficult and hazardous parts in it; sometimes they must be discussed in class, or gone over in considerable detail, with precise, clear-cut justifications, and clarifications. The purpose is to assure that, while the home assignment remains sufficiently difficult—as it should always be—it is within the students' capabilities—as it should also always (as far as possible) be. Furthermore, the best way to teach the students how to carry out those assignments is to do class exercises with common features, provided that the students are gradually but steadily given more and more independence in doing their work, with the least possible involvement of the teacher.

3.7.5. We will repeat over and over again that when a teacher gets a new class, the most important thing is not just to require the students to do their home assignments, but to thoroughly instruct them in the essence of the work—something which a class or individual students always require. Coming to a class and rigidly insisting that all the students do all their home assignments every day of the week is not the best way of launching an effective and instructive teaching-learning process.

When instructing students how to do their home assignments, and when checking those assignments in class, teachers must encourage them (1) to justify the ways in which they approached each stage of the exercise and (2) to set forth the reasons for adopting it. New elements in home assignments must be increased consistently and boldly, but also carefully, looking back to check the class' reactions and the extent to which it has been trained and taught to do home assignments. If all is going well, the home assignments should gradually be made more difficult; if the class fails to keep up with the mounting difficulty, the rate at which it is increased should be reduced sharply. But at all times it is necessary to continuously build up the potential creative capabilities of the students, not only by varying the difficulty of exercises, but also by steadfastly insisting that they all analyze the process of doing them and the reasoning for each stage of the process. Such analysis should also be carried out during all forms of work with the students, including supplementary classes, supplementary assignments covering previously studied materials, preparation for contests and olympiads, and tutoring some students both in and out of class—at consultation sessions and sometimes in the presence of parents, et cetera.

Some mini-researches, both in school and in college, should be devoted primarily to ways of teaching students the art of self-learning.

90

3.8. TWO-WAY TEACHER-STUDENT FEEDBACK.
SOME TYPES OF QUESTIONS

3.8.1. One of the forms of teacher-student feedback is tests. In this section we shall consider other forms of feedback in the classroom.

Monotony in the classroom is one of the worst things that can happen to the teaching-learning process. One invariable reaction to it is a conscious or subconscious effort on the part of the students to create the best impression on the teacher and devise techniques of coming up with good answers. One of the ways of combating such attitudes is to supplement the multiple-choice we most commonly use today with tests that require the students to formulate and justify their answers. We abandoned the latter many years ago when we realized that multiple-choice tests were simpler for us and for the children, preferring to ignore their negative aspects. In addition to this, the classroom should be filled with discussions and debates, with questions on studied and reviewed material aimed at justifying propositions and revealing cause-and-effect relationships, which is something we do not now have. Besides, since general tests are usually given only once in every three to six weeks, to rely solely on them is pedagogical madness.

3.8.2. Classroom discussions should be supplemented as frequently as possible with in-class written assignments for three or four students to be done on sheets prepared by the teacher. The problems and exercises should correspond as closely as possible to the current level of achievement of these students and the current tendencies in their work on the subject. One is despondent, so we offer him an easier—but not too easy—assignment. Another has stopped working, so we give him special written assignments during three or four successive lessons. This should be followed up by a simpler quiz, to encourage his success. The better students should be regularly given creative assignments.

There is no point in giving more than three or four individual assignments during a lesson because there won't be enough time to check them carefully. If you feel that, despite all your efforts, the class has stopped working, you should give it a surprise quiz. This can be followed in a day or two by another quiz, then another, another, and another. However, the teacher must have the moral right for such bold steps, a right realized by him as well as by his students. Otherwise a conflict develops, and the class becomes uncontrollable.

While the three or four students are doing their individual assignments, it is good to give the class a general assignment to solve some problem. If the students seem unable to start solving it on their own you can first discuss it with the class. Or you can walk up and down the aisles and talk to the students in whispers. At the outset or after some introductory remarks you may call one student to the blackboard. He should work in silence so as not to distract the three or four students doing their individual assignments.

Obviously, the students doing the individual assignments do not take part in solving the general problem. There is nothing wrong with this and, besides, it can't be helped.

To enliven the class, you can have one or two—or all—of the students with the individual assignments work at the blackboard. When the students at the blackboard have completed their assignments they should be asked to explain the problems to the class. This is necessary to develop the students' speaking abilities and teach them to justify their work, as well as to let the class see the achievements of those students who need such encouragement, or perhaps to encourage those who have stopped doing their homework. Such work also teaches the students to understand the speech and reasoning of others.

3.8.3. The ability to quickly pose clearly formulated questions is one of the prime pedagogical qualities of any teacher. If the reaction of the class or the student suggests that the question wasn't heard or understood, or if the teacher doubts whether it was understood correctly, he should rephrase it in several variants. This should be done swiftly, clearly, and without simplifying the question (but perhaps clarifying it). By simply rephrasing the question, suitably intoning it, or usually both, the teacher highlights its significant points. If this doesn't help, it is necessary to write the conditions and requirements of the question-problem symbolically, using diagrams, graphs, drawings, and/or tables.

3.8.4. Many students have difficulty understanding not only oral questions, but oral presentations in general. On the other hand, those who quickly grasp oral speech don't always like written work or readily comprehend written communications. For this reason, the most important steps of the lesson should be formulated, if possible, in both oral and written form. It is, however, also essential to regularly practice only oral or only written presentation to develop the ability to readily comprehend spoken communication in those who are slow in this, and the ability to work with written texts in those who prefer to listen.

3.8.5. Virtually every question should be rephrased and repeated several times during all stages of the work and with all types of students. All teachers know how the attention of students vacillates, affecting their ability or inability to immediately grasp the essence of a question. That is why it is so important for the teacher to keep varying the formulation of a question until he is sure that the whole class understands it. He can see this moment easily. All at once the class is alert, all faces showing concentration, thought, effort; some grin triumphantly or flash the shadow of a smile. But until that happens he must repeat the question emphatically, forcefully, but also giving the students time to think calmly, without fuss. The weaker the class or the newer it is to the teacher, the more emphatic and forceful he should be.

It is very difficult to make a class hear and understand your question and then eagerly start looking for the answer, perhaps even in the wrong direction, but eagerly and sincerely.

One has to be on the lookout for those students who make a big show of concentrated attention. This isn't difficult when one has been working with a class for some time.

There are many ways in which students display mock absorption. This is a form of mute deceit which is often the beginning of a person's moral degradation, though it is rarely the student's fault. Far from it. It is the teacher's. You must persist in hammering the question home and working with the whole class when you feel the almost physical sensation of the question hovering between you and the students—and not just hovering, but gravitating from them back to you. You must sometimes fight with might and main to drive it back to the class, deeper into every head. Never leave time for the class to rally and throw it back like a ball. Its impetus can be so strong that your return strike is weaker than the previous one, and you will go down in silent defeat. You were unable to get the question through to all the students, or at least to most of them. You lose not only physically. If such defeats, invisible and unformulated, occur again—not necessarily regularly, but at fairly frequent intervals—you gradually lose your students' respect and esteem.

If several students have still failed to grasp the question while most of the class is bravely attacking it, don't sit back and wait for miracles. Quickly and resolutely go up to the students still pondering the question and talk to them—in a whisper. Help them, prompt them—not by answering the question, but by suggesting how to understand it. If you see that the class is having difficulty understanding the question and will be unable to work on it—even after a more or less prolonged attack with the help of the blackboard, brief notes, charts, and diagrams—ask two or three students to repeat the question. It is also good to ask the weaker students and those with poor speaking abilities to repeat it.

Matters in this respect are even worse in the subjects that involve many complicated problems. We will discuss thorough understanding the conditions of word problems in detail later on. Here we would only like to note that the classical, barbaric, funeral phrase, "Well, and now solve problem number so-and-so," totally destroys any intellectual element in our educational system.

"Solve this problem." "Do that assignment." Such instructions are commonplace. They are, however, usually unaccompanied by concrete requirements or clarifications: What is to be solved? What is meant by "solve"? What is given and what is known? What, specifically, should be done with the given and known quantities? What, finally, is expected? These are things that should be reviewed with the students over and over again, but instead, no attempt is made to explain anything. This alone is sufficient to make the whole teaching-learning process a process of mass stupefaction, of mass production of mindless robots prepared to "solve" they know not what, without the haziest notion of what they have to do. What is the initial data? What can, what can't, and what should be used? Why should it be done this way? Is there some other method not so cumbersome and tiresome? Where does this method lead, to what end, and what for? If all this is not analyzed in class and repeated by the students several times over, millions of thinking people cease to think; they no longer understand what they are doing and what is being done to them, wherefore and why, and why one thing is bad while another is good.

3.8.6. The process of stupefaction and dehumanization of the personality pervades our educational establishments. It is supplemented by the cruelty of unintentionally cruel teachers who haven't the slightest idea of how to pose questions and get the students to really understand them; what can be considered a good answer; how two different answers compare; or whether an answer is right, and why it is or isn't.

One could write volumes about the prevalence of teacher monologues in our country. One can fume about it for years to come, demonstrating and proving all the merits of thought-provoking and controversial lessons, class talks, debates, and disputes—the absence of which is killing the educational system. But it will all be in vain. The vast scope of the study material that has to be covered at every lesson in the mini-math and mini-science courses offered by our schools and colleges allows only for teacher monologues or student self-training. Besides, the level of our elementary or secondary-school teachers' purely academic, and even purely pedagogical, education is such that they are incapable of structuring or conducting lessons going beyond the recapitulation, with greater or fewer mistakes and omissions, of whatever, and no more, than they managed to glean from the school textbook. Besides, the technique of conducting active, debating classes has to be mastered for years, in the course of joint teamwork in school laboratories, school, inter-school, college, county, state, and federal research institutes. What is needed is the mutual, thorough, and long-term training of educators aimed at teaching them how to do as follows:

(a) Pose and drive home questions containing a challenge, involving the whole class in the effort, stimulating the mind, and exploring the essence of the matter.

(b) Immediately discuss the students' responses; praise the really good answers and show the class why they are good.

(c) Reject poor answers, providing justification for every such rejection.

(d) Evaluate the depth of a response.

(e) Immediately detect and identify inaccuracies; offer an immediate general appraisal of an answer.

(f) Summarize several answers or require the students to summarize them.

(g) Proceed to a new series of questions.

(h) Create and immediately discuss new challenging and controversial situations.

Teachers must learn all this and much more all their lives, and they must teach each other, not only when preparing lesson plans and notes, which is hard enough, but during the lessons as well, which is much harder.

3.8.7. A class can sidetrack a lesson from the lesson plan. The teacher must therefore be sufficiently professional to ad lib a lesson forced upon him by circumstances. It is not always right, and rarely possible, to ignore inquisitive students in school or in college without total loss of authority, if not plain respect. A teacher who endlessly promises the students answers and keeps putting them off will quickly lose their respect, and so will his lessons. If this happens, nothing and no one can rescue him or salvage his lessons. Furthermore, students may often suggest better ways and means of discussing problem situations and variants of problem solutions than conceived by the teacher. If he ignores or downplays this, and moreover does so several times, the class will reciprocate by ignoring him. Nothing will save him after that, nothing but the universal brevity of courses all over the nation so prudently imposed on all, or virtually all, educational establishments.

Why aren't we outraged by the disgraceful uniformity, the lockstep marching of all states and the whole nation? We who so tirelessly and indefatigably uphold the uniqueness and originality of every college and every school, defenders of this convenient kind of academic freedom? We defend the freedom and liberty of ignorance and mediocrity, the degradation of the nation.

3.8.8. The overwhelming majority of teachers require special, protracted, practical instruction and training with the help of mini-researches in the great art of conducting thoughtful classroom talks and debates, of instantaneously appraising questions and answers—their own and the students'—of instantaneously reacting to them, and never being debilitated or worn out by this work, repeated every day and every hour. Otherwise they'll lack the energy to prepare for the next day's campaigns against ignorance; they'll lack the energy to love the class for its inquisitiveness and ubiquitousness, for its challenging questions, and for its good as well as bad answers. No group of people is capable of asking more unexpected and maddening questions than a classroom of students ranging from the model to the horrid. The latter, incidentally, may often ask more unpredictable and probing questions than the former.

Some educators acquire the skills and habits of conducting discussions with a class or student subconsciously while still in school, when they mentally imitate their teachers—sometimes deliberately, sometimes unconsciously—if they were fortunate enough to have had one or two good teachers at school.

Naturally endowed teachers effortlessly acquire the skills of conducting discussions with their students even if they never encountered a capable educator. Nevertheless, extensive and thorough instruction of such teachers in their teaching specialty is essential. Without such instruction, fear of the factual material and fear of questions from the students will paralyze the teacher all through the lesson. To formulate a question and quickly react to the torrent of replies and counterquestions, the teacher must feel fully confident in the scientific field he teaches. Children unfailingly sense the presence or absence of such confidence, and they respond to it quickly and fairly.

3.8.9. The school must be based not on force, but on the erudition and professionalism of its teachers. It behooves every educator to display not only rich erudition, but also elements of creativity in the field he teaches, expressed at the very least in an ability to resolve difficult creative problems and establish cause-and-effect relationships between the concepts and propositions of the scientific field of knowledge. Otherwise a discussion with a class, especially a strong and aggressive one, can never be successful. The teacher will be crushed by the class or will strive preemptively to suppress it by insidious methods: deny it the possibility of thinking; belittle and ridicule its ideas; consistently and inhumanely impress upon the pupils the idea that they are good for nothing—a common phenomenon in our educational establishments of all levels.

This is tantamount to the self-destruction of the nation.

However, eventually, and hardly surprisingly, our educators are forced to pay for this. To their horror at their own ignorance, at the absence of an adequate education, and of any real help in the school, is added the ridicule of students who refuse to be dehumanized, which acquires the form, not only of open disobedience, but of violence.

We get from our children exactly what we have earned, neither more nor less. Youth never forgives either coercion or the absence of knowledge and professional skills on the part of the teacher. It lacks the quality which adults call "reason acquired with age." It does not forgive deprivation and suppression of freedom, whether it be physical, spiritual, or intellectual. It is unforgiving of the senseless restraints imposed by locks installed on the doors of schools as well as on the children's thoughts, minds, and thirst for meaningful action, independence, and creativity.

3.8.10. The unfortunate teachers, eternally tired, uneducated, driven to despair, have to drag themselves from one classroom to another six or eight times a day. Hopelessly, with the desperation of people doomed to purely physical extermination, they fight with children demanding love, respect, intelligent and rewarding activity, and the triumph of reason, not of brute force. The intimidation of teachers by children is the consequence, not the cause, of the total degradation and disintegration of what we consider to be the nation's academic system; it is its agony—repulsive, horrible, and extremely dangerous to everyone within its vicinity.

Ignorance cannot be concealed. It makes the voice tremble, the knees knock, and the floor shake underfoot. All the nice, affectionate faces coalesce into a single aggressive visage. An ignorant teacher very quickly succumbs to an incurable persecution complex. He regards every question from the class as a personal insult, as an attempt to entrap, humiliate, and ridicule him. This is hardly surprising, since every question is, for such a teacher, indeed a trap—a cause for humiliation and ridicule.

He is unable to answer it and gropes feverishly and painfully for a way out. He either abandons the school forever or suppresses the class—what we have just spoken of—and turns it into an amorphous mass actively corrupted by falsehood, intimidation of independent thought, base flattery, threats, and the cruelty of students, teachers, administrators, and parents.

Sometimes the teacher finds a *modus vivendi* with the class in assignments, such as (1) students reading from a textbook all through the lesson and answering the questions asked in it, or (2) the solution of numerous problems, preferably in groups, with one student solving and the others writing, or (3) reports are presented at every lesson by the best students, with the total inaction of the others, or (4) whole sections are copied from textbooks while the teacher twiddles his thumbs—and so on, and so forth.

There are many ways of deceiving the children and the society—as many as there are ignorant and helpless teachers. There are television courses and taped courses. The children play with toys; the grown-ups look after their own affairs. They demand respect of their rights and academic freedom, not realizing that both they and their pupils are victims of a national tragedy concealed from the nation.

3.8.11. Among the main skills needed to conduct discussions with students is the ability to respectfully and patiently listen, to the end, to students' questions and answers, commanding all one's courage for this, without being ashamed or afraid of asking a pupil to repeat his answer or question, perhaps more than once. This is absolutely essential if the teacher has not understood something in the answer or question; or if the class hasn't been listening to the student's words; or if the class has been listening but hasn't understood; or when the teacher hopes that in repeating the answer or the question, or in rewording the question, the student will overcome his difficulty himself, without outside aid: This happens, and quite frequently.

If the teacher has understood a student's question, but the class hasn't, because the question wasn't formulated professionally, the teacher must reformulate it in clear-cut, comprehensive terms. He must then ask the student whether that is actually what he had in mind—which may not always be the case. Only when the student confirms that that is indeed what he had in mind should the teacher ask the class to answer the question, or answer it himself, depending on its importance, on how relevant it is to the lesson, or whether the answer would be forthcoming within the coming days or weeks.

A teacher's answer along the lines, "This is too early for you—when the time comes you'll find out," is the most terrible scenario of pedagogical behavior. It causes the students to suspect that the teacher is unable to answer the question, especially if this happens frequently. If a teacher has been adequately trained in his profession he can at the very least answer the substance of any question, if even only schematically and incompletely. He must sometimes explain that the students require additional knowledge to fully understand the answer. And he must do this in a calm, confident voice. There is no need to praise the student too much for a good question. Praise in such circumstances may sometimes be perceived as flattery, as not quite honest payment for the fact that the teacher is unable to answer the question.

It is extremely difficult to teach teachers the art of involving a class, of subordinating them to the need to listen to students' questions and answers. It should become a rule to have students correct any mistakes made by the one answering a question, or to explain and prove why they consider his answer to be the right one. When leading a class in discussion the teacher should speak in a firm voice, without allowing the slightest hint of being afraid of the questions asked by the students, and always with undisguised pleasure and gratification for the very fact of them being asked.

If a question asked by a student or the teacher fails to elicit a readiness from the class to answer it even after it has been reformulated several times, the teacher should delay the answer for a while. He should, if possible, break the question down into a sequence of simpler questions, the answers to which lead up to the answer to the original question.

The teacher should discuss and comment on all the students' answers. He should draw special attention to the merits of the answers, very gently and tactfully note their faults, and—most importantly—point out how to overcome and eliminate those and similar faults.

Discussions of shortfalls in the students' knowledge and the ways and means of overcoming them should be conducted good-naturedly, optimistically, and meaningfully, offering advice and instruction; the teacher must take the opportunity to thoroughly teach every student how to work on the study material and keep from being excluded from the work of the class as a whole. Such discussions should go beyond generalities about the importance of learning and the bane of ignorance. The student should be given small supplementary assignments, with deadlines for carrying them out; the teacher should discuss other ways and means of helping him—he should check the quality of the assignments and insist on their being presented on time. This should be a must with all students who are in danger of losing the ability to work on a course.

3.8.12. Patients don't despise or hate their physicians, and so will it be with teachers. Not every treatment saves from death, or even helps. The doctor, however, is responsible for qualified help, for doing everything he can to save the patient's life or improve his condition. Something like this will happen in the educational system. But until it has happened there will be no educational system, just a natural process of the survival of some and the death of others, with no effective attempts to help the latter.

Where is the way out? What can be done to save the nation's educational system from ultimate catastrophe?

Mini-researches based on studies of the experience of the best teachers, on pedagogical warmth, open discussions, and the collective reason and wisdom of continually taught educators, will lead to the creation of a universal modern academic process: scientifically organized, continually perfected, humane with respect to teachers and students, thoughtful and creative. They will thus help to eliminate the forced dictatorship of modern noneducator administrators, possessing nothing but administrative power and therefore indifferent to ideas, teachers, students, and lessons.

3.8.13. As mentioned before, the training of teachers in the techniques of conducting active lessons, in which questions are fired from both sides ahead of the answers to them, is an extremely difficult aspect of pedagogical education. Naturally, everything should be done to systematize the questions and label them according to their purpose and objective. Such systematization can prove extremely useful to the young teacher during the initial period of his work at school, though not always. Poorly trained teachers, as well as self-effacing, shy, timid, or inert teachers lacking even some elements of independence can diligently learn any method of systematizing questions by rote, but all it will do is constrain them even more. It can deprive them of even those miniscule elements of independent reaction to the work of the class and individual students they had prior to the instruction, received from supervisors and teachers. Overtraining is sometimes worse than undertraining: A teacher with insufficient training can still be taught something new; the overtrained one is impervious. He becomes a clockwork toy which can be either broken or thrown out—there is no third way.

Let us nevertheless try to describe some possible, very approximate variants of questions a teacher can ask his student. Without claiming to be either complete or very accurate, it is an attempt to systematize and suggest them to the young, inexperienced teacher in the hope that they may help him prepare for his next lesson. We shall make no such attempt at systematizing the questions the students might ask the teacher: this is totally unpredictable and undescribable.

Every teacher must systematically ask the class and individual students questions requiring knowledge of the factual material: formulas, the rules of performing operations, the system of axioms adopted in the course, their corollaries, theorems, definitions—all this with examples and, where required, drawings. A twenty-year-old freshman at a highly rated university doesn't know the definition of the sum of two fractions and is therefore incapable of adding $\frac{1}{2}$ and $\frac{1}{3}$; he doesn't know the formula for the area of a circle and is therefore unable to calculate it; he doesn't know the distributive law of multiplication with respect to addition and is therefore highly suspicious of the equality $a(b + c) = ab + ac$; he doesn't know the definition of a fractional exponent and therefore completely ceases to trust you when you write 2 for $8^{1/3}$; he is totally overwhelmed and devastated when you try to explain that $(-8)^{2/6}$ is meaningless, if only because $(-8)^{1/3} \neq (-8)^{2/6}$.

We must constantly confront students with questions requiring the establishment of cause-and-effect relationships between propositions. Inability to establish the relationships between concepts, either defined or undefined; between propositions, whether axiomatically accepted or requiring proof, failure to understand or accept the very fact of the existence and necessity of such concepts and propositions, leads to the forced deprivation of millions of children of the ability to think and of the possibility of learning in college.

Colleges are inundated with helpless beings with no understanding of the idea of definition or the idea of proof. On hearing the definition of a new concept they ask the incredible question: "Why?" These are the people, kind and clever, but totally crushed by our academic system, with whom we have to deal. We must go on teaching them, after "explaining" "why" an improper integral is called "improper" although it has nothing in common with an improper fraction; "why" we can use a negative number as an exponent, who gave us that right, et cetera.

It is, for educational considerations, essential to pose questions requiring comparisons and juxtapositions between newly and earlier introduced concepts and propositions.

An extremely important aspect of pedagogical education is the very difficult and protracted training of educators in the skill of confronting students with questions requiring independent evaluation of the operations being carried out—evaluation of the existing conditions and facts. We have in mind questions of the type: "Why are we doing this?" "Why do the conditions of a theorem contain such-and-such restrictions?" "What can we gain from adopting such a course of solution, such a course of reasoning?" "What are its drawbacks?" Without posing such questions, we tend to create in schools and colleges an atmosphere of incantations and vow-taking, suppression, and obedience, not an atmosphere capable of creating a free-thinking and creative individual.

The next educational stage involves questions that teach creativity and the construction of systems with given conditions corresponding to given requirements. They can be formulated according to the pattern: "What should/can be done to obtain this or that result?" Factorization of polynomials and integration are the simplest examples of this.

Finally, we must instruct teachers in the great art of regularly formulating and, together with the students, resolving questions requiring maximum independence and a steadily growing volume of creativity. Such questions include questions requiring the systematization, generalization, and structuralization of the studied material; questions requiring explanation of new concepts and facts on the basis of those learned before, requiring the construction and systematic development of ever more complex systems and structures with given parameters, for example, questions associated with the development of the concepts of number, operation, algebraic structure, power, coordinate system, geometric transformations, measurement, identical transformations, equations and inequalities and their systems, functions and their graphs, continuous functions, limits, derivatives, convergence and divergence of series, integrals, et cetera.

3.9. ON TESTS

3.9.1. There is nothing wrong with tests and quizzes, if they are knowledgeably compiled from the educational point of view, are not cruel on the students, are didactically humane and kind, and are not the be-all and end-all of the teaching-learning and feedback processes. Written multiple-choice tests are also possible, but they deny the teacher the possibility of seeing the process whereby the student arrives at the right or wrong answer. As a consequence, they also deny him the opportunity of helping the student, of seeing why and where the student makes mistakes, and of helping him to overcome them.

Well-conceived written tests offer a pedagogical cross-section, an excellent means of evaluating the level of a student's knowledges, skills, and habits and intellectual, creative, and cognitive abilities at a certain stage in the teaching-learning process. No one intends to reject them, provided that is what they are: a tool for verifying the level of the students' knowledges, skills, and habits and intellectual, creative, and cognitive abilities. They should confront students with the need to not so much memorize facts and act according to a memorized recipe or algorithm, but to reason, analyze different facts and phenomena, analyze the problems confronting them, plot the ways and means of resolving them, justify their reasoning, get new results in the process of independent, creative work, and analyze conflicting and problematic situations formulated by others or discovered by the students themselves.

3.9.2. Written tests contain an element of chance. The best students can on occasion flunk a test. Some do regularly—not intentionally, of course. The very fact of a restricted time frame and confrontation with a vast array of questions is capable of reducing a normal person, with a normal nervous system, concerned with the results of the test, to a state of horror and panic. Panic can have catastrophic consequences. A series of such catastrophes can cause a nervous breakdown, an inferiority complex, an aversion for school and college, even among talented and brilliant students. On the other hand, plodding mediocrities with rote memories, who manage to memorize formulas and definitions in a few days and have nothing to lose because they seek nothing to gain, impassively check off the responses in our mass tests, which are designed precisely for mediocrities. They get their *C*s, or even *B*s, and calmly and confidently, with never a doubt, climb up the ladder of school and subsequently of a career.

3.9.3. A relaxed study atmosphere in class and at home, with the same teacher over a number of years—under his careful scrutiny and supervision, with his alternately active and passive involvement, and with creatively compiled oral and written tests—is very important for the development of students' knowledges, skills, and habits and intellectual, creative, and cognitive abilities. It is also a natural barrier for the unwarranted advancement of mediocrity and provides natural opportunities for the blossoming and rapid advance of capable, talented, and active people.

3.9.4. We must and can prepare people and forces capable of supervising the development of mass education, in which written testing will be one of the supplementary, secondary variants of the teaching-learning process.

Attention should be concentrated mainly not on tests but on the teacher's work at the lesson, which promotes the intellectual and creative development of all the students. Daily monitoring of knowledge, qualified supervision of student activity, and competent guidance of such activity—this is what will create the academic process, which will reproduce itself. It will impose reasonable but steadily greater demands on teachers, students, managers of the education system, and administrator-educators in educational establishments of all levels.

3.9.5. It is hard to gauge the extent of the cruelty and absence of professionalism within our educational establishments, which often require students to take two tests a day and four or five tests a week on the whole material of a course. Such a testing system is justified only if all students are geniuses or all tests are good for nothing. Countries with a well-developed, effective educational system legally ban more than one test per day and more than two tests per week. Tests administered on the completion of a course are each preceded by two, four, or more free days, depending on the complexity and volume of the course.

3.9.6. Written tests covering the last chapter or chapters of a course should be given at least five or six days before the end of the course, not at the final lessons. The students must have the opportunity to fill any gaps in their knowledges, skills, and habits revealed by that final test.

3.9.7. All tests and quizzes must be first and foremost instructive. They should tell the students and the teacher what has remained unfinished, unlearned, and, perhaps, why. One of the main professional duties of the teacher is to organize his own teaching activity and the students' learning activity in such a way as to eventually overcome all the shortcomings in knowledge, skills, and habits revealed by the test; otherwise, the teaching-learning process is doomed. Ignorance suppresses all its vitality; in the case of short courses this process is irreversible.

3.9.8. An excellent indicator of the quality of the work of both students and teacher on the course is their attitude towards tests. We are least of all inclined to idealize or simplify the academic process, which is unquestionably difficult for both the teacher and the students. On the part of the teacher it sometimes amounts to an exploit, not just a job. The invariable trepidation and excitement in expectation of a test can also be joyful, for both the students and the teacher. When this is the case, all the teachers' and the students' work, which is never easy, is filled with joy and didactic kindness.

3.9.9. We must show our children the inner beauty of science—something which only highly educated people can do; we must teach them how to study; and we must instill habits of systematic and intensive study work. We must prepare for each lesson in such a way as to eagerly anticipate the following day and the lessons to be taught, looking forward to bringing them to the class and anticipating our students' joy during that lesson. During this lesson, everything will be interesting; students will be answering questions tailored to their capabilities; all will be animated by the creative process—by the process of thinking and guessing, by propositions and discoveries. Some will be rejected, others justified and blended into the existing body of knowledge created by hard work and creativity. If a teacher has attained such a level of professionalism, then both teacher and students look forward with joy to tests, quizzes, examinations, and discussions, and the teaching and learning process is a source of tremendous satisfaction for the children and their mentors.

3.9.10. If some mistake is common among the students at a test the teacher should realize that he must share both the blame and responsibility for that mistake: it means he either shortchanged the students, or required too little of them, or both.

If through oversight or exhaustion the teacher includes an unsolvable problem in the test, or if he has made it so involved that it is virtually impossible for the class to solve, he should say as much at the next lesson, without quibbling, and apologize. At the same time, he should realize that the class and his reputation have suffered greatly. The children had struggled with the problem in vain; they had no time left to even try to solve the other ones; they were driven to despair—some sooner, some later, depending upon when they tackled the ill-fated problem. They are genuinely resentful and even contemptuous of a person who failed to take the trouble of carefully going over the test before subjecting the students to it. Both resentment and contempt can be expressed in strong and vivid terms, regardless of the state of relations between the teacher and the class. If the relations were never sincere or up to the mark, the class can develop a deep hatred for their mentor, perhaps forever. Children rarely forgive such things by adults who are not very demanding towards themselves while demanding the attention, diligence, industriousness, and respect of their charges. If relations between the class and the teacher were good, the mutual, temporary coolness and alienation will pass. Not so quickly, perhaps, but it will pass and things will settle down. But you should never make up to the children, never curry their favor to make amends: the thing to do is go on with work as usual. Time will heal the wounds.

3.10. THE SCHOOL AND THE NEW EDUCATOR. THERE IS NO SUBSTITUTE FOR MINI-RESEARCHES

3.10.1. One of the basic duties of colleges of education is to prepare the teacher—to some extent (it is impossible to hope for more)—for independently conducting a teaching-learning process—something he will have to do as soon as he comes to the school, walks into the classroom, and starts his first lesson. However, a good principal of a good school can't place much faith in the college doing this, because not every college is capable of teaching every person even his first steps in the classroom—a state of affairs that is not likely to disappear in the foreseeable future. If you start helping the teacher after a failed pedagogical debut, it may do little to improve his work in that particular class. For that reason, a good school will devote the two or three weeks prior to the commencement of classes to helping the novices to prepare and conduct trial lessons in a class made up of the school's teachers (not necessarily in the same subject). They will be able to offer the novice much good advice as he prepares for and then conducts such lessons. In addition, he will get acquainted with the school's routine and the way lessons are conducted in it. Obviously, no college of education is capable of providing such instruction.

Every school possesses an individuality of its own. It is determined by the makeup of the student body and the faculty, the personality of the principal, its trends as an educational research institute, the interests of the educators, their scholarly activities, and so on. Getting to know the school will help the new teacher make his debut a festive occasion, not a funeral for him as an educator, as is all too often the case. The new teacher should also use those two or three weeks to get to know his future classes to the extent possible on the basis of student files, discussions with teachers, and the joint preparation and analysis of his future lessons and the lessons of other teachers.

3.10.2. One extremely important question arises as soon as the new teacher comes to the school: What if he doesn't want anyone to influence his initial lessons in any way at all? He politely but insistently objects to the presence of anyone at all at his first few lessons, during the first week or two. He wants to win over the class without any outside help, without any influence. He feels that he has the knowledge, strength, and pedagogical abilities to independently set up an operable teaching-learning process capable of yielding consistent positive results. He has been thinking and dreaming of it for many months. He has been able to do it in college, during student training. He absolutely refuses to be lectured on things he is confident he knows. Still less does he care to tolerate anyone's influence at the very outset of his educational career.

Suppose the classes the new teacher is to instruct are not overly aggressive, nor desirous or capable of subordinating him to their will from the very first lesson. That, of course, is something it is hard for anyone in the school to say on the basis of one-year courses. However, whether it was a one-year or many-year course, if different teachers who had formerly worked with some of the students in the new group consider that it presents no great risk for the new teacher's first few lessons, the school administration and members of the school department should give him the opportunity of spending several weeks with it without influencing his pedagogical activity. All that might be necessary is to review the lesson notes and plans he drew up himself or with the help of other teachers.

Results can vary widely in such cases. The teacher may ask for assistance in all aspects of his work after the very first lesson. He may request more active involvement of experienced teachers, supervisors, or administrators in preparing for the lesson. He may want his new teacher colleagues and/or administrators to attend his subsequent classes and then discuss them in thorough detail. He may require indications regarding their merits and demerits and the ways and means of consolidating the positive aspects of the lesson—if any—and introducing new ones to make it definitely effective. The basic effectiveness of the lesson should be considered from the point of view of both the students' attention, work, and activity in class and the lesson's results, i.e., the new and useful things that the students received and felt, and/or may receive or feel thankful for in the future.

The debut of a young teacher confident in himself and wishing to test himself at the outset can be very successful. The students and the teacher may come out very pleased with each other. They may establish a close rapport. The students may do their class and home assignments well and be active in class.

Such a teacher should be treated with great respect, but also with some caution. He is undoubtedly a capable educator, and he knows his worth. During visits to his lessons it is necessary to be very discreet when analyzing them, as well as when jointly preparing for lessons, if he accepts such cooperation.

Our Pygmalion is proud and self-confident; he genuinely teaches the class; he may well be the most talented educator in the laboratory and research institute he joined. It may still be premature to tell him as much nor should he be pestered with trifles: he will object. The laboratory should welcome him with warmth and sincerity. After a while the staff should start attending his lessons, and he should be invited to sit in on other teachers' lessons and take part in preparing and discussing them. His advice and assistance will be very useful for the other teachers. Soon he will begin to teach others with his lessons. He works on his lessons, polishing them to perfection in the knowledge that others want to and will learn from him. He is indispensable in preparing and discussing the lessons of other teachers. At the same time, he always seems to find something new and useful for himself in their experience, though perhaps less than they can gain from him.

105

Quite frequently a young teacher may ask someone to attend his very first lesson and continue to do so for a while—teachers of the same department, the same research laboratory, or representatives of the administration—one by one or in groups, with preliminary and follow-up discussions of the lesson. Such requests should be granted outright, regardless of what the school is like, of the situation in the new teacher's class, and of whether the teachers still rule the school or the students have already taken over.

3.10.3. The learning teacher seeks to participate in lesson preparation by other teachers, and not necessarily in his own subject. He attends lessons and takes part in discussing and evaluating them. He does this diligently; with each passing day, month, and year his participation is more professional and the return is higher, from the point of view of developing the knowledges, skills, and habits and intellectual, creative, and cognitive abilities of both himself and his students. He conducts the teaching-learning process in his classes while continuing to learn from the administrators and other teachers of the school, college, or university. He takes part in educational seminars, conferences, and workshops. He attends lectures on the subject he teaches and on general questions of education and psychology in his own laboratory or in the next-door one—and does so all his life, always, everywhere, in all towns and villages, in all states of the Union.

3.10.4. By creating an atmosphere of mutual and joint learning and educational creativity in every research institute and research laboratory, we will first—after several years—halt the current enduring process of deteriorating standards of education in the country. After that we will reverse it. With the help of mini-researches and other forms of teacher instruction we will start and never cease to push the nation's educational system along an upward spiral, never permitting it to roll down, as we are bitterly and helplessly observing it do today.

Schools, colleges, and universities of different countries exchange and will continue to exchange educators, students, and the results of pedagogical research and educational activities. International exchanges of opinions, ideas, research results, educators, studies, and students, as well as similar exchanges within the country and between states, cities, counties, school systems, and schools—all this is fine and wonderful. But it is all unnatural and absolutely useless without mini-researches, without the daily and hourly sustained efforts of every school and college to promote an effective lesson, without the development and improvement of the knowledges, skills, and habits and intellectual, creative, and cognitive abilities of every student and every teacher.

Over the past few years it has been increasingly suggested that the best thing for a school is when the principal is also the head teacher. It is a view we should reckon with, one we should listen to, but it is impossible to accept the idea of this kind of supervision of the teaching-learning process, and here is why. Firstly, even a highly erudite principal cannot be an expert in all the spheres of knowledge represented in the

106

school curriculum. He is therefore quite incapable of competently analyzing it in the capacity of an instructor-supervisor, either when preparing for lessons or after conducting them. Secondly, even a very vigorous principal is incapable of effectively supervising the academic process in even a small school for the simple reason that one person cannot successfully cope with the huge amount of work involved. Thirdly, it is quite impossible to rely on the leadership of one person, however erudite, in teacher training, because he will subconsciously strive to pattern all the teachers according to a single prototype, using one yardstick for all. In this sense he can cause the school more harm than good. Fourthly, if one person rules an educational establishment he inevitably becomes a dictator.

All of the foregoing is fully applicable to heads of departments and colleges.

Every educator working on mini-researches will inevitably improve his pedagogical qualifications, including the principal. Not administrators, but mini-researches must be the guiding organic component and prime mover of the academic process. Only they can be the brains and heart of the teaching-learning process, because no single person is capable of this to the extent required by the school and college. What is needed is the wisdom of a competent and continuously improving team of educators openly and sincerely collaborating among themselves to achieve a common noble goal.

But then, as Hegel remarked, even bad weather is better than none at all.

3.11. THE TEACHER AND THE LESSON: SOME PROBLEMS

3.11.1. At all lessons, teachers must wage an unrelenting war against brief answers by students of the "Yes"–"No" type. A student's answer must be complete and incorporate its justification, or elements of justification—this goes for all subjects, all lessons, and all stages of education. It is not a question of pedagogical taste, style, or technique. It is a question of "To teach or not to teach," to which our educators and people having nothing in common with education have virtually given a negative answer.

Complete answers will not only develop the students' knowledge, they will effectively upgrade and enrich their speech. Students' oral abilities will become more and more precise and to-the-point—at all lessons, in all the studied courses, under all teachers.

Words like "should" or "must" are meaningless. No matter how many treatises and papers on questions of education we may write, nothing will change for the better until we come to the teacher, into his class, and teach him how to become a professional educator, and until teachers

107

start attending each other's lessons. Then they will prepare those lessons together and share educational experience and pedagogical ideas, methods, and approaches among themselves and other professional educators.

3.11.2. One of the teacher's most difficult duties at a lesson is to imbue the students with firm habits of active listening—listening to and at the same time understanding the teacher or another student answering a question. Study groups in our schools and colleges are not really study groups, because the students are totally incapable of either listening or working in class. They are incapable of following someone's speech, of following the speaker's thoughts, or of working with him. Presence at a lesson doesn't imply teaching or learning.

3.11.3. Very early in life children should be patiently and lovingly taught the art of active listening; that is, listening to, and comprehension of, the message. Instruction in this difficult art should continue through all the stages of education, at all lessons, always and everywhere. But once again the same old problem arises: Who is to tell each of our millions of teachers whether or not he is wasting his time at the blackboard, or wasting his breath and energy in vain attempts to drive even some crumbs of thoughts and ideas home to his flock? Mini-researches, and only mini-researches: they are the brain and heart of a modern educational establishment. The teacher can do a lot on his own, without outside assistance, but only if he is both a naturally gifted educator and a talented researcher.

3.11.4. The active work of educational laboratories in schools and colleges in the form of mini-researches will inevitably lead to the conclusion that it is impossible for students to work effectively in class without constant effective contact between them and the teacher, and without continuous, ongoing feedback between them—explicit or implicit—regardless of the stage of education or the number of students in the group. This work will also show that the creation and investigation of problematic and controversial situations by the teacher, with the participation of the students, is one of the most effective means of active teaching and learning, involving all the students in effective creative activity. Whether the person working at the blackboard is a schoolteacher, pupil, professor, or college student, he is but one of the participants in a joint effort, in joint creativity in class: in part, he is supervisor and organizer of the effort, but never merely an informant, announcer, or dictator.

Not one of the participants in the educational process should be excluded from it for even a single moment. Every student should be prepared at any time to evaluate the work being done in class. To achieve this great pedagogical objective, the teacher must ceaselessly demand the students' attention and effort, enabling them, at any moment, to carry on the current activity in class, or to supplement, correct or clarify it, regardless of who is doing or suggesting the work—the teacher or one of the students. The academic system must follow this great golden rule

108

always, everywhere, under all circumstances. But such a lesson does not develop of its own accord. It is necessary to learn how to organize and conduct it, and to teach others in all laboratories, at all stages of instruction. The basic method is the system of mini-researches.

3.11.5. For an active teaching-learning process involving a class as a whole, and for each separate student to originate and successfully develop in the conditions of this vast country, teachers at all levels must be freed of the duties of baby-sitters in schools and colleges and placed in conditions under which the lesson, preparation for the lesson, and discussion of the lesson are fundamental, not supplemental (and often openly slighted) elements of the academic system. When we learn to create excellent lessons in all subjects, in all schools and colleges, conducted by all teachers, and when we give educators the time and conditions for collectively preparing and analyzing them, then all the problems of the educational system will disappear.

The lesson and the lesson alone is the form, content, basis, glory—or shame—of the academic system. Moreover, this is not only true at some stage in the teaching-learning process, but at all stages and in all educational establishments. Nor is it just lessons as such that we need, but good lessons, with consistent, continuous, and exhaustive formal and emotional feedback; lessons actively involving both sides; lessons which teach and promote the development of both those who are taught and those who teach, imbuing the wisdom and experience of international mass education, continuously perfected and enriched; lessons which are perfected and enriched by the collective experience and practical efforts of school laboratories, school and interschool research institutes, colleges, universities, and the education systems of counties and states. We need an academic system in which the preparation for classes, conducting them, and their subsequent analysis are the basic elements in the operation of educational establishments.

3.11.6. The types and forms of contact between the teacher and his students in class should be diversified. There should be no uniformity or devastatingly monotonous repetition of the same forms of work from one lesson to another. The most interesting, exciting, and effective educational device soon loses these qualities when we begin to overwork it lesson after lesson. When the pupils know in advance what every next lesson will be like they soon come to hate it and the teacher, if only because they, young people who cannot stand boredom or monotony, are subjected to boredom and monotony for long months, if not years—the same old stages of the lesson, the same old words uttered by the poor teacher, who doesn't even attempt to diversify them. He either doesn't realize that this alone can arouse the antagonism of the class, or he does, but simply doesn't care about anything, least of all, the words, the lesson, the students, or even himself. Perhaps he would like to change something in the many years of mutually tormenting himself and his students, but he has no idea how. He once tried to introduce something new and unexpected—it was greeted by the derisive laughter of the class.

109

So he retreated back to the tried and tested form of coexistence in which each one knows his place and part in advance, is ready for it, languishes and suffers, but bears it. It is so much easier than daily plunging into the depths of the unknown, fighting and not always winning. "Fighting and winning" remained unattainable, because there was no one to lend a helping hand.

3.11.7. Struggle and the celebration of struggle, struggle and excitement with the prospect of eventual victory—that is the spirit in which the teacher must launch the education of both the students and himself. With the help of mini-researches, which will come to be the brain and heart of educational establishments, the teacher will keep on learning all his life how to keep the teaching-learning process going by giving the students assignments they can cope with, and by creating obstacles of gradually increasing difficulty, especially during the initial time of acquaintance with the class, and perhaps for very much longer.

While giving assignments of gradually growing difficulty, the teacher must regularly commit the class to overcoming obstacles of sharply differing degrees of difficulty, coping with nonstandard problems. Assignments containing such obstacles are a source of satisfaction and enrichment of the knowledges, skills, and habits and intellectual, creative, and cognitive abilities of both the stronger and weaker students. In this way the students have the opportunity to regularly test their strength on materials of enhanced difficulty and enhance their creative abilities.

3.11.8. Some students seek creative assignments; others have to be encouraged by the teacher. After a while they may start to avoid such assignments, some never to return to them while others may come back. And again, some of those who return will experience success and joy, while others will again retreat into the easygoing environment of gradual, painless, but less exciting studies. They will experience neither flights nor falls and will advance in the stable process of gradually building up knowledge, skills, and habits supervised by a professional teacher. This can be interesting, but devoid of the excitement of creative struggle and replete with the sweetness of victory and the bitterness of defeat.

3.12. THE QUALITY OF THE LESSON DEPENDS ON THE QUALITY OF THE TEACHER. THE PRIME OBJECTIVE OF A LESSON. PREPARING A LESSON. CONDUCTING A LESSON

3.12.1. The teacher-supervised lesson is the basic form of educational work in school and college. This is the inexorable conclusion of a thorough and diversified study of the work of the best teachers, who give children profound and firm knowledge, skills, and habits and high standards of development of their intellectual, creative, and cognitive abilities.

110

The quality of the lesson prepared and supervised by the teacher is the basis of the academic system, yielding a mass, consistent, qualitatively ascending result. A steadily ascending level of intellectual, creative, and cognitive abilities of students and teachers will make it possible, with the help of the lesson, for the academic system to advance steadily up, involving ever new millions of people in this upward motion.

The lesson is the basis of mass education; its quality is a measure of the quality of the teacher. To repeat: If we achieve top-quality lessons in all subjects and in all educational establishments of the nation, we will have resolved all the problems of education. On the other hand, whatever we do, however successful we may be in breeding new projects and new programs, new textbooks and new study aids, as long as we are lacking in mass, high-quality, productive lessons, devised and executed by teachers in all subjects and in all educational establishments, the nation will continue to cheat itself and its children, jeopardizing the present and its future. Alas, the latter process is going through a stage of sadly successful expansion.

All schoolteachers and undergraduate school professors must radically change their attitude towards their basic activity: preparing and conducting lessons. A lesson isn't a hobby, a flight of the imagination, or a leap into the unknown; it isn't made by meaningless teacher harangues or meaningless student activity. A lesson is a creation of the hands and the mind; it is hard, purposeful, intense work on the part of both teacher and student. So when a teacher comes to a lesson just to give it, that is a crime preventing the building up of the nation's educational system.

Before each lesson, the teacher must form a clear and vivid idea of its purpose, of what he, the teacher, and the students will be doing, and what each student will derive from it.

3.12.2. It is much harder, but nonetheless essential, for the teacher to know whether, after the lesson, every student will be able to state what he did during the lesson and what he gained from it; that is, what new and useful knowledge or skill he acquired.

3.12.3. It is very hard to teach teachers to outline and formulate the basic objectives of a lesson. It is even harder—much harder—to teach all educators not to be distracted during a lesson, to not go into a little bit of everything and thus overlook the main purpose, forgetting the lesson's strategic goal and allowing the students to distract him from it.

Unfortunately, the teacher has to fight for every lesson, and to no small degree with himself. It is so easy, sometimes tempting, to get sidetracked from the basic objective of the lesson and take up some very important tasks—we have no unimportant ones—which could be postponed. Besides, a class can consist of thirty or forty, or even 400, students. They ask the most unexpected questions. They can't always be put off with promises to take them up later or during consultation periods. As a rule, we must answer all questions at once. We should, moreover, not only make a point of provoking questions from students as much as

111

possible, but also of creating controversial and problem situations that, by their very nature, would stimulate streams of questions from both teacher and student.

If a teacher realizes all the difficulties he faces keeping a lesson on track and attaining its prime objective, this is in itself a major achievement and important success in his pedagogical education.

3.12.4. When the audience consists of hundreds of students, it is easier to keep from straying too far from the planned and prepared lesson because the lecturer's contact with the students is less tangible in a large hall than in a small classroom, making less likely the prospect of being forcibly diverted from the subject of the lecture. Nevertheless, only the joint experience of educators makes it possible to realize all the difficulties of sticking to the main content of a lecture and to study the ways of overcoming those difficulties, despite the variety of unusual and unexpected developments in class.

3.12.5. In a nutshell, the whole wisdom of a teacher's achieving the main objective of a lesson can be reduced to this not so encouraging formula: In preparing for and conducting a lesson, the teacher must rally all his inner forces, his whole will and resolve to achieve the lesson's main objective at any cost. Keeping the principal objective in sight and achieving it is an act of pedagogical courage, the outcome of a struggle—even when the class has not been reduced to a state of apathy, indifference, inertia, and inability to take part in discussing, or even comprehending, the questions raised.

To involve the class in work—without rushing towards the set goal all alone—the teacher must frequently formulate one and the same question in several variants. But even this may be insufficient. The teacher must know—and we reserve the right to repeat this over and over again—how to break a question down into a sequence of simpler, even elementary, questions so that the sequence of answers to them would lead to the answer to the initial more difficult question. Only mini-researches can help the teacher acquire this great skill.

The teacher must give the students sufficient time to digest each question. Haste in class is extremely dangerous. Nothing can justify it. The time spent turning a helpless, miserable group of children into an active learning and self-learning class is bound to pay off when the students acquire knowledge, as well as the skills and habits of learning in and out of class. However, until that happens, as long as the students lack sufficient knowledges, skills, and habits in the studied subject, as well as skills and habits of studying, they should be abundantly supplied with questions, questions, questions, grudging no time to discuss them.

Whatever forms of work in class the teacher adopts, he should never try to sidestep questions that only he can answer. The very fact of the students' minds working to try and answer a clearly formulated question has an instructive and educational effect on them, even if the answer is still beyond them. But the teacher shouldn't ask too many such questions.

Every teacher must prepare all the students for the coming lesson well in advance (1) by the whole content and all forms of teaching and learning activity; (2) by the depth, sincerity, knowledgeability, vitality, and goodwill of the teaching-learning process; (3) by reviewing beforehand, specifically for the lesson, the material without which it cannot be held or be sufficiently effective.

Of course, no teacher is immune to failure. Most frequently, the lesson doesn't achieve its basic objective or is simply disrupted, degenerating into a farce—a purposeless and useless bustle, if the preceding lessons' objectives did not include preparation of the class for this lesson, or if the lesson was poorly prepared or unprofessionally conceived. One of the main causes of this failure is the teacher's underestimating the difficulty or quantity of the material to be given.

3.12.6. It is necessary to avoid lessons which depend solely on how well the students have prepared their home assignments for a particular lesson, or on how well they understood and digested the lesson immediately preceding it. In such cases the lesson can either be ineffective or collapse completely. To avoid this the teacher must structure the lesson so that the first part consists of discussion and consolidation of (1) the logically-concluded substantive part of the preceding lesson necessary for this lesson, and (2) the portion of the home assignment to be used as the basis for conducting the new lesson.

If the first part of the lesson, which is designed to build the foundation for the lesson as conceived and prepared by the teacher, fails, he should retreat and abandon the original lesson plan. When we say that the first part of the lesson has failed we mean that the students are not ready for the current lesson: they have either not understood the preceding lesson, which passed undetected at the time, or they failed to do the portion of the home assignment without which the lesson cannot be given. Having abandoned the planned lesson the teacher should review with the students whatever remained unclear in the preceding lesson and also have the class do a series of exercises prepared as a standby in case the lesson should fail. The exercises should differ from the exercises of the previous home assignment, but not too much.

If a class is unable to cope with a home assignment, this is usually the fault of the teacher, not the class: either the instructor didn't think it out well enough, or he simply overestimated the strength of the students. In that case the work in class should help the students do the home assignment for that day. They should do it again for the next lesson, perhaps with several supplementary problems and questions. Some of the exercises from that assignment may be done then and there in class, with the help of the teacher and the few students who coped with the assignment. It all depends on the class, the teacher, his style and relations with the class, and the study material. In any case, every lesson scenario differing from the original plan must be pedagogically justified, logical, and effective from the point of view of both the teacher and the students. It should be seen not as a failure or defeat for the teacher, but as something natural that could happen to anyone.

113

Obviously, it is unrealistic to prepare several scenarios of the same lesson. Nevertheless, it is absolutely necessary to teach this in teacher-education colleges and during the first few years in school to give educators an overall idea of how to structure and restructure a lesson off the cuff, if it suddenly appears that the class for some reason rejects the prepared lesson.

3.12.7. The success and quality of any lesson is directly dependent on the success and quality of the whole teaching-learning process promoted in the class in the given—and other—subjects. If all the teachers of the class and all the teachers of the school work as a team, helping and learning from each other and from experienced supervisors and administrators, the students' acquisition of knowledges, skills, and habits and intellectual, creative, and cognitive abilities is increasingly effective. In the process of acquiring the knowledges, skills, and habits pertinent to any given lesson and any given topic, the students expand their general intellectual, creative, and cognitive abilities, learning how to acquire knowledge in general, not only in a specific subject or sphere. The result is a comprehensively educated person with a broad mental outlook, capable of creative endeavor, of learning new ideas, and of continued self-improvement—academic as well as spiritual. While emphasizing the decisive importance of the quality of lessons in any effectively operating and self-improving educational system, we must stress over and over again that the quality of any lesson is directly contingent on the quality of the teacher's work, the quality of the teaching-learning process, and the quality of the overall educational system.

3.12.8. The teacher should conceive and present the lesson as an entity and as an integral element of the educational process. It teaches and educates only when the teacher has thoroughly thought out and prepared every minute of it.

As he goes to every lesson, the teacher must know exactly when and how to prepare the class for its key element, if it was not adequately prepared during the preceding lessons; what questions he will ask the class and which students will be called on to answer the main ones; at what stage during the introduction of new materials he will create and discuss problem situations covering, at least in part, the key element of the lesson; where and in what form the students will be doing independent work, including revision of earlier material unconnected with the new material. The idea is that such revision can be resumed during the lesson, if its key element doesn't take up so much time as to deny the class the possibility of devoting time to the regular revision of the course material, irrespective of its relationship to the currently studied material; when and how long the students will be doing independent or partially independent work designed to consolidate and systematize the newly introduced concepts, ideas, structures, and operations, and their connections among themselves and with previously introduced and studied material; whether consolidation of the new material should be effected in written or oral form; how to structure the checking of written

114

class assignments: orally during the lesson or by checking, say, five or ten of them at home, or combining both methods; and how to prepare for the next and subsequent lessons requiring the restoration of knowledges, skills, and habits that have deteriorated with time but are essential for the new material.

A good lesson leaves neither the teacher nor the students any time to relax. Every minute must be filled with intense work with the aim of involving even the most passive students in active participation. This may not happen at once—not the very first day, the very first month, or even the very first year—but they will eventually get involved.

3.12.9. The teacher's struggle for every student, down to the weakest, is mainly a struggle to have him work intensely during the lesson and actively participate in the work of the class. The teacher should come over to such a student more frequently, and more frequently take his class and home assignments for checking; however, this should be done together with the assignments of the stronger students, not demonstratively, without offending his feelings, but helping him.

When a teacher prepares thoroughly for a lesson he has enough time to come over to both the strong and the weak students. If some students complete their independent assignments faster than the others, they should be given a supplementary difficult problem or problems. Let them work over it, perhaps even over several days. He should not, however, give supplementary assignments if he intends to work with the whole class in a few minutes. In the case of individual assignments given to the stronger students, they can be checked later on, in or out of class—whatever is more convenient.

3.12.10. When most of the students have finished a written assignment the teacher should check it in active discussion with all of them; this can be accompanied by blackboard notes written by the teacher or one of the students. Those who failed to complete the assignment on time must also be drawn into the discussion, thereby helping them to understand how to do the assignment.

3.12.11. There's nothing wrong in interrupting a strong student working on an individual assignment: a strong student should be able to put aside an assignment, discuss another one, and then get back to the initial one. However, this shouldn't be done too frequently. The strong student may grumble that he's required to work on two assignments at once, in spite of the fact that by then he's finished with the first one. The ability to switch rapidly from one kind of work to another, to quickly redirect one's train of thought, is an essential trait of a creative individual, and one which the students cannot acquire on their own.

3.12.12. At home the students do one assignment from beginning to end before tackling a new one. This is very good, a fine personal quality. But if a problem doesn't work out, if the student is stuck and there's still a lot to do for the following day, not every good student, or even educator, may be able to abandon a baffling piece of work in favor of something more urgent. This is a quality we must teach both students

115

and teachers. If there is time left after the more urgent assignment has been done, go back to the abandoned problem, or put it off until the next day, or even several days or weeks. Without problems and assignments that defy completion at one sitting it is impossible to foster a creative individual, possessing willpower, education, and self-confidence, and not afraid of temporary or protracted setbacks. The school must understand this, and the college, too.

We should give special assignments designed for several days or weeks to the stronger and weaker students. This is our professional duty. The assignments should, of course, be quite different for the weaker and stronger students, quite different in every respect, but with the same common objectives: to foster mental activity, independence, creativity, and self-confidence; to develop, enrich, and upgrade the students' knowledge, skills, and habits and intellectual, creative, and cognitive abilities. It may take different methods and devices to achieve these objectives, using different materials and working at different intellectual levels for different students.

3.12.13. The teacher must manage the lesson forcefully and energetically. Everything should be prepared for it well in advance and thought out down to the minutest details. No teacher can permit himself such destructive activity as looking hastily during the lesson for the required problems and exercises, having difficulty solving the problems or doing the exercises, or inventing off-the-cuff examples to explain the concepts or connections between them. Such things inexorably destroy and devastate the academic process. Coupled with endless petty remarks addressed to the students, along with failure to impose realistic requirements which the students are *a priori* capable of meeting—such quasi-pedagogical activity destroys the student's personality and generates an ironic attitude towards the teacher and the school, as well as anger and protest.

3.12.14. Repeated emphasis must be placed on one of the main qualities required of every lesson in every educational establishment. After every lesson, both the students and the teacher should be able to clearly and succinctly answer the following questions: What useful things were achieved at the lesson? What new knowledges, skills, and habits were acquired? What previously acquired knowledges, skills, and habits were expanded and upgraded? What useful purpose was served by the teacher and the students attending the class, and is it worth the trouble of coming again?

As for the teacher, he should set for himself all these questions while preparing for the lesson. He should keep them in mind and be guided by them all through his preparations for the lesson, as well as when conducting it. If all these questions can't be answered, then the lesson was at best useless, and more often than not harmful. It corrupts the academic process and all its participants. But if the questions are easily answered, then the lesson can be rated excellent, or at least good, even if the teacher or the students did make some mistakes when preparing for or during the lesson.

3.13. HIGH DEMANDS ON PUPILS AS A CHARACTERISTIC FEATURE OF THE NEW EDUCATIONAL SYSTEM

3.13.1. Our educators at all levels do not notice that involuntary attention alone is not enough for a student to acquire even a minimal education. They discuss the extent to which different courses or subjects appeal, or fail to appeal, to the students and try to make them more appealing or even alluring. No one, however, is concerned with teaching the students how to study independently, which requires an effort of the will, special skills, and a special knowledge of how to acquire knowledge and how to study. Educators think: Let them fend for themselves. They shouldn't be pressured. The desire to study should come from them. If someone doesn't want to study—so be it. That is freedom. At the same time, these students, whom no one took the trouble of teaching, are required, usually theatrically and demonstratively, and always cruelly and pseudopedagogically, to display knowledges, skills, and habits.

Colleges and even graduate schools go all out to lure people who have been taught nothing and have never learned how to study. They announce open enrollments to throw open the doors of colleges and universities without the trauma of entrance examinations. This is done for the appearance of the equality of all citizens on the one hand, and to fill classrooms and classes on the other. Classes and lessons are assigned to ignorant TAs only two or three years older in ignorance than their students, but more experienced in the art of nonacquisition of even a semblance of knowledge.

States, parents, and the Federal government give money for our children to suffer in transition from one cruel course to another. They lack knowledges, they lack the ability to study, they lack habits or the ability to acquire habits, they don't know how to work with textbooks, and their intellectual, creative, and cognitive abilities are dormant. No one has ever attempted, or intends, to work with our children, yet everyone cruelly attacks them with courses the very nature of which require the students to display qualities no one ever gave them. Such inhuman exactingness, which is prompted by the inexorable circumstances of ever more difficult courses, has nothing in common with pedagogic exactingness as one of the characteristic features of an effective mass education. An analysis of this pedagogic exactingness—its significance, and the ways of imposing it—follows.

3.13.2. Teachers can and should be taught how they can help children by perseveringly, lesson after lesson, preempting and overcoming deficiencies in their knowledge. We can, by applying the system of mini-researches, teach all teachers how to demand daily fulfillment of assignments by all students and help them in their difficult task of learning

117

by judiciously selecting questions and assignments of gradually mounting difficulty.

We must consistently and gradually teach children independence by very judiciously and imperceptibly reducing the teacher's involvement in all stages of their work—before they begin, during, and after completion. Initially, however, as each new question is introduced, we must help the children by discussing the forthcoming work, intervening during the most difficult stages, and then discussing the whole assignment. We must constantly require the students to correct all mistakes made and discuss them with the teacher. We must consistently require them to memorize the simplest and then ever more complex facts, definitions, and propositions; we must give them progressively more difficult assignments, constantly reviewing and recapitulating the material of the last few days, weeks, months, and years; we must require them—gradually and consistently—to memorize it and know how to apply it in various situations.

Nor is this all, not by a far cry. We must gradually introduce elements of creative work into the students' learning activity and gradually instill habits of creative work by creating problem situations and requiring—discreetly and consistently, but with increasing firmness—the children's participation in the investigation of these situations and in resolving problems never encountered before.

3.13.3. The absence of a demanding teaching-learning process backfires in terms of the following: ignorance; inability to learn; incomprehension of what learning is all about; inability to listen and comprehend coherent speech; inability to write, read textbooks, and understand what is written in them; inability to participate in the discussion of questions and situations, or even to comprehend those situations; total absence of factual knowledges, skills, and habits; and a primitive level of intellectual development.

All our children get in the course of their education are assignments, assignments, and assignments, tests and quizzes, tests, and more tests.

3.13.4. One of the very first things pupils have to be taught in school is concentration. At the same time we should strive to make the teaching-learning process interesting and appealing, but not to the detriment of imposing consistently strict, high demands on the pupils. In fact, such teaching must be strict. Without consistent enforcement of strict requirements, an interesting and appealing teaching-learning process can soon lose its appeal—something which many of us completely fail to comprehend.

Being strict is not easy or simple. Rigidly enforced strictness—without the teacher's sincere desire and professional ability to give the children knowledges, skills, and habits and develop their intellectual, creative, and cognitive abilities, without a sincere desire and ability to make teaching interesting and exciting, without the teacher's own continued and successful training in all aspects of pedagogical knowledge, without love and devotion to children—is always cruel, always inhumane, useless, and

118

often dangerous. It evokes extreme forms of protest: hate, attacks against teachers, muggings and murders of teachers, and suicides among students.

3.13.5. The teacher must earn the right to be strict in the classroom by devoted, professional work and interesting teaching. Could that be why we have abandoned consistent, daily strictness in favor of suddenly pouncing on children with primitive or cruel tests?

Strictness is not a game. It should not be applied rashly, and it should always be timely. If a teacher works a lot, if he teaches competently and enthusiastically, enjoys the children's respect and love, but fails to impose consistent, regular demands on them, he may retain their respect and love, but they will fail to acquire knowledges, skills, or habits. That is because there was no one to strictly maintain, upgrade, structurize, and systematize them. Children can never accomplish all this on their own. It is a difficult and responsible pedagogical job, not one for children.

Without imposing strict demands on the students' knowledges, skills, and habits the teacher cannot hope to create an atmosphere conducive to the development of their intellectual, creative, and cognitive abilities. That is because such abilities can be fostered only in the process and as a result of the students' comprehension, active assimilation, and active application of their knowledges, skills, and habits. On the other hand, continued acquisition of knowledges, skills, and habits—at a higher level, on the basis of more difficult concepts, ideas, and structures—is impossible without the persistent development of their intellectual, creative, and cognitive abilities.

In other words, if an academic process is not strict enough it will soon begin to collapse. No amount of interesting lessons or engrossing forms of work with the students will have any effect, because of the inevitable decline with time of the students' standards of knowledge, skills, and habits and of their intellectual, creative, and cognitive abilities. It becomes impossible to encourage such abilities, because the base on which they can be developed has been eroded and the level of knowledges, skills, and habits needed for this deteriorates. This tragedy is afflicting all our children and educators, all our school and college courses, and our entire educational system.

3.13.6. A teacher who lacks experience and has no one to help him reaches out for either a stick or a carrot. Fearful that the students are ceasing to work and to understand both him and the textbook, that they are growing indifferent to the course, the lessons, and the teacher, that they are starting to shirk their home assignments and classroom lessons, he may feverishly grasp the stick. He starts to batter the students with unfair tests, problems, assignments, and sometimes vituperation. But all he gets in response are protests in every conceivable form, usually rude, not the conscientious work that had formerly engrossed the students, because they are no longer capable of it. The teacher's initial failure to impose strict demands has resulted in the students' failure to acquire the

119

knowledges, skills, and habits and creative and cognitive abilities needed to pursue their education.

Or the teacher may resort to the carrot—that is safer, or at least simpler. He starts to flirt with the students, sharing giggles instead of teaching them and demanding knowledge.

This is not to say that all is lost. The teacher may yet be able to restore a successful teaching-learning process by gradually applying more strict criteria and providing thorough, concerned, sincere, and devoted instruction. But left to his own devices, without competent assistance, he will tend to give easier tests a little less frequently, gradually making them easier and easier. His work in class will grind to a halt: it has become virtually impossible to progress, because no one knows anything.

The students will start to despise their teacher. They will busy themselves with their own affairs—in class and at home. The teacher will also forget the once happy days in class; he will try to forget them to ease the pain. The result will be what has by now become the nation's classical form of superficially polite coexistence of the teachers and the taught: they just leave each other alone. Friendly, close relations between teachers and students are rare, because this requires an effort on both sides; lessons are a formality; each side is busy with its own affairs; teachers and students share nothing in common but mutual indifference and the inability to have anything in common.

3.13.7. When work with teachers is conducted in the form of mini-researches—that is, several educators prepare for their lessons jointly, attend each other's lessons, and later discuss them—all participants in the mini-researches should compare the knowledges, skills, and habits the students are expected to possess by that time with the level actually revealed during work with the class.

3.13.8. Even the most experienced teacher often fails to understand why his pupils make serious mistakes; for example, when adding or subtracting fractions with different denominators. This gap in their knowledge keeps them from going on with their work, from tackling more difficult problems, using all operations with fractions within one problem, studying negative fractions, operating with algebraic fractions, solving equations and systems of equations, et cetera. Yet the cause may be quite simple, though never easily overcome.

Most of the difficulties associated with mastering fractions can be gradually eliminated by thoroughly, consistently, logically, and thoughtfully explaining how fractions are reduced to a common denominator, and as thoroughly, consistently, logically, and thoughtfully requiring that every student should master the characteristic property of fractions; that is, that both terms of a fraction can be multiplied or divided by the same, non-zero, number. The teacher should return to this over and over again and select problems, whether they are pertinent to the new material or not, in which it is necessary to perform—with justification—operations with fractions having different denominators.

120

This should be repeated rigorously the following month and following year, but always adding new, more interesting, and difficult material and requiring the whole class and every student to justify all the operations. There is not a single normal child who would be incapable of understanding, assimilating, and acquiring the habits of utilizing and learning to apply the acquired knowledges and habits to similar and more difficult problems. In these problems, the once creative task of reducing fractions to the least common denominator will become a tool of the trade, an elementary habit which becomes more and more complex and automatic as the student advances to operations with negative numbers, the solution of equations and systems of equations, operations with algebraic fractions, irrational expressions, transcendental expressions, and so on.

Not every teacher fully realizes that even in elementary cases strictness should always go together with a profound respect for the student, his difficulties, and his occasional inability to cope with even a simple problem. Reducing fractions containing algebraic and transcendental expressions to a common denominator will always require some effort and concentration. It involves an element of genuine creativity, everpresent in such problems, whatever the level of the techniques the student uses to solve them. We have in mind finding a third expression when two are given; using the algorithm for this—a simple multiplication of the first two denominators—doesn't always yield a result because the whole operation is cumbersome. Furthermore, prior to reducing fractions to a common denominator it may be advisable to first cancel common factors, though again, not always.

3.13.9. We would like to specifically draw the reader's attention to the fact that the consistent building up of elements of independence in problems which are conventionally regarded as purely technical, the consistent building up of requirements for the students with regard to the justification and variation of the solutions makes technical operations a means of developing the students' intellectual, creative, and cognitive abilities.

3.13.10. Failure to impose strict requirements and keep close track of what the students are actually doing, what they actually understand, how they carry out assignments, how they justify each step in their work, what mistakes they make, how they overcome them and how they can be helped, the state of their knowledge, skills, and habits, the level of their intellectual, creative, and cognitive abilities today as compared with last month and last year—the absence of all this makes the academic process uninteresting for both the students and the teacher. It deprives both the students and the teacher of the possibility of evaluating their achievements or failures and mastering ways of improving their work; that is, it totally emasculates the teaching-learning process.

3.13.11. Children actually like consistently strict instructors, but only when the strict standards imposed on them apply equally to the teacher. Occasional strictness can only yield negative results. The students never know what demands they can expect today and what tomorrow. They don't know what to do or what to prepare to please their unbalanced or totally irresponsible mentor.

3.13.12. One of our educational system's gravest crimes against our children is that it demands either too little or too much of them. Both cases are equally dangerous and cruel for both teachers and students.

Our children are not accustomed to meet even the most elementary requirements. For example, they are never consistently required: to understand and memorize definitions and theorems dealing with operations with fractions and negative numbers; to understand and memorize theorems on operations with exponents; to do a sufficient number of exercises for the application of definitions and theorems if, and only if, they are relevant to the problem in hand; to regularly review theoretical material and do gradually more and more complicated systems of exercises aimed at gradually developing automatic techniques and firm habits of handling operations; and so on. Throughout our children's long years at school, either no one regularly makes such demands of them or, on the contrary, every once in a while they are deluged with demands they are incapable of meeting. The teaching-learning process has thereby been universally turned into an idle, corrupting pastime occasionally interrupted by hysterical outbursts of ostentatious strictness, which encourages the students to think that the whole teaching, learning, and study process can be reduced to finding ways of more or less successfully avoiding it altogether.

3.13.13. Millions of unfortunate creatures filled with naive optimism, without a shadow of knowledge or the remotest idea of academic work, gleefully burst into the wide-open doors of colleges and universities. There they are hastily parcelled out in groups according to the results of placement tests, and subjected to cruel torture inflicted by a variety of means: tests; quizzes containing 100, 200, or more questions; the absence of any pedagogical assistance; illiterate, inconsistent, undigestible textbooks filled with haphazardly selected material; a fantastic amount of material to be learned and no less fantastic deadlines for learning it; and the total absence of a thorough teaching and learning system.

Demands, demands, demands. Cruel, because they lack rhyme, reason, or justification, or because they cannot be met and are coupled with total indifference towards the students' fate on the part of TAs and the forced indifference of other instructors.

3.13.14. In the hope of somewhat quenching the students' furious indignation, some teachers give up teaching in general, turning courses into charades. Others resort to homilies, admonitions, incantations, and sermons. Neither recourse will produce any results until the students are consistently subjected to reasonable demands they can reasonably cope with, until objective conditions are created for effectively meeting them, until the manner in which they are met is carefully and competently evaluated, with the most objective and favorable indication of the merits and demerits of all performed assignments. Moreover, the students, together with their teacher, must work out ways of overcoming shortcomings, consolidating and improving upon achievements and using them as the basis for attaining new heights of knowledge and cognitive abilities—this from the very first to the very last year, from the very first to the very last day in school, and then in college.

Today only very few teachers can do this, and even their efforts are reduced to naught by the frequent replacement of textbooks, courses, and study groups; by the vastness and brevity of the courses; by daily classes in the same subjects; by the failure to teach teachers to be creative—that is, the absence of mini-researches in educational establishments; and by the persecution of teachers who directly or indirectly threaten the creators and defenders of ignorance, incompetence, and cruelty.

3.14. THE MAIN TEACHING METHODS TEACHERS SHOULD BE TAUGHT WITH THE HELP OF MINI-RESEARCHES

3.14.1. Every subject studied at school contains material that the pupils can understand, perceive, and assimilate most efficiently from the teacher's narration, explanations, or simply from an academically precise lecture, especially if it is problem oriented. Problem lectures are a must in school when, for example, describing the development of concepts, ideas, and structures, or when presenting or summing up a new method—new from the point of view of its theoretical or practical significance.

The methods of giving lectures should be a topic of detailed discussion when working with teachers in the system of mini-researches. No college of education is capable of teaching this in advance, before the educator starts working in a school. Lectures in the school course can cover many topics: the axiomatic method; the concept of geometric transformations; the concept of isomorphism; expanding the concept of number; non-Euclidean geometry; the solvability of equations in radicals; algebraic operations and structures; algebraic and transcendental numbers; functions; the concept of the limit; and many others.

The art of delivering lectures is not an easy one. Most people take some time to master it. It is a skill that must be taught extensively and thoroughly. The surprising thing is not that so many of our lectures, discourses, and discussions are dull, uninteresting, and pointless, but that we are doing almost nothing to teach people how to prepare lectures.

The system of mini-researches should teach educators how to prepare lecture plans and notes. They should be taught how to formulate problem situations for themselves and the students and how to select the ways of analyzing those problem situations, gaining the attention of all the students—both the weak and the strong—controlling that attention,

123

and making the students listen to the lecture regardless of whether the material is too difficult or largely familiar. Flawless logic of presentation; a carefully thought-out system of notes; interesting examples, which are understandable but at the same time stimulate the brain; involvement of the audience in the investigation of problem situations—all this invites the students' attention. They get involved together with an involved lecturer—they listen attentively when the quality of the lecture deserves attention, when they hear good, literate speech, and when they see the conscientious, thorough work the lecturer has put into the lecture. An audience of students is as perceptive of the degree to which the instructor is prepared for the lesson as the instructor is of the degree to which the student is prepared for it.

Lectures and discourses should be accompanied by questions addressed to the listeners, and not only towards the end. The purpose is to make the lecture or discourse fully comprehensible and understandable to all the students. The lecturer ensures feedback by constantly watching the reactions of the audience—its moods, attention, comprehension, excitement, uplift or, contrariwise, passivity and inertia. But even that is not enough. Even the apparent, obvious interest of all the students may not be enough to make the lecture a success. It is therefore essential for the students to reproduce or expand upon the most difficult and basic points then and there, during the lecture, with the lecturer's help and with the involvement of both the weak and the strong students. Only then can the teacher be confident that the lecture was indeed instructive and useful, not just interesting or entertaining.

The gradual instruction of students in the art of listening effectively to lectures in school should commence with lectures lasting ten or fifteen minutes, followed by a detailed discussion of the lecture and of the reasons why some of the students fail to follow, or have difficulty following, lectures. This should be combined with a gradual but steady buildup of the complexity of the lectures.

It should, however, be remembered and realized that lectures are an auxiliary, supplementary form of academic work in school. Failure to reckon with this will lead to an even further deterioration of the standards of school education. Least of all should the school inculcate and promote knowledges, skills, and habits and intellectual, creative, and cognitive abilities by means of lectures: this requires analyses of problem situations; the performance of problem-oriented assignments, creative tasks, and exercises; and the conducting of problem-oriented discussions during which each student is involved in accessible work, tackles accessible but gradually increasing difficulties, takes part in the general work of the class, learns from the class, and teaches the class. School lectures are but one of several teaching methods. They are gradually, carefully, solicitously, but persistently, blended into the overall structure of educational, teaching, and learning activities. They should also grow gradually but steadily longer. This alone—a most simple device within the means of any school—gradually and successfully teaches children pro-

124

longed attention and concentration on a gradually expanding logical and topical structure, which is the basis of successful listening and comprehension. It is a good idea to preface a lecture with its plan, initially detailed, but not with the lecture notes: if students are given the lecture notes they just won't listen to the lecture.

The lecture plan should be made increasingly more schematic, and it should be written on the blackboard or handed out on separate sheets to the pupils before the lecture, then at the lecture, and then after the lecture. This gradually and steadily helps the pupils to follow the lecture, supplement some things that might have been missed or not understood, and master the difficult art of prolonged, concentrated attention—listening, comprehension, perception, and partial assimilation of difficult lectures. Colleges and universities cannot exist or function successfully if this difficult work has not been carried out with students in school.

3.14.2. Our colleges and universities act cruelly when they fill their lecture halls with hundreds of people who are helpless not only because they lack factual knowledges, but also because they lack the knack of listening to and simultaneously understanding and assimilating lectures and series of lectures. The students sit in the hall, untrained in voluntary attention and voluntary listening for even ten or fifteen minutes. They immediately lose the logical thread of the lecture and cease to understand it. The next lecture becomes even less comprehensible. What this leads to we all know.

If we are concerned with a serious teaching-learning process, the country's colleges and universities must devote many years to come to competently, deliberately, and patiently teaching, teaching, and, once again, teaching freshmen all the things they were not taught or failed to learn at school. This includes the following: the ability to listen, hear, and understand lectures; to attentively follow their own process of perception, comprehension, and assimilation of the things they hear; and to understand the connection between listening, understanding, assimilating, and taking notes.

When delivering a college course, during the initial lectures the professor should interrupt the narrative every ten or fifteen minutes to recapitulate, sum up, and review the material covered, ask the students questions, and invite them to ask questions of their own. During subsequent interruptions the lecturer should again recapitulate and review the material of the past fifteen minutes or of the whole lecture from the beginning to the current point. This again can and should be accompanied by questions from both the professor and the students. The lecture should likewise be concluded with a review of the material, perhaps with some clarification of details, drawing the students' attention to key questions, the basic idea of the lecture, and its principal conclusions and results. This supplementary work by the professor will be barely enough to keep the majority of the students from dropping out of the course.

It is very useful to precede a lecture with a discussion of the material covered during the preceding lectures and regularly give quizzes and tests—written and oral—covering the lecture material. When done regularly, such work provides the lecturer with feedback and helps both sides to evaluate their accomplishments and failures and introduce needed changes in the work. At home, the students will study the content of the day's lecture, filling in details that may have been omitted in their notes or in the plan supplied by the lecturer. They will gather in groups of two, four, or more to pool their efforts to reconstruct the fullest possible picture of the lecture, jotting down all the details so as not to forget them by the time of the examination. They must be encouraged to do all this at home and given instructions on how to go about it.

It's always easier to work in groups of two or four. Whatever one student omitted can be filled in by the others. These groups will shuffle around until they end up consisting of students of approximately the same level. If a group happens to have a student capable of coping with all the material independently he will soon leave it, team up with his peers, or simply do nothing on the subject since he has no difficulty answering the lecturer's questions. He has no need for much work at home or may not even need to work on the course at all.

Usually it is the average and poor students who tend to get together in groups. This occurs spontaneously when the previous material is recapitulated at every lecture and the students are provided with a study room where they can work. The study room for independent work should be in the same building as the lecturer's office, and he should drop in once in a while to see how things are. His office hours should coincide with the students' schedule of joint or independent work on the previous day's lecture. This will bring us closer to resolving the fundamental problem of the individualization of instruction. It will give students of different levels the opportunity to pursue the course equally successfully—though, naturally, with different amounts of effort, time, and work put into it, both before, during, and after the lectures.

3.14.3. Two very serious questions arise in connection with lectures. We have already discussed them on another occasion and will continue to discuss them here.

The first is the duration of courses. If in the first year, a college offers lecture courses lasting only two or three months, they are quite useless, even if the lecturer does his best to teach the students how to listen to, comprehend, and assimilate his lectures. Just learning to listen to lectures takes several months. Two or three months must pass before students can cope successfully with comprehending lectures without the lecturer's help. They begin to work more independently, but even then the study burden should not be shifted completely to their shoulders. In a mass education system this will be cruel and utterly useless for several decades to come. Courses will be losing half their students—which is just what we have today. One-semester courses are acceptable only during the final years of study. During the first two years, the same lecturer should conduct a course for at least a full year, with not more

126

than two or three lectures a week. Daily lectures—like any daily classes in the same subject—should be an exception. They deprive students of a reasonable opportunity to prepare for classes, think for themselves, and seek help from their classmates and professors.

The second of the two questions we meant to discuss in connection with the presentation and comprehension of lectures is the duration of each lesson, including the time devoted to lecture material. This is not a technical issue or a question of pedagogical preference: it is a question of fundamental importance for the country's whole educational system, a question of whether we are out to teach our children or merely record their pitiful attempts at self-education.

One-hour periods in colleges and universities—lectures as well as recitations—deny professors the possibility of teaching and the students the possibility of learning in class. There is not much one can achieve in one hour—virtually nothing, in fact. It is precisely this patent truth which most suits people who either cannot or will not teach our children competently and successfully. During a one-hour period there is no time to think, ask questions, create conflict situations and problem situations, solve difficult problems, assimilate and consolidate what has been understood, and regularly review previously studied material—both to keep the students from forgetting it and to prepare them for the perception, comprehension, and assimilation of new material. This kind of work is totally impossible during one-hour periods, which create only the appearance of an academic process. Their rapid pace creates an illusion of successful activity of both the teacher and the students.

All this is extremely dangerous. It creates opportunities for filling the educational system with totally incompetent people, since it makes no difference who *doesn't* teach the children during the hour. All the instructor and the students have time for is to hastily exchange a few hurried remarks in what has become a great race: a race in the teaching-learning process, a race to develop intellectual, creative, and cognitive abilities, a race to develop the intellect, talents, and latent great thoughts and ideas. This race is a crime. The need is for dignified creativity, lofty thoughts, and thorough, painstaking work; not the reciprocal demeaning of the students and the teachers by the very brevity of their encounter; not fast talk, meaningless bustle, or technical fuss without a shred of thought, ideas, or feelings.

In schools, one-hour periods are necessary mainly because the pupils are, as a rule, unable to concentrate on the material of the subject for too long: they require frequent changes in both the form and content of work. Nevertheless, double periods have proved useful in the conditions of mass education. This practice should be introduced with the purpose of raising the effectiveness of the teaching-learning process, as well as of helping the transition from school teaching and learning to college teaching and learning—in both form and content.

Two-hour periods will give college and university professors a day or two a week when they needn't be present in school. Researchers in the field of education will be able to schedule their time better than they can today, without the need to dash daily from one classroom to another. A well-prepared, efficiently and didactically kind, emotional two-hour period is much better than two one-hour periods, but only provided the educator is competent in his profession and continually upgrades his pedagogical skills. Daily lightning forays into classrooms neither require nor permit the one or the other, especially given the huge volume of the courses to be learned in school and college.

Making professors conduct classes more than three days a week, and schoolteachers more than four days, is an indication of the ignorance of the natural and motivative forces of the academic process. Every meeting of the pupils with their instructor should be an act of creativity and a festive occasion for both parties. We must give our educators greater freedom in the academic process, as well as the time and conditions needed to restore and build up their spiritual strength, positive emotions, and creative abilities, and to engage in self-education and reciprocal education. We must trust them more and demand more of them—that is the strategy for an efficient mass education, which has at present been usurped by competition between educators in the number of hours spent in the school, activities done for the sake of activity, and dangerous games played with courses, curricula, projects, and innovations. We have just about everything *but* professional teachers, professional pupils, effective lessons, and an effective teaching-learning process.

As for college and university students, some will take six, six and four hours of classes per week; others will take four, four and six, or four, six, four, six, and so on. Finally, whoever wishes to can take classes all five days a week.

We need not be afraid of too many hours in one day, and here is why. During two-hour periods there is no rush, no fuss, no reciprocal prodding of teachers and students. On the contrary, they offer an opportunity for organizing a measured process of active, creative, and emotional teaching and learning. Students and professors take such lessons with greater seriousness, because it's harder to devote two hours to just exchanges of repartees. A longer period in itself, by the very fact of its existence, demands of both the educator and the students positive results tangibly felt by both sides. Both educators and students tire less than during one-hour periods at which the feverish, debilitating, mutual incomprehension of teacher and taught is mistaken for a teaching and learning academic process. Two hours offer opportunities to originate a genuine teaching and learning process, study problem situations, launch an emotional discussion-debate, discuss all problem solutions and situation analyses suggested by the students and the teacher, evaluate their advantages and drawbacks, and answer all whys and wherefores asked by the teacher and the students—questions such as what happens when we do this or that, if we substitute the given problem conditions with others, et cetera.

We have digressed from the discussion of teaching methods because the question of the duration of courses and of one- or two-hour periods in colleges and universities is directly dependent on the methods of teaching, which are in turn dependent on it. We are speaking of a strategic question of extreme importance for the whole educational system, and therefore would like to repeat the following: at issue is the creation of an entirely new national educational system that has nothing in common with the existing one. The question is whether to teach our children—in deeds, not words—or leave the solution of this difficult problem to their own devices.

One-hour periods are suitable for elitist education which envisages the strict selection of pupils deemed suitable for going on to continue their education. But in the conditions of mass education—mass not only in form, but in content as well—and given the leading and guiding role of the educator in the teaching-learning process, the very existence of one-hour periods makes it impossible to organize a mass, active, teaching-learning academic process.

3.14.4. Now to get back to the question of teaching methods and how to study them in the system of mini-researches.

We shall consider the narrative lecture, the explanatory lecture, the problem lecture, and the discussion lecture.

In a narrative lecture, the lecturer emotionally and imaginatively recounts, say, the history of the question; he tells about the significant aspects of the newly introduced concepts, and sets forth events in their historical and logical sequence. In short, he does the bulk of the work while seeing to it that he has the audience's continued attention and comprehension of what he is saying and that it remains alert, as an audience should. Otherwise the narrative loses its educational impact.

The narrative lecture should always include an explanatory lecture of a demonstrative character. This should be clearly realized by both the lecturer and the audience.

In every lecture, the lecturer should, with rare exceptions, clearly delineate one type of work from another. This makes it possible for the listeners to psychologically prepare themselves for a specific form of mental activity, a specific form of joint work with the lecturer. Whereas in the case of a narrative the audience should concentrate mainly on keeping track of, and digesting, events and phenomena in their sequence, in the case of an explanation the students should concentrate mainly on the logical relationships between the new and previous material, on the precision and clarity of the lecturer's reasoning, and on valid proof.

The lecturer must make sure to tell the students all they will be expected to do during the coming ten or fifteen minutes. Inexperienced listeners cannot immediately realize on their own what is expected of them at the given moment: Should they follow the precision of the proof and record it? Or perhaps it's all set forth clearly in the book. Maybe they should simply sit back and listen to an interesting story for five to seven minutes—to perk up, relax, and hear something curious and interesting, but which can be subsequently forgotten and therefore needn't be written down.

Lectures of all types can and should be combined with discussion elements, questions to the audience, and a brief but interesting debate. Sometimes the narrative discussion will occupy most of the lecture time. Here, too, the lecturer should state the form of work with the audience, but very briefly: Listen attentively to my questions; try to think how to answer them.

A discussion lecture, narrative lecture, or explanatory lecture can at the same time be a problem lecture: the lecturer creates a problem situation; with the students' help he formulates the problems or sequence of problems, the solution of which exhausts the given situation; together with the students he looks for ways of solving the problems; the problems are either solved in the course of the lecture, or the whole process of finding the ways of solving the problems and their subsequent solution is put off till recitations.

3.14.5. Another method of instruction is the discussion.

Conducting a discussion in class is one of the most difficult tasks for any educator, but it is also one of the most efficient methods of mass education. A competently conducted discussion stimulates the active involvement of all the pupils, the rapid development of their speech and mental facilities, and the acquisition of knowledges, skills, and habits and intellectual, creative, and cognitive abilities, regardless of differences between students or their previous preparation in the studied subject.

Every teacher must realize that new information may not always be suitable for presentation in the form of a discussion: sometimes the educator must introduce new concepts and propositions himself. He has no right to demand this of the pupils, except in cases where it is obviously possible to introduce a new proposition or concept possessing certain definite properties that were clearly formulated during the discussion. These are all things we must teach our teachers in the system of mini-researches: some more, some less, some all their lives.

A discussion requires a certain level of intellect, knowledge, and skills on the part of the pupils that the educator can rely upon—using didactic kindness—to stimulate the mental activity of all the pupils through a sequence of well-considered questions prepared by him in advance. As a rule, but not always, every question should be within the capabilities of at least some of the pupils, and most of them should be within the capabilities of the majority.

3.14.6. If the teacher's question is difficult but basically not beyond the pupils' knowledge, it should be emotionally turned into an investigative question in which all participants in the discussion are equal: no one knows the answer, but everyone looks for it. The educator must have a prepared array of auxiliary questions and auxiliary partial problems so arranged that when solved in a certain sequence, they lead to the answer to the question that had initially been too difficult for the pupils to answer. This kind of activity is a characteristic feature of didactic kindness. It is also an excellent case for applying analysis and synthesis and induction and deduction to instruction.

It is also our duty to offer questions and problems that are difficult for all the pupils, even the most capable. We should do this fairly frequently and regularly.

Difficult problems and questions that can be resolved in the course of a discussion, but can't be handled by any of the pupils within a short time, have a stimulating effect on all of them. The extent of that effect differs according to the level of knowledge, skills, and habits, as well as the intellectual, creative, and cognitive abilities of the different pupils. It is, however, impossible to say in advance the effect this or that problem or question will have on different pupils, or for whom they will be more useful and for whom less.

At the current stage in the development of educational psychology and the psychology of creativity, there are no answers to these questions. In fact, they have virtually not even been formulated. However, we have irrefutable proof that successful mass education, especially in math and science, is inseparable from regular creative assignments, problems, and questions, which are too difficult to be individually tackled by any of the pupils and can only be resolved with the help of the teacher and all the pupils of the class. After several years of such work, the class becomes capable of solving problems and carrying out assignments currently beyond the scope of all the pupils. We would ask our educators to return again to the dilemma they themselves have raised: Should advanced students be taught at the expense of the weaker ones, or the weaker at the expense of the advanced? We are sure that this formulation of the problem is not the last word in the science of education.

The pupils continue to solve difficult problems during their home assignments, sometimes with preliminary and subsequent discussion of the problems in class. Systematic, humane utilization of such a strategy for teaching all the pupils of a class to solve very difficult problems leads to a consistently and rapidly increasing level of the intellectual, creative, and cognitive abilities of all of them, not just the more advanced. Even poorly prepared pupils become active participants in creative discussions.

The class as a collective student is the model student of any school or college. It teaches its junior brothers—teachers and pupils—all together and each one separately. It demands the greatest attention in the academic process; it is ever-present and plays an exceptional, sometimes immeasurable, role in the teaching-learning process.

3.14.7. Nothing can take the place of an active, emotional, professionally considerate, creative discussion: neither a lecture, nor audiovisual aids, nor independent work by the pupils. We could add to what we said at the beginning of our discourse about discussion that, when employed continually and regularly, it effectively facilitates the development of attention, independence, and critical attitudes, as well as the need for learning, creativity, reasoned proof, and activity in all the pupils.

131

The process of consistent, humane acquisition of these qualities by the pupils gratifies both students and teacher. The process gradually extends to independent class and home assignments, supported by preliminary and subsequent partial discussion and, perhaps, partial fulfillment. This is done with or without the pupils' making notes in their notebooks and with or without illustrations on the blackboard. Everything depends on the degree to which the class has mastered the process of learning and creativity, and on its familiarity with the studied theoretical material and the relevant problems.

3.14.8. Teaching teachers how to conduct discussions with a class is not an easy task: it is more difficult than teaching the pupils participation in a discussion. A system of mini-researches—humane and didactically considerate, not only with respect to the pupils, but with respect to the taught teachers as well—is the only way of solving this stupendous task.

A very important prerequisite for successfully conducting a discussion is the teacher's knowledge of the class: his knowledge of the strong and weak points of every pupil and the pupil-class; the level of development; the available body of knowledge, skills, and habits; the level of intellectual, creative, and cognitive abilities; the speed of reaction to oral questions; the need or advisability of translating the question either into written form, or schematically, briefly depicted on the blackboard, and so on. All this requires courses in math and science lasting many years in school and in college, which can assure the second and no less important prerequisite for a successful discussion: the absence of haste during lessons.

3.14.9. It is extremely important for the teacher to know the emotional and academic phase at which the pupil is at the time. This phase can be high or low depending not only on the actual level of his knowledge, skills, and habits, but also on the rate and direction in which they varied over the last few weeks, days, and months. Knowledge of all this makes it possible for the teacher to have the greatest, most optimal impact, for the given moment, on the academic, emotional, and psychological aspects of the individual while conducting discussions.

3.14.10. The questions a teacher asks must conform to certain strict requirements. The art of asking questions is something that will have to be taught for years and years in the system of mini-researches, because failure to follow certain requirements results in a sharp deterioration of the quality of the discussion, if not its total discreditation in the eyes of the teacher and the class.

In the hands of an inexperienced teacher, questions can do more harm than good. They can serve as prompts for the pupils. They can provide indirect indications regarding the ways and means of resolving the problem. This is permissible if the teacher has no cause to suspect that the class overestimates its capabilities and no longer works seriously. If the teacher has no cause for suspicion, it is sometimes necessary to unobtrusively support the rapid forward movement of the whole class and each pupil. But if a teacher regularly solves problems by assisting the pupils in such a way that they remain convinced that they have done all the work independently, he can doom the whole academic process and turn the class into a group of conceited ignoramuses, even if all the lessons superficially seem to be conducted actively. Only a very sensitive teacher can independently avoid this mistake, which is so widespread in our profession. Most teachers require competent evaluation of their work, which must be studied and analyzed; therefore, they should take part in debates and arguments with their colleagues. Without that our work is either useless or harmful.

Questions which require the students to simply reproduce facts are absolutely essential, not only for firm memorization of those facts, but also to enable them to justify their statements and assertions and prove the legitimacy of the operations and transformations they perform. The teacher must, naturally, not only ask such questions, but also firmly and inexorably demand answers to them. Ignorance of basic facts is incompatible with the teaching-learning process.

In those classes in which the pupils tend to limit themselves to comprehending the material without memorizing it, questions requiring the simple reproduction of factual material are absolutely essential at every lesson. The absence of such questions is another widespread omission of teachers at all levels, an omission which totally discredits the whole educational system. "I understand, but can't do it," is a typical complaint, a cry of anguish rising from the throats of millions of today's unfortunate students. In such cases, ignorance of the factual material is usually aggravated by an inability to use it, and the absence of an adequate level of skills and habits and intellectual and creative capabilities. This is hardly surprising: How can students be expected to learn to do something, acquire skills and habits, plus develop intellectual, creative, and cognitive abilities, if they haven't been required to memorize, simply memorize, the factual material after it has been understood?

This work, however, is not an end in itself. Facts are the means, the tools, not the purpose of education—as most educators in our country seem to think today. In effect, all tests are reduced to reproducing factual material. This is a historically unprecedented approach fraught with mortal danger for the nation. Failing to see that such work is useless, all we require of students is to know the factual material. They cannot be expected to be able to reproduce anything if they are taught only to memorize facts: they become stupified, their development slows down, and their memory deteriorates, because there are limits to mechanical memorization. The easiest thing—the reproduction of facts—becomes insurmountably difficult, because the students have no logical memory.

3.14.11. Conducting a discussion in class is an important means of developing new concepts and introducing new ideas through collective work supervised by the teacher. The new concepts and ideas may be extensions or generalizations of ones already familiar to the students,

133

which they have mastered and can apply to the solution of problems and analysis of problem situations. Discussions provide an opportunity for a systematic, step-by-step, purposeful, and didactically kind structuralization and systematization of knowledge—interspaced with lecture presentation.

Discussions must be emotional, and when they are they enable us to create the fundamental type of teaching activity, which is teaching people to think, reason, talk, prove, justify, argue, refute, investigate problem situations, voice doubts and hesitation, reinforce one's view or discover one's mistakes, learn to use books, know how to read and understand them correctly, and learn to acquire knowledge independently.

A discussion is not a teacher's monologue with incidental questions addressed to the audience—there's not much use in this. New concepts and ideas are born in discussions and debates; the connections between them are established, situations requiring investigation arise, problems are formulated and the ways of solving them are determined, and then they are solved by the students, supervised and guided by the teacher, but with his least possible involvement.

This, however, is only possible in an educational system having educated or continually taught teachers. With the help of mini-researches, a viable educational system is capable of teaching its teachers how to ask their students questions that are clear, to the point, and understandable, allowing, as far as possible, no unforeseeable correct answers that do not serve the purpose of the lesson. We will, furthermore, be able to teach all teachers how to formulate questions in such a way that their answers should derive logically from the information assimilated by the students—this is one of the basic manifestations of didactic kindness.

3.14.12. We categorically reject teaching solely by answering questions. By universally relying on students' questions we educators successfully prevent the building up of an efficient educational system, while at the same time striking a pose. Neither schoolchildren, nor college students, nor young teachers, have the least idea what to ask, or how. Asking questions requires a certain level of knowledge and thinking, which neither our students nor our teachers have. We are all fully aware of this, but prefer not to mention it.

A young or inadequately trained, or insufficiently capable teacher doesn't see half the questions he should ask the class. He is unaware of even a fraction of the difficulties the forthcoming lesson is fraught with. It doesn't even occur to him that some of those difficulties could and should be prevented and the others overcome or avoided. Nor does he see that it might well be necessary to create new difficulties for the purposes of the lesson. This is something a teacher must also do to organize an effective instructive lesson.

A young teacher may not even suspect that questions aimed at clarifying the definitions of new concepts through comparisons of several concepts should be formulated along different lines than questions the students are asked for the initial introduction of a new concept. These two types are quite different from questions which require a final formulation of a definition of a newly introduced concept. Questions requiring the recapitulation of properties of previously studied and mastered concepts needed for the current lesson require yet another approach, depending on the following: how long ago they were studied, the degree of preliminary recapitulation by the students, the composition of the class, the state of the students, et cetera. Questions aimed at systematizing and structuralizing the studied material, at establishing the cause-and-effect relationships between the properties of concepts and structures and their mutual interdependence, are of an entirely different nature.

3.14.13. Let us dwell briefly on the main types of student/teacher discussions that teachers can be taught at our mini-researches.

An informative discussion is organized in such a way that the students formulate the new information by answering a series of questions prepared in advance by the teacher. At the same time, they assimilate and digest the information and initially consolidate the acquired knowledge. Thus, the imparting of new knowledge, initial assimilation, and comprehension—and even initial consolidation—occur simultaneously during the lesson, under the stewardship of the teacher, and with the active involvement of all the students.

During an informative discussion, conclusions and hypotheses may be formulated by either the teacher or the students. It all depends on the difficulty of the material, the academic standards of the students, how much time the teacher has worked with the given group, the ability of the teacher and the students to do such work, the quality of the teacher's and the students' preparation for the specific lesson, the mood of the class and the teacher, their relationship, and many other things.

The principal objective of a heuristic discussion is not so much the introduction of new material as the solution of a posed problem by the same ways and means as employed during an informative discussion. The teacher arranges his questions in such a way that the sequence of answers to them represents a problem-solving process that yields either the solution of the problem or a procedure for solving it. A heuristic discussion consistently fosters the development of independent thinking and creativity in all students—the weak as well as the strong. Therein lies its strength and eternal youth, its didactic kindness with respect to the students and the teacher.

The reproducing discussion serves a variety of purposes, principal among them being the consolidation and clarification of the students' knowledge, and the comparison and comparative analysis of concepts, propositions, ideas, and structures known to the students. In the course and as a result of such a discussion there takes place the systematization of the students' knowledge: its consolidation in their memory; its stimulation with the purpose of preparing the students for a new lesson or series of new lessons; the structuralization of the students' knowledge; and the summing up and concluding of the material of the studied section, chapter, or course.

3.14.14. To conclude our discussion of discussions, two comments of major importance are called for.

First: Even the most brilliant student is not a trained teacher. His answers may, naturally, be outside the educational strategy of solving the general problem prepared in advance by the teacher and, naturally, not known to the students. This is sometimes a cause of unfortunate situations, which can affect the teacher's work with the class, both during the lesson and in general, by placing a wall of alienation and hostility between them.

Say a pupil gives a good answer to the teacher's question and offers an excellent independent solution of a partial problem. But the teacher, because of inadequate professional training, fails to grasp the student's answer; or perhaps he understands the answer, but refuses to accept it because it diverts him from the problem-solving strategy he had prepared beforehand. So instead of sincerely praising the student for a correct answer—especially if the student is not at the top of the class—the teacher commits one of the worst conceivable pedagogical mistakes, which is both cruel and irreparable. The student was right—he gave a good answer, though he failed to oblige the teacher by giving the expected one. The teacher frowns with displeasure, sighs, and, if he doesn't tell the student directly that he is mistaken—which also happens—simply ignores him and turns to another student, and another, and another, until he gets the answer he wanted in the first place.

A terrible thing happens. Lessons in math and science become lessons in enigmas, during which good answers are denigrated by ignorance, if not ridiculed; where praise is given for a fortuitously correct answer without any justification save that it leads to the solution of the problem. In fact, the problems themselves become enigmas. Take a closer look at our textbooks for training future schoolteachers.

Second: Too much enthusiasm for dispassionate, dry, logical exercises is as dangerous and fatal to education as is the drive for superficial brilliance to the detriment of thorough study of the material, as is the drive for emotional effects to the detriment of depth and firmness of knowledge and to the active quest for the essence of the studied facts and phenomena. We are speaking of a dangerous and widespread variant of misunderstood class activity with an abundance of superficial, meaningless questions—sometimes dangerous and harmful—which require the introduction of new concepts without adequate preparation of the students. The thoughts of the teacher and the students slip over the surface of the topic—the class is excited, the lesson is interesting and exciting. But the teacher's questions and remarks are so prompting that there is no need for the students to use their brains. There is no penetration into the essence and depth, or even the content, of the material. There is no time at the lesson to consolidate and review the main stages and results of the work, to go into the connections between the newly and formerly studied questions, because the whole lesson has been reduced to a game of words. The students are rapidly guided or even

136

dragged to the solution, to the answers to questions: there is no intellectual effort, no intellectual intensity. If this occurs regularly from lesson
to lesson, the results become tragic. To their surprise and horror, the
students and the teacher soon discover gaps, and even voids, in their
memory and knowledge. The students cease to comprehend the subject.
Their interest and excitement quickly dissipates. The students rapidly
become passive and develop a dislike for the subject and the teacher.

The absence of professionalism on the part of the teacher and the
absence of professional help at the necessary moment give rise to an
irreversible process of student flight from the subject, the teacher, and
eventually from the school.

3.15. HOW TO HELP STUDENTS ASSIMILATE NEW CONCEPTS AND DEVELOP THEIR THINKING AND SPEECH

3.15.1. Educators in all of the country's educational establishments
must realize that it is cruel and useless to expect students to immediately
assimilate new concepts. The assimilation of concepts takes time as, under the competent guidance of the teacher, they expand in content,
acquire more and more significant traits and qualities, and begin to
appeal to the students. Without thorough and competent guidance, most
students never fully assimilate scientific concepts, and they form an incomplete and/or distorted idea of them.

Many of our educators tend to forget that a concept cannot be
assimilated if it is not defined in so many words. For students to clearly
formulate concepts they must be in command of an adequate vocabulary
and the language's grammatical system, acquired mainly in the course,
and as a result of active, creative participation in lessons. However, today
virtually all forms of the teacher's active, creative work with the class
have been superseded by yes-or-no answers and knowledge evaluation
methods which require on the students' part merely mechanical reproduction and application of operations, algorithms, rules, and patterns.
In other words, all that is required of students is what blunts their
thinking, creativity, and intellectual activity, along with their ability to
use grammatically correct and concise language.

The formation of concepts in the students' minds requires the humane and active guidance of the educator. If there is no such activity
in class, no one and nothing in the mass education process is capable of
substituting for it. The students grope independently in different directions, receding farther and farther from the pursued objective; significant aspects of the concepts remain unnoticed; insignificant aspects
take on the dimensions of significant ones. The incomplete or erroneous
assimilation of some concepts leads to the distortion of new ones, because
they are based on an erroneous foundation. The teacher can no longer

137

control the teaching-learning process, which becomes objectively uncontrollable; the students cease to understand the teacher; the teaching-learning process irreversibly declines and perishes.

We must use mini-researches to teach our educators that before new concepts can be introduced the students must be made to realize that the previously introduced concepts are inadequate for solving practical and theoretical problems, performing operations, solving equations, measuring quantities, and so on.

In the course of their studies in college and later on, when they are working on their own and continuing to study with their peers and with the help of supervisors and administrators, our teachers will gradually realize that the assimilation of concepts is a process during which the teacher helps the students to identify the essential, characteristic features of those concepts. We have in mind, specifically, such concepts as equation, inequality, operation, relation, algebraic structure, number, function, graphic representation of functions, limit of a function, continuous function, derivative function, integral, convergence, geometric transformations, measurement of quantities, et cetera. The assimilation process can be very long and difficult, requiring several years of competent, purposeful educational guidance.

In other words, the overwhelming majority of children gain nothing from a formal introduction of concepts. If a concept is not seen in its relationships to other concepts, in comparison and counterposition, it cannot be introduced, will not be assimilated, and most students will display total incomprehension when attempting to apply it. It is in classroom work that the students reevaluate previously introduced concepts and upgrade previously acquired knowledge under the impact of new concepts and knowledge. Many extensive studies have shown that if a teacher fails to conduct such purposeful work aimed at incorporating a new concept into the system of previously acquired concepts, the students will acquire incomplete or distorted knowledge. They will have assimilated not a system of scientific concepts, not the logical system of the course, but a jumble of isolated facts and concepts that cannot be applied consciously and purposefully and are soon forgotten.

In the process of comparing and correlating newly introduced concepts with previously assimilated ones, the students, under the constant guidance and supervision of the teacher, gradually acquire the ability of abstract thinking, which is inseparably associated with speech. This creates the prerequisites for the formal definition of the new concept.

The concept of the area of a figure bounded by the curves $y = 0$, $x = a, x = b, y = f(x)$, where $f(x) \geqslant 0$ and is continuous on $[a, b]$, appears in the course of a discussion on the area of a polygon led by the teacher. It becomes apparent that the known concepts are inadequate, suggesting the need for introducing Riemann sums and their limit. The teacher thus develops the abstract concept of area, formulated with the help of the students, and then by the students themselves. In the course, and as a result, of an active discussion with the students, the previously

138

assimilated and known concept of the area of a polygon is incorporated in the new concept as a special case.

If the teacher, purely formally, has introduced the concepts of inverse trigonometric functions without the long classroom work needed to assimilate them, without correlating them with previously introduced concepts, and without supervising the solution of a large number of problems involving these functions in association with the previously introduced ones, then these concepts will be totally incomprehensible and cruel for the majority of our students. They will develop an aversion to mathematics—even those students who once liked it.

The teacher should supervise the process of assimilation of concepts as a process of advance from incomplete and inaccurate to more complete and more accurate knowledge. This is a complex but controllable process in which the concepts should be presented not in isolation, but as the logical system of the study subject. Such control of the teaching-learning process is beyond the capability of school and college students. It is also beyond the capabilities of motion-picture lessons, programmed learning, or teleclasses—if they are conducted without teacher participation. Nor will just any teacher do, but only one who has learned to (1) continuously follow the students' internal process of assimilation of the system of knowledge, (2) see and feel the process, and (3) emotionally control the process.

One of the prime objectives of pedagogical education in a teacher-education college and, even more importantly, in the educational establishment where the teacher is working, should be to imbue the teacher with the skills and habits of sensing and understanding the inner world of the learner in the process of acquisition of new concepts; in the process of mastering new structures; in the process of acquiring habits and skills of thinking and rationalizing, proving propositions, and justifying statements; and also, in the process of self-instruction and consolidating and evaluating the results of self-instruction.

Teachers should be ceaselessly taught (or, as the case may be, they should teach others) that the introduction of a new concept involves a bold educational act, regardless of who first formulates it in the class—the students or the teacher. This doesn't mean that the formal introduction of a new concept by means of a definition can be achieved with equal educational effect by the teacher and the students. Only in exceptional cases is it hard to give preference to the teacher's or students' variant of formulating a new concept. Usually the differences are obvious. However, teachers must be constantly taught how to evaluate such variants correctly and justify their evaluation from, among other things, the point of view of developing the learners' thinking and speaking capacities.

It is common knowledge that in the lower grades and classes, with unprepared students, concepts should be introduced by progressing from specific examples to the general concept and actively involving all the students in the work. The general trend of the work in class should be along the following lines: With the help of specific examples and

139

under the guidance of the teacher, who provides an example of literate speech and thinking, the students gradually identify the characteristic features of the introduced concept; they formulate a definition; with the help of the introduced definition they solve the problem of the relevance of different entities to the introduced concept; they apply the new concept to different conditions; they then use the new concept to solve a new range of problems, which could not be solved without it, or could only be partially solved or solved with difficulty.

In the course of the teacher's work with the students on the introduction of new concepts with the help of a formal definition, the role of discussion with the class should steadily decline. We should gradually teach all children to accept without protest and understand—even if it takes much time and considerable effort—the purely deductive development of a theory, and not to greet formal definitions with that awful, "Why?"

Our teachers are deprived of the possibility of actively helping the students to develop their thinking and speech and assimilate undistorted definitions of undistorted concepts because none of them were taught how to give such help. We neglect the fact that nothing can ever replace the teacher's oral work when defining and formulating concepts in class. This work can and must be one of the prime sources, one of the most powerful means, not only of correctly assimilating concepts and propositions, but also of developing the students' thinking and speech.

Consistent application of distorted concepts—whether the distortions were due to the assimilation of distorted definitions or to failure to assimilate them at all—leads to the disruption of the system of knowledge, to the use of propositions devoid of any meaning, and to juggling with symbols devoid of any content. Both the course of such operations and their justification and results are totally unpredictable. Instead of fostering creative, analytical, critical thinking, the teaching-learning process stubbornly instills dogmatism. Hence such monstrous mistakes as $\frac{a}{b+c} = \frac{a}{b} + \frac{a}{c}$ which carry over into college in such forms as the following: $\int \frac{x^1}{x^2+1}\,dx = \int \frac{x^1}{x^2}\,dx + \int \frac{x^1}{1}\,dx$; or $\sin(\alpha + \beta) = \sin\alpha + \sin\beta$, or even from right to left; or $8^{15} \div 2^3 = 4^{12}$ or 4^5; or $\int x\,lnx\,dx = lnx \int x\,dx$, $\int \frac{dx}{f(x)} = ln\,|\,f(x)\,| + c$, where $f(x)$ is any function.

We will never be able to completely eliminate such ludicrous mistakes. In fact, that isn't the point. The point is that they are steadily increasing in number and becoming the norm of the academic process. The only way to halt and reverse this process, which is destructive to the whole educational system, is for all educational establishments to sponsor ongoing mini-researches that are didactically kind with respect to the educators and the students.

Our educators at all levels should be continuously and humanely taught that the development of concepts in the students' minds takes time and must be supported by a variety of examples of their applications. The teacher's work on the active assimilation of a concept by all

140

students must commence with introductory examples capable of arousing the students' interest in the concept. This should be followed up by defining the concept, if possible with the help of the students, and then with examples illustrating its applications—the more the better.

The formation of concepts is a long process controlled by the teacher—if we want to make the new concepts a component of the students' system of conscious, operational knowledge. In other words, long work with the students aimed at developing each new concept is a must. Our one-year courses in algebra, geometry, physics, chemistry, or biology in secondary school, and the course in calculus with analytical geometry and other mini-courses (quasi-courses) in college are a consequence either of the total and hopeless failure of those who introduced them to comprehend the essence of the educational process, or of its deliberate denigration, or both.

As long as our children and educators are forced to work in such difficult conditions, we must constantly and very thoroughly help our teachers to improve the methods of assimilation of new concepts by students. We will say again and again that these methods consist in preliminary preparation of the students for the introduction of a new concept long before its formal introduction, followed by thorough work with the new concept in varying associations and relationships with known concepts. In the process of such work the concept is continuously enriched and clarified in the students' minds. By contrast, formal assimilation of a concept during a single lesson may be incomplete, inaccurate, or totally distorted.

The assimilation of undefinable concepts requires many years of extensive work with all students, regardless of their abilities or academic standards.

As the students master the science they are studying, the expansion and refinement of a concept in their minds can lead to its better formal definition—even within the secondary school course. Examples of such concepts are the concepts of function, number, operation, algebraic structure, and continuity. Teachers are unable to carry out such refinement alone. They need mutual, competent, and continuous help and guidance.

3.15.2. A very valuable method for teaching students the ideas and methods of science and developing their thinking abilities is the teacher's thinking aloud. When practiced regularly, thinking aloud fosters relations of profound respect, friendship, sincerity, and confidence between the teacher and the students. It is absolutely irreplaceable in stimulating scientific thinking, preventing misconceptions about the concepts and methods of science, and introducing all students—not just the select—into the edifice of science, where some will stay for a long time, some will remain for good, some will drop in occasionally, and some never. Some students will carry all through their lives a sense of awe for science—its power, beauty, and perfection; some will see nothing special in it; some will feel interested, but will soon forget.

141

One can never predict how a person will react to genuine science and genuine scientific knowledge. Scientific knowledge can never be replaced with home-grown bits of information devised by educators in the name of misconceived interest, misconceived simplicity, and misconceived entertainment.

Whatever our children's impressions of genuine science, they should retain throughout their lives a sense of gratitude for the person who emotionally, sincerely, and patiently, even if not always skillfully, attempted to show them the truth. This is, of course, quite impossible if a teacher is incapable of distinguishing between the truth and naive, pseudopedagogical innovations, between a scientific idea and ignorance.

Thinking aloud—problem-oriented thinking—by the teacher is not a specific device to be employed only in exceptional cases. It is an effective general method of involving students in intense thinking activity, a means of gradually instilling the ideas and methods of science. Educators at all levels must be taught the art of thinking aloud. It differs from the problem-oriented discussion in that the teacher focuses the students' attention on his own thoughts. He invites them to think together with him, but not by taking part in a discussion, because this immediately frightens many children away. Students unprepared for questions by their previous education tend to fear them because they lack the habits of working with questions, don't know how to listen to and understand them, or they can't analyze them even when they do understand them. Moreover and more importantly, a teacher must be entitled to ask the class questions; otherwise, he is a despot and tyrant. Voiced thoughts, even very bold ones, are not cruel.

Another difference between problem-oriented thinking and problem-oriented presentation is that the teacher informs the students that they need not necessarily understand all his thoughts and ideas: they are free to choose whether to listen to his thoughts attentively or not, whether to think together with him or not, whether to try and understand all they hear or just take it as it comes. The teacher must announce this freedom of choice at the outset and then repeat it several times so as to create an atmosphere of complete peace of mind in the classroom and eliminate anxiety—the apprehension that something may not be understood and is therefore dangerous.

Optional participation of the learners in problem-oriented thinking and the absence of any obligation to understand all the ideas set forth gives this form of instruction in creative thinking some universal characteristics—though, of course, there is no such thing as universal method of instruction, nor can there be. The nonrequirement of any explicit reaction, or even any reaction at all, on the part of the students is just what makes such reaction inevitable. It can and should be different coming from different students, which is just what we want. That is why problem-oriented thinking—the scientific substrate of a genuine mass education process—is one of the key methods of bringing up thinking people. However, this can occur only if the teacher fully understands

142

what he ventures to think aloud: if he thinks, not fantasizes; if he resorts to this device constantly, at every suitable occasion, every year and every day; from the children's very first years in school and to the very end. In that case, the number of students taking part in problem-oriented thinking will invariably grow. The most unexpected children will ask the most unexpected questions possessing deep scientific meaning. The problem of teaching and learning individualization is thus largely resolved in work with a group of students. The regular, consistent, tactful, and ubiquitous use of this method, systematically and consistently, makes the teaching process—from primary to graduate school—deeply scientific and differentiated in essence, but without any formal separation of the students into groups according to grades. Problem-oriented thinking makes the educational process humane, kind, attractive to both teachers and students, and, for many of them, exciting. It rids the school of the manifestations of cruelty and unnecessary strictness that alienate our children from us. The more educated and more qualified a teacher, the more is he capable of providing his students with intellectual fare and the less is he surrounded by injustice and cruelty.

The most important thing in presentations in the form of problem-oriented thinking is to communicate to the students examples of thinking that lead to the need to introduce new concepts and ideas. Teachers must be specially taught this kind of thinking.

Continuous thinking aloud in school makes it possible for the students to get familiarized with the idea of axiomatics in mathematics. No lecture or series of lectures would be to any avail, for the students would fail to understand them. The process of fostering the idea of axiomatics should be a process of fostering thinking, a continuous, long-term process of gradually increasing difficulty, in the form of problem-oriented thinking, when day after day the teacher formulates problem situations aloud and then analyzes them himself—for weeks, months, and years. This also holds for the concept of the limit of a function in school and college, the concepts of a real number and continuity, the theorems of existence, and many others.

The students are usually involved in problem-oriented thinking through problem-oriented presentation and problem-oriented discussion. Thinking aloud is also very effective in solving complex theoretical and practical problems under the guidance of the teacher.

Obviously, the longer the teaching and learning process the better the results of problem-oriented thinking aloud. In a system of short courses, it can be useful only for brilliant students; for the others it can prove ineffective.

3.15.3. Our educators do not teach students precision of speech in general, and when introducing new concepts, in particular. Educators should and can be taught this only when preparing for and attending their lessons, and only by drawing their attention to imprecise terms of speech of the students that result in distorted comprehension and distorted assimilation of new concepts and in mistakes when applying them.

143

We have made a big mistake in no longer requiring students to learn poems and prose extracts by heart, in both English and foreign languages. Such memorization, when conducted in all grades from K to 12, can play a tremendous part in the development of the oral and written speech of all students without exception. It will give slow learners the opportunity to feel themselves confident and on a par with the brilliant ones, and sometimes even above them.

Enrichment of the students' speech, enhancement of the standards and body of their knowledge, and perfection and development of the intensity and strength of their thinking cannot be achieved in a short-term process. Ideas, words, concepts, terms, operations, skills, and habits—all these vanish without a trace if the educator fails to carry on continuous, highly competent, never-ending work over many years with the whole class and each student. This work must be aimed at (1) retaining the developed knowledges, skills, and habits of the students and preventing their destruction; (2) continually renovating and upgrading knowledges, skills, and habits; and (3) continually developing the speech and intellectual, creative, and cognitive abilities of all the children.

It would be as cruel and useless to place the burden of this tremendous, never-ending work—which requires the high qualifications, will, and collective wisdom of a modern civilized nation—on the shoulders of every educator, just as it would be cruel and useless to place it on the shoulders of the students.

3.16. MINI-RESEARCHES AND STUDENT EXERCISES

3.16.1. Who can best help the teacher detect the absence or breakdown of a productive system of student exercises? Only his colleagues—teachers and/or experienced professional supervisors and administrators—by attending or video-taping his lessons and studying the procedures he follows when preparing for and conducting classes. Only they can and must help the teacher in drawing up lesson plans and notes—in thinking over every problem, every stage, and every minute of the lesson.

A team of teachers is capable of resolving difficult pedagogical problems beyond the powers of a single teacher, just as a whole class is capable of solving very difficult problems and carrying out other creative assignments still beyond the capabilities of any single student. Teams of teachers and teams of students working together for many years—that is the prime mover of a modern academic process, the teaching and creative potentials of which are virtually limitless.

A question to the students, or a question-problem, is not cruel and becomes a manifestation of didactic kindness only when the class has been prepared for active participation in discussing the question by the

144

preceding lesson or a thoughtfully conceived home assignment. Every question should stimulate the mind and the memory. The answer should be a source of satisfaction to the student and the class as a whole, and a more or less clear and straightforward step towards the discussion of the next question or question-problem.

The ability to compile series of successive, interlinked questions, and question-problems leading up to the solution of a difficult problem cannot be taught in teacher-education colleges. This great skill of active, creative work with the class, in the course of which questions become more and more difficult and laconic, can be acquired only after years of association with a faculty of creative, team-oriented teachers. The absence of such a team—of such daily work of teachers among themselves, and subsequently with the students—cannot be made up by any number of papers, books, lectures, and seminars, courses and reports, or by the warmth or harshness of the school. Teachers must be taught all their lives, as thoroughly as they must subsequently teach their pupils. They must especially be taught the most difficult art of teaching students how to do exercises. Imposing high demands on school and college students and teachers without good, continuous instruction is as cruel, useless, and baneful for the whole educational system as it would be to continuously lower its demands.

The need for qualified, comprehensive training and advanced training of teachers of all grades and levels, as well as for upgrading the skills of their supervisors and teachers, is inherent in the very content of the profession of educator. It is made additionally relevant by the following: (1) the current mediocrity and fundamental impossibility of acquiring an adequate education in teacher-education colleges; (2) the constantly changing demands on schools and colleges imposed by a constantly changing society and the development of technology and science, the science of education included; (3) the undeniable fact that only the active, competent guidance of the teacher, in class and within a system of home assignments associated with the classroom lessons, can give nonbrilliant students the fundamentals of knowledge, skills, habits, intellectual development, the ability to work, and the aptitude needed for pursuing their self-education in the future. As long as the nonbrilliant students fail to get all this from their teachers, and as long as we fail to teach teachers the art of successfully teaching all students, no one will ever be able to change anything in the educational system for the better. The nation's ignorance will strangle every vital spark, and we will continue to live in a country without a future.

It is easy enough to impose demands of varying severity on teachers and students and reduce the whole academic process to this. It requires neither qualifications, nor effort, nor evaluation of the knowledge, skills, and habits of every student, nor consideration of their individual peculiarities or the development of their intellectual, creative, and cognitive abilities. Nor is there any need to know how well the teachers are trained—their pedagogical skills, their strong and weak points, their capabilities, virtues, and shortcomings, their methods and devices of work with students. There is no need to teach either students or teachers—none of this is needed, and nothing of the sort is as yet being done.

3.16.2. For students to do their exercises, each one, at every step in the work, must know why, wherefore, and for what purpose he is making that step.

Does any educator in this country seriously think that the fact of a student doing an exercise and obtaining a correct result is sufficient for him to understand what he has done or why such a course can be adopted? Yet that is the principle, i.e., the principle of checking the correctness or incorrectness of the final result rather than the whole process of performing and justifying the exercise, on which our whole system of teaching students to do exercises is based. The whole pedagogical wisdom of our current mass school and college boils down to giving students worked solutions of problems, if anything at all, and then requiring them to do a long list of exercises and at best check the final results. Hence the total incomprehension by most students of the meaning, purpose, and legitimacy of the operations they are performing, as well as attempts to memorize just the forms of exercises.

We do not totally reject the idea of checking the correctness of exercises done by students according to the end results. But abuse of this procedure leads to monstrous mistakes and the total helplessness of students. Doing any exercises at all without justifying the operations employed and discussing their purpose totally stifles the thought process and suppresses the formation of any habits of self-control. This turns our children into robots, obedient performers of other people's will carrying out purely mechanical operations in which they see nothing but the form and necessity of performing them. Instead of bringing up free, critically thinking, creative individuals, we are consistently and purposefully engaged in creating generations of weak-willed, spineless, subservient yes-people, or bellicose, bitter man-haters who refuse to be the slaves of another person's will.

3.16.3. The tragedy with the study of math and science in our country is in large measure due to the panicked flight from such studies in the system of school and college mini-courses, that bane of this great nation, as well as to misconceived freedom and independence of both educators and students. Bombastic statements about the freedom and independence of students and teachers camouflage unprecedented cruelty towards children and teachers who are helpless and tortured by the existence of an educational process about which neither have a good idea. Moreover, no one even tries to help them—in the name of privacy, the flourishing of democracy, and preservation of its grass roots—all of which are proclaimed most prominently and vociferously by those who, with their own hands, deny education and happiness to millions of teachers and tens of millions of our children.

3.16.4. As regards exercises, at every stage of education the trouble

146

begins with the absence of any system or any careful selection of exercises based on the principle of gradually increasing difficulty. Owing to the absence of mutual assistance between teachers or assistance from more experienced educators and supervisors, and to the absence of pedagogically qualified administrators responsible for the academic process, students are confronted with mountains of insurmountable obstacles in the form of new exercises which have not been prepared for by the preceding ones.

Before being carried away by bombastic slogans about fostering students' inventiveness and creativity, we must teach them how to consciously perform basic operations. After that will come the time for creative problems employing those operations.

Tens of millions of students—except for the most gifted—are incapable of independently mastering the operations and methods of doing exercises. To them the performance of any exercise is from the very beginning—i.e., from the commencement of every new topic—like a circus balancing act, a monstrous game of symbols. Things have reached a state where it has become the rule to solve a problem without even fully comprehending its conditions. More than half the students plunge into the solution before they have comprehended the content or requirements of the problem. They grasp at random numbers and sometimes stumble on the correct result, but even then give the wrong answer. They don't know what the problem asks; they forget what they are looking for, and don't understand what they have found. Students finishing school don't know how to use the equal sign correctly. To most students, problems in math and science are arrays of puzzles and mazes. We keep claiming that the meaningless juggling of empty operations and objects is a way of teaching, instructing, and instilling knowledge and firm habits.

The substitution of instructive exercises with the array of meaningless operations naturally overflows into teacher training textbooks, because that is how their authors were brought up by our educational system. This has become the all but irreversible process of the suicidal self-destruction of the educational system.

3.16.5. We reserve the right to repeat over and over again a trivial truth: The justification of the legitimacy and expedience of every step in problem-solution is the best way to foster student thinking and creativity, develop cognitive abilities, and encourage interest in the subject. This way, every student consolidates his advance and achievements in explicit form and upgrades knowledge and creative abilities on which he can rely in subsequent work—yet another manifestation of didactic kindness.

The use of recipes and stereotypes kills every living thought in our educational establishments. No one interferes with the process: teachers and students have no idea there is any alternative. Students are taught to substitute, replace, solve, transfer, omit, and transform. What remains unknown is why each operation is performed, what purpose it serves, or why it is possible. Other possible variants of problem solutions—their comparative values, advantages, and shortcomings—are almost never discussed.

3.16.6. Analysis of students' mistakes and their causes is a powerful tool in the struggle against ignorance. The ability to perform such analysis is especially important for both working and future teachers. Most of them are incapable of doing this, because no one ever taught them or intends to teach them.

3.16.7. Nor are the troubles of our long-suffering army of teachers and students restricted to the absence of any system, meaning, or justification of exercises. If we are to teach, we must do it "at once," "without procrastination," and "seriously"—that is the cruel principle that governs everywhere with, perhaps, the sole exception of the primary school. If the textbook has thirty problems on the solution of equations in two variables, let them solve all thirty in one batch—let them know that this isn't kindergarten, the learning is serious. If there are forty problems on finding an indefinite integral using partial fractions, give them all at once—learning is a serious thing, let them respect it. The same holds true with convergence of series, differential equations, linear algebra, and everything else.

Those same forty problems on finding the antiderivative by partial fractions should be spread out over at least ten or fifteen lessons; otherwise, teaching becomes a mockery. During the first lesson, no more than two or three problems should be examined, with the whole class actively participating. The questions are directed at all the students; each step is justified and its variants and their relative value are analyzed. After that the best one is chosen.

This way the class is confronted with obstacles it can overcome, stimulating the students' minds and activity. The weaker students should be involved in the work as actively as the rest. Answers to questions should be required not only when they are volunteered. Knowing the class, the teacher should tactfully but persistently require all students to answer: the weak, the average, and the strong. The degree of difficulty of the questions handled by each student is gradually increased, together with the thoroughness of justification required by the teacher. The less advanced students give less justified responses. Initially this can be accepted, while gradually building up demands with regard to the quality of the responses of all the students and bringing them up to the requirements acceptable for the course as a whole. After the first lesson, not more than three or four problems should be given for the home assignment.

3.16.8. The time-distribution of mastered skills and acquired habits is of tremendous, decisive importance in carrying out exercises, as is the time-distribution of the acquisition of theoretical knowledge. Nevertheless, not the slightest attention is given in our country to the one or the other. Students are swamped in one day with more theoretical material than they can assimilate. The material should be expanded over weeks. But the one-year, one-semester, and one-quarter courses which pervade the system leave no time for this. As a consequence, the study material is compressed at every lesson to such a degree that there is no real opportunity to either teach or learn it. For example, take the congruence and similarity of triangles; curves in R_3; nonhomogeneous linear systems of first order equations; trigonometric, logarithmic, and exponential equations; and systems of equations—each of these topics is dumped in one batch on people hearing about them for the first time. Moreover, all the pertinent problems are immediately assigned all at once, so as not to burden the teachers or the students with them anymore.

Students have difficulty understanding the concept of the graph of an equation. For that reason, they are unable to interpret the concept of the solution of a system of two equations as a set of ordered pairs of real numbers that are the coordinates of every point of intersection of the graphs of the two given equations with two unknowns. It takes weeks, if not months, of intense creative effort on the part of the teacher and the students to master these ideas. All these ideas, which are not easy for a nonmathematician, have to be fostered in the pupils' minds gradually, sequentially, and with continuing variations and repetitions over a long period of time. If all this work is not carried out and attempts are made to cram a course covering several years within the space of one year, the result is a hodge-podge of newly and previously acquired knowledges and skills, leading to the utter helplessness of the pupils, who become incapable of understanding even things that had formerly been clear and understandable.

Information A is introduced in class together with worked solutions of relevant problems; only after that should work start on assimilating the new information. Further discussion of information A and the solutions of relevant problems should continue during several subsequent lessons, concurrently with the introduction of new information B, C, D, et cetera. The problems considered in class should be either more difficult than those given for home assignments, less difficult, or approximately the same, depending on the difficulty of the material and the state of the class (in other words, should the class be encouraged at this lesson or, on the contrary, be made to see that there is still much to do). In this way, at the next lesson it is possible to rely on homework while at the same time upgrading its results. This is possible thanks to the fact that at home each pupil has spent as much time as needed in reviewing the class work, on which the home assignment—which must always include new elements—was based, and then in doing the assignment.

The degree of novelty of the home assignment as compared with the class work is to a certain degree dependent on the difficulty of the material. The more difficult the studied material, the fewer new difficulties should the students have to overcome in their home assignments during the initial stages of studying the material. The teacher must see to this, because if the studied material is difficult, the work in class must be supplemented by considerable efforts on the part of the students at home to fully and thoroughly understand it and master the new methods

149

and devices learned in class. Different students will spend different amounts of time at home to clarify and upgrade the work done in class. This is fine, because out-of-class work by students is the principal means of individualizing the teaching-learning process in school and in college.

All the students should come to the next lesson with approximately the same level of newly acquired knowledge, skills, and habits pertaining to both the preceding in-class lesson and the home assignment. That assignment consolidated the results of the class lesson and in part prepared the students for the next lesson, at which one or two problems on the material introduced during the previous lesson should be done at a faster rate than initially. The students can already be required to do more while expecting less explanation. This will teach them to work systematically and thoroughly at home, if, of course, they didn't encounter difficulties that they couldn't reasonably be expected to overcome on their own at their current academic stage. The main portion of a new lesson should be devoted to the introduction of new material, problem solution, and discussion of relevant theoretical questions. The home assignment should again include two or three problems from the preceding section and perhaps three or four from the new section.

This should continue from lesson to lesson. The number of different sections from which every home assignment is given can be from three to ten and more. This should become a system in the work of every teacher in school and in college—if he wishes his students to acquire firm knowledges, skills, and habits and develop their intellectual, creative, and cognitive abilities.

3.16.9. The forty problems mentioned in the section "Integration With the Help of Partial Fractions" should not be exhausted over the first few successive lessons. Reviewing—that is, solving problems from the same section during several lessons—should initially be more frequent and intensive. During the first four or five successive lessons, the home assignments should include three or four problems from the section, one or two of which were partially or completely worked in class. Later, the frequency of review problems should be reduced, as well as the number of problems from the section considered during each reviewing session. One or two problems should be given for homework—first for every other lesson, then after every two or three. In this way, the students study the section under the guidance and with the help, and sometimes active involvement, of the teacher in the course of approximately fifteen lessons.

3.16.10. The students do not know in advance what solution method will produce the desired result if they have to solve problems of the review section; i.e., the section concluding the chapter. These problems should be solved simultaneously with problems whose method of solution is apparent from the topic of the section of the textbook they appear in and where the students are given the method of solution whether they ask for it or not. The problems from the review section confront the students first of all with the creative task of finding the method of solving

150

them. Such activity is purely creative for all students. When engaged in regularly it develops the intellectual, creative, and cognitive abilities of all students, regardless of whether the problem-solving process has an algorithm or not.

The last stage in studying a course involves a review of the theory and the solution of problems from the section covering the whole course. If there is no such section in the textbook it should be compiled jointly by the teachers of the course because the last stage in the study of every course should cover the creative application of all the studied material by the students. The first step in such application is selection from the entire course material of the method of solving a practical or theoretical problem that is entirely new for the students or that includes substantially new features.

3.16.11. What schoolteacher or college instructor is capable—independently, without outside help or joint creative work with other educators—of solving one of the basic pedagogical problems which arises when doing exercises; namely, maintaining the students' continued interest in them? This is especially difficult in those topics in which the character of the studied material requires numerous exercises to be done over extended periods of time to make sure that the students acquire firm skills and habits. We have in mind operations with negative numbers and fractions; identical transformations of algebraic and transcendental expressions; solution of algebraic, differential, and transcendental equations, inequalities and systems of inequalities; solution of word problems; differentiation and integration techniques; convergence and divergence of series; et cetera.

Within the system of mini-researches there should be a special group of teachers working on this problem. One member of the research laboratory will note that to keep monotonous exercises from getting boring they should gradually and steadily be made more and more difficult. Another will note that there should be a sufficient number of them in order to successfully proceed with new material.

But how many are "sufficient," and what does "successfully proceed" imply? These questions can be answered generally, but it is easier to answer them as applied to specific material in a specific class. When this is done extensively, regularly, and over a long period of time, the teacher acquires pedagogical feeling and generalized knowledge of those pedagogical categories. He can then use his knowledge independently, as applied to other classes and other materials, while occasionally discussing his work with other educators.

As a rule, a teacher cannot answer these questions on his own without outside help, even after working with a class for a long time. He will continue to torment and tyrannize children for many years, confronting them with insurmountable difficulties of which he himself is unaware. He will skim rapidly forward in places where it is necessary to sit back, reflect, and solve more problems. Or he will dally and go over things which are known and clear, with which the students are bored stiff, when it is time to rapidly and energetically introduce new material. This causes the class to rebel and get out of hand.

Teachers must be taught—extensively and patiently—that some students may still need time and more practice before successfully going ahead. Such students must be given both the time and the problems, but concurrently with newly introduced material: at supplementary lessons which must be made obligatory for some students; at consultations obligatory for some students; with the help of individual, obligatory, supplementary in-class and home assignments, followed by careful checking and discussion with the students. It is very useful to give some students such compulsory lessons, consultations, and assignments in advance of material shortly to be studied, to forestall their falling behind.

All this should be done firmly, coolly, purposefully, and deliberately. Otherwise, the collective ignorance will snowball, involving both the weaker students and the class as a whole. The weaker students will increasingly hold back the work. The teacher will devote more and more attention to them. Then many of the good students will start to lose interest in the work and soon join the weaker ones.

Or the teacher will busy himself only with the stronger students. Then the weaker ones will roll rapidly downhill, like rocks down a mountainside, dislodging new ones, until they become a landslide.

3.16.12. How many teachers are capable on their own of mastering one more pedagogical skill: teaching how to do exercises that are similar in form but different in content, which are so common and so dangerous at all stages of instruction? Who of us hasn't heard that dreaded statement: "I got mixed up"? That is, the student mistook one for the other thanks to external, superficial similarity. When you tell him he made a mistake he looks at you suspiciously, distrustfully, with a crooked smile, and then delivers the coup de grace with the question, "Well, what is $\log a \cdot \log b$, or $\frac{\log a}{\log b}$, or $\log(a + b)$ equal to?" And when he hears the answer, "Nothing, because these expressions can't be transformed," the initial distrust and alienation is aggravated by coldness, and sometimes hostility. "Well, everything is always equal to something, but here's a teacher who says it isn't." It's very hard to deal with such crippled minds, and we have no one to blame but ourselves for crippling them.

This scourge of ours, i.e., mass mistakes made by students that are due to superficial similarities—the similarity of analytical expressions, equations, inequalities, and geometrical figures in irrelevant, superficial, formal features—can and should be overcome. But it can also be used as a powerful educational tool, as a technique for teaching and learning how to identify the significant features of studied objects, giving students the ability to distinguish the significant from the insignificant. When initially giving students assignments aimed at consolidating a new concept or proposition, it is necessary to follow up at once with series of exercises that are similar in form but differ in content for the specific purpose of using the juxtaposition to fix and consolidate both the old and new knowledge. For example

$a^3 \cdot a^2 = a^5$; $(a^3)^2 = a^6$; $a^3 + a^2 = ?$ — This will peeve them.
Then: $a^3 + a^3 = 2a^3$; $a^2 + a^2 + a^2 = 3a^2$; $3a^3 \cdot 5a^2 = 15a^5$; $2^3 \cdot 2^2$
$\neq 4^5$; $2^3 + 2^2 \neq 4^5$.
$2(a + b) = 2a + 2b$, but $2(3 \cdot 4) \neq (2 \cdot 3) \cdot (2 \cdot 4)$; $2(a^3b^4) \neq 2a^3 \cdot 2b^4$; $(-2)^{-3}$; $(-3)^{-2}$; -2^{-3}; -3^{-2}; $(-\frac{1}{3})^{-2}$; $(-\frac{1}{2})^{-3}$.
$\dfrac{\log a}{\log b} \neq \log |a| - \log |b|$, $\log \dfrac{a}{b} = \log |a| - \log |b|$, $\log(ab) = \log |a| + \log |b|$; $\log(a \pm b)$.
$\int \cos x \, dx = \sin x + c$, but $\int d \cos x \neq \sin x + c$;
$\int \dfrac{dx}{x} = \ln |x| + c$, but $\int \dfrac{dx}{x^2} \neq \ln(x^2) + c$;

$\int 5dx = 5\int dx$, but $\int \ln x \, dx \neq \ln x \int dx$.

Here is another example: $\int_0^{1/2} \dfrac{1}{1-x^2} dx$; $\int_0^1 \dfrac{1}{1-x^2} dx$; $\int_{-1}^0 \dfrac{1}{1-x^2} dx$; $\int_{-1}^{+1} \dfrac{1}{1-x^2} dx$.

This method of constantly comparing and juxtaposing exercises and concepts that are similar in form is one of the most powerful tools of a successful teaching-learning process. This is not "spoon-feeding"; rather, it is a process of instilling basic knowledges and habits. Only after this kind of work, after effective elementary exercises, can one start giving creative exercises.

Many of our educators will find it difficult to understand us. They have never done this kind of work, and they never can within the current system of surreptitious teaching without mini-researches, with the practice of checking only the answers to assigned exercises, and without painstaking work with every student, every day and every minute.

3.16.13. At present, teachers in all educational establishments are simply deprived of the possibility of conducting a successful academic process because they receive no genuine feedback. They don't know their students' mistakes because they check only the final answers of exercises. Therefore, they don't know what they are up against or how to deal with it. What teachers have to deal with; what goes on in the students' heads; what they assimilate easily and what with difficulty; what they assimilate willingly and what unwillingly; where they make mistakes; where they are unable to proceed; why it all happens; how to improve the one, the other, and the third; how to verify whether this has served or harmed the educational process; how to isolate the successful portion of a newly introduced topic from the unsuccessful one; and how to continue to improve the teaching-learning process—these questions have no answers, nor can they have any as long as there are no mini-researches, as long as the teacher does not painstakingly study every step in the exercises prepared by students, as long as there is no constant, continuous, uninterrupted feedback in the pedagogical process. Such feedback is provided by creative lessons involving the active participation of both the teacher and the students, prepared and conducted in a system of mini-researches, and by continuous training of teachers and the upgrading of their professional knowledge and skills.

All these are commonplace truths, but they must be mentioned because neglect of self-evident, classical, commonplace truths, disregarding them only because they are commonplace, is simply irresponsible and detrimental to the educational system—especially if no better alternatives are offered.

3.16.14. The effective supervision of drills and exercises is one of the most difficult forms of educational work. Alone, without assistance, the teacher is unable to judge the quantity and content of exercises necessary and sufficient for the specific class at a specific stage of instruction. Only joint work with other teachers, supervisors, and administrators can give all those involved the general knowledge of the quantity and content of exercises necessary and sufficient for an efficient teaching-learning process.

The number and content of exercises is directly dependent on the course being studied, the makeup of the class, and the stage of instruction. It is also dependent on the effort applied by the teacher and students in doing them; namely, the more intense the effort, the fewer, usually, the number of required exercises, while if the effort is low even a great number of exercises may not do the job. The intensity with which the students apply themselves is, in turn, directly dependent on (1) the characteristics of the individual students—the level of their intellectual and creative capabilities; their love of, or interest in, the subject; their abilities, attention span, learning habits, previous knowledge, fatigue; et cetera; (2) the study material: how abstract it is; its affinity to the students' personal experience; the diversity of exercises—their difficulty and clarity; the logical structure of the material and its novelty for the students; the quality of the textbooks and study aids; (3) the intensity and methods of the teacher's work; and (4) the teacher's pedagogical skills.

The teacher's skills include the following: his ability to keep track of the work of all the students; his ability to hold them in a state of constant emotional excitement and involve them actively in the work; his ability to give the students timely assistance and apply methods of work that will assure a steadily mounting degree of independence of the students and their gradual acquisition of knowledge and firm habits, including habits of learning.

The pedagogical category "Intensity of student work" cannot be treated as merely a corollary of categories (1), (2), (3), and (4). All these categories are interconnected, interdependent, and interrelated. Thus, good learning habits make for greater learning effort, which in turn expands the learning habits. The methods a teacher uses in his work depend on the study material, as well as on the capabilities of the students and their initial training. The level of the students' abilities affects the intensity of their work, while changes in the intensity of the students' learning efforts affect the level of their cognitive abilities. A diversity of

154

exercises stimulates the students' interest and attention in class, the intensity of their work, and effectively develops their intellectual, creative, and cognitive abilities. These abilities are also promoted by comparing problems, by solving and comparing problems with the same conditions but different requirements, by solving and comparing problems with different conditions but the same requirement, and by having the students make up exercises independently.

The intensity of student work is one of the basic indicators of the quality of the teacher's work, provided, of course, that the students' work is correctly oriented and results in the acquisition of knowledge and improvement of abilities.

3.16.15. The system of mini-researches should also be used to systematically train teachers in the skill of independently classifying problems and other exercises from the point of view of their novelty for the students, specifically, introductory, basic, and review exercises.

Introductory exercises can be used to both introduce a new concept and explain and initially consolidate it. In most cases introductory exercises should be done under the teacher's supervision. The degree, duration, and form of this supervision will depend on the difficulty of the newly introduced concepts and the proficiency of the class. The time spent on them may range from a few minutes to several lessons. Gradually, in the process of creative interaction with other teachers, administrators, and supervisors, every teacher develops the ability to see the capabilities of the given class with respect to the assimilation of new concepts and doing the exercises facilitating that assimilation. The selection of introductory exercises, their difficulty, and the time allocated to do them can therefore be determined differently for every specific case. Only a lesson or series of lessons can help to verify the aptness of the choice of introductory exercises from the point of view of their number, difficulty, and emotional impact on the students.

The basic exercises serve as the means of consolidating a new concept or proposition and establishing its relationship to previously learned concepts and propositions. They are the principal means of developing the students' intellectual, creative, and cognitive abilities, as well as a means of forming and developing firm habits. As a rule, they are structurally more complex than introductory exercises, and often difficult. They must be targeted on the students' creativity and independence and on their independently choosing and applying the concepts, structures, and techniques.

Review exercises can be given concurrently with the basic ones, i.e., during the same lesson, or whole lessons can be devoted to them. Doing these exercises requires the application of concepts, structures, and techniques previously studied by the students. They prevent time's destruction of knowledge, skills, and habits; help restore lost knowledge; and structuralize, generalize, and consolidate knowledge. Review exercises also have the purpose of making knowledge active, retrievable, and read-

155

ily usable as a means and tool for solving theoretical and practical problems.

The classification of exercises as introductory, basic, and review—i.e., their classification from the point of view of novelty for the students—is highly arbitrary. One and the same exercise, in the same class, with the same students, at specific stages in teaching and learning the material, can be introductory and after a while used to review the material. One and the same exercise can be basic and review at the same time, if it includes both new and reviewed material. Furthermore, one class may require five or eight basic exercises to be done in class and at home. In another, this may not be enough, and it may take ten or twelve basic exercises before going on to a new concept or proposition. The same diversity is true of the number of review exercises, their difficulty, the time to be devoted to them, and the degree of independence to be displayed by the students in doing them. Much depends on the composition of the class, the study material, and the personality of the educator. However, despite the diversity of conditions needed for a specific educator to successfully teach a specific material to a specific group of students, a highly important prerequisite is the teacher's ability to draw up three sets of exercises covering a specific question for his class, and to justify his choice; these sets may, of course, intersect. He must also be able, in the course and as a result of mini-researches, to evaluate the merits and demerits of his work and the work of other teachers, both before and after the lesson.

3.16.16. Finally, what follows are a few more important remarks to conclude our discussion of how to teach students to do exercises.

(a) It is very important when doing introductory exercises to eliminate reviewing; otherwise, the lessons can do more harm than good, if the students encounter numerous difficulties.

(b) If the teacher is not taught how to gradually but steadily increase the students' independence in doing exercises, he will inevitably place them in an inextricable situation, a phenomenon at present so typical of all our educational establishments.

(c) There are many ways of torturing students when doing exercises instead of teaching them, and they all obey the same inhuman law: students are required to do things they have not learned and, more likely than not, were never taught.

Some teachers give their pupils only copying assignments; that is, they make them copy and rewrite exercises from samples written by the teacher or the best students on the blackboard. If at the same time no home assignments are given—which happens all too often in our country—or if they are given but not checked by the teacher—a common thing in our country—the whole process of so-called teaching is restricted to copying, with the consequent deadening of our children's mental abilities. The first time the students ever have to attempt doing exercises on their own is during examinations. Only the most gifted and capable can cope with this successfully. The rest gradually—but consistently and inexorably—get used to the idea that they are second-class people and education is not for them. They drop out and seek, not unsuccessfully, the society of people—including criminals—where they are less tormented and better appreciated. Others are humiliatingly dragged from grade to grade, and then on into college: unhappy, obsequious, crushed, and often criminal.

On the other hand, some teachers are unaware of the possibility, and sometimes even the necessity, of copying assignments. Such educators restrict themselves to listing exercises. This places most students in a no-win situation long before examination time. Very often the students try to teach one another: in general, this is not a bad thing, but only if it doesn't substitute for the whole teaching-learning process.

Finally, some teachers give only copying or reproduction exercises. In reproduction assignments the students do exercises independently, but only those like the ones done earlier under the supervision, or with the active participation, of the teacher. If only such exercises are given, the students memorize them. At examinations they are prudently given identical exercises. But that isn't all. To keep the students from burdening the educators and themselves with work, they are given a preliminary sample exam; that is, a virtual prototype of the upcoming examination. This deprives the teaching-learning process of its powerful means and its great purpose—the cognitive activity and creativity of students. It is replaced by a farce of terrifying proportions and tragic consequences for the whole nation.

Only in exceptional cases, when the form and technical aspects dominate over content, can copying and reproduction work be justified. We are duty bound to drive this truth home to our educators and not leave them helpless, miserable, and alone in the unequal struggle against ignorance.

But realization alone is not enough. To build up a teaching academic process we must not only give all teachers modern pedagogical knowledge; we must also, with the help of mini-researches, give them the skills and habits of such teaching activity, so that every exercise can be a creative effort for the students and well within their capabilities. The degree of student creativity should increase together with their mastery of the method of science, its ideas, concepts, structures, and technical apparatus.

(d) To supervise students doing exercises, as well as to engage in other elements of the academic process, the teacher must be trained in efficient guidance of the class as a whole and the work of each individual student. We must teach all educators that, when working with the class as a whole, when different stages of an exercise are done and reported to the class by different students, the appearance that the lesson is progressing nicely can be misleading. There can never be full confidence that all the students are working successfully and that they understand every stage of the work—even when they think they understand it and don't ask any questions. That is why work with the whole class should be accompanied by stages of independent work, which should gradually grow in duration and difficulty as the class assimilates the new information. Furthermore, when the teacher continuously evaluates the level of knowledge and quality of the skills and habits acquired by the students, he can individualize the teaching-learning process with the help of special questions and assignments at the lesson, in home assignments, and during special sessions for the stronger students, or for those with gaps in their knowledge.

(e) The positive effect of exercises done by the students also depends on the teacher's ability to help them develop habits of self-control—an important component of the teaching-learning process. It depends, among other things, on the teacher's ability to anticipate possible difficulties and the most common mistakes of the students. In some cases, when help and support are more important than exactingness, the difficulties and mistakes should be prevented—perhaps even in ways that leave the students unaware that they are being helped. In other cases, the teacher should clearly state his requirements and demand that they be met, only, of course, if he is morally entitled to this; that is, if the students have been prepared by all the previous work for independent, albeit perhaps tiresome, overcoming of encountered difficulties.

3.17. HOW TO USE THE SYSTEM OF MINI-RESEARCHES TO TEACH TEACHERS TO CONSOLIDATE STUDENTS' KNOWLEDGE

3.17.1. The never-ending training and mutual training of educators in the system of mini-researches, with and without video-taping, should be devoted, among other things, to the process of reinforcing and consolidating the knowledge acquired by students.

The initial concepts that form in the students' minds during introduction to the new information quickly and irreversibly destruct if the teacher hasn't been trained to organize their consolidation. Even the most talented and gifted children are not competent educators. They cannot teach themselves. With the virtual absence of a qualified teaching-learning process in our country, some manage to acquire an education solely by virtue of innate talent, but at the cost of a tremendous, unproductive waste of time, effort, and health. Others get it with the help of money, while some, often very gifted people, remain uneducated despite tremendous expenditures of time, work, health, and money—thanks to the absence of competent teaching.

Our school and college teachers don't even try to organize initial consolidation of knowledge during the lesson in the form of the simple reproduction by the students of the information they just received. This is because they either don't realize the need for such work, don't know how, or don't wish to organize it. Whatever the case may be, the end result is cruel treatment of our children and their total ignorance.

Initial consolidation of knowledge should take different forms, depending on the students' age, the difficulty of the new material, and their personal qualities. In junior and weaker classes—and at all stages of instruction when the material is difficult—we cannot avoid purely mechanical repetition of the definition of the new concept and its properties, both proven and unproven. Many educators, even after extensive work with them, fail to realize the importance and necessity of simple reproduction of the information just acquired by the students. They frequently place both themselves and the students in an untenable situation by trying to establish relationships between concepts that cannot be established, solve problems that cannot be solved, or prove propositions that cannot be proved, because the students have simply not yet memorized all that was just said in class. No lectures for teachers, however good, no university courses, workshops, seminars, et cetera, can change anything for the better. What is needed is the teacher's regular involvement in practical daily work and regular practical assistance for him.

Here is an example. The teacher gives a definition of even and odd functions and immediately asks whether $f(x) = \sin x + \cos x$ is even or odd. This can be done only with a very strong class, and even there one of the top students should be asked to answer the following: The function is neither even nor odd, because for some x, $f(-x) \neq f(x)$ and $f(-x) \neq -f(x)$. In average classes, however, the question would be useless and cruel for most of the pupils. Some simply still haven't memorized the definition of even and odd functions. Others have, but they need to see the new information applied initially in the simplest cases, such as $f(x) = x^2$, $f(x) = x^3$, $f(x) = \cos x$, $f(x) = \sin x$, where the answer to the question requires only direct application of the new definitions, namely, $(-x)^2 = x^2$; $(-x)^3 = -(x^3)$; $\cos(-x) = \cos x$; $\sin(-x) = -\sin x$, for all real values of x. Hence, the first and third functions are even, and the second and fourth are odd. Without consolidation of the concepts of even and odd functions by reproducing their definitions, it is not only useless but also extremely harmful to require all students to offer a knowing and justified response to an even/odd analysis of the function $f(x) = \sin x + \cos x$. Unjustified, false exactingness stemming from pedagogical ignorance breeds a sense of uncertainty and apprehension in the student, suppresses the individual and his desire to study, is psychologically damaging, pushes the student to deception and protest, and, when continued regularly, breeds bitterness and vindictiveness.

3.17.2. Supervisors and administrators of all levels can provide our teachers with the assistance they need by helping them prepare for

159

lessons and by attending, taping, and discussing those lessons. They must painstakingly and patiently teach our educators the great skill of initial consolidation of knowledge and subsequent consistent and courageous enhancement of the complexity and difficulty of the questions, problems, and exercises offered the students. In the conditions of mass education, with a force of millions of educators and tens of millions of students, this work requires tremendous efforts, but there is no substitute for it. On their own, our instructors will never become educated, able, skillful, or happy. They can never make their students educated and happy if they themselves are not systematically, universally, and ceaselessly taught; if they are not given constant assistance in preparing and conducting as many lessons and classes as possible. As the educator masters the difficult art of teaching, the help he gets invariably decreases, but it should never, under any circumstances, disappear. Having become experienced, able, and skillful, the once helpless educator, in the process of discussing forthcoming and past lessons—his own and his colleagues'—invariably and subconsciously evolves from mainly student to mainly teacher status (although he never completely ceases being a student). Not a single educational establishment or a single educational system can operate normally without such a system of ongoing reciprocal training of educators. Such training of educators is neither just a wish nor one of several possible variants of successfully teaching our children: it is the only possible variant, insofar as we are speaking of the present stage of development of educational theory and practice. Naturally, the search for other, better, and more efficient ways of promoting universal mass education will go on continuously, and no one can ever stop the process. But before improving an educational system, it first has to be built up—which is what this book is all about. One can't improve on what doesn't exist—this is just what our country is currently engaged in. Hence the torrent of studies based on nothing, for there is nothing to base them on; therefore, these studies are totally useless, with the exception of the researchers themselves. Hence, too, the "deschooling society," "goodbye, teacher," and so on.

3.17.3. Incapable of independently getting to the essence of the matter, our educators include initial consolidation of knowledge in the students' independent assignments, which is fatal for the students and for them. The students are cruelly denied one of the most important stages in the teaching-learning process and, as a consequence, are unable to continue work on the course. It is especially dangerous for our children when the teacher hurries to pass on to difficult material or harder exercises in the name of a misconceived principle of encouraging the students' independence and creativity, or as a consequence of his total pedagogical incompetence.

Examples of this abound.

If a teacher has not worked sufficiently with the class during the introduction of the concepts of trigonometric functions and failed to consolidate them in the students' minds by means of a carefully developed system of questions, problems, and exercises—spanning not just one lesson, but the time it takes to cover the whole topic—he has contributed to the total failure of the students to comprehend the whole course of trigonometry. It is hard to correct anything when students confuse the symbol of a trigonometric function with a factor and take it outside the parentheses. This, moreover, is no fault of the children, something our educators cannot or will not understand.

Without consolidating the idea of fractionating units into quarters, fifths, sixths, and so on, with the help of a sufficient number of questions and special exercises, the teacher requires the students to do operation (7): $7\frac{1}{5} - 2\frac{3}{5}$. This is cruel with respect to the students and useless for most of the children if they have not first thoroughly learned subtraction, such as (1) $1 - \frac{3}{5}$; (2) $7 - \frac{3}{5}$; (3) $7\frac{1}{5} - 2$; (4) $1\frac{1}{5} - \frac{3}{5}$; (5) $7\frac{1}{5} - \frac{3}{5}$; and (6) $7 - 2\frac{3}{5}$. Here, more is needed than giving one or two examples which the teacher solves on the blackboard, even if he takes his time and calls out some students to help answer questions. It is absolutely essential for the students to independently solve problems of this type, and in numbers sufficient to firmly consolidate operations (1) through (6), which provide the basis for performing operation (7); in other words, didactic cruelty should be replaced by didactic kindness.

This is not to say that all obstacles should be removed and courses in math turned into lessons in imitation. This should certainly be prevented. The students try to do, say, operation (3). The teacher helps them only if they have some difficulty and to sum up the results. The same holds for operations (4) and (5). In the case of (7), the students independently apply the results of operations (1) through (6) to the more difficult case, which requires the ability to carry out particular elementary operations.

The fact that there may be two or three students in the class capable of carrying out operation (7) independently, without initial consolidation of the elementary operations, is no reason for omitting stages (1) through (6), and here is why. Operations (1)–(6) are necessary for all the students to amplify and consolidate habits of subtraction of fractions and mixed numbers. The fact that these operations are a necessary stage towards the execution of a more complex operation for some students but not for others is but added justification for a qualitative analysis of their educational value for different students. The same questions, problems, and exercises given to different students lead, naturally, to different results. Most students require exercises (1)–(6) both to acquire habits of subtracting fractions and mixed numbers in six different situations, and to prepare them for carrying out operation (7), the most difficult one in subtraction of mixed numbers. The more capable students require the first six types of exercises to a lesser degree to prepare them for operation (7); some may not need them at all. For such students, exercises (1)–(6) are largely or exclusively useful in acquiring skills and habits of performing the operations flawlessly—something which, incidentally, most gifted people in our schools and universities have never achieved. Subsequently, during follow-up lessons, those students who feel themselves sufficiently prepared to handle problems (1)–(7) without mistakes need not be required to do exercises (1)–(6) for their home assignments. The assignments must, however, remain obligatory for students who themselves feel the need for such exercises or whom the teacher obliges to do them—in confidence, so as not to hurt the child's ego, perhaps by penciling a remark in his copybook.

3.17.4. Many years of special studies lead to the conclusion that for children under nine or ten initial consolidation of knowledge must invariably involve simple reproduction and repeated reviewing of the acquired and comprehended information, coupled with gradual, very careful enhancement of generalization and systematization elements. Starting from about the age of ten, sometimes earlier, the complete reproduction of material just received at the lesson should gradually be replaced by reproduction of only the most important key facts and concepts. This should subsequently be replaced by establishing and reproducing in class the system of facts, concepts, and logical relationships between individual facts, phenomena, and concepts. Then comes the time for establishing the structure of knowledge; both in the course of the introduction of new material and immediately after its introduction, as well as during subsequent reviewing. This is something teachers must be taught constantly, by attending their lessons, preparing for lessons together with them, and discussing the attended lessons (including sample lessons given for teachers by the best educators, administrators, and supervisors). This work is essential both in school and in college, especially in the system of elementary courses. Neither the school nor the college can function successfully without such work and they are doomed to die a slow death as educational establishments.

3.17.5. Consolidation of study material always presents considerable methodological difficulties for the teacher, because the absence of novelty can sharply reduce the students' interest in it. Furthermore, the students have, to varying degrees, already digested and assimilated the newly introduced material prior to the moment when the teacher proceeded with its consolidation. Moreover, and most unfortunately, for some students the stage of initial consolidation of knowledge may be only the stage of perception and understanding, either because they were not attentive enough when the new knowledge was being introduced, or because the teacher was unable, or perhaps didn't try, to involve them in active mental and technical activity. Some students may think that consolidation is unnecessary and a waste of time because they grasped and memorized all that was said, seen, and discussed during the lesson.

What should be done? What is the solution for one of the most difficult pedagogical problems? What should the inexperienced, or even

162

very experienced, educator do? What should he learn to make the consolidation of knowledge in class interesting and useful for all of the students?

The methods of consolidating knowledge depend on several factors: the students' age; the composition of the class; the difficulty of the material; its novelty; its theoretical and practical significance; the method adopted by the teacher to present the material; how successful the instructor was in the presentation; the mood of the class during the lesson; the teacher's ability to work; and his skill, relations with the class, conscientiousness, and devotion to children.

During attendance of lessons and participation in preparing and discussing them, attention should be paid to making the consolidation of knowledge in class obligatory not so much in form as in essence. In other words, if the students have assimilated the new material while it was being introduced, there is no need to consolidate it formally; if the teacher nevertheless persists in going ahead with consolidation he will make the lesson unpleasant and boring for the students, thus doing more harm than good. It will arouse protest, cause attention to deteriorate, and breed dislike of the subject and the teacher, as well as an unwillingness to work on the subject either in class or at home.

One effective method of consolidating knowledge in class is the merging of two stages of the lesson: introduction of the new material and its consolidation. This merger can be partial and require an independent subsequent stage of consolidation in the areas not covered by the teacher's work with the class.

Here is an example. The topic is the product of the segments of two intersecting chords. The theorem is not initially given. The teacher, with the students' help, establishes whether the triangles obtained by joining the endpoints of the chords are similar or not. As they answer his questions, the students come to the conclusion that two angles of one triangle are respectively congruent to two angles of the other; they justify their answers. This is followed by the conclusion that the triangles are similar. The corresponding sides of the triangles are identified. The students suggest how to write the ratios of similar sides and come to the final result. The teacher asks them to formulate the proved theorem.

In the course of the proof the students voice propositions, which are discussed by the class, and the best ones are adopted. The whole class is involved in the work and questions are addressed to both the strong and weaker students. Some of the most important stages of the proof are repeated, the final conclusion is formulated by the students themselves, and then repeated by the weakest of them. After this, two or three simple problems are solved. The first one is solved with the participation of all the students; i.e., the questions are addressed to the class as a whole, several students are required to answer, and the stages of the solution are written on the blackboard. The next problem is then solved by the students independently. The solution is checked on the blackboard, with several students taking part.

163

In this and similar cases, the initial consolidation is interwoven with the imparting of new information because the students are actively involved in the search. They themselves discovered the proposition, which they hadn't known before, by going through its proof. They took part in discussing the different stages of the search, solved two or three problems, and discussed their solutions. Only at this point can the teacher give a home assignment to be done by the students independently—only at this point, not earlier. This is something our teachers will have to be taught very patiently and at great length. They are eternally in a hurry and will be in a hurry to complete their mission as quickly as possible and give the home assignment.

3.17.6. The home assignment must include consolidating material studied during previous lessons and learning the new information discovered and justified at the latest lesson. The home assignment should also include problems similar to the ones solved in class, so that the weaker students would have a base for advancing and the stronger for acquiring habits of technical work. The home assignment should also include harder problems requiring the students' independent thought and creativity. It may take some children an hour, others two or three hours. This is only natural and what individualized teaching and learning is all about. Both will come to the next lesson prepared, though to different degrees.

At the next lesson, or soon thereafter, the students must be required to formulate and prove the proposition they had established in class. The teacher should also analyze, together with the students, the solutions to problems in the home assignments, especially the more difficult ones. And the students should know that this is how it will always be at every lesson, in connection with every new proposition and every new problem they get. There is nothing cruel about such an approach; on the contrary, it is humane, concerned, and didactically kind. We are cruel and unfeeling when we don't do this for our children.

3.17.7. Without repeated, multiple consolidation of newly acquired knowledge—of course, in as many different forms as possible—it would be naive and hopeless to expect our children to learn successfully and acquire an education. Our schools and colleges are plagued by universal ignorance because we are, or pretend to be, hoping for a miracle, for a mysterious, supernatural, never-before-witnessed process of mass self-education. Forget it, dear politicians and educators. It's only a figment of your imagination. It is at best a monstrous misconception. It has never happened and never will. There are no miracles, especially in the world of education. Not only will our students know nothing without ongoing, competent training, but our teachers can also know nothing about a teaching educational process without ongoing, competent training. Many centuries of worldwide experience—including American experience—and especially the experience of the last few decades are convincing proof of this.

3.17.8. Getting back to the example of intersecting chords and the consolidation of students' knowledge of such a simple question, let us show possible ways of further consolidating and enhancing that knowledge by working with secants drawn to a circle from one point, with a secant and a tangent, and with two tangents. The students will come to a conclusion that would seem naive from the point of view of a mathematician, but is useful from the point of view of the teacher and students: in all six cases of segments radiating from a common point and intersecting, or tangent to a circle, the result is the same regardless of the location of the point with respect to the circle. According to its pedagogical intention, this work is like thinking aloud, of which we have spoken before. The strong students will find it gratifying and interesting, like any generalization which serves to systematize different and apparently unrelated things. The very fact, the very possibility, of such a generalization and its result is gratifying to a person with mathematical abilities. It frees both strong and weak students of the need to memorize several statements instead of one. The cases with tangents are also extremely important from the point of view of implicit familiarization of the students with the concept of a tangent to a curve at a given point A as the limiting position of a secant passing through points A and B, if point A is fixed and point B moves along the curve toward A; that is, B approaches A. This is one of the many cases which should fill every math course at all stages of mass education in all educational establishments. It can be understood by all students. It arouses their interest and attention. And its consideration and study is useful to all students.

All six variants should be considered when the students encounter a case of degeneration of one of the secants into a tangent. Cases when the common point of two chords is on the circle—which, like other cases of degeneration, are very instructive for the stronger students—should not be rushed. They require special courage on the teacher's part, because he risks not being understood by anyone and perhaps even being ridiculed. This depends on the composition of the class, the number of good students, and, most importantly, on who holds sway in the class, who commands authority, and who is held in greater respect: the good students, or the weak but aggressive ones.

The case of two tangents automatically yields the theorem of the quality of two tangents drawn to a circle from one point; a theorem that is frequently invoked but which students tend to easily forget. Incidentally, the students virtually never arrive on their own at the theorem's corollary: the sums of the opposite sides of a quadrilateral circumscribed around a circle are equal. At this point, the teacher can use the opportunity to offer several problems making use of this statement. For example, a circle is inscribed in an isosceles trapezoid with bases 2 and 8; find the diameter of the circle (obviously, only if the students know the Pythagorean theorem).

3.17.9. Let us consider other examples. Teaching the properties of exponential and logarithmic functions without adequate consolidation

165

of the material leaves no trace in the students' memories, seems unnecessary and useless, and serves merely to widen the gap between the students and mathematics. Yet there are many ways of making the study of these functions in secondary school and in the university course in calculus both interesting and effective, leading to a stable, positive, mass result.

The solution of, say, the inequality (1) $\log_{1/3}(1 - x) > - 2$ will prove extremely useful for both strong and weak students from the point of view of consolidating their knowledge of the properties of logarithmic function, (2) $\log_{1/3}(1 - x) > \log_{1/3}9$, because $\log_{1/3}9 = -2$, (3) $0 < 1 - x < 9$. This is because, firstly, when the base is less than 1, smaller numbers correspond to larger logarithms: the logarithmic function is in this case decreasing; secondly, logarithms exist only for positive numbers, hence $1 - x$ is a positive number. Furthermore, (4) $0 > x - 1 > - 9$ and, finally (5) $1 > x > -8$, bring us to (6) $(-8, 1)$, the answer. Since it is easy to prove the equivalence of every pair of inequalities (1)–(5), the solution can be considered complete.

Here is another example: Solve inequality (7) $|x|^{x^2 + 5/2x - 3/2} < 1$.

Case 1: $|x| < 1$, then from the property of an exponential function with base smaller than 1, the exponent $x^2 + \frac{5}{2}x - \frac{3}{2} > 0$; that is, $2x^2 + 5x - 3 > 0$;

$$x = \frac{-5 \pm \sqrt{25 + 24}}{4} = \frac{-5 \pm 7}{4} \; ; x_1 = -3, x_2 = \frac{1}{2}.$$

(8) $\begin{cases} x < -3 \\ |x| < 1, \text{ no solution, or} \end{cases}$

(9) $\begin{cases} x > \frac{1}{2} \\ |x| < 1, \text{ i.e., } \frac{1}{2} < x < 1. \end{cases}$

Case 2: $|x| > 1$, then $x^2 + \frac{5}{2}x - \frac{3}{2} < 0$; that is,

(10) $\begin{cases} -3 < x < \frac{1}{2} \\ |x| > 1; \text{ that is, } -3 < x < -1. \end{cases}$

Since the solution set of inequality (7) is the union of solution sets of the systems of inequalities (8), (9), and (10), the answer is:

(11) $(-3, -1) \cup (\frac{1}{2}, 1)$.

If the teacher has not reviewed quadratic inequalities with the students for some time, and if the class is weak, such an example should be preceded by an exercise like this:

Solve the inequality (12) $|x|^{x-3} > 1$.

Case 1: $|x| > 1$, then from the property of exponential function we have

(13) $\begin{cases} x - 3 > 0 \\ |x| > 1 \end{cases}$;   (14) $\begin{cases} x > 3 \\ |x| > 1; \text{ that is, } x > 3. \end{cases}$

166

Case 2: $|x| < 1$, then

$$(15) \begin{cases} x - 3 < 0 \\ |x| < 1 \end{cases} ; \qquad\qquad (16) \begin{cases} x < 3 \\ |x| < 1; \text{ that is, } -1 < x < 1. \end{cases}$$

Since the solution set of inequality (12) is the union of solution sets of the systems of inequalities (13), (14), (15), and (16), the answer is (17) $(-1, 1) \cup (3, +\infty)$.

After this the solution of quadratic inequalities should be reviewed, and then the inequality (7) given to the students.

Formal instruction in exponential and logarithmic functions in our educational establishments at best includes a list of their properties, the drawing of only elementary graphs, and solution of the simplest exponential and logarithmic equations—and even that not too frequently. It is all very soon and irretrievably lost by the students, because teaching procedures lack the stage of consolidation of knowledge by all students, weak as well as strong, under the strict supervision of the teacher.

Abandoning children in mid course, after formally providing them with formal information, has become the rule in our country's educational system—if we can speak of education at all. School teachers and college instructors are totally unaware that their responsibilities do not end there; in fact, that is where they just begin. And even if some gifted students—very few and very rarely—manage to acquire sufficiently deep knowledge in some field, this is in no way an achievement of our educational system. It is its tragedy, because incompetent people, or people hostile to the idea of universal mass education, exploit the fact of successful self-learning by talented, brilliant students to justify the preservation of the status quo. Our educational system does not give extensive, comprehensive education to anyone. Even the most gifted students are forced to grope along blindly, some of them comparatively successfully, but at the cost of tremendous sacrifices on their part. Every year it leaves tens of millions of children in a world of ignorance, hopelessness, and despair, inflicting irreparable moral, material, and political damage on society as a whole and each of its members in particular.

Let us return to our examples. Inequalities (1), (7), and (12) are neither difficult nor, still less, incomprehensible to normal, healthy students—in school, in remedial courses, in college calculus courses—if the teaching is systematic and is not ignored. They are neither exceptional nor original. Like all the other cited examples, they were taken only to illustrate a general pedagogical or specific methodological proposition. These examples and others like them are extremely important for developing the mental ability, independence, and creativity of all students—weak, median, and strong—while simultaneously consolidating the material. This consolidation is carried out along with current revision, utilization, and consolidation of previously acquired knowledge: in the present case, we refer to knowledge of first- and second-order inequalities. However, the review of linear and quadratic inequalities here differs radically from their initial learning. They are no longer a target of cognition: they are its tool, a means of cognition. Elements of independence and creativity are required from the very first step, i.e., in going over from inequality (1) to inequality (2). To develop inequality (2), the student must perform an independent analysis, something which not all can do at first. In order to solve an inequality of type (1), it is sufficient to solve an inequality of type (2), which reduces to an algebraic inequality, the solution of which is known.

Many students have some difficulty solving inequality (2). Some, maybe even most, instead of inequality (3), $0 < 1 - x < 9$, will write (3a) $1 - x > 9$, considering it equivalent to inequality (2). Some will rush to the assertion that (3b), $1 - x < 9$, leads to the solution. All these difficulties are quite natural; in fact, problem (1) was conceived precisely to cause them. But that isn't its only merit. The students' difficulties, the obstacles they encounter at every stage in solving the problem, stimulate thinking because they have been prepared by all their preceding instruction to overcome such difficulties, which are in fact surmountable: this is a very important manifestation of didactic kindness.

We insist that when the time comes for studying exponential and logarithmic functions, all the students must be prepared—to varying degrees, naturally, but prepared—to overcome the obstacles they encounter. They must indeed be prepared, though not necessarily independently. The latter is only for very few students. The former can and must be the duty of all our teachers—a duty they can cope with, if we teach them instead of just talking about such teaching.

If the teacher finds that none of the students are able to proceed from (1) to (2), or if, walking silently up and down the aisles, he sees that only a few have coped with it—nothing unusual for a problem of this kind—he can adopt several variants of continuation of the lesson. He can ask one of the students who has done the first stage of the solution to write inequality (2) on the blackboard and require the class to justify both the possibility of going over from (1) to (2) and the advisability of such a transition. The possibility is justified solely by the fact that $-2 = \log_{1/3} 9$. The advisability is supported by the possibility of utilizing the decrease of the logarithmic function in (2) to go over to (3). The existence of the number $\log_{1/3}(1 - x)$ is postulated; otherwise, the whole argumentation is pointless.

Regardless of how many students have independently developed (2), the teacher can try a new tack to stimulate the thinking of all the students and encourage them to develop inequality (2) independently. Namely, he should offer a series of inequalities, each of them giving rise to surmountable obstacles. The inequalities should be immediately solved by the class as a whole, say, in the following sequence:

(2a) $\log_3 x > \log_3 7$, whence $x > 7$; $(7, +\infty)$, Answer.

(2b) $\log_3(1 - x) > \log_3 7$, whence $1 - x > 7$, $x - 1 < -7$, $x < -6$; $(-\infty, -6)$, Answer.

(2c) $\log_{1/3} x < \log_{1/3} 7$, whence $x > 7$; $(7, +\infty)$, Answer.

(2d) $\log_{1/3} x > \log_{1/3} 7$, whence $0 < x < 7$; $(0, 7)$, Answer.

(2e) $\log_{1/3}(1 - x) > \log_{1/3} 7$, whence $0 < 1 - x < 7$, $0 > x - 1 > -7$, $1 > x > -6$; $(-6, 1)$, Answer.

After solving a series like (2a)–(2e), the expedience of going over from (1) to (2) becomes obvious to all the students without exception.

3.17.10. When discussing with teachers a lesson including problem (1)—in either preparing the lesson or when subsequently analyzing it—it is necessary to discuss the question of the place of problems (2a)–(2e) in the lesson; i.e., should they be given before inequality (1) has been presented, or during its solution?

It is not customary for our educators to go into such details. They regard such questions as lesson technique, which can be highly diversified—a point with which we fully agree. In practice, they don't regard these questions as important—something we cannot accept. Technical, or rather methodological, methods of teaching make for the success or failure of every lesson and the course as a whole. They are determined fairly rigidly, though not uniquely, by the nature of the study material, age of the students, composition of the class (i.e., the number of strong and weak students), the lesson's objectives, its place in the sequence of lessons in the given subject, the pedagogical capabilities of the teacher, and his ability or inability to effectively utilize specific forms of work with the students. The method used in conducting each lesson, and every detail of each lesson, is determined by the teacher's general pedagogical philosophy, his pedagogical outlook, his love of the academic process, and faith in its power and success—all sentiments we should instill in teachers. Or it is determined by apathy and total indifference—if not antipathy—towards the academic process, those who supervise it, and the students. This is something we must try to alleviate and, if possible, eliminate.

A bold and capable teacher can and should start with inequality (1) regardless of the composition of the class. Coping with the lesson in this case may not be easy. That is why the supervisor or administrator should suggest that the inexperienced or less capable teacher adopt the sequence (2a)–(2e) and only after that (1)–(6).

The sequence (2a)–(2e) will go smoothly, easily, and usefully for all students, the weak as well as the strong. Superficially, the exercise will not seem boring if it is sufficiently fast-paced and the questions needed to justify each stage of the solution are asked intelligently, clearly, and forcefully. But the same lesson can arouse much greater interest and emotional and intellectual fervor in the class and have much greater teaching and developing significance if the teacher starts with (1), and only then, if necessary, inserts the sequence (2a)–(2e) or individual elements of it between (1) and (2).

3.17.11. The question is: What is preferable in school, remedial courses, and college?

The fundamental purpose of our school and college is to foster and develop the mind and the intellectual, creative, and cognitive abilities of the students, and in the process to give knowledge and instill skills and habits, including the skills and habits of independent acquisition of knowledge. That is why a sequence of the type (1)–(6), including (2a)–(2e) (only as needed, and perhaps only partially), should be preferred in all regular educational establishments with a regular student body—i.e., students who have had no interruption in their education and are unencumbered by family, work, or age.

There is nothing that can ever make up for the education and development a child receives in school. The solution of inequalities of types (1) and (7) should come naturally to school children. The current one-year courses in algebra I, algebra II, geometry, physics, chemistry, and biology provide no opportunities for fostering thinking and creativity; however, they do make it necessary to fill children's minds with recipes and facts, which is both useless and cruel on the students and the teachers. Just showing problems of types (1) and (7) in class without solving them together with the students can do nothing to foster thinking and creativity. In a school that gives life and rears thinking people, problems (1) and (7) should be posed forcefully. They need not necessarily be solved the same day and can be postponed, not for lack of time, but to give the students time to carry them about and think about them and then at the next lesson argue about possible solutions and their justifications.

Something along the same lines with the solution of inequalities (1) and (7) should be practiced in college; provided the course covers a sufficient number of hours—i.e., many more hours than are now devoted to the course in calculus. The four years in college should, as in the secondary school, be dedicated not so much to factography and imitative activity on the part of the students as to fostering and developing their thinking processes, creativity, independence, urge to continue their education, and habits of self-learning. That is why prime attention in the college academic process should be given to problem situations, and only in this connection to specific methods, operations, recipes, and algorithms—which are also doubtlessly very important but are available in handbooks.

Remedial courses and night groups in college are an entirely different matter: in these situations, the students have to cover extremely time-compressed courses, they have a very low level of knowledge, and are encumbered by a long break in their education. Such students should never begin with inequality (1), just as no attempt should be made to take up problems on mixtures and alloys or start with $5\frac{2}{7} - 2\frac{3}{7}$. Pseudorevolutionary, bombastic statements are especially dangerous when teaching weak students, adults, and people after long breaks in education. They are triply dangerous when people of all these categories are

170

merged in one group, coupled with terrible reductions in the time devoted to instruction.

That, however, is precisely the state of our remedial courses. And it is precisely in the teaching of such courses that ultrarevolutionary statements about modern science and the development of student creativity are the loudest; where the problem $5\frac{2}{7} - 2\frac{3}{7}$ should be seventh on the scale of difficulty and where the sequence of transcendental inequalities (1)–(6) is deadly if not preceded by the sequence (2a)–(2e).

In remedial courses—regardless of whether they are taught in the senior classes of school or initial years at college—the question can be mainly of knowledge, skills, and habits, not of developing the students' intellectual, creative, and cognitive abilities. The development of intellectual, creative, and cognitive abilities requires many years of systematic, active teaching and learning. The basic purpose of instruction in remedial courses should consist in the development of knowledge and, mainly, skills and habits of practical operations; of course, only if the students fully understand them. In the case of remedial courses, such understanding can be achieved by the careful selection of material that the students are capable of digesting—mainly necessary for studying subsequent courses—with the most thorough and pedagogically justified removal of everything else and observance of the principle of gradually and consistently increasing the degree of difficulty of exercises. These exercises stimulate the mental activity of students of remedial courses, thanks to the existence of obstacles in them. They should not be allowed to discourage thinking by making the obstacles insurmountable or presenting the students with problems they can't understand.

Problems (7) and (12) require the simultaneous overcoming of several obstacles associated with entirely different sections of the course; namely, the solution of exponential inequalities (the objective of the exercise), utilization of the properties of an exponential function (the material to be consolidated and a tool of the exercise), and the solution of systems of inequalities with absolute values (a tool of the exercise). Like the transition from problem (1) to problem (2), the transition from (12) to (13) can be either preceded or accompanied by the following sequence of problems:

(12a) $2^{x-3} > 1$, whence $x - 3 > 0$; $x > 3$, $(3, +\infty)$, Answer;
(12b) $2^{x-3} < 1$, consequently, $x - 3 < 0$; $x < 3$, $(-\infty, 3)$, Answer;
(12c) $(\frac{1}{2})^{x-3} > 1$, consequently, $x - 3 < 0$; $x < 3$, $(-\infty, 3)$, Answer;
(12d) $(\frac{1}{2})^{x-3} < 1$, consequently, $x - 3 > 0$; $x > 3$, $(3, +\infty)$, Answer.

In remedial courses the sequence (12a)–(12d) should precede problem (12); otherwise, the creative stage—consideration of the two cases in (12)—would have to be imposed on the students from outside instead of being developed by themselves. For that reason, the sequence (12a)–(12d), which explicitly includes both the cases which in problem

171

(12) require independent identification and solution by the students, is absolutely essential in remedial courses.

3.17.12. As mentioned before, whatever the type of lesson—in school as well as in college—consideration of new material should include a series of questions prepared by the teacher in advance to consolidate the new information. The questions may be aimed at summing up the new information and the main results of the lessons, with a clear indication by the teacher of what has been achieved in class, how it relates to the preceding material, what must be learned and memorized for upcoming work, and what need not be memorized. For example, it isn't necessary to remember the shape of the curve $y = \frac{1}{x^2 + 1}$, but the student must be able to justify its development; on the other hand, the shape and position of the curve $y = x^2 + 1$ should be remembered. It is virtually impossible to remember the shape of the curve $y = \frac{1}{x^2 - 1}$; however, the students can be taught to reason logically when constructing it. At the same time, all students must remember the position of the curve $y = x^2 - 1$ on the coordinate plane.

After the introduction of new information it may be necessary in class to read from the textbook the definition of the new concept and proof of the new proposition and answer any questions the students may have. Such consolidation is essential if the material is poorly presented in the textbook and may not be understood at home, even following the active work of all students in class during the primary introduction of the material under the teacher's supervision. It is also necessary if subsequent work in class requires that the students memorize what they have just understood; for example, the properties of logarithmic functions or the properties of the functions $y = \text{arc sin } x$ and $y = \text{arc cos } x$.

Special studies have shown that new information is memorized best when, in addition to giving the students exercises and asking questions requiring the active, conscious utilization of that information, the teacher also clearly instructs them about the volume of new information to be memorized. All teachers must conduct this work, not only during the lesson at which the new study material is introduced, but also throughout numerous subsequent lessons with the purpose of forestalling any destruction of knowledge. Teachers must be taught this work very diligently and patiently during the preparations for, and conducting of, mini-researches. It is one of the basic prerequisites of a successful academic process. Teachers should acquire firm habits of such activity under the guidance of competent supervisors and the best teachers of the school system, the city, and the state if we really intend to teach our children, and not just dream about it. Moreover, teachers at all levels should be taught how to supervise the memorization process and the process of learning new information, regardless of where the students engage in this learning and memorization: in class or at home. We are speaking, basically, of the need for the teacher to identify logical justification points. For example, why the range of the function $y = \arcsin x$ is $[-\pi/2, \pi/2]$, and that of $y = \arctan x$ is $(-\pi/2, \pi/2)$; why it is better to choose the interval $[0, \pi]$ rather than $[-\pi/2, \pi/2]$ as the range of the function $y = \arccos x$; why for the function $y = a^x$, $a > 0$, $a \neq 1$, et cetera, even though formally the definition is given and the question "why" is meaningless.

Another important element in assuring the successful memorization of material is for the teacher, with student participation, to logically correlate the material to be memorized with already known material, and also logically group the material. This work is absolutely essential during all stages in developing the concepts of number and exponent, the concept of equation and inequality and their equivalence, the concept of function and its graphic representation, and so on. Teachers must learn all this, all their lives, from each other and from leading specialists in the field of teaching methods. Otherwise, our children will keep forgetting not only the formulas of trigonometry—as a consequence of which they waste half the time devoted to the study of calculus—but even the formulas for solving quadratic equations. The blame for this rests not with the children, but with us, their educators.

3.18. USING THE SYSTEM OF MINI-RESEARCHES TO TEACH EDUCATORS HOW TO REVIEW STUDY MATERIAL

3.18.1. Although many of our instructors still talk with students in vain efforts to give them new knowledge, virtually none of them have ever undertaken that special kind of work with students without which it is impossible to preserve and improve knowledge. We are speaking of review; that is, never-ending special efforts to (1) prevent the destruction of knowledge, (2) restore lost knowledge, (3) deepen and expand the overall body of information in the students' possession, (4) structurize and systematize knowledge, (5) improve skills and habits, and (6) develop the students' mental, creative, and cognitive abilities in the course and as a consequence of such an academic activity.

3.18.2. Review of studied material should go on continuously throughout the academic process. Only then can one of the prime objectives of review be achieved: preventing the destruction of existing knowledges, skills, and habits and their upgrading, together with the development of intellectual, creative, and cognitive abilities. As regards math and science, one of the simplest forms of this work is to stretch the students' work on the material of every section, chapter, part, and course over longer spans of time.

For example, suppose the section "Graphs of Equations in Polar

Coordinates" is being studied. If the students are familiarized with the drawing of straight lines, circles, limaçons, roses, spirals, and lemniscates during one class, no good and only harm can come from such work, regardless of how many problems the teacher gives for homework, five or forty-five. If the teacher has at least some concern for his students' knowledge and knows how to go about his task, he will extend the work involving their initial familiarization with all types of curves in polar coordinates for at least four lessons—concurrently, of course, with the study of new sections. But that isn't all. From time to time he will come back to it, if only to solve one or two problems in class and assign as many for homework. Furthermore, he will group the exercises in such a way that the students can see the similarities and differences between curves due to the similarities and differences in their equations. For example, $r = 2 - 2 \cos \theta$ and $r = 2 + 2 \sin \theta$, or $r = 2 \cos \theta$ and $r = -2 \sin \theta$, or $r = 2 + 2 \cos \theta$, $r = 3 + 2 \cos \theta$, $r = 2 + 3 \cos \theta$, et cetera. He must make a point of discussing in class the type of relationship between a and b when equations $r = a + b \cos \theta$ or $r = a + b \sin \theta$ generate a cardioid or a limaçon with a loop; what graphs are generated by equations $r = a \sin n \theta$ and $r = a \cos n \theta$ with n even and n odd; et cetera.

Such work should be resumed from time to time. Its intensity, however, should vary, together with the degree of teacher participation and the forms of teacher supervision. Initially, the students should work actively in class under the active supervision of the teacher; the home assignments should only consolidate the work, largely repeating it, with some minor inclusions of new elements. Approximately half the problems of every section should be covered in this way.

Gradually, as work on the material of the next chapter progresses, greater emphasis is placed on students' independent work with the material being reviewed. Discussion of assignments (including the reviewed material) prior to their being done is replaced by discussion *after* they have been done, and subsequently only during consultation sessions. Gradually, the problems in the third quarter of the list of problems of the reviewed section are covered; individual problems are taken from the review list.

Conducted systematically, such review of previously studied material serves to deepen, expand, and consolidate the students' knowledge. The result is a productive, humane, and didactically kind mass education with stable results for all students, the highly as well as the less talented. This is in part because the same home assignments require different amounts of time, intellectual effort, and mental activity on the part of different students, as well as varying degrees of teacher participation.

3.18.3. However, the teaching-learning process is not by far restricted to home assignments. Home assignments can only supplement, not replace it. The basic teaching and learning work takes place in class. We have said this many times before, and will repeat it over and over. Review and consolidation of knowledge is in large measure achieved in the system of home assignments, although not exclusively. Otherwise, both the revision and the home assignments will be discredited. However good preliminary and subsequent discussions of home assignments might be, the educator must regularly, in class, with the help of special assignments and exercises, consolidate, summarize, systematize, and generalize each specific stage of reviewing and improving acquired knowledge. These half-control, half-teaching assignments and exercises should be done in class with the most active participation of all the students, for the weaker students this will substantially help them improve their knowledge and skills. For the stronger ones it offers an opportunity to check themselves, get some generalizing and systematizing help from the teacher, and show examples of creative work, which will be discussed under the teacher's supervision by all the students and be of great use to all—the weak as well as the strong. The teacher, for his part, will get detailed information about his students' mental abilities—their thinking, knowledge, skills, and habits—at the given stage of their schooling and development. Furthermore, such pedagogical activity is accompanied by a continuous flow of information from the teacher to the students regarding the merits and demerits of their knowledge and the ways of overcoming the demerits while preserving the merits.

3.18.4. Continuity of the teacher's professional academic activity, which organizes and guides the continuous activity of the students in the acquisition and consolidation of new knowledge, as well as its subsequent systematization, structuralization, consolidation, and continuous updating, results in continuity of the knowledge assimilation process of all the students. Continuity of the process of acquiring, consolidating, and upgrading skills and habits leads to a mass process of continuous mastery of firm skills and habits. This pedagogical wisdom must be driven home to all our educators and administrators of the educational system.

3.18.5. Thus, systematic, teacher-organized review of study material is one of the educational devices aimed at ensuring continuity of acquisition of knowledge by all students. This device is available to all teachers without exception, but not without special instruction and learning in the system of mini-researches. Furthermore, regular review, restoration, and renovation of the material under the teacher's supervision results in deeper comprehension and rapid and firm consolidation of the acquired knowledge in the students' minds, which makes it part of their general erudition, culture, and personalities.

3.18.6. The most ancient and primitive method of review consists in the continuous restoration of knowledge the students specifically need to comprehend new material. If the teacher hasn't been taught how to organize and continuously supervise such work, his academic activity is doomed. Politicians and educators needn't be surprised that our mass education exists only in words and cash flow, because no one takes the trouble of teaching our teachers anything, even such primitive activity.

175

Millions of students in educational establishments of all types attend introductory classes in, say, the concept of inverse trigonometric functions, understanding nothing and simply memorizing the form, because they have already forgotten the concept of function, the concept of inverse function, and everything else needed for the current lesson. All this happens because the instructor hasn't been taught that several lessons prior to the introduction of new concepts he should tell the students about those on which the new ones are based—concepts which they should have known but may have forgotten by then. It is only natural for students to forget things learned long ago to which the teacher had never returned. This must be taken into account, without blaming the students for everything—it is no fault of theirs if we don't know how to teach them.

Previously studied material should be reviewed tactfully, without accusing the students of having short memories, but also efficiently, requiring them to read specified material and carry out specified exercises for the next lesson. At that lesson the teacher should make a point of discussing with the students both the theory they reviewed and the exercises they did. Depending on the complexity and specifics of the new section, in preparation for which the review has been undertaken, the work may be conducted during one or two classes, or substantially more. For example, problems employing all operations with algebraic fractions should precede problems involving all operations with radicals. Students cannot solve the problem of simplifying $\dfrac{1}{\sqrt{a} - \sqrt{b}} - \dfrac{1}{\sqrt{a} + \sqrt{b}}$ because they can't simplify $\dfrac{1}{a - b} - \dfrac{1}{a + b}$, or even $1/3 - 1/4$.

3.18.7. Teachers should realize as early as possible in their educational careers—and we must help them with this—that the purpose of review may be the restoration and upgrading of knowledge needed by the students not only to understand the new information, but also to establish connections between the knowledge they are acquiring and the previously acquired knowledge. The establishment and expansion of such connections—the construction of a system of knowledge—is one of the basic study objectives of school and university courses.

For example, in establishing the properties of the diagonals of a square, it is necessary for the students to review the properties of the diagonals of a rectangle and a rhombus. When introducing powers with the exponent m/n, the students should review the definition of a fraction and prove that m/n as an exponent is a fraction. A similar approach must be taken when introducing powers with the exponent $-m$; that is, it is necessary to review the definition of a negative number and prove that the exponent $-m$ is a negative number ($m > 0$). When introducing the concept of function with the help of a set of ordered pairs of real numbers, the teacher should discuss the definition of function with the help of the concept of correspondence between the elements of two sets.

176

When introducing the improper integral the notion of the definite integral from a to b should be reviewed, and so on.

3.18.8. We must, within the system of mini-researches, also teach all our educators that one of the main objectives of review is to prevent the destruction of knowledge. It is, of course, impossible to prevent the destruction of some previously acquired knowledge in the conditions of an ongoing process of acquisition of new knowledge. The essential thing, however, is that the continuing teaching-learning process should provide a steadily growing and continuously changing body of active knowledge, skills, and habits for every student that the student can independently and consciously use when solving a wide range of problems. Otherwise the process of acquisition of new knowledge can lose any meaning, which is what we can see everywhere in our country today, but quite incredibly prefer not to discuss.

Review does not, of course, resolve all teaching and learning problems, but its systematic and purposeful application in conditions of mass education of students and teachers will result in a stable increase in the level of active knowledges, skills, and habits of all learners—instructors and students.

Regular, continuous review of the main concepts, ideas, and structures of the course, as well as of the basic relevant operations, skills, and habits, is carried out independently of the introduction of new material, in parallel with such introduction, and as far as possible in keeping with the logic of the science represented in the course. Such review is carried out in class and in the system of home assignments, in the form of discussions, teacher and student reports, conferences, debates, written assignments—taking ten minutes or ten days—problems, exercises, questions, computer programs, motion pictures, video and audio tapes, radio, et cetera.

3.18.9. Coming to a lesson to talk semicoherently about a new section of a textbook, then asking the students several questions and hastily giving them their home assignments; doing the same the next day; for the sake of variety, forgetting either the new material, questions to the students, or both; once in a while shamefacedly giving the so-called learners lengthy, learned-looking but insultingly primitive tests requiring no more than mechanical memorization of information: this and the likes of it is not mass education—it is mass delusion. It isn't even a shadow of education, but rather a consistently enforced rejection of education and a cruel slighting of millions of teachers and tens of millions of children, done under cover of bombastic slogans about defending the grass roots of democracy, freedom of the individual, and equal opportunity for all.

Without an ongoing, stable process of reviewing studied material and consolidation of the students' knowledge effected in all forms, by all teachers, in all the nation's educational establishments, there never was, is not, and never will be a genuinely mass education. Without con-

177

tinuous mutual instruction of teachers in how to organize and carry out such review in all forms there has never been, is not, and will never be a teaching academic process based on the following: student independence and creativity; continuous upgrading and consolidation of knowledge, skills, and habits; active and effective development of their intellectual, creative, and cognitive abilities.

3.18.10. Teachers must be continuously and extensively taught that not every kind of review is useful for the students. Mechanical review of the same material without exerting the mind, which is not accompanied by the gradual expansion of the material's content in depth and breadth, can at a certain stage breed the students' dislike for the subject, emotional and mental inertia, drowsiness, and apathy. Such symptoms of an extremely dangerous state of affairs in the class should be very carefully watched by the teacher and *his* teachers: a young, inexperienced teacher may not always notice them on his own. On the other hand, the expansion of the content of the course during the review process should not be too tiresome for the students. Otherwise, there will be no time left to learn and consolidate new material or instill new skills and habits. For this reason the reviewed material should be updated mainly through the medium of various generalizations and through the structuralization of knowledge and establishing and consolidating the connections between the reviewed sections of the course, as well as the preceding and subsequent material. Reviewed material should also be updated by introducing more complex and difficult exercises and new types of exercises. These exercises may not have been considered at all during the initial introduction and consolidation of the material, or they may have been considered, but not sufficiently enough to assure firm mastery of the factual material, its idea content, or the techniques of carrying out operations. The exercises may have been inadequate for developing the students' independence and creativity within a new structure of concepts and operations, in unity or juxtaposition with previously studied structures.

For example, the solution of logarithmic and exponential equations and inequalities for the purpose of upgrading the students' knowledge, skills, and habits in the field of exponential and logarithmic functions, algebraic equations, and inequalities and their systems requires a high level of intellectual activity made necessary by the more complex connections between the reviewed topics as well as by the novelty of the material itself: logarithmic and exponential equations and inequalities. The same can be said of trigonometric equations and inequalities; irrational equations and inequalities; equations and inequalities with parameters; the investigation, graphic representation, and differentiation of composite functions; differential equations; and many others.

3.19. MINI-RESEARCHES ON TEACHING STUDENTS LEARNING STRATEGIES AND STUDY SKILLS AND TECHNIQUES

3.19.1. Learning is not restricted to the acquisition of knowledge, skills, and habits and the development of intellectual and cognitive abilities with the help of that knowledge: it is a function of the students' learning strategies and study methods.

The success or failure of education depends on the quality of the learners' learning strategies. Education should, therefore, include instruction in study methods, the development and perfection of study skills, techniques, learning strategy and style. Then, and only then, will education be a continuous, self-reproducing process, because the knowledges, skills, and habits acquired by the students will provide the basis and prerequisite for acquiring new knowledges, skills, and habits. As they acquire and perfect them, the students will assimilate and perfect the very process, the very method, of acquiring and upgrading knowledge in general, not just specific knowledge. If that doesn't happen, people stop learning not because of any lack of abilities, but because of an inability to work at the higher stages of learning. This is yet another cause of the American educational tragedy.

3.19.2. Teaching the strategy of learning presumes continuous mental activity on the part of the students, deriving from the fact that the teacher always strives to leave to the learners exactly that amount of intellectual and technical activity that they are capable of performing. The ability to maintain the mental activity of all the students—to varying degrees in different students, but always activity—is what distinguishes didactic kindness from cruelty, a skilled educator from an inept one, a good school from a bad one, successful schooling from self-learning attempts. Moreover, the interest aroused by the teaching-learning process is dependent on the degree of mental activity and seriousness of the ideas presented at the lesson, not on attempts to entertain the children without relevance to its contents.

Teaching the strategy of learning and study methods means more than just gradually and continuously creating and maintaining mental activity in class. It also means stimulating thinking and the need to think; it means teaching children to think, reason, juxtapose, compare, analyze, identify the main points, memorize, draw conclusions, generalize, prove, justify, voice doubts and convictions, give examples and counterexamples, refute and clarify. All educators must do this as they pass on knowledge and instill skills and habits in their respective subjects. All educators must be taught this at all stages of instruction, by attending, video-taping, and discussing lessons and pooling the efforts of supervisors, teachers, and administrators to work out lesson variants aimed at developing the thinking abilities, independence, and creativity of both learners and teachers in various spheres, including study methods.

3.19.3. When preparing and subsequently discussing lessons with supervisors, administrators, and instructors at all stages of education, special attention should be given to the students' ability to simply listen to the teacher's explanations, something not all students have been taught. They wait impatiently for the end of what they see as a useless waste of time. Some occupy themselves by leafing through their books; others rummage in their bags, openly demonstrating their impatience or even protest. They have never heard a problem-oriented or simply useful presentation and have no idea that such a thing can exist. Educationally qualified and efficient work with them is extremely difficult until they can be convinced that the teacher's work is both necessary, useful, and, in fact, irreplaceable; until they are taught to listen to the teacher and acquire habits of listening without being distracted; until they participate in the problems set forth by the teacher—sometimes only mentally, which is hardest of all. We must teach children to keep constant track of the teacher's train of thought, to try to understand him, ask questions and think of examples—mentally or out loud, if requested—to agree with the teacher or try to refute him; compare the new material with what was learned at previous lessons; to make sure, in the absence of the teacher's instructions, what should be written down and what shouldn't, and so on, and so forth.

Children usually learn the great art of listening when they are still very small and haven't yet lost hope of hearing useful and interesting things; either in primary school, if the teacher isn't too incompetent, or sometimes in elementary school, if the teacher is good. Later on, when they get into the hands of an endless succession of instructors little concerned with what they are saying or whether others are listening to what they have to say, children soon lose the habit, not only of actively listening to the teacher—that is, listening coupled with simultaneous comprehension, assimilation and analysis—but of listening in general. They hear sounds—not meaningful, problem-oriented speech. It takes much time and much deliberate effort on the part of educators to arouse or resurrect children's ability to listen, hear, and respect the words of the teacher. One of the basic educational techniques of achieving this is a continuous succession of questions coming from the teacher, the problem orientation of his discourse, and the gradual and continuous buildup of the volume and difficulty of the information, which the students have to analyze immediately—at one go, during one session.

3.19.4. An extremely important task on which all educators must concentrate when preparing, conducting, and analyzing a lesson is the gradual emotional instruction of the students in one of the fundamental, most important, and absolutely essential forms—not only of learning strategy, but of human activity in general. We are speaking of the ability to succinctly, consistently, logically, and with correct grammar, set forth ideas, views, and observations, in both oral and written form.

Mastery of oral and written speech is an absolutely essential prerequisite, tool, means, and result of the application of learning activity, irrespective of the studied subject, the age of the students, or the complexity of the studied material. It is directly dependent on the quality and methods of instruction. It is not just one of several possible forms of the educator's teaching activity; it is not a suggestion that one may either heed or ignore. The development and never-ending improvement of the students' oral and written speech at all stages of education is as inseparable from the academic process as the students themselves, the study subject, and the tools and techniques of teaching and learning. Teaching succinct, clear speech—by having the students memorize textbook examples and learn poetry by heart; by correcting mistakes and discussing the best variants of statements and wording, explanations, proofs, refutations, doubts, questions, and misunderstandings; and by ensuring complete comprehension—this is inseparable from didactic kindness. All this must accompany every lesson, every class, in all educational establishments, always and everywhere. Such teaching activity is possible if the real, not just proclaimed, purpose of education is the development of the individual: the development of a person's thinking, independence, and creativity; the ability to express one's thoughts and desires; the ability to understand others and to understand the worlds of knowledge, science, and art; the ability to live a full-blooded human life.

Mastery of oral and written speech is a means and result of instruction and education; the one is impossible without the other—this is self-evident. So how do we manage to keep not just normal but even naturally very gifted people in school for twelve years who cannot speak, read, or write? By what mysterious means and in what incredible ways do teachers give their charges knowledge in math, physics, chemistry, and biology? How do they teach them language, literature, and history? What means and devices do they use to achieve the students' complete understanding of their ideas; the laws of development of nature and society; the plot of a literary work or its artistic images, expressive devices, and features of speech of the protagonists and the author? How are they able to hear all this from their students? In what mysterious ways do they explain the factorization of polynomials and the necessity of introducing negative numbers? How could they judge if the unfortunate children understood them, and, if so, to what extent? How could teachers judge what their charges found difficult, what they didn't understand, and what they misunderstood? How do supervisors and administrators help the teachers, guide their work, and evaluate their achievements and failures if the students are incapable of expressing themselves in ways understandable to themselves, to say nothing of others? They are incapable of writing anything coherently; they cannot explain how to find the area of a rectangle; they can't comprehend the conditions of a problem; they are incapable of saying anything about the dependence between distance, velocity and time in uniform motion; and so on. Hasn't the only version of the whole twelve years of schooling been the total absence of any

181

schooling whatsoever, the total absence of any teaching or learning activity, the total neglect of the whole academic process in all its manifestations, even the most primitive?

3.19.5. Teaching students the strategy of learning and study skills and techniques—like teaching educators teaching strategy and teaching skills and techniques—is based on the principle of systematic, conscious assimilation of theoretical material coupled with exercises, while steadily and gradually building up the complexity of the activities of both learners and instructors. This instruction in learning and teaching strategy is also based on continuous variation of conditions, circumstances, and targets, as well as teaching-learning methods, operations, tools, and techniques. The whole course and the results of the preceding education should prepare the students and the teacher for the requirements presented by each new stage with respect to the ability to teach, study, and employ educational and study skills and teachniques. If teachers and students are not prepared for this, the blame is with the educational system. To lay the blame on the children and teachers is cruel, useless, and detrimental to the nation.

3.19.6. School and college teachers must work regularly with all the students, the weak as well as the strong. When only the teacher or the best students work at the blackboard, this destroys the teaching-learning process. The lesson is fast-paced. A good pupil dictates while at the same time writing. The rest only write. They write and write all those years, hearing and not hearing the person at the front of the class, seeing and not seeing the notes on the blackboard. And this is called active instruction—reliance on the best students. Indeed—but with the purpose of turning the teaching-learning process into a farce, into a coy game between the teacher and the students, instead of intense work on the part of both: the students on the studied subject, the teachers with the students.

To finally conceal his helplessness, assuage his guilty conscience, and at the same time neutralize the students—some of whom intuitively feel, while others clearly realize, that they are not being taught and not being given new knowledge, and that it's all just a superficial appearance of propriety—the teacher mumbles barely coherently: "Any questions?" He then hastily leafs through the textbooks and mutters, more clearly this time, "And now we will. . . ."—his face quickly renovated, happily concerned, promising something very interesting which he will now find in the textbook, all for the sake of discouraging the class from asking any questions. Our helpless, unhappy teacher acts exactly like the photographer promising, together with the broadly smiling parents, that a little bird will fly out of the lens, just wait a minute.

3.19.7. The teacher must love and teach both the good students and the weak students. He must work selflessly to promote the development of all the children; he must courageously teach study skills and techniques to them all—the smiling and the dour, the happy and the

182

embittered. They are all human, and it is up to us whether they will remain human. By systematically, emotionally, lovingly, and caringly teaching the child study skills and techniques; by giving him assignments he can measure up to and discussing with him in detail the study procedures and obtained results; by pointing out and showing how to correct shortcomings in his work; by unremittingly observing all his subsequent work—how he improves it and manages to control himself; by helping him again wherever he has as yet insurmountable difficulties; by imbuing him with the need for and habits of self-control—in behavior and in work—and with confidence in his strength; by praising when necessary, sometimes even if the child hasn't earned it, yet—thus, day by day, year by year, the teacher didactically and affectionately creates a *thinking* person. This child thus becomes a creative person and a loving person, not an empty guffawing clown or an embittered beast incapable of study or work, and capable only of violence and cruelty.

3.19.8. Studying is neither simple nor easy. In school as in college, the students hasten to hand in written assignments without checking them and therefore they are full of foolish, accidental mistakes. No one has ever even tried to teach them to check the quality of their own work or how to improve it along each step, each operation, and each word. Our children could avoid so much unhappiness, so much humiliation, so much suffering if they were taught the difficult art of being able to check the quality of their work, the ability to soberly and objectively evaluate it. This tragic ineptitude in self-control is the consequence, not the reason for, an illiterate, irresponsible, and cruel process, which we call an educational process.

Those pupils who have received at least crumbs of knowledge and study skills are not usually in a hurry to turn in their papers. The others, however, rush to get out of the classroom, hastily correcting the most stupid mistakes which accidentally catch the eye, not in the least discouraged by the natural thought that they could probably find many more such mistakes.

So many of our children keep repeating, sincerely and sadly, gulping back tears, "But I did study, I really did!" But they were never taught what it means to understand; what it means to learn what you understood; what is means to check yourself; what it means to review the newly learned again and again, and over again, today, and tomorrow; what it means to use new knowledge to acquire skills and habits and achieve new results, including new results in study skills and techniques.

3.19.9. People lacking in education are incapable of appreciating their capabilities, knowledge, and skills, or of realizing their weak points. They are know-alls and do-alls, dilettantes and ignoramuses, who consider themselves capable of any job (if it pays well) and who are extremely dangerous to society. There are others who suffer from a different mania—an inferiority complex. They think they know nothing and are incapable of doing anything, yet they possess outstanding knowledge and skills, both particular and general.

The national educational system can and must prevent the inundation of society with untalented, illiterate, self-confident crushers of all the good beginnings they happen to get involved with and which they immediately seek to control, as well as with shy, timid, hesitant do-nothings with no initiative, even if they do possess knowledge and skills, as well as creative and mental capabilities. The latter see nothing of this in themselves; they don't realize the wealth they possess and so squander it on useless projects and undertakings. They are afraid of taking to the road of full-blooded, active, creative endeavor, which brings pleasure and happiness to people and to themselves, success to their undertakings, and strength and prosperity to the society.

An effective, qualified, honest, sincere educational system should give our children not only knowledge in certain spheres, nor should it only develop their abilities; rather, it should also continuously and painstakingly foster skills and habits of sober self-control and qualified self-evaluation. This will make it possible for our children to see the opportunities they possess today, evaluate the real requirements for obtaining and upgrading new knowledge, skills, and habits, and achieve higher levels of intellectual, creative, and cognitive abilities—at all stages of their lives. This will help them approach the ideal of human happiness and human wisdom: to do or claim only what you can cope with and what is in reach of your will, wisdom, creative abilities, knowledge, and skills, including the ability to acquire new knowledge; not to claim things you are incapable of doing, in which you lack adequate knowledge or the capability of obtaining it at this time.

3.19.10. The necessity and habits of self-control can and should be fostered in students from the earliest age and up to the end of their schooling. One of the forms of such work is involving them in frequent in-depth debates, arguments, and discussions on prearranged topics, dealing with questions for which the students—or groups of students—prepare their answers in advance, controlling and evaluating the level and quality of their knowledge. In the course of the debate, conducted by a qualified and educated teacher, several students or groups of students set forth their views, opinions, and answers to the same question and explain how they obtained the results. The teacher refrains from any comments, opinions, or evaluations—explicit or implicit, direct or oblique. Several other students, individually or on behalf of a group, evaluate the statements, answers, and judgments, comparing their good and bad points, seeking to establish the connections between them and the procedure of academic work. The authors of the initial statements and the other students challenge the evaluations; argue; cite examples and counterexamples, proofs, and refutations; analyze and synthesize the discussed statements; and introduce variants and suggestions. The teacher supervises this work energetically and actively.

This procedure should be used to analyze as many theoretical questions as possible, as well as the solutions of problems—both creative and algorithmized—both prior to, during, and after the formulation of the algorithm. This format should also be used to discuss all home and class assignments, both practice and control assignments, creating and discussing problem-oriented situations.

If this work is conducted from the earliest age the children acquire self-confidence: they are bold in their statements, critical and self-critical, and get used to evaluating their work as they do it and after it is done, thereby developing habits of control and self-control. It is absolutely necessary for the teacher to ask special questions, such as: Why do you think so? How did you arrive at this conclusion? How would you answer this question, and why? How did you check yourself at this point? How did you control yourself when doing this exercise? How can you avoid such a mistake in such-and-such a situation? How and why did you discover this inaccuracy? What led to the next wrong step and mistake in your reasoning, proof, and justification of the solution? How could all of those errors have been avoided? And so on, and so forth. Without all of this, with the help of only written answers—moreover, answers requiring merely a choice of the correct one out of several offered, without analytical and synthetic reasoning, justifications, and proof—there is no educational process. All there is is another variant of useless or harmful time-wasting for tens of millions of our children, which may be more or less unpleasant, according to the personal qualities of the teacher.

3.20. HOW THE TEACHER SHOULD SUPERVISE THE STUDENTS' WORK ON HOME ASSIGNMENTS

3.20.1. However thoroughly questions of theory requiring good understanding and firm memorization by the students were discussed during the lesson, work at home with the textbook or with notes made in class is virtually always necessary. If the students listened, and even if they actively participated in the discussion of theoretical questions during the lesson, their homework should be aimed at learning new information, memorizing it, and establishing the connections between the newly and previously acquired knowledge.

3.20.2. Understanding doesn't necessarily mean knowing. The overwhelming majority of our students sincerely believe that if they understand what is said in class, this is sufficient for them to know all they have to about a chapter of the course.

During the first few years in school the teacher requires the children to go over and memorize the taught lesson at home. Gradually, however, this requirement declines. Where there was one teacher several take over. They change every year, if not more frequently. The teachers are indifferent to the students' successes or failures, to their knowledge or absence of knowledge. The students become indifferent toward their helpless mentors. This means the disintegration of the academic process, the teaching process, and the learning process.

3.20.3. Firm knowledge of concepts and their properties—of propositions, operations, and structures and the ability to handle them correctly; firm knowledge of algorithms; the ability to see a problem situation, formulate a problem, and find the ways of solving it—these and many other forms of knowledge, skills, and habits are acquired to varying degrees by different students equally applying themselves, depending on their personal qualities and abilities. That is why giving all students, without exception, the opportunity to align to some degree their respective levels of knowledge, skills, and habits acquired during the lesson by doing home assignments is not the teacher's private affair, nor a manifestation of his academic freedom, but rather the foundation of the whole academic process, if it has any claim to success.

This leads us to the formulation of one of several extremely important objectives of home assignments: individualization of the learning process in school and college with the help of independent homework based on the students' work in class. The lesson, for its part, is the basic form of the teaching, learning, and educating process, the main source of knowledge, skills, and habits acquired by the students, and the main tool for developing their intellectual, creative, and cognitive abilities.

3.20.4. Flirting with home assignments and discussions regarding their usefulness or harm is a consequence of incomprehension and total failure to understand the nature and techniques of both teaching and learning. Where one student will require fifteen minutes to do the portion of the home assignment that is a variation rather than a review of the class work, another may spend thirty minutes, and another even forty-five. The result, however, can well be that all three students will come to the next lesson with the same levels of knowledge and skills in the specific question considered at the previous lesson. On the other hand, those same students may come to the next lesson with different levels of knowledge and skills. Our teachers must realize this, as well as the fact that a more capable student may not necessarily be the best prepared if he overestimates his powers and abilities and underestimates the requirements of the course.

Regular discussion of home assignments in class is an effective means of assuring the required minimum of knowledge and skills at every segment of the academic process called the lesson. Such instructive discussions provide the teacher with feedback from the teaching process and the students with feedback from the learning process, coupled with the improvement of their skills, the generalization and systematization of their knowledge, the clarification of questions, and the addition of new knowledge.

186

3.20.5. Work on home assignments is not a question of the teacher's tastes or whims; it is one of the basic laws of mass education. It makes it possible to organize a teaching-learning process in class that gives knowledge, skills, and habits and develops the intellectual, creative, and cognitive abilities of all the students—the more capable as well as the less capable, the sluggish as well as the nimble. Work in class, discussions, oral and written exercises—including material from previous lessons and previous home assignments—provide the opportunity for virtually all students to master the basic material of the course to the extent required for successfully continuing their education. This by no means implies that the level of knowledge, skills, habits and intellectual, creative, and cognitive abilities of all students should or can be made the same—certainly not. In fact, it would be criminal with respect to the students and, happily, virtually impossible. All we are saying is that home assignments—or rather, that portion of home assignments which is directly associated with the preceding class work—give all students the opportunity to work at home, set their own pace within their own time frame, and come to the next lesson prepared to discuss and upgrade the results of the preceding lesson and the fulfilled home assignment. Thus the students are prepared to successfully assimilate the contents of the new lesson.

On a larger scale, work on home assignments, coupled with active work in class, which is the basic form of teaching and learning, is one of the manifestations of didactic kindness. It gives virtually all students the opportunity to complete the course with satisfaction, with results making it possible for them to tackle the next, more difficult, course.

3.20.6. A comment of extreme importance to all educators and students is in order.

Daily classes in one and the same subject (with the exception of music, languages, some sports, and marching drill) in school and in college are foolish and cruel. They destructively affect the individualization and effectiveness of the academic process. What can be changed in the students' knowledge and skills with another lesson coming up the next day?

Let student A be highly capable in math but incapable of putting two words together when it comes to history. Let student B have no trouble at all with history but find the going hard in math. Let, furthermore, both A and B require the same effort and time to handle the other study subjects. If math and history are given daily, student A hasn't the time to cope with his history, while student B can't tackle math in a single afternoon. They both come to school or college every day with guilty expressions and a hidden fear which turns a person into an eternally guilty, unhappy creature—often for life.

Student A is tormented by the history lesson—not even by the teacher, just by the lesson. The same is true of student B during the math lesson. If by chance, by some evil quirk of fate, student A has a very knowledgeable, capable and demanding history teacher, while student B has the same hard luck with his math teacher, then life for both becomes a daily torment. There is neither the time nor physical or moral strength to prepare for five classes a week in a subject you don't care for. One evening is not enough for student A to prepare his home assignment in history. He needs more freedom. He should be able to come home after the lesson and carefully study his notes made in class and the relevant pages in the unloved textbook. The next day he must learn and memorize it all and correlate it with the previous lesson. Perhaps he should read ahead in the textbook, knowing that he has difficulty remembering all that is said during the lesson. Towards the middle of the lesson he forgets what was at the beginning, and by the end all that is left is usually a bitter mixture of ignorance, fear, and despair.

Meanwhile, student B is going through the same troubles. The first day, the day of the lesson, he tries to go in detail over all that happened at the lesson; he reads the textbook and compares the account there with his notes made in class. He once again goes over the concepts and propositions newly introduced at the lesson and the connections between them and previously introduced concepts and propositions. He tries to do several exercises, some successfully, others not. There have been quite a few new concepts and propositions over the last few days. They are stubborn and student B is unable to set them in their right sequence or see the connections and relations between them. Using them to solve problems or analyze problem situations seems quite impossible.

During the weekend both A and B patch up the remaining holes, one in history, the other in math. Patching up five lessons is all but impossible; two or three may not be that hard.

Daily lessons rustle by like the leaves of a book, turning into a continuous blur. Prior to the test, the teacher gave a sample test, which they jointly managed to master, getting help from their friends, as well as the teacher. Their memories have retained some of the course material of the last few days. The main thing now is not to forget. But there's no time to forget. Tomorrow is the main test, a replica of the sample test.

3.20.7. Let us speak again of students' skills and habits of doing home assignments. All students should possess these skills and habits, but most don't. It is our duty to commence work with new students by teaching them how to do home assignments, regardless of how young or grown up our students might be, or how low or high their level of knowledge, skills, and habits—including the skills and habits of doing home assignments.

By starting out with purely imitative activity in home assignments, we gradually but inexorably deprive the students of the opportunity of saying, "I don't know how to do the home assignment. I don't know this or that, so I couldn't do my assignment." If prior to falling into your hands the student had virtually never tried to do his home assignments, or he did them only in elementary school, i.e., many years ago, it takes a long time to get rid of such responses, uttered half-sincerely, or even quite sincerely, however talented and experienced the teacher. There is an obvious reason for this: All through the student's previous schooling, his teachers, upon hearing such a statement, invariably supported by a dozen or more other children, would plunge with desperate resolve into repeated revision of obvious things which had been discussed time and again during previous lessons. Such scenes invariably were accompanied by the triumphant grins of students pretending they are attentively listening to their naive or simply unqualified teacher. They listen triumphantly because yesterday, and the day before, and many days before that, they had been able to force the teacher to do this with the same invariable success as today. And it will be the same tomorrow, and the day after, and many days and months after that. Why sit at home and do your homework when the teacher does it for you so readily and selflessly? He is really happy that we've been poring over our homework. So what if we can't do everything or even anything? And there's our good, kind, responsive teacher who so readily repeats things over and over in class that it seems a shame to deny him the pleasure.

3.20.8. There is a difference between what a student may not be able to do today and what he must be able to do. He must be able to subtract $\frac{5}{7}$ from $3\frac{2}{7}$, if the class went through subtracting, and say, $\frac{1}{5}$ from $4\frac{1}{5}$ and $\frac{5}{11}$ from $5\frac{3}{11}$, if the work was conducted with the full attention and active participation of all the students and accompanied by detailed explanations out loud of every step in the operations. Subtracting $\frac{1}{5}$ from $\frac{1}{5}$ is impossible, because the students still haven't heard of negative numbers. We have to subtract $\frac{1}{5}$ from $4\frac{1}{5}$, i.e., from the sum $4 + \frac{1}{5}$. This sum can be changed so as to obtain as one of the addants an improper fraction with the denominator 5. Then we subtract the fraction $\frac{1}{5}$ from the improper fraction, because to subtract a number from a sum it is sufficient to subtract it from any of the addants. Thus, $(4 + \frac{1}{5}) - \frac{1}{5} = (3 + 1 + \frac{1}{5}) - \frac{1}{5} = (3 + \frac{6}{5}) - \frac{1}{5} = 3 + \frac{2}{5} = 3\frac{2}{5}$.

This reasoning can be presented in other variants. However, we doubt whether every teacher can present a series of questions the sequential answers to which yield the solution. Can he reduce this series of questions with the solution of new similar examples? Can he summarize the steps in such a way as to have the students do the example much more quickly while being capable of justifying each step? Can the students on their own, without mistakes, go through and justify all the steps of the solutions to examples differing from the cited one, but essentially similar to it? For example, $5\frac{3}{11} - \frac{5}{11} = 4 + 1\frac{3}{11} - \frac{5}{11} = 4\frac{9}{11}$. There is no need to follow exactly the same procedure; similar ways can be found. The joint work of educators will be very useful here.

3.20.9. The first home assignments given to a new class should include only exercises similar to those which have been solved and/or thoroughly analyzed in class. During this initial period give the closest attention to checking the fulfillment of home assignments. Make a point of collecting home assignments—not necessarily all at once, but the more the better. Give them marks. Meet the parents, first of the good students,

189

then of the rest. Don't start out your acquaintance with complaints and pleas for help. That way you will reveal your helplessness in the eyes of both parents and students; the students may also see this as picking on them and as a lack of integrity—"He hasn't taught anything yet, but he's already complaining." Invite parents to school, visit them at home, call them up, or write letters, but keep these discussions brief and use them mainly to praise a student. This can be done even if the student hasn't yet earned your praise—you won't tell anybody that—but you feel he can and should.

3.20.10. Never spend too much time on home assignments that repeat assignments done in class. Even if you haven't yet managed to get all the students to do their homework regularly, you should gradually include new elements in home assignments. Initially, you should tell the students the following: such-and-such exercises will be more interesting than those done in class, but also more difficult; you may not be able to do them at once; try, perhaps several times, today and tomorrow; try getting together or calling up classmates to ask advice or argue a point; in class we'll discuss the exercises in detail.

Don't give too many exercises for homework, especially during the initial period of work with the class. This can be fatal. You still haven't earned the right to require the students to take too long to do your home assignments. Every teacher and professor must earn this right to require work and discipline from students of all ages and educational establishments by sincere, conscientious, competent work. No parent can help you with this—have no illusions on this score. Why is it that with one teacher the students do all their home assignments while with another those very same students don't? You can earn the right to make demands by your devotion to and love of the students; by your firm resolve to teach them everything you explain in class; by being strict, but fair towards yourself and your students, without picking on anyone; by being serious, but not boring; by boundless good will towards the students, and stinting no effort for them.

While gradually including new elements in home assignments, you should at the same time even more gradually give up detailed analyses of home assignments in class, both before and after the students have done them; otherwise, you will have no time left for active instruction in class and the whole teaching-learning process will deteriorate into assignments and a pretense of discussing them—a tragedy that has engulfed our country and is almost unequalled in the world history of education. However, you can never look forward to a successful academic process if you don't discuss selected exercises from home assignments in detail and regularly (preferably after every lesson) and thoroughly check the home assignments of several students. How many assignments you check is up to you. Sometimes you may collect half the home assignments, sometimes two or three, sometimes all of them. Check all the assignments for solutions but only a few thoroughly, giving marks especially to those students who tend to have trouble with their home assignments. The best system for checking home assignments is the absence of any system—but not the absence of checking. However, never let your noble, well-intentioned work assume the character of picking on individual students, still worse of persecution. This will doom you in the eyes of the class. You can never justify cruelty. Picking and hounding is an abominable manifestation of cruelty, even if your demands are legitimate but too straightforward and absolutely inflexible. Never be carried away by your professional activity to the extent that you forget that you are not only a teacher but also a decent, honest, fair, and kind person.

3.21. USING THE SYSTEM OF MINI-RESEARCHES TO TRAIN TEACHERS IN THE ORGANIZATION OF STUDENTS' CREATIVE ACTIVITY

3.21.1. We will speak of the creativity of the learners in the academic process in those cases when, working independently or with the help of the educator, they obtain new results by using methods and techniques they selected themselves. When we speak of methods and techniques selected independently by the students, we imply that for the given situation there are no general rules or algorithms which, when used correctly, would necessarily lead to the correct result: they either just don't exist or are for some reason not known to the students.

One should distinguish between student creativity and student independence. An assignment done independently may not contain any elements of creativity, if each step is predetermined by a known rule. For example, the multiplication $17 \cdot 7$ or $(a - 2)(a - 3)(a - 4)$ contains no elements of creativity even when the student performs the operations independently, because the multiplication algorithm leads to the result automatically. But factorization of the number 119 or of $a^3 - 9a^2 + 26a - 24 = a^3 - 5a^2 + 6a - 4a^2 + 20a - 24 = a(a^2 - 5a + 6) - 4(a^2 - 5a + 6) = (a^2 - 5a + 6)(a - 4) = (a - 2)(a - 3)(a - 4)$, done independently or even with the teacher's help, is a complex and difficult creative process. If students on their own suggest the representation $9a^2 = 5a^2 + 4a^2$; $26a = 6a + 20a$ to obtain the common factor $a^2 - 5a + 6$, or if they participate in such a representation supervised by the teacher, they are engaged in a creative process.

The problem $\int \dfrac{xdx}{x^2 + x + 1}$

$$(1) = \tfrac{1}{2}\int \frac{[(2x + 1) - 1]dx}{x^2 + x + 1}$$

$$(2) = \tfrac{1}{2}\int \frac{(2x + 1)dx}{x^2 + x + 1} - \tfrac{1}{2}\int \frac{d(x + \tfrac{1}{2})}{(x + \tfrac{1}{2})^2 + (\sqrt{3/2})^2}$$

$$(3) = \tfrac{1}{2}ln(x^2 + x + 1) - \tfrac{1}{2} \cdot \frac{1}{\sqrt{3/2}} \text{ arc tan } \frac{x + \tfrac{1}{2}}{\sqrt{3/2}} + c$$

$$(4) = \tfrac{1}{2}ln(x^2 + x + 1) - \frac{1}{\sqrt{3}} \text{ arc tan} \frac{2x + 1}{\sqrt{3}} + c$$

191

is a creative problem. It requires creativity from the very first step. The intermediate result (1) cannot be obtained with the help of a rule known to the student. The term $2x + 1$ has to be developed independently, and this is a creative element. It is introduced so as to represent the result (1) as the sum of two integrals, each of which can be easily computed, because $D_x(x^2 + x + 1) = 2x + 1$. Therefore it is possible to make use of the basic formula $\int \frac{du}{u}$ in the next intermediate result, (2).

Furthermore, the integral in (2) again requires creative development, creative steps. The student has to represent $x^2 + x + 1$ as the sum of two squares. He must develop $(x + \frac{1}{2})^2 + (\frac{\sqrt{3}}{2})^2$ while asking himself, "Why am I doing this?" and "Why can I do this?" If the student doesn't know how to do it—how to complete the square of a binomial—he cannot handle this problem at all. The connection between $\int \frac{dx}{x^2 + x + 1}$, $\int \frac{du}{u^2 + a^2}$ and the completing of the square of a binomial can be actualized only if all the connecting elements are there. Besides, different approaches can be used. There is an infinite number of ways of identical transformation of $x^2 + x + 1$, and each time one can answer the question, "Why can I do it this way?" However, without answering the question, "Why should I do this?" there is no creative element in such independent operations. This must be done with $\int \frac{dx}{x^2 + x + 1}$ because the next creative operation, namely the representation of dx as $d(x + \frac{1}{2})$—which, incidentally, invariably arouses the students' suspicious distrust—together with obtaining the sum of two squares in the denominator of the fraction, yields the basic formula $\int \frac{du}{u^2 + a^2}$.

Of course, dx can also be represented as $d(x - 5)$ or as $\frac{1}{2}d(2x - 5)$. However, in the problem $\int \frac{dx}{x^2 + x + 1}$ such transformations would be indications of helplessness rather than creativity. They can easily be justified from the purely formal point of view. There are countless transformations, and the very fact of their being used by students without any purpose, just because they are possible and permissible, not because they are expedient or necessary, usually indicates the absence of any attempt to teach them creativity or, for that matter, anything at all.

Instead of teaching our children to do what is required and admissible in a given situation, all we teach them is to do what is not prohibited, without any apparent purpose in mind.

But that isn't all. Teachers have virtually given up using the students' speaking faculties in the teaching-learning process. As a consequence, they make no attempt to teach them how to distinguish between understanding and misunderstanding or incomprehension. Instead, they involuntarily teach them yet another form of monstrous activity: to do totally impermissible things, which cannot be explained or justified by accepted agreements or proved propositions.

3.21.2. The very transition from x to $\frac{1}{2}[(2x + 1) - 1]$ used to be a creative experience for the students. The experience of identical transformations, carried out by the students over many years, should make the validity of the identity $x = \frac{1}{2}[(2x + 1) - 1]$ self-evident; otherwise, the computation $\int \frac{xdx}{x^2 + x + 1}$ cannot be a creative process. The student is incapable of performing it; at best he may understand it, with more or less difficulty, after someone else does it.

The same should be said of the identities $x^2 + x + 1 = (x + \frac{1}{2})^2 + (\sqrt{3/4})^2$ and $dx = d(x + \frac{1}{2})$. The necessity or expedience of using them to solve a problem—that is, the very process of referring to these identities over others and selecting them above all others—is a creative task when solving the problem of computing $\int \frac{xdx}{x^2 + x + 1}$. However, the justification of the validity of these identities in integral calculus should not be a creative process; rather, it should be a habit acquired earlier and retained. Otherwise, the problem can't be solved. In turn, after a while the problem of computing $\int \frac{xdx}{x^2 + x + 1}$ will also cease to be creative; i.e., it will no longer require the students' creative efforts—after they have acquired sufficient experience and habits of computing indefinite integrals.

3.21.3. The question of whether a specific problem requires a student's creative effort depends on the stage in the teaching process when it was offered. This gives us unlimited opportunities for developing the students' intellectual and creative abilities during all stages of education.

As the students acquire experience, habits, and new knowledge, problems and assignments which were once creative cease being so. They become technical problems. The algorithm for solving them is developed by the students themselves as a result of experience, practice, or new knowledge, even though the algorithm may never be explicitly formulated—as in the case of the problem $\int \frac{xdx}{x^2 + x + 1}$

Problem: From point A to a circle are drawn a tangent AB and a secant ACD. Determine AB, if $AC = 4$ and $AD = 9$. This problem is creative and fairly difficult before the students are taught the theorem of a tangent and a secant drawn to a circle from the same point. When the theorem has been proved the problem becomes a purely technical one: $(AB)^2 = AD \cdot AC = 9 \cdot 4 = 36$.

Problem: $\int \sin^3 x \, dx = \int \sin^2 x \cdot \sin x \, dx = -\int \sin^2 x \cdot d(\cos x) = -\int (1 - \cos^2 x) \cdot d(\cos x) = -\int d(\cos x) + \int \cos^2 x \, d(\cos x) = -\cos x + \frac{\cos^3 x}{3} + c$. This is a creative problem until the students are given a more or less general rule for solving problems of the type $\int \sin^n x \cos^m x \, dx$. After

193

such a rule has been formulated explicitly in the course or mastered by the students implicitly, it is no longer creative and no longer requires a creative effort or serves the purpose of developing the students' creativity.

3.21.4. It is legitimate to ask the following: 1) Should a teacher be able to distinguish between a creative and a technical problem? 2) Can a teacher be taught this? 3) Should the teacher strive to turn creative problems into technical ones?

The answer to the first question is, obviously, positive. If we want a teacher to be humane, give our children knowledge, and provide intellectual and creative development, he must understand the causes and character of difficulties encountered by students in their studies. If a teacher fails to understand this he inevitably becomes a useless or extremely dangerous participant in the educational process, depending on how active he is. Instead of giving his students time to think over a creative question he either distracts them with fussy, clumsy prompting, oblivious of their disappointment or irritation, or he demands an immediate answer, causing fear, anger, and subsequently depression. Instead of naming a new concept—i.e., instead of formally introducing a new term—such an illiterate teacher will adopt some incredible approach, smiling mysteriously and encouragingly while sweetly asking the children to "guess" or "figure out" how the concept "should be called." He doesn't understand that this is not a question to ask, it is not something to offer the students as a challenge, and it is his duty to name the new concept and inform them that it can be called by another name. Otherwise, he causes his students unimaginable harm. He deprives them of the practical opportunity of continuing their education and of distinguishing between a formal definition and a proposition that has to be proved. He will teach his students to ask the question "Why?" in places where it is meaningless, from both the pedagogical and the formal, logical point of view.

Instead of requiring all his students to quickly and precisely prove that the absolute value sign in the expression $ln|x^2 + x + 1|$ can be omitted, because $x^2 + x + 1 > 0$ for all real values of x, an inexperienced or ignorant teacher will launch a protracted and highly dangerous debate, thereby legitimizing the students' moral right not to know or try to memorize things they should have known and memorized by then. It goes without saying that whatever the students' level, they should be made to understand and remember for the future that $ln|x^2 + x + 1|$ $= ln(x^2 + x + 1)$, and in general, $ax^2 + bx + c > 0$, if $a > 0$ and the roots of the function $y = ax^2 + bx + c$ are not real numbers. A course in integral calculus, however, is not the place where this question can be considered creative. There is no room for an investigation of this: firstly, because you will have no time left for the calculus itself; secondly, at all stages in their education the students should be clearly and forcefully told what they must know, what they should be capable of doing, and

194

what they should both know and memorize. We must be professionally consistent, responsible, competent, strict, and fair—both when laying down our requirements and demanding their absolute fulfillment. This is hard for us and hard on the students. But teaching and learning have never been and never will be entertainment. They can and should be exciting work, filled with didactic kindness, creativity, and thought—for both the students and the teachers.

3.21.5. The question of teaching educators the extremely difficult ability of distinguishing between a creative and a technical problem can be successfully resolved on the scale of the country and of mass education, but only provided the nation really intends to teach its teachers. Only people totally ignorant of the nature of educational work, regardless of what they have been doing, and for how long, can seriously expect even the best college or the graduate school to cope with this task.

The ability to see and foresee, to sense and anticipate possible difficulties encountered by students, as well as their causes and the ways of overcoming or removing them, is an essential prerequisite of didactic kindness and success in teaching. This ability requires many years of systematic training of the teacher in the conditions of a natural educational process implemented by the teacher himself. Such teaching should be promoted by the joint efforts of teachers and administrators in the system of mini-researches. It also presumes opportunities for getting consultation—oral or written, published or unpublished—in neighboring schools, colleges, and universities, as well as in the best schools, colleges, and universities of the country.

Only in his own class, which he has studied and come to know, can a teacher know whether a problem like the following, for example, is creative or not: How much does a paperback book cost if it was bought together with a hardcover book for $22, and the hardcover costs $5 more than the paperback? Our noble and justified condemnation of problems which are difficult for the students before they come to equations is undoubtedly noble, but hardly justified with respect to the students. A child of eleven or twelve is capable of reasoning, or learning to reason, that if he bought two paperbacks he would have to pay not $22, but $5 less, i.e., $17. Hence, one paperback costs $8.50, and the hardcover, which is $5 more expensive, costs $13.50. Belittling such a solution of the problem is unfair with respect to the student, because we want to rid ourselves, not the students, of the need to find logical solutions of problems instead of the formal $x + x + 5 = 22$ in which logical reasoning and justification is reduced to a minimum by the use of algebraic methods. Here we pretend not to notice the lost opportunity of using simple and understandable problems involving small numbers (two books together cost $7, one costs $1 more than the other, how much does each cost?) to guide children to the solution of such a combinatorial problem: A class consists of 30 students; 2 of them are girls. In how many ways can committees of five students be formed so that each would

195

include both girls? The obvious solution is very close in both logic and form to the solution of the two books problem, namely, if the committees are made up of only 3 boys each, with the 2 girls then added to each such committee, we obtain the number of all possible groups of 5 out of 30, each with 2 girls; i.e., the answer to the problem is the number of combinations of 28 elements taken 3 at a time. If the class has 4 girls, and each committee should have 2, the answer is $_4C_2 \cdot {}_{26}C_3$.

Take another problem: A ship traveling down a river from A to B at a uniform speed covers the distance in 5 days; from B to A it takes 7 days. How long would it take a raft to drift down from A to B? It isn't hard to get a child to understand that if he eats an apple in four bites of equal size each bite is $\frac{1}{4}$ of the apple; if he eats the apple in eight equal bites, each time he eats $\frac{1}{8}$. If the ship takes 5 days from A to B traveling at the same speed, then each day it covers $\frac{1}{5}$ the distance; from B to A it covers $\frac{1}{7}$ of the distance a day. The difference between the speeds downstream and upstream is $\frac{1}{5} - \frac{1}{7} = \frac{2}{35}$ of AB per day, which is double the speed of the current. Thus, the speed of the current is $\frac{1}{35}$ of AB per day. Sincè the raft covers $\frac{1}{35}$ of the distance per day, the journey from A to B takes 35 days. The latter step is similar to the answer to the question: How many days will a watermelon last if each day one eats $\frac{1}{2}$, $\frac{1}{3}$, $\frac{1}{4}$, et cetera., i.e., how many times does $\frac{1}{2}$, $\frac{1}{3}$, $\frac{1}{4}$, $\frac{1}{35}$, et cetera, fit into 1?

When first given to a class, all three problems—on buying 2 books, on the committees of 5, and traveling by raft—are creative, because they require the students to independently develop the steps leading to the answer. The teacher must realize the degree of difficulty of each problem for the students in a given class. It depends on the students' knowledge, intellectual level, the level of their creative abilities, and their ability or inability to complete each of the specific steps in the sequence leading to the solution of the whole problem. If a class is unable to immediately answer the formerly creative question—What portion of a distance does a uniformly moving body travel in one minute if it covers the whole distance in 2, 3, 4, 7, 11, or 29 minutes?—then it is cruel to give such a class the raft problem. This is what teachers must be taught. If the students are at a stage in their training and development when they are incapable of readily determining the number of days needed to do a certain job if each day $\frac{1}{2}$, $\frac{1}{3}$, $\frac{1}{4}$, $\frac{1}{7}$, $\frac{1}{27}$ of it is done, then the raft problem will be humiliating, not creative. Teachers must be patiently taught this; in specific classes, with specific students, taking note of the teacher's questions and the students' questions, as well as their emotions, behavior, and mood. Later this must be discussed with a group of educators who have attended the lesson, calling upon all members of the group to take part in the discussion, in order to argue, prove points, and prepare new lessons in the same class or in other classes with different variants of pedagogical solutions of controversial issues.

One can argue whether the raft problem, for example, should be given before or after the students can absolutely consciously, quickly, and without mistake determine the speed of the river current knowing the speed of the boats up and down stream; i.e., before or after the particular problem has moved from creative to technical. This does not mean that all the participants in the teacher seminar group should hold the same view or even arrive at a consensus after protracted arguments and trial lessons. This is both undesirable and impossible. Some will hold that the particular problem of determining the speed of the current as half the difference between the speeds of the boat downstream and upstream should remain creative for the students at the time they solve the problem of the rafts. Others will seek to somewhat simplify the raft problem by first transferring the problem of determining the speed of the current to the category of technical problems. Both are right and both can and should stick to their pedagogical views. But both should also understand and be able to formulate the additional difficulties or simplifications both variants present to both the students and the teacher, which variant should be preferred for a given class, and what positive or negative consequences the choice may yield at the lesson and during the series of subsequent lessons.

Transferring the problem of determining the speed of the current when the speed of the ship downstream and upstream is given from the creative to the technical category will not make the raft problem a technical one. In either case, the students will have to independently perform the creative operation of actualizing and formulating the particular problems that they know how to solve in such a way that solution of these problems in a sequence developed by the students themselves will lead to the solution of the initial problem. Of course, the greater the number of particular problems which the students solve purely technically, i.e., without any creative effort, the simpler the initial creative problem is to them. Another important aspect is the temporal proximity within the teaching-learning process of the particular problems and the creative problem being solved with their help. But even if the students solve every one of the particular problems without any effort, the compound problem is not just a sum of the particular problems. It is a qualitatively new problem that may require some major creative effort and may even be too much for the students to solve independently at the current stage of development of their creative forces and abilities. For example, the problem—Determine the domain of a function $y = ln(\sin^3 x + \cos^3 x - 1)$—remains difficult even after thorough assimilation of the particular technical problems to which its solution reduces.

3.21.6. Teaching how to solve creative problems does not reduce to teaching the students how to solve the technical problems that are elements, steps, or stages in the solution of the creative problem. It does, however, imply such teaching. This is precisely what our educators try to disregard, and this is just what they must be taught in college and after finishing college. The absence of such instruction has resulted in the virtual impossibility of teaching courses in math and science not only in school, but in college and university as well.

We would like to cite some well-known examples.

The technique of differentiation, once a favorite with weak students, is causing more and more difficulties in view of the absence of the technique of identical transformations of algebraic and transcendental expressions. Most college students are incapable of representing $(-2)^{-3}$ as a number. The derivative of the fraction $1/x$, which, to be sure, always provoked mistakes for understandable reasons of a psychological nature, is now all but incomprehensible to many students. The whole technique of integration, the fine creative arsenal and pedagogical pride of classical calculus, is being consistently excluded and eroded from colleges and universities by the total inability of students to cope with even the most elementary problems, thereby making integral calculus humiliatingly inaccessible to the students. The problem of finding $\int \cos^4 x \, dx =$

$$\int (\frac{1+\cos 2x}{2})^2 dx = \tfrac{1}{4}\int(1 + 2\cos 2x + \cos^2 2x)dx = \tfrac{1}{4}\int(1 + 2\cos 2x + \frac{1+\cos 4x}{2})dx,$$ which is not difficult but undoubtedly creative, requires

the ability to see the square of a binomial, which many of our students already lack. It requires two actualizations of the identity $\cos^2\alpha = \frac{1+\cos 2\alpha}{2}$, and in the first actualization the student should anticipate, that the next step will require another actualization of the same identity in somewhat more complex form, when α is substituted by $2x$, namely $\cos^2 2x = \frac{1 + \cos 4x}{2}.$ But most of our college and university students are simply incapable of actively utilizing the latter identity, because in school no one dealt with this conscientiously and competently.

We would like to draw special attention to the fact that studying math in colleges and universities has become impossible not only because students don't remember formulas, make mistakes in identical transformations and perform them hesitantly. In school the use of identical transformations should be brought to a level at which the students can mentally reproduce them in their hypothetical solution of a creative problem without or before writing them down. They must operate with them mentally, sometimes subconsciously; obviously, they need not always bring the mental operation to the end result, which is possible only in comparatively simple cases. If a student has mastered how to square the binomial $x + y$, he needn't be overly concerned if he has to square the binomial $3a^3 - 5a^2$. Despite the existence of the algorithm $(x + y)^2 = x^2 + 2xy + y^2$, he at one time must have independently and creatively made the discovery that $3a^3$ can be substituted for x, and $-5a^2$ can be substituted for y. Thanks to a sufficient number of exercises the problem of squaring $3a^3 - 5a^2$ has ceased to be creative. It has become technical

198

and the student can, in principle, anticipate its solution. Therefore $\int(3x^3 - 5x^2)^2 dx$ will cause no difficulties, especially if the use of $\int ax^n dx = \dfrac{ax^{n+1}}{n+1} + c$ when $n \neq -1$ has also ceased to be creative. But what do we expect if we demand that millions of students solve problems that are quite traditional for the course in calculus, but accessible only provided they had some minimal training, which neither the schools nor remedial courses offer? For example: $\int \tan^4 x\, dx = \int \tan^2 x (\sec^2 x - 1)dx = \int \tan^2 x \sec^2 x\, dx - \int \tan^2 x\, dx = \dfrac{\tan^3 x}{3} - \int(\sec^2 x - 1)dx = \dfrac{\tan^3 x}{3} - \int \sec^2 x\, dx + \int dx = \dfrac{\tan^3 x}{3} - \tan x + x + c$. The identity $1 + \tan^2 \alpha = \sec^2 \alpha$, which is essential for this problem, cannot be made a creative tool in the course of one or two lessons, even if they are devoted solely to trigonometry and not to integral calculus. This identity becomes a part of a person's operational method and can be applied automatically only after repeated and protracted applications—with intervals and reviews—in the course of trigonometry when proving identities, solving equations and inequalities, and sketching graphs. Since we have given up offering children a thorough course in trigonometry in high school—half a year is just not serious—the only thing to do is give up the whole of integral calculus: there is no other way. Moreover, besides integral calculus, colleges and universities will have to get rid of series, analytical geometry, elements of differential geometry, and many other subjects. It's not hard to imagine what will become of our universities. All our professors fully realize this. But they have other things on their minds. The chariot of quasi-education is rolling irresistibly forward over millions of human lives. Please reflect on the sacrifices it will demand tomorrow and the future it promises to what is still a great nation.

Even integration of rational functions by partial fractions—which is such a purely technical integration method with not much of a creative element—though understandable, remains totally beyond any practical utilization by most of our students owing to their inability to operate with algebraic fractions and systems of equations.

Polar coordinates, followed by cylindrical and spherical coordinates, have been turned from a means of developing students' mental and creative abilities into a tool of suppression and torture. We spend great efforts on persuading and adjuring students that the graph of the function $r = 2a \sin \theta$ is a circle. There is no use proving this, still less expecting creative involvement of the students, because the very idea of a graph as a locus is unknown to them. And even if it is familiar, the knowledge is purely formal, without the ability to apply it. An angle inscribed in a semicircle instead of being a tool is an unexpected target of investigation. The equality of the two angles in this problem arouses their suspicion. The dependence between the sides and angles of a right triangle is known to a minority of the class—and even then at the level of polite

199

acceptance, not application. Because of that a beautiful and lucid elementary problem which invariably sparked the grateful involvement of, especially, the weaker students in solving it, has disappeared as a simple and creative problem from our courses. It has either been replaced by the purely technical operation of plotting points and joining them with a curve, or it overwhelms both students and professors with its unexpected and monstrous inaccessibility. We try to find the area enclosed by two loops of a limaçon at a time when the students can't comprehend where the loops came from.

In this way all our math and science courses in college have been turned, not into a means of developing student creativity, independence, and activity, but into homilies and invocations. They sometimes resemble children's games with curious symbols in which the students shamefacedly and ridiculously imitate adults, blindly carrying out their seemingly meaningless demands. This monstrous mass amusement would never have swept through our educational institutions had we undertaken to teach educators in the course of their professional activity.

3.21.7. The transition from creative to technical problems is continuous within the educational process—provided that process is not substituted by the teacher's mere presence at the lesson. A competently organized and controlled transition from creative to technical problems never ends, because the sequence of creative problems can continue endlessly. Unfortunately, time often reverses the transition, and technical problems may revert back to creative. However, this can be avoided to some degree, and we will discuss later how this can be done.

3.21.8. With the help of more experienced educators and his own experience, a teacher can gradually learn to carefully handle the students' slightest learning difficulties, especially those caused by creative processes. He must be able to anticipate these difficulties when preparing for the lesson and understand their nature and causes. At the lesson he must sense the moment when any of the possible difficulties has stopped the work of individual students or the class as a whole, creating insurmountable obstacles for some or misdirecting the activities of others. Occasionally—depending on the level of the class, on how long he has been working with it, the difficulty of the problem, and the objective of the lesson—the teacher should carefully and tactfully intervene in the class' work and, together with the students, attempt to overcome the difficulty. To this end he can resort to a creative discussion, which can be brief and not necessarily exhaustive, to give the class the opportunity of thinking it over and acting independently, consciously, and responsibly.

For example, if one of the first elements in solving a problem is the transform $\sqrt{(1 - \sqrt{2})^2} = \sqrt{2} - 1$, and the teacher sees that the majority of the students are making a very bad mistake, say, when canceling out the fraction $\dfrac{(1 - \sqrt{2})\sqrt{3}}{\sqrt{5}(1 - \sqrt{2})^2}$ they write $\dfrac{\sqrt{3}}{\sqrt{5}}$, he should discuss the theorem

200

$$a \cdot \sqrt[2n]{b} = \begin{cases} \sqrt[2n]{a^{2n}b} & \text{when } a \geq 0 \\ -\sqrt[2n]{a^{2n}b} & \text{when } a \leq 0, \end{cases}$$

or the theorem $\sqrt[2n]{a^{2n}b} = |a| \sqrt[2n]{b}$. Otherwise, half the lesson will be wasted on work that will most likely be done wrong and when checked will make the students feel depressed—though sometimes this, too, may be necessary. If such a transformation occurs towards the end of the problem or is encountered again after several days, there is really no reason for the teacher to intervene in the students' work: let them tackle it on their own. All the teacher should do is carefully check in what way the class has solved the problem. If the class is sufficiently strong and doesn't like outside interference, then it's best not to intervene too much. It may perhaps be necessary to go over to some of the students who need help and will accept it. Afterwards, the teacher should, of course, check all the stages of the solution with all the students.

When solving the equation $\sin x + \cos x = 1$, it is useful to conduct an active discussion with the class, taking up all the merits and demerits of two variants of the solution—one involving squaring both parts of the equation followed by verification, the other without squaring. The comparative value of the two solutions should also be discussed. When the discussion should be held, and in what detail, depends on the composition of the class and its mood during the lesson, and on the way the lesson goes, which cannot always be accurately foreseen but which can and should always be correctly and soberly evaluated. This is something educators must be taught, during their own lessons and at lessons conducted by other teachers.

3.21.9. The best way of avoiding many difficulties in problem solving is to discuss the problems with the class before and in the process of solving them. We will never be able to teach creativity in class if we don't intervene in the students' work, because that is how creativity is taught, provided the teacher gradually lowers his profile. Besides, without such intervention one problem may take a whole lesson and not even be solved. This is permissible, but very rarely. First of all, there isn't enough time, and besides, the students are invariably dissatisfied if class work remains unfinished or, still worse, not a single problem has been solved.

The widespread and very comfortable view that the best way to overcome difficulties—including difficulties in the creative process—is to give the students the opportunity to overcome them independently can be very harmful in the conditions of mass education. Guided discovery in class, initially only partially independent but gradually building up elements of independence and creativity, is essential. Such work, coupled with enhancement of the difficulty of problem situations, provides virtually all the students with the opportunity to acquire the capabilities and habits of creative work. It also encourages their creative activity, which must be consolidated and developed by regularly carrying out independent home and class assignments.

In other words, students can acquire and perfect their creative abilities only when they are prepared for independent creative work by the whole system and content of the teacher's educational activity in class. Creative assignments done by the students should be discussed in class—sometimes before, sometimes during, and always after the work is done. This involves consideration of possible variants of attaining the end result and their comparative value. The next step is consideration of variants of greater complexity, with partial changes in the conditions of the problem or problem situation, as well as activity leading to the solution of the partially changed problems or partially changed situation.

3.21.10. Progress in school and college math and science requires the introduction of more and more complex problems and problem situations, the solutions to which require greater creative efforts on the part of the students. In the process, the problems cease being creative and become technical, while problem situations become trivial. This makes it necessary to set certain guidelines to be followed when drawing up math and science curricula for secondary schools and colleges. Such traditional topics as identical transformations of algebraic and transcendental expressions, development of the concept of number and function, equations and inequalities, Euclidean geometry, trigonometry, elements of analytical geometry, and calculus, will remain in our school curricula for a long time to come. Failure to understand their role in modern education has had tragic results. These topics are an essential element of the technical methods of mathematics and science. They also provide limitless opportunities for developing students' intellectual abilities and creativity, depending upon when they are employed in the teaching process and how pedagogically competently they are used by the educators. Furthermore, the development of the students' intellectual abilities, creativity, and activity can be pursued more effectively when the school offers material necessary for continuing education. In this case, the students' creativity is developed, among other things, by the development of the study material and in the process of its development. On the other hand, the material to be studied is developed and enriched together with the development of the students' creative activity and intellectual and cognitive abilities, along with their ability to see, formulate, and resolve creative problems and study problem situations.

If identical transformations of algebraic and transcendental expressions haven't become technical problems in school—i.e., if they haven't evolved from creative to technical problems—in college the students will be unable to use them as a tool and will perceive them as creative problems. That is why students are unable to use them to solve creative problems, such as integration, convergence of series, and the solution of differential equations. The question is thus that identical transformations of algebraic and transcendental expressions should be used as mathematical tools already in school, and for this, identical transformations alone are not enough, even in great numbers. What is needed is creative problems employing those transformations, such as (1) polynomial equations, (2) fractional equations, (3) irrational equations, (4) exponential equations, (5) logarithmic equations, (6) trigonometric equations, (7) inequalities, (8) systems of equations and inequalities. If (1) and (2) alone—i.e., only polynomial and fractional equations—were enough to make identical transformations of algebraic expressions an applicable tool, after which they would never be needed in subsequent education or in practical life, there would be no need to go beyond them in school. But since (1) and (2) must be employed as a tool for solving irrational, logarithmic, exponential, and trigonometric equations, inequalities, and their systems, and also to continue education in college, it is necessary not only to solve very many polynomial and fractional equations in school but to use them when solving (3), (4), (5), (6), (7), and (8). The choice of equations and inequalities (3)–(8) for programs and textbooks depends wholly or in part on the extent to which (3), (4), (5), (6), (7), and (8) contribute to making (1) and (2) a tool, the extent to which they will be needed during the subsequent education as a tool, and on the importance of the mathematical ideas and structures they represent. Without solving exponential, logarithmic, and trigonometric equations and inequalities and their systems—both analytically and graphically—it is impossible to make exponential, logarithmic, and trigonometric expressions and functions a tool in secondary school. This is because all the properties of exponential, logarithmic, and trigonometric functions are employed when solving exponential, logarithmic, and trigonometric equations, inequalities, and their systems, and we have as yet nothing that would be more suitable and acceptable in school or abound more in transcendental functions and expressions.

College and university students will rarely have the occasion to directly use exponential, logarithmic, or trigonometric functions, inequalities, or their systems. However, our children cannot be graduated from school without them. Remedial courses will not help. It takes years for elementary functions and algebraic and transcendental expressions to become not just a topic to study but a means and tool for studying mathematics and science in school and in college. No special chapters in calculus courses devoted to logarithmic, exponential, and trigonometric functions will help, however well they are written, even when bolstered with a vast array of fine exercises. No one and nothing will help if algebraic and transcendental expressions are not thoughtfully, gradually, and competently transformed during five or six school years from a subject of study and investigation into a tool and means of study and investigation of the concepts of a set, correspondence, relation, function, graph, number, operation, algebraic structure, geometric transformations, isomorphism, et cetera.

Furthermore, the skills and habits of using algebraic and transcendental expressions, equations, inequalities, and functions as a tool in school equip the students with the skills and habits of utilizing mathematical methods in general. They give them generalized skills in solving theoretical and applied problems which they hadn't encountered before, and foster a self-confident personality possessing dignity and creative abilities.

3.21.11. The foregoing equally applies to plane and solid geometry. If the skills and habits of solving plane and solid geometrical problems were not required in subsequent stages of education and if they contained nothing to promote the students' intellectual and creative capabilities, they could be omitted in the school curriculum. But in calculus we measure lengths, areas, and volumes, work with polar, cylindrical, and spherical coordinates, and use solids of revolution which students don't and can't see. We find the centers of mass of plane figures and solids which the students don't and can't see. A few words in the calculus course will not help.

The school can and should over many years give students knowledge in geometry, together with an idea of the deductive structure of science. This is a cause and consequence of the development of the students' intellectual and creative abilities. In college we can give an additional boost to the intellectual and creative abilities of students toward a new height, in the calculus course introducing them to the method of calculus, which they also learn to apply actively.

If calculus is to be used as a mathematical tool—i.e., if we teach it to people who will need it to study higher courses and work after graduating from college—it should only be taught to those who feel at home with school-level math. Otherwise, neither a year nor three years will suffice to teach how to use calculus as a tool. Moreover, adequate preparation of students for the course in calculus does not relieve us of the need to continue during that course to develop their intellectual, creative, and cognitive abilities and to gradually turn what were once creative problems into technical ones, thereby making calculus an active tool without which it is impossible to master the higher courses of mathematics.

If, on the other hand, calculus is offered only for the sake of general education and not for use in subsequent courses, then it can be offered to people with minimal high school preparation. Such students, however, should be taught separately, in special groups not involving future engineers, teachers, or scientists; that is, those who will continue their mathematical education and will need calculus in their future professions. Future housewives need not be given the rigorous epsilon-delta definitions in the course of calculus, because they can be made to work and listen without them simply by playing with differentials and integrals. Of course, even in this course there should be a certain level of conscientiousness and sophistication with problems capable of stimulating the mind and creativity. Otherwise, the course will be still-born, dull, or ridiculous, certainly not a college-level course. The students will avoid it and tell others to stay away as well.

3.21.12. In high school, the classes offering math and science are to a large degree specialized, if only because not all students opt for courses in science or regular courses in math. That is, selection of students in school math and science courses does take place. For that reason we can teach school math at a sufficiently high level. If we gave the methods and ideas of science in elementary school as well we would have many more children taking math and science courses and then going on to college departments requiring extensive work in math and science.

3.21.13. It is our duty to use the system of mini-researches to teach all our teachers how to spot student creativity and guide it in solving even the most elementary problems, like $5 - \frac{2}{5}$, after the child understands and knows how to perform the operation $1 - \frac{2}{5}$. It is our duty to teach teachers to anticipate the time when the students themselves—down to the last one—make this one of their first discoveries. Help some, praise them all, then give them $2 - \frac{2}{5}$, realizing that this is more dangerous, if not more difficult, than $5 - \frac{2}{5}$, just as $(a + \frac{1}{2})^2$ is more dangerous than $(a + b)^2$, than $(a + 1)^2$. Here is another example: $\sqrt[12]{a^3} = \sqrt[4]{a}$, but

$$\sqrt[12]{a^4} = \begin{cases} \sqrt[3]{a}, & a \geq 0 \\ -\sqrt[3]{a}, & a \leq 0 \end{cases}$$

The teacher should firmly require all students to be quick enough giving $\log x$ if $x = \frac{5a^2b}{3c^4}$, because there exists an algorithm which gives the solution at once. However, he should wait patiently until the students give $\log x$, if $x = \log \sqrt{\log 3}$, and be even more attentive to the children when looking for x if $\log x = \log 5 + 2 \log a + \log b - \log 3 - 4 \log c$, or when solving such an equation as $\frac{2 \log x}{\log(5x - 4)} = 1$. Anything can happen if the children aren't prepared for such a creative move; the teacher hasn't prepared them for it. They may write $\frac{x^2}{5x - 4} = 1$, or $\frac{x^2}{5x - 4} = 10$, or $x^2 - (5x - 4) = 1$, or $x^2 - (5x - 4) = 10$.

As many as 80 percent of all students solve the equation one of these ways after high school, where they took Algebra I and Algebra II, and after five remedial courses in college. Neither equations—even the simplest—nor the properties of logarithms have become mathematical tools for them, because one-year math courses are basically incapable of helping them master those tools, and besides, the teacher was never taught how to transfer problems from the creative to the technical domain with the help of a system of carefully selected exercises. Yet those students are expected to pass all through calculus, linear algebra, differential equations, and often much more.

Students are unable to distinguish between the quotient of logarithms and the logarithm of a quotient because no one was able to teach them, just as no one was able to teach them the difference between $a^m a^n$ and $(a^m)^n$, or between the difference of squares and squared difference of two numbers or algebraic expressions—from which moment all their troubles began.

3.21.14. High standards of teacher training and of the courses offered in school and in college are not the only necessary conditions for stimulating the intellect and creative activity of students. A prime requisite is high standards of firm knowledges, skills, and habits actually acquired by the students. As we mentioned before, the teaching-learning process cannot seriously rely on knowledges, skills, and habits the students should possess but in fact do not. There is in our country a wide gap between what students should know and what they actually know, a gap spanning all levels of education which can be overcome only with the help of universally conducted mini-researches.

We shall never be able to develop students' creativity as long as they, for example, sketch graphs of functions with only the haziest idea of what graphs and functions are all about. They are unable to define a function or the graph of a function. All they have been taught is how to tabulate numbers, place dots on a coordinate plane, and join them with a more or less smooth curve—even where it is sheer madness, as for example, in the case of the function $\{(0,0), (1,1), (2,2), (3,3)\}$. Confronted with the graph $y = f(x)$, they are unable to indicate point $(a,f(a))$. The same can be said of graphical solutions of systems of equations.

Students have absolutely no idea of the meaning of identical transformations and are therefore unable to distinguish between the process of identical transformations and the process of solving equations and inequalities, because no one has ever consistently and competently taught them this. Nor has anyone ever taught their teachers how to teach them. What kind of creativity can we expect if the monstrous mistakes made by students throw some teachers into the depths of despair and others into rage, while some don't understand them and the overwhelming majority don't even suspect them because all they do is check the answers? We have in mind, for instance, dropping the denominator in identical transformations of analytical expressions and an inability to perform the simplest operations with numbers or analyze functions, solve algebraic and transcendental equations and systems of equations, or solve inequalities. Our children have such low standards of knowledge, skills, and habits, their intellectual and cognitive abilities are inadequate for them to see the difference between situations which have nothing in common but a superficial similarity.

3.21.15. One of the reasons of this all-American tragedy is that our students fail to understand and adequately assimilate scientific concepts and structures from the outset of their education. Their very first steps in education require active intellectual involvement, which is impossible without the universal, daily teaching of educators, because children can develop and gradually build up creative activity only under the competent guidance of teachers in conditions of didactic kindness.

Our politicians, educators, and administrators are lulled by the superficial appearance that all is well in our elementary schools because there are no sharp forms of protest on the part of students or teachers. They do not understand that the state of affairs in those schools is one of the main reasons for the sorry state of our junior and senior high schools. After starting out school in the hands of uneducated and untaught elementary teachers, our students are incapable of continuing their education in the senior grades, where no one teaches them professionally, either. That is why the creation of the country's educational system, a system of effective—genuine, but not ostentatious work with teachers and students—must commence with the very first years at school, from kindergarten on; otherwise, we will be building a colossus on clay legs.

If the only goal is to develop student skills and habits—which some educational establishments are still miraculously doing—without giving scientific knowledge or developing intellectual, creative, and cognitive abilities, our students will never acquire either firm habits or flawless skills because they will have acquired pseudoskills and habits: skills and habits of playing with symbols and words, which turn into unpredictable mistakes or total helplessness in nontrivial situations.

3.21.16. Teachers can and must be taught the great creative profession of teaching only in the course of work, making use of specific situations involved in the academic process. Educational administrators, university professors, and the best school and college educators must help teachers by supervising them in the system of educational research institutes and laboratories constituting the nation's educational system. They will teach teachers by offering guidance; by prompting, arguing, and discussing, and accepting or rejecting their suggestions; by instructing them in how to supervise (with didactic kindness) the processes of student assimilation of concepts and structures and systematization and structuralization of scientific knowledge. With the help of mini-researches we will develop problem situations in class and reduce them to trivial ones; we will argue and reason with the students, proving and requiring them to prove their points—agreeing with them or rejecting them. We will give them the technical tools, and the skills and habits of working with those tools, as a corollary of systematic solution of creative problems; we will develop their intellectual abilities and creativity, their cognitive abilities and skills and habits of study and creative work. We have none of this today, but we will have it all in the new educational system, in the system of research institutes and research laboratories—a self-evaluating, self-regulating, and self-reproducing system.

3.22. THE TEACHER'S WORK AND THE STUDENTS' INTEREST IN THE SUBJECT

3.22.1. Students are virtually unconcerned with the social role of education. In other words, the fact that the mastery of scientific knowledge by rising generations is essential for the development of society is no incentive for them to acquire knowledge at any stage in their education. In senior high school and college, the desire to acquire knowledge is usually associated with the desire to acquire a profession. But even then interest in learning is usually overshadowed by concern for successfully passing examinations and meeting all the other requirements needed to get a formal education at each successive level. Only a very few naturally-endowed students sincerely seek to acquire in-depth knowledge in their favorite subjects, regardless of the quality of the teacher's work. For all other children and adults, the incentives for learning can be created only by the very teaching-learning process under the stewardship of an erudite teacher.

But where can such a teacher be found?—where can we get him, and who will train him for us? Only we ourselves and our educational system—organized and structured as a self-reproducing and self-regulating system—can.

3.22.2. One of the objectives of training schoolteachers and college instructors in the course of their pedagogical activity is to teach them how to supervise the process of assimilation of knowledge by students; i.e., the transition from specific notions to concepts, from simple concepts to more complex ones, and on to systems of concepts. Students cannot make this transition independently. It requires competent and active supervision and guidance.

Even the process of expanding the concept of an exponent leads to the most unexpected and distorted knowledge if it is not carefully guided through every stage, starting with the first generalization when the exponent is 1. At every new stage in expanding the concept of exponent the teacher must establish the need for introducing the new concept, its connection with previously mastered concepts, and its characteristic features.

3.22.3. The assimilation of knowledge by students should be regarded as a continuous process of building up a system of knowledge in the students' minds. Every new element in this system is logically connected with the previously assimilated elements and contains the potential of establishing connections with knowledge to be introduced later. At each stage in the assimilation of new knowledge the teacher organizes the students' work to consolidate the new information in their memory, establish its connections with previously acquired information, and develop and upgrade the skills and habits involved in applying the new knowledge in connection with formerly acquired knowledge.

The teacher must be taught how and by what ways and means that connection can be actualized, and how the pupils should be prepared for the active assimilation of new knowledge. One of the most effective ways of achieving this goal is the creation of problem situations, the analysis of which reveals the limitations of the existing system and requires the introduction of new information and expansion of the constructed system of knowledge. Numerous commonly known examples can be cited. They include the following: the expansion of the concept of number to facilitate performing operations; solving equations and measurement; introduction of the concept of derivative in connection with the construction of a tangent and the determination of instantaneous velocity; introduction of the concept of a definite, and later an improper, integral in connection with the problem of calculating area; and so on.

3.22.4. We would like to draw attention not to the examples as such but to the ways of utilizing them in the educational process. If students read even the best textbook all by themselves, this breeds very passive cognitive activity, and even then only among the few who are up to the mark. Such students can gain some good, perhaps even a lot, from work with the textbook, but still it is immeasurably less than they could have gained from work with an educated and capable teacher. Only a teacher can require and get clear-cut, error-free answers from his students and nurture and develop their speech and intellect; only a teacher can establish why a student has taken such a course and not another similar and perhaps more suitable one for the given case; only a teacher can, when discussing a problem situation, ask for possible variants of investigating it and get the students to offer an emotional comparative evaluation and analysis; only a teacher can prevent partial understanding or total misunderstanding of new concepts and structures, which lead to distorted or totally misconceived ideas of new concepts and thus plunge a student into horror and despair. There are many other things which only a teacher can achieve. That is why the virtual absence of an active teaching-learning process in our country's schools and colleges, supervised by a trained and continuously training teacher, inflicts irreparable damage on the level of our children's knowledges, skills, and habits, even in those special cases when the children are naturally gifted and capable of working independently. For all the other students, the appearance of education created in our amateurish school system and toy colleges yields only pain, despair, the appearance of knowledge, and an abundance of excellent grades and attractive diplomas.

3.22.5. As the students work under teacher supervision, observing new structures and getting to know new concepts, they gradually learn to pinpoint the characteristic features which distinguish them from already known, previously introduced structures and concepts. Active, emotional, creative work, supervised and guided by a teacher, gives students the skills and habits of independent study work. A systematically implemented, active teaching-learning process, involving a steady reduction of visual elements and a gradual increase in both the complexity of the introduced concepts and structures and the independence of the students, is an irreplaceable incentive for inspired study and intellectual activity and creativity for *all* students—not only the brilliant—both in class and when preparing for lessons.

3.22.6. Students should not get their new information from just one source (which may happen to be in vogue), or from the one that is the most convenient and least demanding on the educator (requiring no pedagogical qualifications and no pedagogical effort), or from the one most publicized by the companies manufacturing study aids. The use of this or that source of direct perception of new information by the students is always a corollary of the methods of instruction, content of the study material, and degree of its novelty and difficulty for the students. It also depends on the students' age, their ability to concentrate on every specific source of information and productively work with it, the degree of intellectual and physical activity of the class, its excitability or sluggishness, the objectives of the lesson, the frequency with which different means of imparting information were used during previous lessons, the possibility for using them at subsequent lessons, et cetera. In other words, the teacher's choice of methods of imparting information is prompted by a variety of factors and considerations highly relevant to the teaching-learning process. These factors and considerations, some of which were listed above, should be a target of constant scrutiny, study, and analysis by the teacher.

3.22.7. In the system of mini-researches, educators of all levels will acquire the following abilities: to see, evaluate, and analyze their classes and the study material, as well as the general and specific objectives of studying it; to learn and understand the methods of primary perception of new information by the students; to consolidate, expand, and systematize their knowledge, instilling skills and habits; to reinforce knowledge, upgrading skills and habits. The quality of education, the students' interest in the studied subject, and the success of the academic process are contingent on all these knowledges and skills of the educator, in conjunction with professional conscientiousness. The latter is in some measure determined by the standards of the teacher's college training and, in decisive measure, by the content, form, and quality of the never-ending reciprocal learning of educators at all levels. It is also contingent on training administrators in educational skills, competent guidance of the educational process by professional supervisors and administrators, and on continuous, didactically humane and kind assistance given to educators by the professionals of the educational system, the best and most experienced educators, and special institutes and departments for advanced training of educators of all levels.

3.22.8. In the new educational system, organized along the lines of an educational research institute, teaching will be turned from an inevitable and hated pastime, imposed by force or circumstance, into the selfless and inspired teaching of tens of millions of our children. It will become the purpose and meaning of life for millions of educators who will find in it the joy and happiness of cognition, the joy and happiness of continuous creative effort and creation. Their life will be as full, meaningful, and interesting as the life of our fine researchers in all other (noneducational) fields. At the same time, we must never contrapose noneducational research and teaching, that is, educational research. The one should not exist at the expense of the other.

3.22.9. It is widely held that what primarily determines a student's interest in a studied subject is the subject itself or the student himself: his predisposition for the subject or his natural ability to study this or that sphere of science. We can accept this, but only in part. Why can a student's attitude towards a subject change drastically with a change in the teacher who teaches it? A class that once liked a subject now hates it. The students attend lessons grudgingly and do their home assignments unwillingly, if at all. The lesson is dull, uninteresting, and boring; the students wait impatiently for the bell, they ask few questions, and the teacher himself is not very talkative.

Sometimes we have a student who knows that his mathematical abilities are very average, is afraid of difficult problems, and doesn't always understand the material at once. Nonetheless, he likes math, he likes the lessons, he likes to work in class—though it isn't always easy—and he likes and wants to do home assignments, although his success and achievements may vary. He likes to think over the questions asked by the teacher and raised by other students in class. He derives pleasure from reading the textbook at home and discussing math with friends. He also likes literature, reads many books, and writes essays and reports well. But he doesn't care for the lessons. They are dull, boring, and unenlightening. They contain neither thoughts, nor ideas, nor characters. All they offer is the debilitating babble of an instructor indifferent to literature, children, and teaching—even though he may know the subject.

3.22.10. Teaching is neither easy nor simple. Nor is sparking and maintaining the students' interest in the studied subject. Capable teachers sense intuitively (and the others can be taught) what each student needs and what the main student—the class—needs to derive pleasure and satisfaction from learning and to never fear difficulties, approaching them as something natural which should and can be overcome. How does one teach people to make mental activity and mental creative work gradually become a habit? How does one teach teachers to keep technical work, without which it is impossible to teach, from arousing the active protest of some—those who would only like to think without doing—or the overly enthusiastic attitude of others? The latter are so used to performing monotonous technical operations without stopping to think or reason that they can transfer operations required in some circumstances to fundamentally different circumstances, thereby making monstrous mistakes. How does one distinguish between the development of a student's natural inclinations—for instance, a disposition for abstract thinking—from a one-sided, lopsided development of the personality?

3.22.11. The students should be able to work through every year in school and every section of the course; they must come to each lesson already prepared to understand and digest the theoretical and technical material to be studied and consolidated. If they are unable to understand the material or handle the technical devices encountered at the lesson, their attention will concentrate on their inability to work and their inability to comprehend the new information. In such cases a considerable portion of the lesson should be devoted to the restoration—not always successful—of lost knowledge. The class's mood plunges sharply, making it incapable of working on the lesson material, even if it isn't difficult or new. The lesson turns into a voluntary or involuntary, explicit or implicit, disgrace of some and a boring do-nothingness of others. The students' desire to work is superseded by an ardent desire to escape from the lesson and the course; to avenge the teacher for the humiliation he forces them to endure from lesson to lesson; to avenge the school, parents, and everyone who forces them into that idiotic establishment, while at the same time admonishing that learning is light and ignorance is darkness.

3.22.12. The teacher must know each student within his class; his weak and strong points; whether he likes or dislikes the subject; whether he can reason logically and perform creative assignments at the level the teacher expects; whether he can take an active part in resolving problem situations or can only repeat the ideas of others—which isn't that bad, either; his ability and willingness to do technical work; his preference for working independently or participating with the class as a whole; and so on.

If the teacher doesn't know at least the aforementioned qualities of all his students, his lessons will be a torment to most, if not all, of the class. Instead of teaching his students, he will be systematically, albeit without realizing it, humiliating them. Not knowing a student who isn't prepared for strict logical reasoning and who has to be taught this gradually from lesson to lesson, suggesting that at first he should independently rationalize simple situations and repeating and rewording the conclusions of others, the teacher will instead require this student, perhaps even sharply, to work out a complex conclusion. The teacher will thereby put the student in an untenable position, exposing him to ridicule. He will immediately try to help the student out, perhaps taking some time. Almost everyone will be bored; other students will suggest variants of their own, some of them very good. The first student is disgraced; the ones who came up with good answers are ecstatic and the only ones with at least a minimal interest in the lesson. A successful answer can come up only by chance, because the teacher didn't know what to expect from the next student he asked. The student who was asked first glowers resentfully at the successful one. Interest is replaced by an atmosphere of mutual impatience, envy, hate, and resentment, which pervades the class.

By now most readers are probably indignant. Indignant not with the teacher who aroused the resentment of his students, but with us. Do we mean to say that the teacher should ask only those students who know, and only what they know? That he should demand only what they like and avoid any confrontation with lack of knowledge, difficulties, unwillingness, or impossibility—and you call this a teaching-learning process?

No, certainly not. You, the administrators of local school systems and colleges, are the ones who regard this as education, use it as a surrogate of education, and have turned teachers and students into implacable enemies. You have replaced the nation's education with flirting with children, parents, and courses. You emasculate the courses of whatever may require the students and the teachers to exert their minds or wills. You offer mini-courses that you try to wrap up before the parents and the students have time to discover that nothing has been learned. Teachers are afraid of having the same students for more than a year for fear that they will protest even louder against the teachers' inability to work with them. Teachers don't even attempt to review past material, because it is too tiresome for them and for the students. Nor do they attempt to systematize and structuralize the students' knowledge, because they don't know how. You rant about universal education instead of universal ignorance. You don't teach teachers—either in college or during the lesson—how to teach in such a way so that all children would be doing work both interesting and accessible to them. The next day's work would then be at a somewhat higher level while remaining both interesting and accessible. If that doesn't happen, the student should be made to go back and go over variations of the assignments done before—all under the competent stewardship of teachers whom you educators must courageously teach every day. The new assignments may be identical in content to the ones done before, but different in appearance, form, and the combination of unessential features, which the student is as yet incapable of distinguishing from essential ones. That is how the teacher must work every day, both with each student separately and the class as a whole.

The teacher must vary questions, problems, and problem situations. He must vary creative oral and written assignments in such a way as to effectively and humanely supervise the work of every student through every minute of the lesson, and get feedback by creating difficulties the continuous overcoming of which—with the teacher's assessments and commentaries—is a source of gratification to the student.

3.22.13. The teacher should address questions to the class in such a way as to spare every student the shame of disgrace, and instead give them all the opportunity to think, reflect, and argue with the other students at the level the student has attained and which the teacher is aware of. He must do this systematically. To him, each of the forty people is an open book which he reads as he pleases and in which he knows where what is written, and how. He gradually corrects this book, erasing some things and changing others. And he goes on writing the book about each student individually for years and years and years: his knowledge and blank spots; the level of his intellectual abilities and oral and written speech; his parents, family, and interests; shortfalls in his knowledges, skills, and habits; the level of his creative and cognitive abilities. The teacher creates forty such books in each class. But for this to happen, one-year courses in math and science must disappear like a bad dream, like a dark age in American education. The sum total of forty such books is more than a set or stack of volumes. It is a new book in the teacher's mind and thoughts, in his heart and brain, a book of the entire class, without the details about each student but with all the details of the class as an integrated student. The number of words in that book is not the sum of the number of words in the forty books of the class. But the number of thoughts, observations, teacher plans, and intentions is about the same as in each book about each student.

3.22.14. There are different types of teachers—there always have been and always will be. The greatest crime is trying to make all teachers the same. In magnitude, this crime is comparable only with attempts to make all students the same. We may try to console ourselves, believing that for many reasons neither is possible, so there is no cause for worry. But there is. There are schools where the principal is a dictator who strives—successfully enough—to shape all teachers according to his image, just as some despotic teachers do with their students. There can be no interest in the subject in such a class.

When we speak of different types of teachers we have in mind the ability of some teachers to work with the class and proceed from the class to each individual student—clarifying, adjusting, and sometimes altering everything in the knowledges, skills, habits and intellectual, creative, and cognitive abilities of each student as a result of work with the class.

Other teachers feel themselves more confident when they concentrate mainly on each student separately—when working in class as well as in their thoughts and when preparing for the lessons. Such teachers have numerous individual assignments, cards, and forms, comprising a file for each student in their heads, and in the office. During lessons they avoid working with the whole class at once. They are unable to encompass forty people at once with their attention and work. They work with the class only occasionally—i.e., they proceed in their teaching from the specific to the general, though not neglecting work with the whole class at once; otherwise, it is impossible to teach anyone anything, for one teacher is incapable of teaching 150 or 200 students one by one.

Teachers should be free to choose what route to adopt. That is their right. Most teachers prefer to alternate between collective methods of work with the class as a whole and individual work with students. They individualize home assignments and supplementary lessons until they manage to build up a common pool of knowledge, skills, and habits and a general level of intellectual, creative, and cognitive abilities shared by all the students, which enable the class to advance as a whole, more or less simultaneously, with greater or lesser results that are, however, clearly tangible to both the teacher and the students.

3.22.15. Keeping constant track of each student's achievements is an inseparable element of the educational process. The teacher's appropriate response to those achievements is important to ensure the students' interest in the subject: supplemental assignments, explanations, questions, additional reading suggestions, work with parents, work with students at special seminars and lessons, additional tests, and so on. All these forms of work should involve not only the lagging students but, in different forms, virtually the entire class.

The amount of such work should vary for different students. Some need to be asked two or three questions a week, others ten or more; some should be required to read out loud from the textbook and answer questions, others should be given simple problems from preceding chapters of the course to solve independently, with the teacher, or together with other students, then submitting them to the teacher for checking if he thinks it necessary; some should solve contest problems with the teacher or in a study group for students from several schools; et cetera. Such close contact between the teacher, the class, and each student individually, as well as the teacher's unfailing sincerity and his constant concern for the level of the knowledges, skills, and habits and intellectual, creative, and cognitive abilities of each student, is essential for a successful educational process and ensures the active, creative involvement of every student, interest in the work being done, and the enthusiasm that should prevail among the students both in class and when doing their homework.

3.22.16. An atmosphere of didactically kind collective and individual work of the teacher with the class and each student can be created only in class, only during lessons. This atmosphere breeds involvement in the lesson, interest in learning, the joy of overcoming surmountable difficulties, and the joy that comes from creativity, advance, success, well-deserved praise, and independent achievement. The teacher can and should be taught all this—our great profession, the great wisdom of our trade—only in class, only during lessons.

The students' intellectual, creative, and cognitive abilities and interest in the subject can be fostered and encouraged mainly in class and during lessons by creating problem situations to be tackled collectively, involving all the students in discussing them. For this it is necessary to consider very thoroughly and in advance the specific problems each student will be given to solve, as well as how to react to possible failure

215

or partial success, to possible errors, insufficiently generalized reasoning, insufficiently convincing proof, and technical difficulties.

3.22.17. It has become a tragic tradition to change our children's teachers every quarter, semester, or year, giving them more and more new teachers incapable of distinguishing the faces of their charges, to say nothing of their knowledges and skills. We totally refuse to acknowledge the common truth that it is impossible to conduct an instructive academic process based on the gradual, reasonable, individual, and universal development of the students' knowledge, intellect, and creativity—a process capable of causing emotional uplift and creative inspiration on the part of both the teacher and the student—with an endlessly changing student body. Within the short time allotted to him the teacher is unable to get to know his students. He is therefore incapable of assessing their achievements or controlling the process of improvement. He is incapable of being humane and didactically kind and is instead stiff, formal, and cruel.

3.22.18. Total incomprehension of the essence of mass education and the resultant total indifference of both students and teachers to the study subject is reflected in the offhand, unprofessional attitude of the teacher as to what to teach. Let us explain this.

Teaching the same course the first two or three years is extremely difficult for the teacher and not very useful to the students. To continuously and competently control the process of developing the knowledge, skills, and habits and intellectual, creative, and cognitive abilities of every student and the class as a whole the teacher must devote all his attention (1) to the students and their difficulties, however minor and however frequently they crop up; (2) to the emotional and psychological state of the class as a whole and each student in particular; (3) to the students' achievements and failures, both technical and fundamental; (4) to fluctuations in the class' attention, mental concentration, and alertness; (5) to fluctuations in the class' capacity for work and interest in the lesson in general and in problem situations in particular; (6) to the gradual buildup of the response of each student and the class as a whole to the lesson, breeding either interest and satisfaction or indifference and apathy. The teacher must devote all his energy, all his attention, all his strength, and all his sensitivity, wisdom, and love for the students to all this—in part when preparing for the lesson, and totally during the lesson. That is why teaching a course for the third, fourth, et cetera, times can be harder on the teacher—because it's harder to teach well than just talk—but much better for the students.

That is probably why our unfortunate school and college teachers are never left to their own recourses. To keep them from preparing and conducting instructive, competent lessons they are made to change courses as frequently as possible. The novelty of courses is supplemented by the undying enthusiasm of changing texts—usually from bad to worse—and reworking curricula and syllabuses: this is an endless process which invariably results in the failure of courses and whole sequences of courses, in the shuffling of the contents and names of courses and the number of hours assigned to them without any serious justification or the slightest hope of success. Teachers are denied the possibility of working on the same series of courses and textbooks for the two or three years it takes them to realize all their educational merits and demerits, all the difficulties the majority of students encounter in them, and the ways of overcoming those difficulties.

A teacher has to (1) see how to create problem situations in class and in home assignments and the ways of studying them; (2) create a set of useful and interesting problems and drills and develop the principles of compiling tests and quizzes; (3) find ways of making the work interesting for those students who have flaws in their preparation for various sections of the course; (4) find the ways and means of working on the course with the best prepared and most capable students; and (5) develop questions and series of questions requiring the mental and creative efforts of all the students, both in class and when doing their homework. And there are many, many other things that a teacher needs to successfully teach a course—of which we have been speaking and will go on speaking about over and over again.

By the time the teacher is more or less ready to involve his students in creative studies, he is given a new course, new students, new textbooks, or new programs, all together or in various combinations.

3.22.19. The army of TAs, lacking effective pedagogical help, is unable to provide our undergraduate schools with courses capable of interesting the students. Moreover, this army is being increased with people holding no degrees at all: undergraduate students. The undergraduate school is literally teaching itself and reproducing itself. There are too few graduate students to fill the classes with teachers. This is hardly surprising, since even the most desperate college graduates don't care to risk the rigors of graduate school by reason of their growing ignorance. The educational system is destroying itself; some find this intriguing, others are appalled.

The replenishment of the ranks of TAs with undergraduate students has a terrible logic which ought to horrify us all. We educators are truly undaunted. No one is surprised any longer by our inventiveness and dangerous optimism, still less we ourselves. Indeed, does it matter who sits in the hall and doesn't teach?

3.22.20. As we said before, for a teacher to be able to prepare and conduct lessons that generate enthusiasm, interest, the constant attention of students, excitement, and creative activity, he must know the class and each student's capabilities, strong and weak points, the trends in the development of his knowledge and abilities, the blanks in his knowledges, skills, and habits, his relations with his classmates, and so on. But that is not all. The quality of an instructive and edifying lesson and the involvement of the students and the educator in it depend to no smaller

217

degree on the depth and scope of the teacher's knowledge of the science he teaches, on his knowledge of the courses that preceded the current one as well as those to follow. It is absolutely essential for the teacher to have a good idea of who he is working with, on what basis, and what is required of him for the students to successfully master the courses that will follow. He must know all this to have the moral right to conduct a lesson and hope for its success and the students' interest in it.

To create an interesting lesson an educator must carefully consider the objective ability of the class to cope with the difficulties that may arise during the lesson. He must identify in advance the problem situations as well as the students who will be called upon to discuss them at the lesson. The teacher must also plan whom he may call upon to help in the solution and how, if the need arises, he will involve the whole class in a discussion of the issue. He must have a thorough and profound grasp and understanding of all the details of the forthcoming lesson and all the minutiae of the factual material, problems, problem situations, and creative and technical assignments. He must be able to foresee the whole process—copious and multifaceted, spontaneous and controlled—the process of introducing each student to the new lesson. He should mentally imagine the work of each student, with all his individual traits, during the lesson and the work of the class as a whole.

A class is a highly complex organism—mobile and interesting, lively and apathetic, joyous and unhappy, thoughtful and thoughtless, serious and frivolous, educated and ignorant. At work is the highly complex process of introducing each student and the class as a whole to new knowledges and new information—dull and engrossing, dry and interesting, filled with profound ideas and tiresome technical requirements. The teacher must evaluate, weigh, experience, and come to love all these scores of components of each lesson in advance. He must dramatize mentally a confrontation of the class with the content of the lesson in all its details, both boring and exciting—the ideas, trends, and possible variants of the introduction, discussion, and representation. Moreover, this must be done not for an abstract class, but for a specific one, with specific students, whom the teacher knows or honestly strives to know and teach. He mentally introduces into the forthcoming lesson situation after situation, pupil after pupil, question after question. He thinks over the combinations of different students with different problem situations and the reaction of each student and the class as a whole to his questions, to the content of the material, and the difficult stages of the lesson. He sees the possible difficulties for each student, anticipates their questions and the ways of encouraging them, and decides upon the means of avoiding too many questions which could sidetrack the lesson, distracting him and the class from the lesson's objective. The latter is dangerous, because if you start grabbing at everything the course will never be learned. It will turn into a succession of free debates on free topics.

What TAs, from what universities—even from among the best graduate students, but lacking effective pedagogical guidance—can cope with

218

this? How can all this be entrusted to undergraduate TAs? How can this work be imposed on an eminent productive scholar engrossed in his noneducational science? How can we expect a high school teacher to give thirty lessons a week without turning his classes into bunches of do-nothings? How can we replace teachers every year, semester, or quarter without totally losing the educational process? How can we expect to change courses, textbooks, and programs with such incredible flare and energy—just to create an appearance of organizational activity—without totally destroying the academic process, especially one that is instructive, humane, and promotes knowledge, intellect, and creativity?

3.22.21. Let us dwell on several more well-known qualities that every lesson should possess. Neglect of these qualities in preparing and discussing lessons is always detrimental to the degree of involvement of the students in the lesson and their interest in the subject. Without unswerving concern for conducting lessons possessing these qualities, the whole course becomes amorphous, dreary, and endlessly painful for the teacher and the students, who force themselves to study only because they have to; that is, if they don't give up studying altogether.

The teacher should give special attention to the beginning of the lesson. To be sure, a good beginning may not necessarily ensure a suc-cessful lesson; on the other hand, a bad beginning almost certainly leads to failure, especially as regards getting the students interested.

The students must always be told in advance what they will be doing during the lesson. This makes them respect the lesson and the teacher for his attention, for having prepared the lesson specially for them, for wanting to impart them knowledge and teach them something new, even if it may not always be very exciting. This, too, is something the students should be warned of in advance, not apologetically, but in a businesslike, optimistic manner: not everything is always interesting in every job, sphere of knowledge, or profession. There are many technical things to be done, some of them dull and boring, but which one must know how to do. Without such skills it is impossible to achieve any results in the course or the following lesson, in related courses, or in work. Don't pretend, for example, that the factorization of a number can be exciting or that representing an algebraic fraction as a sum of partial fractions is remarkably interesting. You must tell them frankly that yes, this is a bit tedious, monotonous; not many profound ideas, problem situations, or creative operations are involved. However, it's necessary, just as one has to know how to brush one's teeth and wash. With time it ceases to be such a drag, and then you stop noticing it.

The introductory words about the forthcoming lesson should not be just a repetition of the lesson plan. This can depress the students from the outset instead of arousing their interest and attention. You should start out by preparing the students for the degree to which the material may be boring or interesting, the degree to which it may prove difficult, the degree of their creative involvement and the need for, or impossibility of, such involvement. For example, when introducing factorization of polynomials, antilogarithms, integration methods, or investigation of series for convergence or divergence, you should explain very thoroughly, showing respect for the student and the subject, that this is creative work. You must ensure them that they have done other creative work before and therefore there is no need to fear it now, even though at first they may encounter difficulties.

It is absolutely essential to point out to the students some of the types of creative work done before and their difference from algorithmic operations. Some of the best examples of creative work are problems in geometry. Is that why we have virtually abandoned them? But recall the mystical horror aroused in college by the problems of the falling ladder, the man receding from the light source, and all other material associated with geometry. Were we in too great a hurry?

The class should also be warned that many will find the work very difficult, especially initially. They should be told that the teacher can offer only limited help: giving exercises, some advice, and generalizations. He cannot, however, offer any universal advice. One, of course, can and perhaps should be disappointed with failures, but not to the point of despair. Practice and experience are the best ways of overcoming such difficulties, though the process can take some time.

Teachers can be taught the art of delivering a brief, interesting introductory talk, lasting perhaps only a minute or two, but this must be done only at an actual lesson. Moreover, only those teachers can be taught who are capable of appreciating the structure of the forthcoming lesson, its value and place in science, its educational difficulties, and its specific features, which may be exciting for some and tragic for others. If, for example, a teacher introduces the concepts of real number, function, limit, derivative, integral, and convergence of series with the same emotional fervor as the concepts of, say, proper and improper fractions or the elimination of irrationality in the denominator of a fraction, that means that he doesn't understand the ideas, structures, or content of mathematics—things we don't teach in college, or after, either. Such an instructor may well prefer the latter two trivial questions. He will impatiently object to the answer being given in the form of an improper fraction just because it is improper, provoking the suppressed hate of the students. He will rejoice triumphantly when the radical is not retained in the denominator—perhaps without any explanation, but arousing much the same negative emotions of the class. Such quasi-educational activity, which deprives lessons of their scientific content, is one of the many manifestations of pedagogical helplessness and irresponsibility that denigrate and humiliate both mathematics and the teaching profession in the eyes of the students.

The present tragic situation in the forty-two states experiencing an acute shortage of math and science teachers is a natural development. Moreover, it is only the beginning. The country is at the brink of catastrophe as far as teaching mathematics and science in schools and colleges is concerned, with all the social, economic, and political consequences thereof. Even the most irresponsible people are beginning to understand this.

When a teacher is good, loves his profession, and gives highly scientific and interesting lessons, half his pupils dream of becoming teachers. Our pupils flee from us in horror—horror of becoming like us, horror at the very thought of being involved in any way in the academic process. This is a national tragedy: the educational system is actively destroying itself.

We reserve the right to repeat the following over and over again: As soon as we start giving good, instructive, and interesting lessons in every school and every college—which is totally precluded without universally and continuously functioning mini-researches—all the problems of the educational system will immediately disappear. What we need is not baby-sitting, not entertainment, not softness or harshness in school, not cruelty; we need continuously upgraded pedagogical skills, lessons all filled with meaning, giving students and teachers the opportunity to develop their intellect and creativity, realize their thoughts, acquire new knowledges, skills, and habits, and improve those acquired before. We need serious lessons at all stages of education, lessons that also have superficial beauty and are pedagogically esthetic and emotional. Every lesson should contain highly scientific material, accessible to every teacher and student, which they can gradually master—this is the foundation of an eternally living, exciting, instructive, and educational teaching-learning process.

3.22.22. Indifference to the work of teachers in schools and colleges breeds the teachers' indifference to the work of students. Cruelty and unreasonable and unfulfillable demands imposed on teachers breeds cruelty with respect to the students. The ignorance of teachers in the subjects they teach and pedagogical ignorance leads to the universal ignorance of students. The absence of humane, systematic teacher-training and qualified help in the schools and colleges results in the absence of an instructive educational process in the classroom.

When administrators and supervisors do not know the strong and weak points of their teachers and their standards of knowledge; when they know nothing of the teachers' interests, capabilities, intentions, objectives, moods, relations with their pupils, and attitudes towards their profession—it becomes virtually impossible to conduct successful training of inexperienced teachers having substandard qualifications, low professional skills, and inadequate education. On the other hand, ongoing comprehensive educational work conducted by administrators and supervisors with school personnel and each teacher individually—mainly in the form of mini-researches—provides such knowledge, including knowledge about the creative, cognitive, and intellectual abilities of the teachers and the trends in their development. The latter makes it possible to control a unified process of teacher and student education and con-

221

tinuously expand and improve it on the scale of the class, school, college, school system, city, state, and the nation. The more informative and interesting we make the continuous advanced teacher-training process, the more informative and interesting will the teachers be able to make the educational process for their students.

3.22.23. The system of mini-researches should be used to teach educators the art of teaching in such a way as to keep themselves and their students in a constant state of suspense. We can never hope to teach all teachers this great art. But the very process of such instruction is the only form and principal way of preserving the educational system's viability.

This doesn't mean that we should teach only the things the teachers and students are directly interested in. The interest of teachers and students in a subject can be stimulated and maintained by the following: a never-ending process in which the teacher creates and the students overcome reasonable obstacles; the teacher's knowledge of the individual capabilities of all his pupils and his ability to offer them timely assistance; his guidance and constant encouragement of the students' independence, activity, and creativity; alternating types of student activity during lessons and combining collective work in class with individual work geared to the degree of novelty and difficulty of the material; the teacher's ability to see the purpose of every lesson, its difficulties, and place in the system of lessons, as well as the system of development of the students' knowledge, skills and habits; imbuing every lesson with substantive meaning and making sure that the students understand this; sincere concern for the acquisition of knowledge and perfection of intellectual, creative, and cognitive abilities by all the students; eschewing rhetoric and hollow homilies about the importance of thinking, creativity, and diligent work; enforcing reasonable, moderate, but consistent requirements in class; constant concern for the students' performance of their homework and independent assignments and for their oral and written speech; giving timely and competent help to those students who need it; the teacher's concern for the continued upgrading of the educational standards of outstanding students—both in and outside the class—as well as of students with below-average capabilities; love of children, the class, and each student in particular; deep respect for children, with all their qualities and shortcomings; consistently showing the students the inner beauty and logic of science and its basic concepts, ideas, and structures; the teacher's desire and ability to make every student confident that he has everything necessary for continued intellectual growth.

3.22.24. The teacher should use a variety of special devices to stimulate and maintain the students' interest in learning in general and learning a specific subject in particular. We will speak of the main such devices.

An imaginative exposition of the role of science in the development

222

of society and of the most important and interesting stages in the development of science invariably arouses the interest of most students. For example, the stages in the development of the concepts of number, function, differential and integral calculus, and so on. However, this can and should be done only by teachers possessing the gift of speaking well; otherwise, the effect can be quite the reverse. Furthermore, such expositions, however interesting, shouldn't be delivered in classes that haven't yet come to learn, understand, and love the subject: squaring a circle or trisecting an angle is of interest only to those who have developed an interest in math.

A well-prepared and earnest oration on, say, the solvability of equations in radicals can arouse condescending or even scoffing smiles, if not laughter. The teacher must first win the right to such narrations by dint of long, devoted, selfless, competent work. He must also win the right to tell the class about the not too distant prospects of its work on the course: the main elements of the course they will learn—not should learn, but will learn—during the semester and the year; what questions will be left over for the following years; what knowledges, skills, and habits they will acquire during the course. This should not be delivered in the form, "If you study well, do your assignments, and behave well, I'll give you all this, but those who are bad won't get anything." You should state things clearly, with words like, "You will 'get,' 'acquire,' 'learn,' 'be able to.'" Include no "ifs," because "ifs" imply permission, if not an instruction, not to do something.

It is very important and useful to warn the students about possible difficulties they will encounter in the course, the current lesson, or the next semester. These should be recounted calmly, in a businesslike manner, without threats or admonitions. Students aren't afraid of threats, which they see as an indication of weakness and helplessness; children sense this intuitively. You should speak optimistically, which will arouse respect for the lessons and the course, as well as greater attention, dedication, and respect for the teacher, who the students see as caring for them, understanding their future difficulties, and thinking about them, confident that the difficulties can be overcome and knowing how to help them do it.

An important pedagogical device for arousing the students' interest in a subject is the discovery, or perhaps creation, of a conflict in the sphere of the knowledges and skills the students already possess. This should be in the form of a demonstration that is not too formal and may sometimes be accompanied by an expression of regret about the inadequacy or insufficiency of the students' current store of knowledge, skills, and habits. It should be followed up by a calm, sober, businesslike, and clear demonstration of the ways of overcoming the conflict (provided it has been clearly understood by the students), or of the inadequacies and insufficiencies of their knowledges, skills, and habits.

One good way of maintaining the students' interest and attention is for the teacher to help the class establish, and each student to thoroughly understand, the logical ties between the studied concepts and propositions, as well as between the newly and previously introduced data. If a subject is presented as a set of separate, isolated facts it is incapable of arousing their interest. One way of establishing those connections is by explaining previously learned facts and concepts from a more generalized point of view and using new, more sophisticated methods to solve problems done earlier.

A readily available and effective means of maintaining the students' interest in the case of long, many-year courses is a well-thought-out system of continuous revision of the material, each time and every year at a new, higher, logical level. This work is conducted with the introduction of new, more generalized, and diversified examples, reinforced by the teacher's constant concern for genuine assimilation of the material by all the students and for the ability of each student to set forth the newly acquired information and knowledge in good English—oral as well as written. This helps every student see his own growth and the changes taking place in his knowledge, skills, habits and creative and cognitive abilities. The teacher should regularly—calmly and in a businesslike way—sum up the results of the students' work without heaping praise on himself, the students, or the course. He shows the students what they had not known and could not do; that they were incapable of even understanding the problem. But now, thanks to their collaboration with him and each other, they have mastered new study methods and techniques, acquired new knowledges, skills, and habits, and attained a new level of intellectual, creative, and cognitive abilities enabling them to advance successfully and independently.

3.23. EDUCATIONAL WORK WILL MAKE OUR CHILDREN AND TEACHERS HAPPY

3.23.1. While still in college the future teacher must realize that students who have failed to cope with their assignments are not necessarily to blame. They may have failed to understand the teacher's explanations during previous lessons, or the explanations may have not been given in sufficient detail. The teacher may, for some reason, have decided not to organize consolidation of difficult material in class. Perhaps the teacher was engaged in a very active and very interesting discussion of the new material during the previous lesson, but only with a few students instead of the whole class. Or perhaps the home assignment included almost all the problems on the studied section in the textbook, and while the students were more or less able to cope with the first half, each successive problem required knowledge of material long since studied but never reviewed and therefore forgotten. Finally, the new section may not yet have been assimilated sufficiently for the students to apply it for problem solution.

3.23.2. How do we educators manage to conduct one lesson after another—bravely, confidently, and cheerfully—while relying not on what the students actually understand, know, and can do, but on what they should understand, know, and be able to do?

Both the students and the teacher, in school and in college, must fully realize the level of the students' knowledge, skills, habits, and shortcomings; the teacher must have a good idea of the process whereby the students assimilate knowledges, skills, and habits; he must know the processes involved in the gradual advance from lower to better, fuller, and firmer knowledge, skills, and habits. For this, the teacher must conduct daily active discussions with his students and as regularly as possible study how they carry out their assignments. Only thus can the teaching-learning process be made purposeful and effective at every lesson and fill the lives of both teacher and student with a sense of pride in themselves and others, imbuing them with the joy and happiness of joint work and joint movement towards common goals.

What the students acquire in school and in college, and the state of their inner forces, depends on us. We are responsible for whether they will grow up to adorn or intimidate society. No civilized society, no educational establishment, no educational system can function successfully or even exist (if we don't regard dying as a form of existence) without a thorough, competent, ongoing learning process with the simultaneous enrichment and upgrading of the knowledge and creative and cognitive abilities of both teachers and students.

3.23.3. Endlessly repeated, helpless complaints about poor discipline, inadequate development, and low standards of knowledge of students and the poor training and helplessness of teachers are misdirected; these are not the causes of the final disintegration and demise of our educational system but rather the manifestations of that demise. Teachers—except for a select few—will continue to be helpless and deeply unhappy as long as they are isolated from each other and their professional supervisors. Denied education, professional help, and guidance, cruelly and irresponsibly thrown from one set of courses, programs, and textbooks to another, from one group of students to another—every year, if not several times a year—they are incapable of studying and knowing all their students. Teachers are incapable of knowing what a student doesn't know, and why; what he can do and what is difficult; the student's capacity for work, perseverance, attention, and willpower; what positive traits can be relied upon to help the student in his studies; his interests and inclinations; what positive qualities can be fostered for him to rely upon and give him faith in his strength; what should be gradually but persistently eradicated. When a teacher displays concern and attention for every student over several years, when he regularly presents clearly formulated, fully feasible requirements while gradually increasing them in difficulty and scope, when he offers sincere help and support whenever the student needs it—this teaches the student to work regularly and helps develop his speech, intellect, and creativity. Gradually, students come to enjoy their work; they experience the joy of success and gain confidence and pride in themselves. This creates an atmosphere of amity and trust among the teacher and the class and fosters in the children responsibility, sincerity, industriousness, and the ability and desire to study and learn.

Our teachers must be taught the skills of organizing an instructive teaching-learning process. To this end, mini-researches should confront teachers with clear assignments that can reasonably be carried out, as well as with steadily more difficult and extensive requirements, while at the same time imbuing them with confidence in their strength and giving them the joy and happiness of creative work. Mini-researches could transform those very teachers who are today so ignorant, helpless, and unhappy.

If a teacher has thirty periods a week and spends eight hours a day, five days a week in school, no one and nothing will ever make him happy. He has no opportunity to prepare for his lessons and will never give a good lesson. In colleges this is doubly so. The absence of competent, instructive lessons—something everyone in school and in college is well aware of—breeds heightened but purely formal attention towards consultation sessions as the panacea for all troubles. But only the best students are not afraid of attending consultation sessions. Only those capable of coping with the main portion of the course venture to attend consultations. The overwhelming majority of high school and college students remain without knowledge, skills, habits, and speech abilities, at eternally the same level of cognitive abilities. This level comes into conflict with each new course, destroying the personality of both the taught and the teachers. Instead of developing an instructive and educating teaching-learning process, schools and colleges destroy it completely. Because of some misunderstanding, the blame for this is heaped on the teachers and the students.

3.23.4. Under any, even the most humane and perfect educational system, there will be people who have been unable to obtain a high level of knowledge, intellect, and creativity. Some of us will inevitably be higher up, some lower, on the social ladder. Some will be content with their position, some not. But our undereducated compatriots who were unable to acquire a good education should feel that during all those years in school and in college, their teachers strove to help them in their studies, loved them, sincerely rejoiced at their successes, and, together with them, were sincerely sorry at failures. Their parents and the school did not lie or mislead them all those years; on the contrary, they did all they could to give them the best possible education. Educators honestly evaluated their knowledge, without currying their favor with high grades in attempts to stifle their protest and assure their own peace of mind. The school, the college, and the parents did absolutely everything to help them and teach them, the same as all the other students. That way these people will not come to hate other people and the society they live in; they will live alongside the others, grateful to those who wished them goodness and happiness and did all they could to make them so. Some will try and advance in society: they feel the need. Others will remain where they are. But neither will accuse their parents, teachers, or fellow students for their troubles; instead, they will take a look at themselves and wonder whether they had done everything for their happiness when receiving and accepting the help, support, and exactingness of others.

LETTER FOUR

HOW TO CREATE THE LESSON

[Schools are] the foundation of our freedom, the guarantee of our future, the cause of our prosperity and power, the bastion of our security, the bright and shining beacon that was the source of our enlightenment. . . .
—Robert M. Hutchins

Thirty-nine percent of all high school seniors are problem drinkers.
—*U.S. News & World Report*, 23 December 1985.

4.1. THE LESSON AS THE BASIC FORM OF AN EDUCATIONAL PROCESS. ON PREPARING AND CONDUCTING A LESSON

4.1.1. Every teacher must be able to competently structure the lessons for his classes as well as to evaluate lessons developed by other teachers. The lesson is a great and powerful creation which is capable of everything. It is sometimes capricious, sometimes smooth and tranquil, and always majestic. Its form and content cannot always be predicted. It is always living and changing, resistant to uniformity and stereotypes; cheerful and joyous or gloomy and deadening to everything and everyone in its vicinity; kind and affectionate or aggressive and criminal; a creation intelligent and eternal as the world, giving joy and happiness or sorrow and grief; either creating or corrupting the personality of the student and the teacher; giving the nation peace and tranquility, strength or weakness, life or death.

A lesson can be either educationally moral or educationally immoral. It can make young people believe in honesty, kindness, justice, and the triumph of good over evil and of justice over perfidy. It can foster industriousness and a sense of duty and responsibility. But it can also create people with no moral precepts who are incapable of distinguishing between good and evil, justice and injustice. It can foster hate and contempt for people and create implacable enemies of society—everything is in its hands.

Our erstwhile hopes for the omnipotence of education were, obviously, mistaken, because education alone is incapable of resolving all the problems of society. On the other hand, the absence of education can create insoluble problems. One of the reasons for this is the replacement of education with a militant, formidable process of anti-education, the transformation of the lesson into a school of ignorance, bitterness, falsehood, injustice, fear, depression, helplessness, cruelty, hopelessness, envy, and the moral and physical corruption of tens of millions of learners and teachers.

To be logical and consistent, we should lay to rest all pedagogical meetings, congresses, conferences, journals, papers, and books as quietly

231

and somberly as lessons have been laid to rest.

4.1.2. Instead of analyzing the problems and questions of a test held on the previous day, instead of analyzing the problems and questions of the class and home assignments, instead of introducing new material and reviewing old material at the lesson, and instead of many other important things, most of our recluse teachers seek some convenient mode of coexistence with their students. Whatever devices they come up with, their effects are that of monstrous deceptions, resulting in depriving whole generations of education.

These devices are very convenient and natural—if not the only ones possible—for a helpless, untaught teacher who stands in mortal fear of his students. He is afraid of their questions and of their methods of solving problems, which differ from one another and lead to different results.

Math and science teachers are unable to distinguish the correct from the incorrect; they freeze with horror when a student asks, "What was my mistake?" Accordingly, they adopt a strategy of marking time instead of teaching the course, a strategy that only a specialist can expose. Instead of conducting thoughtful lessons capable of giving knowledges to all students, they create an appearance of work, an appearance of educational activity.

Without the help of administrators and more experienced and skillful teachers and supervisors, these frightened teachers will never be able to conduct debates with their students. They will never create an active lesson because they are incapable of dealing with student activity and discussing things with them. In the absence of knowledge in the subjects they teach they are incapable of answering the students' questions or asking them questions. The results are sermons, homilies, and monologues instead of an educational process.

This monstrous teacher-strike at lessons has been going on, most incredibly, for decades. From the beginning to the end of the lesson, millions of teachers engage students in flurries of pseudoeducational activity and games instead of teaching them. In fact, they have no idea what teaching is all about.

Teachers loudly proclaim their duty to their weakest students—yet they continue to give all students the most trivial questions, the most primitive and naive problems, repeating the same things over and over again. They require none of their students—neither the strong nor the weak—to have any knowledge of theory or any ability to reason, prove, and refute. They do not think of developing the knowledges, skills, and habits or the intellectual, creative, and cognitive abilities of either the weak or the strong students.

Over and over again they trumpet their humanitarianism with the purpose of muting the protests of the stronger students, as well as of parents and, perhaps, their colleagues and administrators. They analyze a trivial problem for the tenth time and repeat the proof of the same

232

theorem for the fifth time. They tirelessly declare that children from poor families are denied the possibilities of doing their home assignments because there is no one to help them at home. For that reason they either do away with home assignments altogether or give monstrously naive assignments which only deaden the children. The idea that the students can be prepared to do their home assignments, that assignments can be analyzed at the following lesson by asking questions and confronting all the students with problems and problem situations, is new and foreign to such teachers. They are incapable of asking questions that can give the students knowledge, develop their mental abilities, and involve both the weak and the strong students in the work—so they don't ask such questions. Some of our educators spurn such work because they don't know how to conduct it, they have never seen it, and even if they have heard of it, they were unable to comprehend it. Some teachers, especially those in colleges, have no time to prepare and conduct a lesson as a creative, teaching-learning process requiring selflessness and courage to the same degree as any other form of research work.

The foregoing picture has become the law of life of teachers, classes, schools, and colleges.

Our school systems mislead parents even more successfully than children. They demagogically appeal for the assistance of mothers and fathers to convince them of the excellence of the work of teachers and school administrators and shield them from student attacks.

Children are more discerning than their parents. They detect pretense and deception in the school and refuse to obey orders in spite of threats and the possibility of being penalized by our wise rulers of schools and school systems. Others naively believe all through life that their ignorance is due to their stupid and lazy schoolmates who deprived the teachers of the possibility of conducting an instructive teaching-learning process.

We would like to repeat once again that the reason why teachers are incapable of teaching purposefully and energetically is that in college they were taught neither the subject they were supposed to learn nor how to conduct an instructive and educational lesson. In the school, they are assigned to teach thirty or thirty-five classes per week, and no one even thinks of helping them. School administrators and school-system officials keep knowledgeable people out of lessons to prevent them from seeing how millions of our children and teachers are uselessly marking time. Teachers timidly try to teach our children half, if not one-third, of the course in the time allotted for the complete course. Because of their total incompetence, as well as the physical impossibility, they are incapable of giving the students knowledges, skills, and habits or of developing their intellectual, creative, and cognitive abilities. All of this is assiduously concealed behind a smoke screen of bombastic words about the grass roots of democracy, about the need to teach weak children—which means to teach nothing—about equal opportunity for all, which today turns into equal opportunity for all to acquire no knowledge and no education.

4.1.3. Today it may sound trivial to say that the information explosion in all spheres of knowledge, education included, has made it impossible for schoolteachers and college instructors to raise their skills on their own, without the collective effort of other educators.

Let one member of the department follow the new world literature on, say, using the lesson to develop students' intellectual abilities. He attends classes and lessons in his educational establishment as well as in others, paying attention mainly to this aspect of lessons and the teachers' and students' activities. He speaks on this question at meetings of his own department and the departments of other schools and colleges. He will be the expert in this field at discussions and evaluations of lessons conducted by his colleagues and student teachers. This doesn't mean that everyone will or should always agree with him. This is unrealistic and unnecessary. He will, however, in any case represent contemporary science in his field of learning, its development and trends. He may or may not write papers on the subject—that is his personal affair. He must and will read journals and books, not only in his narrow field, but in all other educational fields. Otherwise he will turn into a narrow specialist in a narrow field and will cease to be a creative educator capable of giving his peers and his students knowledges, skills, and habits and of promoting the development of their intellectual, creative, and cognitive abilities.

We cannot permit an educator who has selected a narrow field of science for investigation to stop knowing the trends and practical advances in world pedagogy in, say, the development of an active lesson, the independence and creativity of students during the lesson, et cetera. Meetings of one's EdRL or EdRI alone are not enough, even if some other expert in, say, the development of an active lesson, speaks about this expertly and authoritatively, analyzing and evaluating it from the point of view of his lessons, the lessons of other teachers, and the lessons of student teachers at the school. This alone may prove insufficient to remain a researcher in one's narrow field, still less a comprehensively educated, erudite educator. In other words, all educators must continually upgrade their skills and enrich their erudition with the help of not only mini-researches, but good libraries as well.

4.1.4. Nothing we have today is comparable with what a lesson should be like in respect to the effectiveness of teachers' teaching activity and students' learning activity. Work in class should be supplemented with obligatory homework for all students, individual home assignments and activity in interest groups, clubs, conferences, et cetera. However, these forms of work with students can be effective only when they are coupled with thoroughly prepared and competently conducted lessons.

The lesson system presumes (1) the teacher's continuous awareness of improvement of the quality of lessons; (2) the teacher's and students' awareness of expansion of the volume and quality of the students' knowledge, skills, and habits; (3) the teacher's awareness of continuous upgrading of the students' intellectual, creative, and cognitive abilities.

Schools and colleges can exist—i.e., offer students and teachers knowledges, skills, and habits and develop their intellectual, creative, and cognitive abilities—only through the medium of continuously upgraded lessons. Lessons, in turn, can exist and be upgraded only when the knowledge, skills, and habits and intellectual, creative, and cognitive abilities of teachers and students are involved in a process of steady development and improvement.

The educators and administrators of every educational establishment bear full responsibility for the quality of lessons and their organic integration in the teaching and learning process. The quality and character of the lesson directly affects not only knowledge, skills, and habits and the level of the intellectual, creative, and cognitive abilities of students and teachers, but also the molding of their personalities.

Participation in the preparation and discussion of lessons will enable teachers to note the features and qualities of the lesson and the study material in which they specialize—which they like most and know best. This will promote exchanges of pedagogical ideas and study material among the teachers and the administrators involved in the research laboratory. They will be tested pedagogically and then discussed. Educational establishments will develop a style of work as a succession of mini-researches, in which all teachers learn from one another while each specializes in his narrow field.

As we have said before, every new lesson created by the collective efforts of several experts in different educational fields constitutes an experiment, a mini-research. It meets all the requirements of a pedagogical experiment: discussion and formulation of the scientific hypothesis—the lesson plan; the experiment itself—conducting and videotaping the lesson; and discussion and evaluation of the results. In the course of the mini-research, each researcher will accept some propositions of other members of the laboratory, reject some, and in some recognize things he had been using for many years, either retaining them as they are or updating them. It is our contention that such ongoing scientific activity—both theoretical and experimental—is imperative for any educational establishment to function successfully in the system of mass education.

4.1.5. The teacher must decide for himself whether to prepare one lesson after another or several lessons in advance. After every lesson the teacher sees what turned out well, what was not so good, what went wrong. In either case, therefore, it is necessary to prepare for every subsequent lesson. Nor can one say offhand what will take more time and effort: preparation of a sequence of several lessons or one at a time. In real life, any member of that sequence can turn out to be quite different than had originally been contemplated. For example, the teacher ventures, together with the class, to attack new material without preparing the students for this in advance—which is, generally speaking, permissible. But, as a consequence, most of the lesson is devoted to vain attempts to advance. This makes it necessary to omit everything relating to the questions which remained unresolved at the lesson from the home assignment for the follow-up lesson, since the students will not be able to cope with the material. Furthermore, with the time lost on the new material, none is left to review earlier, but by now forgotten, material for the next lesson.

In such a situation, which is quite common in our profession, the follow-up lesson should be revised, regardless of how thoroughly it was originally prepared, in order to dovetail it with the lesson that preceded it. Changes in one lesson and consequent changes in the assignment for the next one make it necessary to prepare anew for the follow-up and subsequent lessons. The more thoroughly the follow-up lessons are prepared in advance the harder it is to revise them. It is often more difficult to reject or revise elements of a lesson prepared in advance, for which the teacher has already developed an affinity, than to create a new lesson.

4.1.6. As we have said before, one of the difficult tasks facing a teacher when preparing for a lesson is that of thoroughly considering and clearly formulating its basic objective. Most good teachers will formulate the lesson's basic objective both for themselves and for the students, and they will commence the lesson with it. It is, of course, impossible to tell the students all the details of a lesson still to come, but it is necessary to describe it briefly and clearly, confidently and forcefully. This makes the students feel as if the teacher has a purpose.

Such statements should also be made, firstly, to give the students an idea of what to expect of the lesson and, secondly, to enable the teacher to sum up the lesson together with the students and evaluate what has been done and what has yet to be done at the following lessons. Even without a summing up by the teacher or the students it should be obvious to them all that the lesson has given them new knowledges, skills, and habits. In other words, both the teacher and the students should come away from every lesson with a feeling of satisfaction with themselves and the lesson, with a feeling of gratitude for the lesson, the effort that went into it, and the preparation for it.

Imparting the feeling of satisfaction is harder at lessons, the main purpose of which is preliminary familiarization with new ideas and concepts which can be introduced only later. These concepts are so profound and difficult that it is impossible to master them in one lesson. In such cases the teacher should clearly state at the very beginning of the lesson that the work may at first appear to be meaningless and useless; it is, however, essential for the subsequent introduction of the new concept, idea, structure, or proposition.

4.1.7. The greatest danger to the whole academic process in school and college is a monotonously structurized lesson, a stereotype that the teacher repeats day after day. Logically, the best opening to a lesson is a discussion of the portion of the home assignment pertinent to the introduction of the new material. Then the teacher presents the new topic with the active involvement of all the students. This is followed by consolidation of the newly acquired knowledge by jointly doing several exercises. Finally, the teacher establishes the difficulties the students encountered when reviewing the previously studied material, which is not directly associated with the new material. Such review should be done according to a strict system and sequence, paralleling the development of the new ideas, concepts, operations, and structures.

There is nothing wrong with such a lesson structure, provided it is one of several. If the students are forced to attend the same type of lesson day after day they will gradually get bored by the monotony, even if the lessons had initially seemed interesting. Their interest will slowly, but surely, wane. For some time, neither the teacher nor the students may even realize what is happening; they will not know the cause of the gradual, mutual cooling toward one another.

A good educator varies lesson structure not only out of fear of boring the students by sticking to one and the same scheme. The diversity of objectives and contents of lessons simply cannot be fitted into a standard lesson structure, which may be fine for lessons pursuing one objective and totally inappropriate for lessons having other goals.

4.1.8. If you plan to devote a lesson to introducing subtraction or multiplication of negative numbers, the concept of logarithm, a new coordinate system, the concepts of inverse trigonometric functions, convergence, or other things requiring thorough work in class—forget about checking the home assignments for that lesson. The introduction of the new material will require the utmost concentration of the class and take all the time you have; the whole class must be brought up to a state of, at the very least, primary perception of the new and difficult concepts. That perception should then and there be accompanied by exercises. These should be carefully checked, pointing out the pitfalls encountered and praising the students for success. The new home assignment should include several fairly simple exercises from the new section, with the idea of gradually increasing their difficulty in subsequent lessons and assignments.

To avoid having a difficult lesson start with questions on the home assignment you gave the students at the previous lesson, do not include anything difficult in the assignment; otherwise, you may well doom the lesson to failure. If some students are nevertheless eager to ask questions, try to put them off. Tell them to save their questions for the end of the lesson or for the next lesson, because today they will be studying a difficult concept which will take a lot of time to make sure that they all understand it. Besides, things that were unclear in the homework may be clarified in the course of the lesson. If there are other questions, put them off, too, or invite the students to a consultation session.

Never let the class acquire the strength and right to steer you. You should respect the class, consider its opinion, and earn its respect. But you are the only one who can decide such questions—firmly, with dignity, with respect for the class, with brief comments, but by no means apologetically.

4.1.9. If the material needed for the students to understand the new material was reviewed earlier, you should start the lesson with a discussion of the new material. This should be done in a stern, forceful voice. A forceful beginning immediately draws the students' attention to the lesson. This gets it off to a flying start within the first few minutes, exerting necessary pressure on the class, especially if it isn't used to getting down to work at once, as soon as the task has been formulated. In our case, the task is one of listening, hearing, understanding, and being ready to respond to the teacher's questions.

By launching the lesson with a forceful, emotional introduction of the new concept, structure, or operation, you immediately capture the class. The students' attention is targeted on the new material, the new problem, the new problem situation. If within those first few minutes you see or feel that not all the students have begun to work, listen, and think actively, you must draw them into the work, not overlooking a single person. You direct your glance, clearly formulated questions, and demanding voice from one student to another. Even if this is sufficient to get the whole class to actively follow your words and thoughts, you should realize that in any class the first few minutes of the lesson may not be enough to build up the maximum activity of all the students. Some may miss something, as a result of which they may fail to understand the whole lesson; many may fail to understand some of the lesson.

The first stage of the lesson should be consolidated with a clear-cut, concise recapitulation. This is achieved by requiring the students to answer a series of simple questions. If you recapitulate the first stage of the lesson yourself, the students will get into the habit of expecting you to do it always; they will gradually stop listening to you, at least during the first part of the lesson.

Attempts in the middle of the lesson to apply results acquired during the first part often reveal that many of the students have missed the point—frequently through no fault of their own. They know the material they had to review for the lesson and they know how to apply it. But during the initial part of the lesson they were unable to concentrate on working with the teacher and the class, or strange thoughts kept drifting through their heads. This may have happened not only initially but several times in the course of the lesson. To prevent this, a good teacher will summarize the material, ask the class questions, and comment on the students' answers all through the lesson. He will repeat the most important statements by the students. Moreover, he will require other students to repeat those statements.

All educators must be taught this kind of work during mini-researches; this is an embodiment of education that is didactically kind, active, effective, emotional, interesting, mass accessible, and capable of developing intellectual, creative, and cognitive abilities. It will instill knowledges, skills, and habits in all students and all educators whether they are present at the lesson or not, because such teaching will become the rule. All teachers will take note of it and make use of it.

4.1.10. After the new material has been introduced comes the time for consolidating the newly introduced concepts, propositions, and operations.

If you alternate the introduction of new material with consolidation during the lesson, there is no need for a formal consolidation stage, provided you organize the introduction of the new material with the active involvement of all the students. In this case, formal consolidation of the material is boring and a waste of time. More importantly, it is harmful, because it annoys the class and generates sarcasm. You become tedious and lose the children's esteem.

If you have selected exercises making use of the material presented at the lesson, use them to consolidate the new knowledge.

If the lesson material proved difficult and the lesson progressed slowly, if the students had difficulty comprehending and formulating the new information—and then only under strong pressure from the teacher—it is absolutely essential to consolidate the new material by asking questions. Without such thorough consolidation, half the students will be left with no idea of what the lesson was all about. This will make the subsequent lessons even more difficult and less successful. Two or three weeks later a distance will form between the teacher and the class, developing mutual misunderstanding and, subsequently, incomprehension. The distance will increasingly resemble a chasm or a wall, which will be very difficult to bridge or break down. Disruption of businesslike relations between the class and the teacher imperceptibly develops into a breakdown of good, or even polite, relations between them. This process is virtually always irreversible.

4.1.11. We would like once again to dwell on the need for the teacher to carefully think over and clearly formulate for himself the basic objective of the lesson he is preparing. There can be several supplementary or incidental objectives associated with the recapitulation of previously studied material, but there should never be many, lest the lesson become kaleidoscopic. It gets fussy and hasty—one very widespread variant of a useless lesson. The teacher and the students careen from one topic to another without dwelling sufficiently on any. In such cases, the basic objective can be forgotten; the lesson loses all meaning.

In other words, before starting a lesson the teacher must clearly formulate its objective, the purpose of his coming to the class. If he means simply to solve some problems, or discuss fractional exponents, or give the students an assignment from the book, or review the solution of equations, or anything like that, there is very little hope that the lesson will do the students any good. There is no hope that they will find it interesting; both sides will find the lesson dull, boring, and mediocre. Most of the class will not derive the feeling of satisfaction that should fill every student after every lesson—if we wish to have a successful academic process. Following each lesson, every student should be able to answer such questions as: Why did I spend an hour in class? What useful things did I gain during that hour? What did the teacher do for me during that hour? What did I do myself? What did I learn during that hour? Would it have been simpler and better for me not to have attended the lesson at all? Is it worth coming to this teacher for the next hour? Will the next lesson help me in my work on the course with this teacher?—and so on and so forth.

Sometimes the teacher must fight with might and main to achieve the lesson's prime objective. He must prevent the class from leading him and the lesson away from the set goal. The only justification for a lesson not achieving the primary objective can be the teacher's total conviction that in an unforseen situation it is useless to even attempt to pursue the lesson's primary objective. The lesson, the teacher, and the students will merely be striving in vain to attain the unattainable.

Such situations usually arise when introduction of the new material relies on a review of the previous day's homework, which the students failed to cope with. As a consequence, reviewing the material takes up too much time and the students derive little from it. In such cases, the teacher should tell the class that, because they have failed to do their home assignments, the lesson is useless. They will have to do the assignment again. Perhaps they will be more successful, in time for the next lesson. Meanwhile, they can do exercises or solve problems, or the teacher can let them answer such and such questions and hand in their papers.

In such situations—as always in the academic process—the teacher should not appear to be vengeful. The students never forgive this. It leads to the continuous, implacable hostility of the whole class. Besides, if the material that had to be reviewed was studied some time earlier, the fault is the teacher's. Knowing that the upcoming lesson would require preliminary work at home, the teacher should have given the students home review assignments at least twice: two lessons before the one in question and immediately preceding it. Moreover, each time the reviewed material should have been discussed in class.

There is no point in giving difficult assignments in place of a failed lesson. The students will wrongly perceive them as the teacher's revenge. Nor is it necessary to check the classwork of all the students. It is sufficient to check only that of the students who require special attention. Checking can be done in class by asking the students different questions, perhaps writing down some points on the blackboard. This can be done by the teacher himself, prompted by the students, or, if there is enough time, by the students in turn.

If the class is overly active, volatile, and fidgety it is better for the teacher to be at the blackboard. An excitable or excited group can be controlled only by controlling its work. Incidentally, the latter is true of any group. But the forms of control, and the forms of work with the group, depend on the study material, as well as on the group's specific traits and its current state of mind.

4.2. THE LESSON AS A MEDIUM FOR TEACHING THE CLASS, THE STUDENT, AND THE TEACHER

4.2.1. The members of any body of students possess their individual capabilities, inclinations, interests, qualities, and shortcomings. Our duty is to know those capabilities, inclinations, interests, qualities, and short-comings, and to study them constantly. It is our job. Teachers don't know how to do this, and they must be taught it constantly.

We should encourage and cultivate certain traits in our students: the ability to form considered judgments, erudition, thinking ability, high standards of creativity and cognitive abilities, and the like. We must try to reduce or eliminate others: inability or unwillingness to listen to the views of others, inability or unwillingness to justify one's point of view, inability to formulate a question, fear of embarrassing oneself in the eyes of the teacher and the class with an ill-put question, fear of a subject, test, any question from the teacher, et cetera.

4.2.2. The members of a student body are also involved in a constant, diversified relationship among themselves and with their teachers. They influence each other, the teacher, each lesson, and the educational process as a whole. They constitute a living organism, a teaching-learning system. We may not understand or notice this, or we may pretend not to understand or notice it.

We are forced to abandon the idea of teaching each student separately. Nevertheless, when teaching a system comprising thirty or forty individuals, we hope to teach each one. Furthermore, we are duty bound to preserve the individual, the independent development of each personality; that is our job.

Every class, every study system, possesses traits similar to the traits of an individual. We distinguish different kinds of classes: (1) excitable or inert; (2) well-prepared or ill-prepared in the subject over the preceding years; (3) capable of incapable of listening; (4) capable or incapable of participating in the discussion of problems; (5) those that like and those that do not like such work; (6) capable of, and wanting to, study problem situations or lacking these qualities; (7) with or without a sense of humor; (8) good-natured and likeable or hard and prickly; (9) aggressive or passive; (10) possessing high or low standards of intellectual development; (11) having or lacking an aptitude in the subject; (12) those that like technical work and those that hate it; (13) those that seek to tackle creative assignments and those that eschew them, and so on.

As with every person, a class's moods and condition are subject to change. One day it copes with a complex creative problem easily, the

241

next day it fails, even when the same procedure can be used to solve the new problem. What is the reason, what has happened? The teacher alone is incapable of coping with such questions.

One day the students participate actively in a discussion, readily answering questions and asking their own. The next day they are silent, inert, distracted, do not hear the questions, and if they do, they fail to react to them. Here, too, even an experienced teacher cannot understand what has happened.

4.2.3. We must constantly attend each other's lessons and/or videotape them, discuss them, and analyze the teaching-learning process and the behavior and state of the class during the lesson. We must determine the lesson strategy and the causes for everything discovered within it: (1) the role of the teacher—passive or active—during the lesson, and the extent to which he was prepared for it; (2) successful or unsuccessful choice of the lesson type and/or teaching methods; (3) dependence of the lesson structure on the nature of the study material, its complexity, and the degree of comprehension by the students; (4) dependence of the content of the lesson on the level of training of the taught system as a whole and each student in particular; et cetera. The teacher must be able to analyze all this competently, otherwise he will never be able to teach successfully. He will prepare a lecture lesson which his students will ridicule because they are unprepared for listening to lectures on such subjects. Their knowledge is so meager that they are incapable of following a logical presentation of difficult material. After several minutes they cease to understand what the teacher is talking about and start to laugh at everything. They laugh at the teacher, his lecture, and his promises that it will all be needed in the near future and that without the lecture the students will be unable to understand things later on. But they already don't understand. They laugh at the seriousness of the lecture; they laugh at their incomprehension; they laugh through tears, out of despair or desperate merriment. They laugh because they are young, cheerful, and bubbling with life, while here they are being treated for a whole hour with profound homilies they are incapable of understanding. If the teacher doesn't quickly realize that he should abandon the lesson, if he doesn't start laughing together with the students at the formal proof that a line segment has the only midpoint or that right angles are equal, the whole academic year will be lost. The students won't study; moreover, they will never even listen to the teacher again—even if they can still understand some things.

Another time the teacher decides to conduct a discussion and ask questions of students whom he doesn't know. They may be tolerant and obliging but unused to questions and discussions. They are at a loss. They don't understand spoken questions, especially if they involve unfamiliar terms. It is even worse if the teacher calls upon a student to answer a question before asking it. The student knows that he will have to answer a question, but he doesn't yet know what it is and fears it may turn out to be very difficult. He has been singled out. He has been forced

242

into the role of a respondent to something unknown. One such mistake by the teacher can arouse the student's protest, confusion, or both.

Questions during a lesson should be addressed to the class as a whole, to the taught system as a whole. Moreover, the system should be given time to grasp and completely understand the question. The question should be paraphrased, or several students should be asked how they understood it and what the teacher expects of them. After discussing the question—not the answer—the system should be given time to think it over. Perhaps some students would like to discuss it among themselves, swap answers, or argue softly. Other members of the system hate this. They stop their ears to keep from accidentally hearing the answer. Both should be given the opportunity to think and work. You can then go up to the more timid and talk softly to them. You should also go up to the more vociferous students and very quietly calm them down. Only after that should you listen to several answers—first only the answers alone, without requiring them to be justified. Then ask for the justification—not necessarily from those who gave the answers. You can listen to the justification of those who simply agree with the answers. In that way more students will be involved in the discussion.

Having failed in a lecture and a discussion, an inexperienced teacher recalls that one of the ways of developing the students' intellectual, creative, and cognitive abilities is by creating problem situations. He gives the class an abstract situation with which the students can't cope. They can't comprehend the problem. They can't understand what the teacher is so excited about. For instance, is there such a thing as the area of a circle or not? Everyone knows that there is, since you can cut a circle out of a piece of cardboard and that piece covers an area on a plane. From a child's perception, that is its area. At this point that is all they are capable of. But the teacher doesn't understand this, nor can he without outside help. The third lesson in a row ends in utter defeat. None of the teacher's colleagues have come to his lesson and none intend to.

After three failures, the teacher comes to the class at his own risk. Even a strong and knowledgeable teacher may be unable to change anything. Our young teacher wilts before our very eyes. Nothing is left of his youthful enthusiasm and pedagogical fervor. Children and lessons generate irritation, animosity, and sometimes silent depression. Having heard of written assignments in class, when everyone does what he wishes, he resorts to this variant of contemporary pedagogical wisdom. Or he invites the children to play with TV sets and tape recorders while he waits patiently for the lesson to end; he occupies himself with grading the previous test and writing the next one. Everything falls into its horrible place. The students read or don't read, they carry out or don't carry out their assignments. Yet lesson follows lesson and tests are held according to schedule. The children mind their own business, the teacher minds his. No one interferes with the other. Everyone is polite. Once in a while they attack each other, fight, kill, hang, or shoot themselves. But that is society's problem: the causes are all social. After all, there is no such thing as a perfect society, or perfect children, or perfect teachers, or perfect lessons.

4.2.4. All over the world, conducting a lesson in a poorly known class is considered a calamity. But not in our country.

It is universally acknowledged that the first year of work with a class is the most difficult one for both the teacher and the students, and the most inefficient from the point of view of quality. As for the development of the students' intellectual, creative, and cognitive abilities, this is something that can't even be seriously considered. Disregarding this, we have voluntarily cut the system of many-year education of a creative personality into annual segments, which we call courses in algebra, geometry, trigonometry, calculus, physics, chemistry, biology, and so on. It takes at least a year for a teacher to get to know his students, their inclinations, and the level of their intellectual, creative, and cognitive abilities. By the time he manages to put together the thousands of invisible links between himself and each student and is able to start teaching the class as a whole and each student separately, the course is over.

4.2.5. For a teacher to know a class he must know every student, be sincerely concerned for and respect the fate of every student, be able to discern and encourage everything positive in every student, and see the negative and work patiently to help the student overcome it. Such an approach establishes sincere relations of goodwill between the teacher and the class, which is an essential prerequisite for the existence and perfection of the lesson and a teaching, learning, and educating academic process.

Studying the class is not easy, and many teachers never really get to know it. A student's shyness can be interpreted as stubbornness, as a challenge; this is a typical reaction of teachers lacking confidence in themselves. Excessive energy, vitality, or activity on the part of a student is another challenge for the teacher who is afraid of everything—because of his inexperience or because he is shy. This can result in a peremptory or insulting reprimand, increasing the number of adversaries in the class. An aggressive, sharp response to a student's joke or quip—and the number of teacher's friends dwindles again.

We should not be cruel to our teachers; we should not be irresponsible with our children by committing them to a confrontation knowing that no good can come of it.

A young teacher must be forewarned against disrupting relations with the class. He cannot deal with this himself. He makes irreparable mistakes. In our profession, few mistakes can be rectified. Even if relations with the class during the lesson appear to be friendly, businesslike, and good-natured, this may be an indication of only their superficial, not workaday, aspect. They may be based on the teacher's subconscious attempts to ingratiate himself with the class with reduced demands and exaggerated high grades. Other frequent causes of superficial well-being in a class and in the teaching-learning process are reduction of the class's theoretical standards; denying the students needed creative activity requiring effort, work, and will; the absence of efforts to cultivate the students' intellectual, creative, and cognitive abilities and their replacement with entertainment, pseudoactivity, and clowning.

The degree to which the teacher and the students appreciate the quality of lessons and their mutual relations can vary depending on the personal qualities of the teacher, the composition of the class, and the teacher's experience. The only people capable of judging the real qualities of a lesson and the academic process as a whole are the teacher's peers who study the work and the academic process. As long as the nation refuses to accept this, the spiritual corruption of whole generations and the deterioration of educational establishments (to the level of institutions promoting the intellectual and moral degradation of both children and adults) will continue at an accelerated pace.

4.2.6. In order to formally legitimize the joint work of schoolteachers and make it possible for young teachers to demand to be involved, they should be issued permits to teach independently, not immediately after college but only after three to five years of successful pedagogical activity. We are not inclined to overrate the role of formal operations in building up the educational system, but neither do we intend to reject them.

4.2.7. In the initial stages of the teacher's work, help from qualified and skilled supervisors, teachers, and administrators can be highly intensive. It depends on the degree to which the new teacher has been able to gain an insight into the makeup of the student body: the level of knowledges, skills, habits and intellectual, creative, and cognitive abilities; the ability to work during lessons, listen to teachers, and comprehend questions and participate in discussing them. The scope of active assistance teachers can expect also depends on the extent to which they have from the outset been able to establish personal and professional relations with the students; this enables them to supervise the academic process with at least superficial accuracy, with the involvement of the majority of the students. The academic process must yield more or less positive results, which should be a source of at least some gratification to the students and the teacher and permit them to digest at least some of the new study material; for a beginning, that is sufficient.

Attendance of a new teacher's lessons by his colleagues, administrators, and supervisors will do much good, especially during the initial stages of his work with the class. They will advise him whether to continue the good work or to change the form and content of his lessons and the teaching-learning process as a whole. Such advice may cover the degree of the teacher's participation in analyzing problem situations and creative problems in class, his work aimed at helping the students restore knowledges needed to study upcoming questions of the course and the course as a whole, and at instilling firm knowledges, skills, and habits relating to the newly studied material, and so on. It is extremely important to draw the attention of inexperienced teachers to the extent of the de-

245

mands they can make on their students and to the need to recognize shortfalls in their knowledge, pinpointing and reacting to them. It is extremely important for the teacher to react calmly to cases of students' total ignorance of some questions and failure to comprehend questions asked by him or by other students. It is absolutely essential for the teacher to be able to involve the class in a discussion, conduct and sum it up, and introduce a new topic for discussion; this is especially difficult with a new class. All of this contributes to making the academic process at least temporarily suitable and successful in its external manifestations, forms, and reactions of the class, individual students, and the teacher.

Day after day, lesson after lesson, the teacher gains an ever deeper insight into his students' capabilities. He seeks to adjust the complexity of the studied material to the level of comprehension of all the students, while at the same time maintaining an adequate degree of concentration and interest. This is achieved by thoroughly studying every student, up to and including (1) individual work with some students after class; (2) visiting students at home; (3) talks with students and parents; (4) individualized assignments; (5) thorough checking of quizzes and tests and every step in them; and (6) including in quizzes and tests questions requiring comprehension of the essence of the basic concepts and ideas of the course, creative questions, and problem situations. Such thorough work with the class is supplemented with attendance of the new teacher's lessons by other teachers and their participation in preparing and discussing them. It includes preparation of different types of lessons, with the greater or lesser involvement of the strong and weak students, with more or less independent work of the whole class and individual students.

The new teacher attends the lessons of other teachers. He takes part in preparing and discussing them. He discusses the merits and demerits of the lessons of experienced teachers—their failures, successes, and the reasons thereof. He compares his work with the work of other teachers and critically evaluates what is applicable or inapplicable to his class, and for what reasons: the extent to which his students are prepared, their temperaments, the number of very strong and very weak students, the ability of the teacher and the students to work with the class as a whole, their ability to work independently, their willingness and ability to solve difficult creative problems, et cetera.

Gradually, invisible ties form between the teacher and the class, ties that are sensed only by the teacher and the students, as well as by experienced people attending lessons. By this time the teacher sees before him, even mentally, not rows of heads but a class: its features, faces, characters, souls, intentions, knowledges, achievements, and will; its ability to work, think, and react to questions; its sincerity, reticence, activity, ability or inability to ask questions; its perseverance, swiftness of motion and answers, or sluggishness; its individual situations at home—relations with parents, brothers, and sisters, friends, and so on. All those thirty or forty students comprise a new living entity, a complex organism: the

246

knowable and controllable Class. It is hard to teach this class effectively—much harder than teaching a single person—but it is possible. All teachers, with rare exceptions, can learn this.

4.2.8. It is especially difficult to teach a class initially, during the first few months, or sometimes up to a whole year or even more. In the hands of a teaching-and-learning teacher, the class gradually becomes more than a teaching subject: it becomes an effective means of education of both the students and the teacher. It becomes the teacher's powerful and faithful ally for many years. Our educational system's rash, thoughtless rejection of many-year courses rejects the idea of creating a class-teacher entity. This is one of the causes of its tragic demise.

The class and the student are different living beings. They have much in common, but also many differences. The teacher must be capable of seeing, understanding, feeling, and teaching both the class as a composite student and each student separately, and he should be constantly aware of each individual student and of the composite student-class.

While the class is taught by teachers, supervisors, administrators, and students, it also teaches—the students, the teachers, the supervisors, the administrators. As it acquires new knowledges, skills, and habits and raises the level of its intellectual, creative, and cognitive abilities, the class exerts a profound influence on all its members, both those who have forged ahead of it and those who are lagging behind. If the former begin to painfully feel the class's resistance, its inertia and sluggishness, the teacher should discern this at once and come to their help.

For decades it was believed that the only way to help the stronger students was to provide them with creative assignments and problem situations capable of satisfying their cognitive abilities and needs without detriment to the rest of the class. This view, however, was not shared by all. The better and more talented teachers simultaneously set their sights on raising the other, slower part of the class to the level of joint creative work with the more gifted students. Two or three times a week they conducted special lessons with the weaker part of the class after regular hours. They gave special out-of-class assignments accompanied by detailed discussion with the purpose of restoring knowledges eroded by time or incompetent instruction. At the same time, during lessons they would give the whole class creative, problem-oriented situations not requiring the reproduction of knowledges that might have been lost, but requiring fresh ideas, energy, courage, and innate capabilities. Such efforts fairly frequently and fairly quickly changed the class beyond recognition.

The thing is that the stronger part of the class does not necessarily comprise the more gifted students, but rather the more diligent and studious ones. The weaker students are more often than not those who don't know how to study or have gaps in their knowledge. This situation can be rectified by giving to all students creative assignments and problem-oriented situations requiring a minimum of formerly studied factual

247

material, by introducing new, comprehensible methods during the lesson, and by confronting students of all levels of training and capabilities with challenging questions. This way the teacher injects energy and courage into formerly totally neglected, intimidated, and forgotten children. The less prepared students catch up. The class becomes more energetic and capable of creative and technical work. Within several months—up to one year—many formerly weak students come to rank among the strongest.

The stronger students continue to work at full capacity. Special sessions for students wishing to go beyond what is done during lessons should become a law for every class and every educational establishment. They can be individualized or conducted in groups, depending on the individual aptitudes, requirements, and abilities of both the students and the teacher.

4.2.9. The teacher should be the most erudite and active student in the class. He takes part in solving problems and studying problem situations not only as their creator and supervisor of the class but also as a rank-and-file student. Furthermore, each day, during each lesson, the teacher-student receives ever new information about each student and the teaching-learning process, that is, new experience of work as a. teacher-supervisor.

The presence of the student-teacher, who is more educated and experienced than the other students and possesses the qualifications and authority of a supervisor of the academic process, makes the class a fundamentally new organism as compared with a group of students studying without a teacher.

People sitting in the same room, doing the same things, and independently studying the same things do not constitute a class. Nor does it matter how long they have been sitting in the room or how long they have been engaged in their work. If day after day each student only reads his textbook and answers the questions in it, this is not a class but simply a group of people who happen to be in the same room. If during the lesson the teacher gives his students a list of problems to solve and even permits them to ask him questions, thinking that he has fulfilled his educational mission, that, too, does not make a class. If during the lesson each student listens to his tape recording or watches a TV monitor, taking or not taking notes, carrying out or not carrying out assignments, taking or not taking tests, appealing or not appealing to the teacher—this does not make class.

The characteristic feature of a class and a lesson is the presence of the teacher who supervises it and engages in continuous, competent educational activity. This activity is aimed at the acquisition of knowledges, skills, and habits by all the students and the development of their intellectual, creative, and cognitive abilities. The teacher-supervisor ensures that the students acquire in-depth, firm knowledges at an accessible scientific level and teaches them to intelligently apply the acquired knowledge. He also helps prevent the destruction of acquired knowledge and

248

supervises its systematization and structuralization. The teacher-supervisor ensures the connections between the studied subject and other, related spheres of learning; he ensures the development of the students' oral and written speech. Under the teacher's guidance the students develop a thirst for knowledge and the desire and ability to study, including independent studies with the help of textbooks and study aids such as radio, television, tape recorders, and motion pictures. The teacher uses the lessons to ensure continuous awareness and feedback between the students and (1) their comprehension and intake of new material, (2) their mastery of new material, and (3) the overall level of their knowledges and creative and cognitive abilities. During the lesson the teacher provides continuous, competent guidance to eliminate shortcomings in the students' knowledges, skills, and habits and in the system and structure of their knowledges. He also ensures that the students work regularly on independent home assignments on the subject. He starts to supervise this work in class before the students do it; later he checks its quality and ensures its continuous upgrading.

Schools, colleges, and universities are not just assemblies of thousands or tens of thousands of people sharing curricula, textbooks, and schedules requiring them to spend specific hours in specific classrooms. An educational establishment is a system of lessons and a system of classes, a system of interdependent courses. It is a living organism which is taught and teaches. It is taught by teachers, professors, administrators, systems of courses, lessons, individual classes, and students. It also teaches teachers, professors, administrators, individual classes, and students.

A state educational system or the national educational system is more than a set of schools, colleges, and universities in which each element of the set may be, or not be, a system of interrelated lessons and classes, a system of interdependent courses. A state or national educational system is a set of interconnected educational establishments. A state or national educational system is a system of educational research institutes, a system of educational establishments, each of which is an educational research establishment as well as a system of lessons, classes, and courses.

4.2.10. On rare occasions the teacher may pick out one student in the class to discuss the solution of a problem one-to-one. The class benefits to some extent because some of the students listen and a few may even try to work together with that student.

The degree of the class's participation in the teacher's work with one student depends on the methods he employs—something which is virtually ignored in our country. Today the basic pedagogical problem of the lesson is how to teach every student without missing a single one and how to teach the class so as to fuse it into an organism, a force more powerful than when the teacher teaches individual students, both the strong and the weak.

The mini-laboratory—that is, the taught group—is a "vector" (5), which is a sum of four components, or four "vectors": (1) the teacher-educator, that is, the teacher-supervisor; (2) the teacher-student; (3) the class-teacher; (4) the class-student, consisting of forty students. This is an objectively existing structure. It is the foundation, the basis, a mini-structure existing and developing, regardless of whether or not we recognize its existence or comprehend its nature. As elements of a taught group—i.e., a mini-laboratory—the students, teachers, and class learn from each other, teach each other, support each other, and lead each other.

At different stages in the development of the mini-laboratory, depending on the lesson's objective and the nature of the study material, its four component vectors have different directions and different magnitudes. However, at every moment of every lesson we must be capable of controlling the teaching-learning process in such a way that the class-student vector, which is a sum of forty vectors, is directed positively and its magnitude does not decrease. Each of those forty vectors represents the level of development of the knowledges, skills, habits and intellectual, creative, and cognitive abilities of one student.

The teacher-educator, teacher-student, and class-teacher vectors must also always be positive and their magnitudes must continually increase; we also consider them to be noncollinear.

All forty vectors, each of which offers an idea of the degree of education of a single student, are in constant contact with each other and the other three vectors of the mini-laboratory. They have different magnitudes and are differently directed during different stages of the lesson and different teaching-learning stages of the class and the teacher. However, unlike vectors in linear algebra, our "vectors" continuously interact emotionally, intellectually, and pedagogically. All of them—the large and the small, the strong and the weak—are constantly influenced by the aggregate vector, that is, the mini-laboratory. The purpose of an effective teaching-learning process is to keep that aggregate vector always positive and greater in magnitude than any of its component vectors. We would like to repeat that while we consider these "vectors" to be positive, we do not consider them to be collinear.

4.2.11. The existence of the lesson and the class in the academic process are not the drawbacks or calamities many think them to be. They are powerful and indispensable tools in our hands.

A difficult creative assignment, which no single student in the class can fulfill, can be successfully tackled by the class as whole, working collectively under the guidance of the teacher. This makes it possible for us to teach all the students of the class with the help of study material beyond the individual capacities of even the best of them. Therein lies the invincible strength and virtually unlimited possibilities of teaching students as members of a mini-laboratory.

The invisible links existing between the teacher and each student make it possible for the teacher to supervise the students' work in class in such a way that each one contributes something to the solution of the

250

common problem. Each student answers particular questions which all, including the teacher, are trying to answer.

Such joint work of forty students—plus the class-teacher, plus the teacher-educator, plus the teacher-student—gives rise to dozens of diversified methods and directions of teaching-learning activity.

The study group—that is, the mini-laboratory—is the strongest, most intelligent, most educated student in the academic process. Together with the taught children and the class-teacher, the teacher-student and teacher-supervisor create a new quality, a new organism, a new pedagogical category.

All the students are in constant interaction—personal, educational, or businesslike—with the teacher-student and the teacher-educator. In addition, the teacher and the class continuously and actively influence every student, regardless of our will or the will of the students. Whether the class can and will be an influential student and teacher, and to what extent, depends on its qualities. Whether the teacher-supervisor/teacher-educator is good or bad also depends on many factors.

Very few teachers know how to make the best use of all the forces and capabilities of the class as both a teacher and a student, as well as of their own forces. The objective, of course, is to give the teacher, the class, and each student the maximum knowledges, skills, and habits as well as development of their intellectual, creative, and cognitive abilities. Most teachers have to be taught this extensively and diligently.

When we speak of the knowledges, skills, and habits and the development of the intellectual, creative, and cognitive abilities of the teacher and the class, we have in mind the teacher-supervisor as well as the teacher-student, the class-teacher as well as the class-student. And again and again we return to the same old theme: All school and college teachers must learn from each other. They must discuss lessons before and after they are given, seeking to improve them in every possible way. They should suggest to each other ways of overcoming difficulties encountered during lessons involving both individual students and the class as a whole. They are duty bound to jointly discuss and analyze the causes of positive and negative aspects of the lesson, its various stages, sequences of lessons, and the course as a whole. They must jointly determine the ways and means of overcoming shortcomings, consolidating and expanding the success of individual lessons as well as of whole topics, courses, classes, schools, and colleges. They should conduct and videotape model study lessons and research lessons, work on the literature for weeks and months, and seek the help of the best schools, colleges, and universities. They should discuss, systematize, and generalize the monthly and annual results of work on individual subjects and the work of individual classes, schools, and colleges. They should make decisions and review the academic process at new levels. They should invite the best teachers, administrators, supervisors, and qualified educator-politicians to take part as consultants in research and educational work—every hour, every day, every year in every school, college, and state throughout the country.

251

Such activity is virtually unknown in our country. It has never had education and doesn't know what it is. It is a whole, vast, new sphere in the nation's life, a sphere of scientific knowledge, a sphere of extensive and intensive activity—pedagogical, political, and social. It involves lofty ideas, in-depth research, science, and practice on a scale our people, our children, and educators cannot even imagine. They have never had this and don't know—or in many cases don't want to know—how the nation can acquire all this.

4.2.12. Many of our educators overrate the possibilities of individual or individualized instruction, i.e., instruction of students not in a class atmosphere but one-on-one with a book, tape, film, calculator, or teacher. This is what alternative schools are based on; many of us like them because they are better than other public schools, which is to say that they are better than nothing. It is the rationale behind classes of 700 people and the vogue for tele-teaching, programmed and computerized instruction and the like, which is sweeping the country, but not in the name of the nation's education. Irresponsible innovations are overwhelming our schools, colleges, and universities, while the nation looks on enraptured, not seeing that tens of millions of its children are being trampled under by self-styled creators of the educational business.

Work in class should always be interesting for all—for the teacher, in the first place. The class is a school of joy and happiness for all—for the teacher, in the first place. The teacher is taught, he is helped; he gains confidence, strength, joy, and happiness from his instructors. In turn, he infects the children with confidence, strength, joy, and happiness. No inanimate toy, even the most expensive, is capable of being enjoyed for so long. This is done by the class and its constantly inspired teacher. Therein lies the secret of our eternal strength, youth, and impact on children, society, and its spirit, intellect, soul, and morals.

It goes without saying that children must gradually be taught to work independently with books, programmed aids, calculators, tapes, and TV monitors. The teacher is not omnipotent. He can be feeling bad and fail to get a point across to his class. Besides, there are home assignments, which imply independent work. A student may miss several lessons. He may wish to review what he heard and saw during the lesson. He may want to read about it or try to test himself with the help of a programmed aid. He may need to catch up with the class because he was unable to concentrate—something happened at home, or he was simply daydreaming. Television lecture films, tapes, programmed aids, books, radios, and all the rest are absolutely essential for all these purposes. All these study aids individualize the class system in those cases and for those children who are in need of this, and when they need it.

The sole *raison d'être* of our thousands upon thousands of school systems and other organizations endowed with legislative powers seems to be to engage in bustling activity over questions in which they are totally incompetent. Nevertheless, our school systems, colleges, and universities are capable of swiftly and effortlessly producing mad but

252

bombastic results. They give rise to spates of new, asinine, incompetent, harmful curricula. They give rise to mountains of monstrously naive or illiterate textbooks and study aids. They give rise to thousands of miles of worthless, naive, or illiterate audio and video tapes—just to be innovative, just to be creative. A few private schools provide education, and that's enough. Whoever wishes can attend them. We have freedom of choice; the system is flexible and adaptable to the needs of all. If tens of millions can neither read nor write, that's their own fault. They are oriented in the wrong direction. No matter how much you teach them they will learn nothing. The main thing is no uniformity—never be in step. Each bakes his own pizza or makes his own bicycle, his own TV set, or his own automobile.

4.2.13. One of the main prerequisites for a teacher to be able to work successfully with all his students during a lesson is thorough preparation of the lesson for the specific student-class. This includes the choice of teaching methods and devices in accordance with the individual features of the class—its capabilities and requirements; its level of knowledges, skills, and habits; its intellectual, creative, and cognitive abilities; its character. It also includes the right choice of teaching methods and devices in accordance with pedagogical logic, prompted by the specific content of the lesson, its objectives, and its place and role in the system of other lessons of the topic, section, and course.

The choice and variation of teaching methods includes such devices as having the students themselves analyze and plan the forthcoming stage of the particular activity. The teacher can go over to some students and talk to them one-to-one, perhaps pointing out something or prompting them. This way he is able to take stock of the state of the class several times during the lesson at specific stages, and then conclude with a quickfire, animated discussion of all possible variants of the work carried out by the students. He or the students, possessing different levels of training and abilities, show the variants on the blackboard and evaluate their comparative value. Opportunities appear for the teacher to work, voicing out loud his thoughts and ideas, which are understandable to all the students, albeit to varying degrees.

4.2.14. Every successful teacher must know the class and each student. He must thoroughly study the students' qualities and shortcomings, their weak and strong points, conditions at home, their hobbies and interests. This is a teacher's duty, not just a wish.

Analyzing the work of mini-laboratories with the help of mini-researches, coupled with a considerable extension of the time devoted to studying different courses, will immediately reveal those of us who are in need of assistance and what forms it should take. Such analyses will show whether the teacher realizes the great need for a serious, in-depth study of each student. It will show whether he knows how to do this—in class and during lessons as well as in talks with parents in the school and at home. Such talks can be held in the presence or absence of the student, depending on the child's character and the nature of the difficulties that arise when working with him in class.

Illiterate and desperate students can be transformed from being our apparent or potential enemies and enemies of society into our close friends and good students. After several talks with a student and his parents, conducted competently and in a spirit of goodwill, after attentive and caring help given him, he becomes grateful to the teacher and the school for all his life. The talks reveal that the child never studied, for instance, percentage, algebraic fractions, negative numbers, or all this together. At the time there was a sports contest, or he was sick, or something else had prevented him. Now he is in a state of panic at the mere mention of percentages, algebraic fractions, or negative numbers. Meanwhile, the class has moved on to fractional equations and matters have gone from bad to worse. The student is afraid of the textbook, the school, the teacher. He engages in a desperate preemptive war with his parents, teachers, and administrators. He flees from lessons and seeks solace in the company of drunks or drug addicts. It's so easy and simple there, so pleasant. He realizes that he is going under, that there is no way out. But alone he is incapable of escaping from the quagmire, the quagmire of percentages, fractions, equations, and quagmire of drunken singing and narcotic oblivion. What he needs is for the teacher to sit with him one-to-one, together with those percentages and fractions, for as long and as frequently as possible, or in a small group of others like him. It isn't hard to find such people, and he won't feel so lonely. Or perhaps he would prefer being with the teacher without witnesses, if he is shy, proud, and doesn't want to have witnesses to his shame. In class, the teacher should ask him questions that he can answer confidently and proudly in front of the whole class. This must be done for weeks and months, if not more. The person changes. From a mire of ignorance he enters a world of respect for knowledge, confidence in himself, and hope for the future, a world of pride, productive work, creativity, thought, and honor.

There are especially many victims of our pedagogical helplessness among people who lack self-confidence, who are by nature timid, indecisive, and shy. They require long and extremely tactful support, assurance, and encouragement. This is essential until the children acquire the necessary minimum of knowledges, skills, and habits and gain self-confidence and composure—composure and the resultant joy of achievement and cognition, the joy of creative work in the company of well-wishing educators and a wise, tactful student/class and teacher/class.

The absence of close people capable of rendering active and preventive assistance reduces our children to gloom and despair. This assistance should be continuous, for some students lasting perhaps several years.

The absence of many years of contact with the same teacher; the fantastic agglomeration of study material in math and science courses; the absence of competent activity of mini-laboratories and mini-researches; the consequent impossibility of creating lessons and a successful teaching and educating academic process—these are but some of the causes and effects of the absence of an educational system in our country.

4.3. THE LESSON AND THE INITIAL STAGE OF ASSIMILATION OF NEW KNOWLEDGE. ONCE AGAIN ABOUT THE TEACHER

4.3.1. For teaching to be successful it is essential to show the students the connections between newly introduced material and previously acquired knowledge. For that, the teacher must prepare the lessons long before conducting them. It may take years to prepare students for the introduction of some concepts and ideas, such as the limit, irrational numbers, functions, the method of mathematical induction, and others. This requires having a very well-educated teacher in elementary school.

The revision of the material that is needed to introduce the new information, or that is a previously studied component of that information, may sometimes require several lessons. However, a full lesson, still less several lessons, can rarely be devoted to such revision. Usually there isn't enough time; the students must go ahead and study new material. The restoration of knowledge destroyed by time and the prevention of the destruction of new knowledge must be done along with the study of new material. The work need not be in any way associated with the basic material of the lesson. Its purpose is to bring the students, step-by-step, closer to the introduction and comprehension of the new topic or section.

Initial familiarization of the students with the new information is an extremely important stage of the educational process. The reaction of the class to the new material, which may be quite uninteresting or perhaps difficult or cumbersome, depends solely on the teacher. He must foresee his students' reaction to the lesson. Obviously, his anticipation can be erroneous.

The experienced educators and administrators must show the greatest tact and energy so as not to abandon the young teacher if he finds himself in trouble in his unequal confrontation with what may be a difficult class and a certainly difficult lesson. The inexperienced teacher often goes down in defeat in such confrontations. This starts an irreversible process of destruction of the academic process while it is still in embryonic stage.

Experienced educators know how difficult it is to conduct lessons at which the laws of growth and decay are introduced; they know the confusion which the method of mathematical induction introduces after many years of guessing without subsequent proof; they know the extent to which students dislike virtually everything associated with percentages—the mystery of the century. More or less proper introduction of the concepts of a circumference and area of a circle and the formulas for calculating them are usually difficult and unpleasant for both the teacher and the students. To this list can be added: the concept of locus;

255

introduction of the concept of function in middle school; introduction of the concept of coordinate system; the initial lessons devoted to graphic representation of functions; inverse functions, particularly inverse trigonometric functions; the limit of a sequence and a function; theorems of limits; work with Riemann sums and introduction of the concept of definite integral; the concept of differential and its applications—and, unfortunately, many other things. The beginning teacher cannot know that these lessons are extremely difficult to conduct and require especially thorough preparation.

4.3.2. The teacher must be helped, thoroughly and consistently. Otherwise, half the class, if not more, will understand nothing. The students will feel frustrated, protest vociferously, and make the poor teacher's life a hell. Soon he will be forced either to leave the school or to virtually stop teaching anything or demanding anything—which most of us have already done.

There is one more terrible variant of the nation's educational tragedy: the transformation of the lesson into a show where everyone is in high spirits and no one is bored. The teacher offers several simple problems requiring simple operations. He tries to entertain the students or busies himself with his own affairs, leaving the students to entertain themselves. Everyone is happy; there are no home assignments and none in the offing. The teacher has grown wise and doesn't introduce any new concepts: he once tried to introduce the concept of graph of a function or inverse trigonometric functions and got burned. He doesn't know how to do this professionally, and no one has taught him. The class got completely out of hand, so he will never repeat such a foolish mistake. All he now does is give a new symbol and show what to do with it in the simplest, most elementary, special cases. There is no hint of any explanation of the scientific content of the new concept, no hint of any justification. Just make substitutions, go by trial and error.

Driving the content of a newly introduced concept home to every student, showing its relationship with previously introduced concepts, asking yourself and the students questions of the type, "What will happen if we change this condition?, "What will happen if we change this condition thus?", "What is this condition for?", "Why does $a^{m/n}$ have meaning only for positive a?", et cetera, are things that have disappeared from our schools and colleges, or are disappearing rapidly wherever they still miraculously survive. Many colleges have transferred the laws of growth and decay from calculus, where they are extremely difficult, to the initial remedial course, where they are totally inaccessible.

Fewer and fewer attempts are made in school and college to strictly prove anything. Most teachers don't even try to teach anything seriously; they either don't know what it means, don't know how, or don't care—or all three. Droves of people are coming to graduate schools with not the slightest idea of the methods of science. They are immediately assigned teacher positions; everything follows the terrible, tragic routine.

4.3.3. The initial introduction of a new concept should serve to get the students interested in the studied science, knowledge, the school, and the teacher. This can be achieved only if the teacher is prepared to make the introduction interesting, understandable, and attractive and if he is helped to prepare for such work. After a series of failed lessons it's too late to try to salvage his doomed reputation.

While learning (under the teacher's guidance) new concepts and propositions and establishing the interrelationships between them, the students also learn to spot the essential features of concepts. They learn to establish connections between propositions and the interconnections and interrelationships between concepts and propositions. They learn this not only in cases similar to the considered ones but also in essentially new cases and situations. In other words, under the guidance of an educated teacher, the students learn the elements of scientific research and how to study independently.

The initial stage is of special importance in the general process of assimilation of knowledge. Every more or less successful educator knows this. During this stage there is an inevitable confrontation, and sometimes conflict, between previously learned information, which has become part of the student's inner world, and the material invading that inner world and inevitably altering it. Sometimes the new information simply enriches the student's inner world, complementing it with new data having familiar connections with familiar concepts, operations, and ideas. Sometimes it complements previously learned knowledge and concludes a definite stage in their development. Sometimes the new information systematizes and structuralizes previously acquired knowledge with the help of new, more general, and more effective methods. Sometimes it sets up a system of knowledge by subordinating the studied material to a systematizing and structuralizing idea. Sometimes it causes revolutionary transformations in the students' habitual notions, arousing protest and opposition on their part. But in every case, the initial assimilation of new knowledge must be most thoroughly and competently organized by the educator or a group of educators in such a way as to enable the whole class and each student to see and feel the newly studied subject. They must discover and learn its essential traits, manifestations, and connections with other subjects.

4.3.4. In our educational establishments, initial assimilation of new material is conducted formally and cruelly with regard to the students. Most frequently, the students have to read the textbooks themselves, without the slightest teaching effort on the part of the teacher. The teaching-learning process is stripped of its teaching, analyzing, structuralizing, ideational-scientific, problem-oriented purpose. All that is left is reception learning and imitation, mechanical memorization and reproduction of the study material. Such an academic process cannot provide education. It devastates and embitters a person, without developing his cognitive, creative, and intellectual abilities. The student is crushed by the lesson, crushed by the suffocating amount of new complex scientific information which he is not prepared to comprehend or master.

257

With rare exceptions it crushes him both morally and physically. The exceptions are especially gifted students or the students of a talented, self-taught teacher who has desperate courage, unyielding willpower, and incorruptibe honesty.

4.3.5. The methods of initial introduction of new knowledges, skills, and habits are diverse. That is one of the reasons why they must be handled with great care. In dealing with specific courses, specific student bodies, and specific lessons, we must teach our educators to make the best use of the methods of initial introduction of new material.

One of the prime conditions of successful teaching and learning is the students' active involvement and concern. Student activity can be effectively encouraged by the teacher if the teaching-learning process provokes questions from the students and provides answers.

It isn't easy to arouse the students' interest in material they don't know and encourage questions, attention, and active involvement. Teachers must be constantly taught how to win the students' attention from the very outset of the lesson and how to make them think and get actively and energetically involved in the work during the lesson. One of the principal methods is a clear, swift, energetic formulation of methods, ideas, facts, propositions, problems, and problem situations with the help of rapidly asked, exacting questions. Such questions are appropriate when the teacher is confident that the answers will usually be correct and fairly clearly formulated. Otherwise, he will have to waste time and distract the class by elaborating upon the answers, which can be protracted and boring.

An energetic, exacting, problem- and conflict-oriented beginning creates a dynamic atmosphere of quest, research, debate, and advance at the lesson. This atmosphere captivates the class and immediately turns it into a unified student organism. It produces a student-class in which all the students are equal and alike in respect of activity, dynamism, and absence of indifference and apathy.

4.3.6. One extensively employed and successful method, especially in the junior grades, is assignments that prepare the pupils for the conclusion to be drawn during the lesson. However, as the students grow older, more emphasis in the assimilation of new knowledge should be given to the development and perfection of scientific methods and structures; the development of concepts and scientific ideas; the logic of science, and the justification of propositions and operations, their legitimacy and importance.

The development and formulation of a problem situation requiring immediate, urgent analysis and the formulation of problems, the solutions of which require the students' active involvement and arouse questions, arguments, proofs, and refutations during the lesson, are things that, from the outset, draw the students' attention to the lesson. This can be supplemented with vivid description of the significance of the question to be studied for the solution of theoretical and practical problems, as well as with a brief recounting of the history of the question.

258

The educator must be adequately equipped to be capable of stating the history of development of all of the following: negative, real, and complex numbers; logarithms; solvability of equations in radicals; function; limit; derivative; integral; differential equations; linear algebra; Euclidean, Lobachevskian and Riemannian geometry; et cetera, as well as their importance for science. He must be able to discuss such interesting problems as the squaring of a circle, trisection of an angle, the theorems of Fermat, and many other things. The graduation from college of elementary and secondary teachers incapable of preparing an interesting, exciting, and competent lesson is a crime before the nation; it misleads parents and students and consistently implants ignorance, which leads to protest and crime.

4.3.7. Historical digressions to prepare the class for active, interesting work during the lesson should be used sparingly, and they should be very well prepared. Such pedagogical devices should not be endlessly rerun, like classical operas or plays, to keep them from losing their eternal freshness and from reducing the force of their impact on the audience.

To a lesser degree the foregoing also applies to the creation of conflict and problem situations at the very beginning of the lesson, and here is why: The school and the college are not places for pleasure and entertainment; they are places of work. Students should not be led to expect that every lesson must necessarily be entertaining. The only entertaining feature in the lesson should be, without any restrictions, the students' work: accessible, active, and meaningful. It should provide a feeling of gratification derived from the feeling of overcoming accessible difficulties, from the acquisition of new knowledge, skills, and habits, from a realization of the power of thought and creativity. Children like work when it helps foster their ability to independently achieve new results and independently acquire new knowledge, as well as enabling them to apply that knowledge to the solution of new, more difficult, and therefore more interesting practical and theoretical problems. The widespread view that all this is accessible only to naturally gifted and talented people, which is stubbornly cultivated in our country by the powers that be in science, is deeply erroneous. People not endowed with special abilities, talents, or even high intellect, derive interest and profound personal gratification from any subject that is taught knowledgeably and competently.

Some people like the strict logic and order of mathematics. Others enjoy the ability to solve problems known as transform techniques, as well as solving equations. When competently and knowledgeably taught, both can be intertwined with each other and with other concepts of fundamental importance and provide great satisfaction and joy to the people studying them. This is true, for instance, of identical transforms and the solution of equations and inequalities against a background of studying the properties and graphs of the corresponding functions.

Some people like only geometry, though not on too strict a level.

They regard the proof of theorems with tolerance, but they are more concerned with the justification of the solution of geometrical problems—something not to be found today. Everything is increasingly oriented toward the primitive levels of the teachers we ourselves have created.

Some will appreciate problems in solid geometry, which are not given in school but which every course in calculus requires most cruelly. But all students like the feeling of moving ahead: they like to acquire new knowledges at every lesson under the competent guidance of the teacher; they like to see themselves as growing, capable, and advancing—not deteriorating to the accompaniment of teacher wisecracks.

4.3.8. Primary among all the objectives of the school is to give children an education; we must give them knowledges, skills, and habits in the natural sciences and the humanities with the help of an active, creative, teaching-learning process. The most important means and product of this process should be the fostering and development of lofty human qualities: thinking, cognitive abilities, a positive work ethic, creativity, independence, activity, individuality, respect of adult society, and so on. Primarily, we have in mind respect for the teachers who instill students with the joy of creative learning endeavor and the joy of cognition from early in life—with the help of simple but wise assignments which are within their capabilities and require active thought and action.

Work during a lesson should be creative and active from the outset. There should be no mechanical memorization, especially during the initial stage of assimilation of new knowledge, during which mental alertness, intellectual effort, and creativity should reign. Learning by rote humiliates and insults our children, for which they revenge themselves on society throughout their lives. Memorization by rote eliminates thought and creativity from our schools and colleges, as well as smiles and joy.

4.3.9. The preparation of students for the acquisition of new knowledge is not an obligatory, explicit stage in the study of a new topic, still less a stage in every lesson. When teaching standards are high this stage usually goes unnoticed by the students. New knowledge arises out of existing knowledge so naturally that there is sometimes no need to draw the students' attention to the novelty. Rather, they can subsequently be asked—after the lesson or after completing a small section of the course—what new things they learned, what new ideas entered their minds and the system of their knowledge. Such *post factum* formulation of a newly acquired—perhaps fundamentally new—method, concept, or proposition closely approximates the academic process to scientific research during which intuition guides the creative process until the achievement of a clearly apparent, or even hypothetical, result.

4.3.10. Teachers must be constantly and tirelessly taught the art of preparing students to grasp new knowledge during the lesson. We must correct and forestall their mistakes and imbue them with creative teaching habits. Instruction in pedagogical creativity cannot be replaced by any workshops, consultations, or lectures for teachers. We have said this before and will continue to repeat it in the future. Such creativity can only be acquired by years of work in school or college. It is impossible to bring up a performing musician by making him read or write new scores. We need teachers who are capable of teaching actively and energetically, who know and understand the class and possess habits of pedagogical technology. The latter implies an ability to plan every lesson to assure that every child is actively involved with the maximum application of his intellectual and creative efforts. These efforts ensure the gradual, steady development and improvement of the students' knowledges, skills, and habits and their intellectual, creative, and cognitive abilities—which are independent of their abilities and inclinations. The degree of such development, however, is very dependent on both.

4.3.11. We are not afraid that teaching teachers of all ranks in all educational establishments will turn them into clones: this is impossible in view of differences in abilities, inclinations, and personal qualities. Teachers must be given the opportunity to create their own educational strategies, which would be qualitatively new in comparison with all the strategies they had ever seen or studied. It is, however, cruel, useless, and dangerous to force every educator to create anew what civilization has created over the ages.

Obviously, we are now speaking of the degree of influencing teachers, of the degree and methods of their instruction and education, not of the fact. The fact exists—if one can call what is going on in our schools and colleges today a fact of pedagogical education. It is harder to gauge activity than to state a fact. The existence or absence of a fact can be proved. Gauging activity is more difficult. The only yardstick for gauging a teacher's preparedness for educational activity, or rather, the proof that he is prepared, is the fact of successful educational work. This fact can be established by professional educators. But even if the fact of successful educational activity has been established, the educator should not be abandoned. Firstly, he may, unnoticed by himself, gradually cease to upgrade his skills and become less qualified. Secondly, he may become less qualified and try to improve, but to an insufficient degree. He will start forgetting the subject matter and, one after another, omitting successful teaching methods, even though he may occasionally read professional journals. He will learn independently from other teachers, but not always the things capable of effectively enhancing his qualifications. In this way, he gradually deteriorates from being a fine specialist into an ignoramus and corrupter of our children. Thirdly, all successfully working teachers—successful in the sense that they achieve good results—must be sought out, identified, praised, paid, supported, taught, developed, and encouraged with the aim of turning them into leading experts and supervisors capable of leading and prodding upward other educators one by one, or even whole schools and department faculties. They will comprise that mass of teachers and professors whose main profession will be that of continuously teaching other educators as well

261

as children. They will create the backbone of that gigantic, educational research institute—the federal educational system—which will be continuously strengthened, upgraded, and expanded.

4.4. LESSONS DEVOTED TO CONSOLIDATING SKILLS AND HABITS

4.4.1. Special attention must be given to lessons devoted solely to the consolidation of the students' skills and habits. We are speaking of lessons at which no new concepts, ideas, or structures are introduced, but which do contain new things for the students; otherwise, there would be no point in conducting them. This is to say that lessons devoted to revision and to the consolidation of skills and habits must contain new elements, including a higher level of difficulty of the material.

Most teachers, especially the less experienced, erroneously think that such lessons are easy for both the students and the teachers. This is a terrible mistake, and for many teachers it is their last one, after which they are forced to give up their profession, especially if they teach subjects requiring many lessons devoted to the consolidation of knowledges, skills, and habits.

Teachers usually prepare for such lessons less seriously than for lessons containing new information. They erroneously and very naively assume that if the students are familiar with parts of the lesson it will be easier to conduct than a lesson containing only new study material. That is why lessons on the consolidation of skills and habits usually turn into a torment for both students and teachers. They yield no positive result and are extremely dull, boring, monotonous, and uniform, for which the teacher is solely to blame. The students feel unhappy and doomed to suffer, as does the teacher. Both sides wait impatiently for the end of the lesson.

Once again, lessons not introducing new material are extremely difficult to prepare and conduct. Difficult—not easy, as many people think. They are much more difficult than lessons containing new information, and here is why: The very fact that the material is new is of great help to the teacher—thanks to its logic and to the process of unravelling it in the course of the lesson, thereby giving the lesson its educational force. It sparks the interest of at least some, and hopefully all, of the students. It carries a large share of the lesson's instructional impact, which in the absence of new material has to be borne by the teacher.

Dear educators, beware of lessons containing no new material. They are extremely difficult—if you wish to do your students any good. Beware of them and prepare for them very thoroughly.

4.4.2. One of the worst things a teacher can do is to bounce into the classroom and hastily write the numbers of problems to be solved in class on the blackboard. This is no way to launch an academic process. Such a beginning can only be justified if the teacher deliberately and justifiably intends to devote the whole lesson or part of the lesson to independent work by the students, to be followed by checking its results.

Dividing the class into groups of three to five students, taking care that every group includes at least one good or excellent student, is a sign of total pedagogical ineptitude. The good student will end up doing all the work in his group while the rest copy him, often without understanding what they are doing. In such cases the teacher usually complements the picture of pedagogical madness by reading a book, paper, or magazine . . . or checking a test . . . or sitting over a typewriter. This happens quite frequently and everyone knows it—students, teachers, and parents—but no one declares, clearly and forcefully, that this is open humiliation of our children, deliberate corruption instead of instruction.

4.4.3. The children realize only too well that we are deceiving them. They know that such work is useful and necessary for us, not for them. Instead of teaching and training them we merely look on with ingratiating smiles. We simply sit in at lessons where helpless students remain helpless. We refuse to do a thing to help them, or we don't know how to help them. If anyone dares ask a question we make no effort to conceal our displeasure. Most students, however, don't ask questions because they don't know what it is that they don't understand.

Our work is not oriented on the lesson, the children, their knowledges, skills, or habits. We cannot, therefore, expect the children's attention and respect, because we haven't earned it. They despise and hate us for our helpless, empty lessons and will continue to despise and hate us until we learn to teach them. They have even begun to attack us physically when we dare impose demands on them.

4.4.4. Dear teachers: You have come to the classroom to work both with each student separately and the class as a whole. The children will work by themselves in study halls, at home, in libraries, and laboratories—they have every opportunity for this. During lessons it is your duty to teach them the most difficult lesson: how to work and study independently, how to study without outside help. When they have learned this—not necessarily in general, but within a specific topic—then is the time for independent work in class. But even then it must be under your supervision. That is why you are in the classroom; that is your job. The children have come to the classroom to learn from you; they can learn from each other without you, outside the classroom.

4.4.5. One of the main troubles, if not the calamity, of our education is that even when students do something, they don't know why they can do it. They don't know what justifies a specific course of action, what is its purpose, whether there are alternative ways, and what is the optimal variant. Without daily and hourly mass instruction of teachers and students in all of this, the educational system cannot function successfully.

263

As we proceed from one topic to another and promote the students from one grade to another, we leave them and their teachers at an unchanging level of development of their intellectual, creative, and cognitive abilities—deliberately or not, but most certainly.

4.4.6. The students' skills and habits can be consolidated by steadily building up their independence and creativity according to the difficulty and novelty of the study material.

Let us discuss this in greater detail.*

When the class faces an altogether new problem of a kind the students have never solved before, they cannot, of course, be expected to solve it unassisted. Nevertheless, the teacher should refrain from solving it himself or having one of the better students solve it on the board so that the rest of the students could copy the ready solution. It is desirable to employ such a method of teaching as to have each student make his contribution to the complete solution of the problem and eliminate passive participation and mechanical writing. Students take turns suggesting steps of the solution; they do it either by responding to the instructor's leading questions or without such questions, and substantiating their suggestions. Each suggestion is discussed by the class, and the best one is taken from all the alternatives. Thus the problem is solved by the entire class; the questions are put to all the students. Each subsequent step of the solution is written out on the board only after it has been elucidated to the whole class. Let us conventionally call this method "frontal."

Frontal work should be accompanied by board work only if the problem is too difficult or if the students are not yet familiar with the form of the written presentation. In case of a difficult problem, even after discussing and clearing up a given step, one cannot be sure that the students will carry out the solution correctly. At this point, in order to verify the correctness of individual steps in the solution, one may resort to writing the matter on the board. Care should be taken as to proper timing: the presentation on the board must appear somewhat after the same point has been written by the students on their own in their notebooks. As the students master the solution of a given type of problem, we can dispense with the board presentation of separate simpler steps, gradually shifting to frontal work without board presentation: at the teacher's request the students put forward their suggestions; these suggestions are discussed and perfected; the students write them down in their notebooks.

To develop and consolidate the students' skills and habits, it is also of use to conduct the following type of work. Let a certain number of steps be singled out in a given problem; some of them are done in

*J. Goldberg, "On Methods and Techniques Employed in Teaching Students to Solve Mathematical Problems," *Papers of the USSR Academy of Pedagogical Sciences*, No. 3 (1962), Moscow.

succession by one student at the board, the rest may be done by a different student or students. We call this work "semifrontal." This method should be preferred when certain steps in the solution are more naturally grouped together rather than separated from one another.

The teacher's objective is to teach his students to be able to solve problems on their own. Therefore, all kinds of frontal and semifrontal work should alternate with partially unassisted and fully unassisted work. The usual order in introducing a new type of problem would normally be: (1) begin with frontal work, (2) pass on to semifrontal, (3) then through partially unassisted to (4) completely unassisted.

At the partially unassisted stage the students do the more familiar part of the problem on their own; if necessary, the instructor supervises and guides the progress of the slower students. Then the more difficult part of the problem is done frontally by the entire class, with or without subsequently writing it on the board. Depending upon the structure of the problem, the unassisted work comes at the beginning, in the middle, or at the end.

As the students obtain a certain minimal level of skills and habits with regard to the solution of this or that type of problem, the share of unassisted work gradually increases. In the transition to complete independence, it may be of help first to discuss the outline of the solution and then have the students carry it out by themselves. At the fully unassisted stage the students perform the whole solution on their own, asking occasional questions. Greater help is rendered to the slower students. When the solution is completed, a frontal checkup is done, with or without the blackboard.

Various forms of class work can be alternated in different sequence from that described above. In weaker classes, and/or when handling a more difficult problem, the transition to unassisted work should be done with caution and reservation. In a stronger class, and/or when dealing with a simpler problem, certain forms of class work can be omitted.

4.4.7. Provisions should be made for special preparatory assignments for almost every chapter. They should be given in advance, well before the chapter is introduced in class, and should include matter from previous chapters and courses that will be made use of in the forthcoming chapter. For example, multiple integrals should be preceded by a thorough review of techniques of integration, polar coordinates, conic sections, quadric surfaces, and basic chapters from high-school solid geometry.

4.4.8. Regular home- and classwork should embrace problems from several sections. This system of daily recapitulation is designed to maintain a higher level of theoretical knowledge and develop necessary skills and habits. It helps the students to review and consolidate the various aspects of the course. This, in fact, is the system we have in mind when elsewhere we consider methods of classwork for solving problems that are more familiar and less familiar to the students.

As far as daily home assignments are concerned, it is useful to discuss the more difficult problems in advance. This should be done when the teacher realizes that the students lack sufficient skills and habits to cope with them on their own during the limited period of time before the next class. Needless to say, one is not compelled to assign such problems at all; however, it is of great use to expose the students to more challenging problems gradually, discussing certain points with them and at the same time giving them a chance to try and carry out the solution on their own.

A preliminary discussion is indispensable for problems and questions that give the fundamental concepts of the course: function, limit, derivative, differential, integral, continuity, convergence, the mean-value theorems, basic facts about vector space and the real-number system, and others.

4.4.9. The bigger and more difficult the home assignment, the more time it takes during the class session to analyze and discuss the assigned problems. As a consequence, very little time is left to the teacher for actually teaching the students in class. Now, since not enough is taught during the class session, the home assignment inevitably grows in size; then at the next session more and more time is spent explaining homework problems; and as a result still less time is left for teaching, for actual development of a general understanding of the course, for consolidating the students' skills and habits.

It is suggested that the students' homework be returned together with the instructor's solutions of the more important problems. In some cases the solutions should be presented in such a way as to require a certain effort on the part of the students to understand them. In most cases, however, the description should be detailed enough for any student to follow every step, thus allowing each student to understand the solution of the problem he had failed to solve, or at least to compare his solution with that of the instructor. It is essential that the key is given to the student only after he has handled the problem himself.

It might be worthwhile giving the key in at least two variants: a few directions for the better students and more detailed step-by-step descriptions for others.

If a student hands in his homework with only a few problems completed, the instructor should return it for completion without suggesting any solutions of his own. At times one has to do so with the entire class.

The suggestion of variants of solutions does not rid the teacher of the necessity of subsequently discussing the more important or the more difficult problems in class with the purpose of testing the students' overall comprehension of the material and helping them to appreciate its meaning and purpose better.

Sometimes one should also discuss problems in which students are apt to make bad mistakes.

4.5. THE LESSON AND THE DEVELOPMENT OF STUDENTS' COGNITIVE ABILITIES

4.5.1. Learning the study material is a process that we must teach our students gradually and continuously. Without this process, supervised by the teacher, teaching and learning is impossible.

In the junior classes it is easier for children to learn individual facts, rules, or new words. Their mechanical memory dominates over logical memory. Perhaps that's why we start teaching foreign languages just when the children lose that ability, and then we wonder why we have endless failures in foreign-language instruction.

One of the school's prime tasks is to gradually teach children the skills of logical learning. Students must not only be able to establish connections and relationships between different concepts, facts, phenomena, and structures—they must also know how to learn them, how to retain them in their memories, and, on this basis, learn and develop new concepts and structures, establish new facts and laws, reveal the connections between them and previously developed structures, and define ways and means of further developing and improving them.

Children are incapable of handling this process on their own. They are incapable of even implementing it more or less successfully without competent, outside guidance. It is necessary for an educator to record the progress and results of this work. He must thoroughly study the learning process implemented by each student and point out mistakes in learning activity which result in inadequate standards of knowledge, skills, and habits and retard the development of intellectual, creative, and cognitive abilities.

4.5.2. All educators must extensively study and learn from each other the art of supervising the study activities of children and college students, both in and out of class. We must study the schools, colleges, and individual educators who cope with this task successfully. Some educators achieve this intuitively, subconsciously, by virtue of special talents for this kind of work. Some are successful because of their great educational experience. Some find this work especially interesting; they devote special attention to it, attach special significance, and study the special literature.

Master's theses, Ph.D. dissertations, and research papers by college and university professors—especially in departments of education and psychology—should be devoted to positive teaching experience, notably experience in developing students' cognitive abilities.

4.5.3. Some teachers insist on their students' memorizing the definitions of concepts, provable and unprovable propositions, verbatim from the textbook. This gives the students examples of immaculate, precise, and grammatically correct speech, and it should not be rejected—provided the textbook is good and that the whole teaching-learning process is not reduced to this. However, if such a teacher fails to

267

establish the students' true comprehension of what they have memorized, if he doesn't try to vary questions in such a way as to make a student depart from verbatim reproduction of the memorized material, he will be teaching his students not to think.

We must constantly and persistently teach children to give voice to their thoughts and formulate them independently; otherwise, the natural inclination of, especially, younger and weaker students to memorize mechanically will become an article of faith. For a while it will save them and even be a source of gratification and joy. But ultimately mechanical memorization may triumph, not only over logical learning, but over logic and meaning, over comprehension of the memorized material. Mechanical, verbatim memorization of a textbook will turn a child into a thoughtless automaton rather than a thoughtful, critically minded member of society capable of analytical thinking and creativity. The inclination for mechanical memorization should be courageously and consistently replaced by a need for justified statements, analysis, and reasoned proof. It is the educator's duty to guide this complex process.

4.5.4. Children are not only incapable of guiding the process of their education; they are, naturally, not even aware of the possibility of such guidance. They simply do what they happen to find simpler and more natural. They memorize things that should be analyzed, justified, proved, understood, compared, and correlated, and for which cause-and-effect relationships must be established between events, phenomena, processes, concepts, and propositions.

Academic freedom has turned into the academic death of whole generations. Children are hopelessly mutilated. They have been denied the possibility of thinking and living happily.

Our system of written multiple-choice tests, coupled with the total passivity, and more often total inaction, of the students during the lesson is profoundly fallacious. The absence of any guidance of independent work, the absence of guidance of the work of teachers, and the absence of competent help for them, all yield whole classes, schools, and school systems in which children do not know, do not learn, and have never learned even basic facts, propositions, and concepts. Of what cognitive abilities can one speak?

Some students remember some propositions, definitions of concepts, proofs, and problem solutions while totally lacking in comprehension of those propositions, proofs, or the solution processes of those problems. Try interrupting such a student during his work; try formulating a question differently. Give him the same problem differently formulated, or a simpler one which is but a special case of the problem he has just stated without a flaw. Try asking him "Why?", or even worse, "For what purpose?", or "What will happen if the condition is changed this way?" He is rendered totally helpless. For him the study of math and sciences is but a process of mechanical memorization of definitions, propositions, proofs, justifications, and solutions. All those years he stud-

268

ied things without ever attempting to understand their interrelationships and interdependences, the difference between basic and defined concepts, between definitions and theorems, between axioms and propositions that must be proved. Such a student can easily reverse cause and effect in the course of his reasoning. He may well commence proof of the proposition, "If there is A there is B," with the proposition, "Let there be B," and then triumphantly conclude with the statement, "Therefore B exists." And there is no way to convince him that he has proved nothing.

4.5.5. Dear educators, administrators, and researchers: Go to lessons. Visit schools and colleges. Sit in on as many lessons as you can. Talk to our teachers and students, to our future teachers, engineers, officers, generals and admirals, mathematicians and physicists, chemists and biologists, congressmen and presidents. Take a closer look at how they are taught and whether they are taught at all. See whether they are taught how to study. When children study mainly on their own, even if they study a lot, but without the active educational involvement of a professional teacher, even if they take tests very successfully—naive, primitive tests requiring only the memorization of facts—this in itself means nothing. Most students remain hopelessly illiterate all their lives without a trace of cognitive ability, yet completely confident of the infallibility of their knowledges and abilities. This is because, on their own, students are incapable of seeing and understanding how they were taught and what they have been taught.

4.5.6. In all the country's educational establishments, in all classes, teachers must explicitly and implicitly supervise the development of the ideas and methods of science; they must create problem situations for the students to analyze. Every student must be required, at lessons and when doing home assignments, to overcome reasonable difficulties. He must participate in debates and in establishing cause-and-effect relationships between events and phenomena. He must be taught induction and deduction, analysis and synthesis. The academic process must be filled with discussions and debates involving all the students and endless questions: "Why?" "Wherefore?" "For what reason?" "For what purpose?" "What if there is no A?" "What if instead of A we take B?" Clearly defined requirements within home assignments; determination of what should be done according to the textbook, and how; analysis at the next lesson of the theoretical and practical parts of the home assignment, with those same endless questions, justifications, refutations, proofs, examples and counterexamples—these are the forms and content of the development of students' cognitive abilities. If this is lacking in a teacher's work system then there is no teaching-learning process: The students acquire no knowledges, skills, or habits and there is no way they can develop their intellectual, creative, and cognitive abilities.

Students do not know how to work with textbooks—even if some of them still remember many things, even if most of them can answer a hundred worthless questions in the course of an hour. Our cruel, helpless, primitive, illiterate, so-called educational system, which is most harmful to society and corrupts the minds and souls of both the taught and the teachers, makes no attempt to offer more. It is incapable of more.

A study of the work of schools, teachers, and students—with the help of other teachers, administrators, supervisors, college and university professors, and graduate students working on their master's papers and Ph.D. dissertations (not just once in a blue moon but daily and hourly)—would reveal a terrible picture. Neither teachers nor students would be able to describe how the students work on textbook material during lessons and at home, the technique of working one-on-one with the book. Moreover, the overwhelming majority of our schools and teachers have simply given up the idea of home assignments, and virtually all—with rare exceptions—pay not the slightest attention to the students' ability to work with books or to the results of such work. The surprising thing is not that the level of our children's knowledges, skills, and habits, as well as their intellectual, creative, and cognitive abilities, is declining with each passing year. The surprising thing is how, at the cost of enormous sacrifices—physical and material—some of them manage to acquire some semblance of knowledge: primitive, naive, incomplete, distorted, unstable, narrow, fragmentary, unsystematized, scattered, ungeneralized, chaotically jumbled. These miserable shreds of knowledge are unrelated to the students' skills and habits—if any trace of the latter can be detected. They miraculously survive at a primitive level of intellectual, creative, and cognitive abilities unworthy of a member of modern civilized society.

4.5.7. We once again repeat that the naturally gifted, talented, great scientists reared in our land and outside its borders have nothing in common with what we call our system of mass education. Such people virtually independently, with the most passive participation of educators—much less knowledgeable, gifted, and capable than their pupils—acquire, not primitive and naive, but comprehensive, genuine, diversified, systematized, generalized, and structuralized knowledges. On the basis of these knowledges they simultaneously build up firm skills and habits and develop their intellectual, creative, and cognitive abilities. They achieve all this alone, by virtue of their gifts and talents, using excellent books written by similar talents. They work in numerous libraries and laboratories without any supervision, sometimes in collaboration with other brilliant researchers. They appear, not thanks to our educational system, but outside and in spite of it.

4.5.8. Different students quite naturally take different approaches to work in class and at home on the teacher's assignments, both oral and written. This work is necessarily individualized, and the methods used should not be imposed. It is unquestionably a matter of the student's preferences and personal qualities. But equally unquestionably, most students erroneously and tragically tend to substitute the learning of new information with what is but an appearance of comprehension and perception of elements of far from primary importance. Moreover, they have no idea of the difference between learning and memorizing, because no one has ever taught them. Children don't know when they can let up, at least for a while, and tell themselves that the new material has been learned, at least initially.

The teacher must conduct daily, detailed discussions of study material presented at the preceding lesson and initially memorized by the students at home. These discussions must include questions of learning and memorization procedures involving good and bad answers by the students. The practice of mass education and experience of the best teachers will reveal that in this way the students learn from each other how to study, while at the same time developing and expanding their cognitive abilities. This way, at every lesson, the students, under the supervision and with the active participation of the teacher, exchange their learning experiences and procedures, not just their results. We repeat once again the following: Such exchanges should take place in the case of both successes and failures of the students.

4.5.9. The systematic development of students' cognitive abilities should start during the very first years of instruction, and should go on continuously. It should be an element of every active, instructive lesson.

Exchanges of learning experience carried out regularly during lessons will reveal that some students immediately attack the written part of an assignment. Such students hope that they have understood and even memorized all the teacher has taught and told them.

For the stronger students this approach is not only acceptable but also preferable—if they have adopted it spontaneously. They like it. Encountered difficulties arouse a pleasant sense of struggle. They seek to independently justify each step in the exercises before carefully studying the theoretical explanations in the textbook. They are confronted with difficulties of a purely theoretical nature and with difficulties in finding the ways and means, methods, and general strategy of solving problems and doing exercises. They see the solution of problems as a scientific investigation. Some strong students even try, subconsciously or deliberately, not to listen to the lecturer before doing a written assignment. They listen absently, indifferently, or even skip classes, especially in college. They don't want to hear in advance how they should perform their independent work. Of course, they get some information from the textbook, but they seek a minimum of such information before tackling the problem.

Do not interfere with such people. They are our future researchers. Imitation is not for them. They are born to be creators. However, do not leave them alone in the struggle with the course. Insistently require them to work studiously with the textbook—not only in cases of difficulties in performing the written, creative portion of assignments, but

271

in all cases. Thoroughly and patiently explain to them why this is necessary. Firstly, students' justifications can be incomplete and imprecise. The textbook gives examples of solutions with complete and precise justification of the legitimacy and necessity of each step. Even a very talented student may be much below the author of a good textbook. Secondly, the student must study the theoretical portion until he is capable of independently reproducing all the theoretical material without peeking into the textbook.

This, of course, is not the end. It must be followed by a series of reviews, systematization, and general assignments. The students will return to the section again and again. In the absence of specific instructions by the teacher that certain material can merely be glanced through, some must be read, and some can be omitted for the time being, all the students, the weak as well as the strong, should thoroughly study the whole theoretical section of the assignment.

The teacher should insist that the students bring their studies of the theoretical material up to the level of independent analysis. They should be able to identify the main, basic elements necessary for solving practical and theoretical problems. They should be capable of establishing the connections between the new material and preceding sections. They must be taught this continuously, in school and in college.

Students should universally and invariably be given guidelines for studying each section, asking them questions abounding in "whys," "wherefores," and "what ifs," both before and after the section is studied.

4.5.10. Courses grow more and more complex with each passing year. The students must therefore constantly improve and enrich their ability to analyze and study the material, otherwise they will remain at a primitive level of cognitive ability. However, they sit in classrooms where they are required—naturally but hopelessly—to have a much higher level of training, including training in ability to study.

4.5.11. Unfortunately, not only the strongest students but also the weakest pounce upon the written part of assignments without sufficient theoretical knowledge. This is very dangerous. They literally trace a finger along the problem while hunting with another finger for a similar example considered in the book. In this way they manage to create a kind of symbiosis of two superficially similar structures. Without knowing what they are doing, they insert two or three formulas that catch the eye—just to make sure.

This is what we should fear most of all. It dooms classes, schools, school systems, colleges, universities, and whole generations—at least as far as learning physics, chemistry, and mathematics is concerned. Yet in the majority, the absolute majority of cases, our children are not to blame. They have simply not been taught; no one attempts to teach them how to understand and apply mathematics and science. All that is required is reproduction, imitation, and work according to samples and stereotypes. They are pitted against books, usually bad, and against teachers, usually helpless.

The system of work with a textbook by poking a finger from a problem to the book must be avoided and eliminated from the very outset of school studies. Furthermore, it is essential to teach children how to study in general, how to develop their intellect, creativity, independence, activity, initiative, and, on this basis, their cognitive abilities. This must be done from the outset of studies—but it also happens to be just when they are in the hands of utterly helpless and illiterate elementary-school teachers. This alone is enough to destroy any educational system.

4.5.12. When teaching children how to work independently, the procedure for preparing the theoretical part of an assignment should be approximately the same for both the more capable and the less capable: First read the assignment thoughtfully, unhurriedly, without digressing. Some students, you will find, prefer to read the theoretical part of an assignment several times. They may or may not make notes. After that, they independently reproduce what they have read, then read it all over again to check what they have reproduced. Let such students continue to work that way—of course, only if the results are positive.

Other students will prefer to read and study the theoretical part in segments. They will read one segment several times until they understand it. They will try to analyze what they have read, then reproduce it without referring to the textbook, recalling whatever they think to be the most important and essential. After that they will reread the reproduced portion to compare it with the textbook. They will follow the same procedure with each segment. After that they will read the whole assignment and reproduce it, striving to recall the general content, Finally, they check the reproduction with the textbook by reading the theoretical part of the assignment once again and comparing the textbook material with their reproduction. This is done by memory, orally.

Sometimes, when reproducing the consolidated material in segments or in full, a student will make brief notes and generalizations. This way it is easier to verify the quality of comprehension and learning of the information. Besides, this requires greater mental activity and stimulation. The learning process is less likely to turn into a mechanical process of memorization to the detriment of comprehension. It is easier to reread several times than to read and try to recall what has been read. This is why the weaker students try to read several times and reproduce less. All students should be taught to try to reproduce the new information several times, while cutting down on the number of readings.

4.5.13. We repeat and will continue to do so over and over again: You must teach children how to study all the time, from the moment you have received a new class. The degree of thoroughness of such instruction may vary for different students. The specifics of a course and the gradually increasing difficulty and complexity of courses as the years go by will invariably suggest to the educator or group of educators what advice and instructions regarding work with the textbook should be given to the students.

The methods of work with a textbook may vary. We will not even attempt to discuss them in detail. For example, one method is preliminary segmentation of the whole assignment into logically complete parts—first by the teacher, then with the help of the class. Next, some students join the second portion with the first and reproduce them both. Then they work on the third part, writing down new terms, unfamiliar words, and reproducing either the last two or all three parts, and so on. Let those who like to work that way do so; they find it easier. It is, however, essential that every student should understand the sequence of the individual parts and the connections between them.

As mentioned before, other students will quickly read through the whole assignment one or two times. They think of it and try to understand and remember what they see as the main, most important points. After that they will start with the written portion of the assignment. This, too, should be welcomed; the ability to distinguish between the primary and the secondary is a great skill—it should always be taught to all. If work on the written part stalls, they go back to the textbook. Perhaps they were unable to identify the main points. After this, such students tackle the written part again. This can happen several times until the written assignment is finished.

Then, perhaps after working on other subjects, the children go back to studying the theory until they can reproduce it completely and knowingly in their own words. There are many such students, too. Let them work that way. It means this method is more in line with their personal tastes, capabilities, and character. They are fearful of studying up to the very end. They are afraid they won't have enough time for other assignments in other subjects. Besides, they instinctively feel that it's better to return to the same material several times, even in the course of a single day, than to learn it all at once, even very firmly.

4.5.14. It is important for all students to know (1) that these and other variants exist; (2) that all variants can be effective, provided they devote themselves constantly and studiously to the work; (3) that all variants should be concluded with complete self-evaluation, i.e., independent reproduction of material in the student's own words; (4) that the student should at the same time self-evaluate the quality of his reproduction.

Furthermore, it should become a law for all students that they must continue to work on the same material today, tomorrow, and the day after. This will become possible when we finally come to our senses and give up daily drills in the same subject, both in schools and in colleges. Furthermore, locking up students for the whole day in school instead of giving them assignments they are capable of coping with and firmly requiring their fulfillment is cruel and useless.

4.5.15. One of the basic tasks of the educational system is to teach all students the art of sober and objective self-control and self-evaluation of their knowledges, skills, habits, and even the level of their creative and cognitive abilities. This is an enormous social problem imposed by society on education. Its resolution is directly contingent on the quality and comprehensiveness of feedback in the teaching-learning process. Inability to evaluate one's condition—inability to distinguish between knowledge and ignorance, apparent knowledge, incomplete knowledge, erroneous knowledge, misconceptions, and militant ignorance—is the source of numerous tragedies—big and small—experienced by many people. The most dangerous members of society are those who always consider themselves right.

4.5.16. Initial review of study material should be more frequent than subsequent review. Both teachers and students will learn this in EdRLs and EdRIs. They will be sure to discover that if the material in difficult or voluminous the intervals between revisions should be increased. On the other hand, extending the learning time for too long when studying the same information can be dangerous. It is also dangerous to extend for too long the time devoted to the acquisition of skills and habits pertaining to a certain amount of material. When the time intervals are too long so much is forgotten between sessions that most of the effort goes into recalling and restoring what has been lost rather than into consolidating, expanding, and developing the acquired knowledges, skills, and habits. Some effort should go into this inevitable restoration under the general conception of extending revisions in time. In the process of such extension, revision helps consolidate knowledges, skills, and habits, but it must yield optimal results.

4.5.17. It should be understood that the teaching and learning process is individualized, as are the students' cognitive abilities. Therefore, schools and colleges should provide different opportunities for both teachers and students. For example, giving 200 hours of college calculus daily, for four quarters, to all students, is madness. There should be variants of courses, with double periods, covering 400–600 hours over two years, in every college and university. The existence of courses in advanced calculus changes nothing: the student has already been destroyed, morally and physically, by the mad four-quarter course.

We'll see how many brave people will choose to go for 200 hours of calculus a year. Some will, and that is wonderful. Why should they spend two years on something they can do in one? But the overwhelming majority, for whom calculus is insurmountable and a cause of dropping out of college, will not do that. They won't remain enemies of those who forced them to remain ignorant. Nor will they be enemies of those who managed to overcome the course, because they, too, will overcome it. They will remain in college and complete calculus and other courses successfully. Today our children are incapable of coping with these courses because they are implemented within time periods and at a level requiring entirely different school training—something which is lacking and will be lacking for many years to come.

4.6. THE ACADEMIC PROCESS AND TESTS.
TEST LESSONS AND TEST ANALYSIS LESSONS

4.6.1. High schools could offer not 180 hours in chemistry, but 580; not 180 hours in physics, but 680. The same could be done with algebra, geometry, trigonometry, analytical geometry, calculus, and foreign languages. But if they did only that—and nothing else—the students' education would not change much, and who knows in what direction?

It isn't really relevant to the acquisition of knowledge, skills, and habits in, say, physics if a student does nothing at physics classes for 180 or 680 hours. The purely mechanical operation of increasing the volume and length of courses will only serve to increase the boundless sea of suffering of both teachers and students. Instead of one short year of skimming over the headings of several chapters in the textbook—usually its first part—they will have to spend several years hacking their way through dense thickets through which neither teachers, supervisors, nor students are at present capable of making their way.

In other words, it is much harder to create an appearance of education in a course lasting three or four years than in a one-year course, but the result may well be the same. Doubling or tripling the number of years and hours devoted to a course can yield little or nothing without (1) replacing the bureaucratic dictatorship in all educational establishments with the dictatorship of the academic process, and (2) replacing the dictatorship of tests in all educational establishments with the dictatorship of the academic process. We will show how this can be done.

4.6.2. The teacher must thoroughly think over the whole teaching-learning process. Every lesson must be painstakingly prepared and competently conducted. Only then can the teacher and every student develop the same evaluation of the difficulty and complexity of the problems, questions, and exercises which the teacher considers should be required of the class at the time.

The teacher should be especially careful and fair with respect to the students in those cases when the questions, problems, and exercises he is giving are not intended to be analyzed in class. We are speaking of those cases when the teacher firmly requires the students' independent work in a test, individual assignment, or a discussion having the features of oral testing.

Before requiring the students to do anything they must be taught how, in the course of the academic process. If the teacher fails to do this he creates not professional students in his class but enemies—bitter and later criminal.

The gradual accumulation in the class of students hostile to the teacher can result in the total destruction of the academic process in that class, either gradually or, occasionally, suddenly. The teacher rapidly loses the class's respect and attention. The students start talking back and then advance to more aggressive actions. If the school does not practice regular attendance and reciprocal attendance of classes by administrators and educators, a teacher working alone may remain unawares for some time that his class is heading for catastrophe. If, on the other hand, the teacher does see that his relations with the class are gradually collapsing but refuses to appeal to his peers for help, the destruction of the academic process may also become inevitable. The teacher will either be forced to give up that class or he will be forced by his helplessness to grovel pitifully before the students. Both sides—the teacher and the students—may take militant positions. The class and the teacher will torment each other with mounting cruelty.

4.6.3. The teacher must organize the work of the class in such a way as to supervise the students' assimilation and repeated application of new operations, concepts, and propositions. Only then will he have the moral right to require the students to be creative and to independently apply the material they have assimilated and already used repeatedly when studying new problem situations, solving new problems and doing exercises, and answering questions that are new in content and require independent analysis and selection of the methods of resolving them. When solving a problem, the students should also be able to independently develop the sequence of partial problems whose solutions lead to the complete and independent solution of the given problem.

The extremely important ability of maintaining such relations with the class is mastered by very talented educators at once, starting with the first few lessons in school. The rest—virtually all—must be extensively taught this great skill. There is only one way to do this: mini-researches and video-taping including mini-researches that take the form of test lessons and test-analysis lessons.

4.6.4. Perhaps some readers may be experiencing a mounting feeling of protest against what has just been said about students independently solving problems and doing exercises. There can be many causes for such dissatisfaction, but of one we can be practically certain: Will this not continue to make our children simple imitators? Will it not teach them to do only what they had been doing under the supervision of the teacher?

Such a danger exists. It will exist as long as one person attempts to teach another. It is impossible to totally avoid such a possibility in a teaching-learning process—nor should one strive to do so. Elements of imitative activity are inherent in the teaching-learning process. The thing to strive for is to prevent imitative activity from dominating the teaching-learning process, to give the students ever-greater independence with ever-increasing elements of creativity—in class, in home assignments, in tests.

4.6.5. The extent to which we give people the opportunities to independently analyze problem situations, solve essentially new problems, and do essentially new assignments depends only on us. Only we can teach them to independently choose the way and carry out the process

277

of problem solution in the broadest sense of the word. Only we can teach our children creativity, enriching their lives with creative individuality, and give them the joy and happiness of independent creativity for life.

Educators must commence this titanic labor in kindergarten and build it up until completion of graduate school. Otherwise, if five- or six-year-old children are in the hands of ignorant teachers, the process of fostering a creative individual will be extremely delayed and become totally inaccessible to most—even talented—people.

4.6.6. A modern nation must teach and educate its children in such a way as to achieve at every lesson a merger of the teaching and learning process into a single process of creative activity of the teacher and the students. This process will rear creatively thinking people capable of creative activity. These people will acquire diversified experience of creative activity in school and in college. They will be able to feel the joy and happiness of creativity in at least its elementary manifestations in all forms of independent work. These people will then attempt to imbue every step of their professional activity with independence, active thought, and creativity. These are the people who will be capable of preserving modern civilization.

4.6.7. Our children are unable to write in their own language as well as in the language of mathematics. They are incapable of distinguishing between the representation of, for example, the solution of an equation and the proof of an identity.

Our education has experienced a catastrophe, the scope and tragedy of which is unprecedented in the world history of education. Students don't know how to use the equal sign—and this is the rule rather than the exception. No one has ever taught them this, either in or outside of class. No one has ever verified their solutions step by step, either in class or in home assignments. They rush to the answer, in their haste omitting symbols and losing sight of the content of the problem.

Often a correct answer results from the student's manipulation with symbols without the slightest idea of what is taking place. Students do not understand the type of problem, neither its form nor its content. They don't understand why it can be solved a certain way. If both sides of an equation can be multiplied by a number other than zero, why not multiply an algebraic or transcendental expression by such a number? They don't understand why it can't be done. Why can't an algebraic or transcendental expression be raised to a power to simplify it? How can the solution of a problem be improved using permissible methods and operations? What operations are permissible in some circumstances and impermissible in others? What are all these circumstances and all these operations?

These are the people we keep on giving tests and tests and nothing else. When analyzing a problem after a test there is no possibility of achieving anything useful: the student is incapable of comprehending where he went wrong.

4.6.8. Ongoing training of teachers and students and the daily and hourly requirement that they meet certain reasonable demands—not by means of tests alone—should be the law of the academic process. Active participation in all lessons enables the students to fully and comprehensively understand the need for and legitimacy of every step in the work being done. Such work, when supervised by the teacher and combined with efforts to fill in the gaps in the students' knowledges, skills, and habits, yields results that few inexperienced teachers expect.

As mentioned before, many weak students catch up with and outpace stronger students. The reason is that they became weak in the first place not through any deficiencies in their natural abilities but through the fault of ignorant teachers who failed to teach them how to study, through the fault of that essentially reactionary creation that we call the country's educational system. Many formerly strong students begin to lag behind formerly weak students because their natural qualities are, in fact, lower. They were simply fortunate enough to acquire knowledges, skills, habits and standards of intellectual, creative, and cognitive abilities that had been inaccessible to the others through no fault of their own.

4.6.9. During the initial years of their educational work teachers must make a point of discussing with more experienced educators the extent of the requirements they impose on their students, including the level of tests. This should be done in the mini-research format, otherwise the students will be dissatisfied that the course is either too simple and primitive or prohibitively difficult. They will quickly come to ignore and even despise both the course and the teacher.

Demands upon students may have to be urgently varied. This should never be done hastily or abruptly. When requirements are raised the teacher should devote a maximum of attention to the weaker students both during and after lessons. However, it should be remembered that after firm relations have been established with the class it is always difficult to change them in any direction, whether towards increasing or reducing requirements.

4.6.10. Every lesson, test, and home assignment should contain questions and problems that are difficult for all the students, the strong as well as the weak. By their very presence they make the course intensive and sufficiently interesting for all the students. Don't be disappointed if initially only a few students display interest in and respect for such problems. If you work with your students regularly and keep their tasks and assignments within their powers, they will gradually develop a liking for your subject and your tests. They will get to appreciate your exactingness toward yourself and toward them. They will experience the joy of success, the joy of victory over the course and themselves, and the happiness of independent creative activity.

Our purpose should be to have every student look forward to each test with anticipation. No pseudoscientific and quasi-scientific games, charades, or show lessons can replace the honest, intense, competent work of the teacher and the students, work which is by its very nature difficult. That is why we must dwell in special detail on certain aspects of education. To the layman this may seem boring or incomprehensible. To the specialist it should, at the very least, be comprehensible.

4.6.11. Dear educators! Your students should realize that during previous lessons you gave them about as much as you will require of them today and in the future. In that case, your analysis of the test will be interesting and bring joy and satisfaction even to those who got lower grades. This will most surely happen, because the students know that under your system of work with them—honest, devoted, and conscientious—and under your system of testing—exacting, strict, but fair—they will perform better on the next test than they did on the last.

In other words, a student's performance throughout the whole sequence of tests should be dependent only on how diligently, effectively, conscientiously, and honestly both of you work during the lesson and at home. Every student should be confident that all your tests will be within the power of all of them and just hard enough to make them interesting for all—the weak, the strong, and the average.

4.6.12. Several problems in the test should be beyond the powers of most of the class, but within those of the top students. The teacher should inform the students that such problems exist, stating their numbers if the class as a whole is not very strong. If the class is strong let the students decide the relative difficulty of the test problems for themselves.

In other words, all tests should include problems that do not have to be solved by all the students. The students themselves should decide whether to solve them of not. If you don't include such problems in your tests many of the stronger students will stop working altogether.

4.6.13. Several initial problems should be easy so as to reduce nervous tensions. The other problems, of sharply varying degrees of difficulty, should be scattered randomly throughout the test, and not in the order in which the relevant theoretical material was studied, otherwise the number of a problem in the test will indicate its difficulty and method of solution. One of the difficult stages in the solution of any problem is the evaluation of its difficulty and selection of the ways, means, and methods of solving it. This is a purely creative process, if the problem isn't so obvious that its solution is automatically associated with a known algorithm. For example, add $\frac{1}{3}$ and $\frac{1}{2}$; find

$$D_x \frac{2x + 1}{x}; \quad \int d\sin x, \int \sin^2 x \, dx;$$

solve the equation $\log_3(x^2 - 1) = \log_3 x - \log_3 2$, and so on. We refuse to see even elements of creativity in all these and similar problems.

4.6.14. At present we reduce analyses of tests to having students copy the solutions of problems they failed to solve and answers of questions they failed to answer. This work is usually boring, leaving many students with nothing to do and gradually building up feelings of resentment in them.

4.6.15. One desirable feature of a test is a diversity of methods of solving problems and analyzing problem situations.

We fully realize how difficult it is for an educator to find such problems and problem situations when preparing a test and how difficult it is to check it. This is when the students come most unexpectedly to our aid. Educators with sufficient experience of compiling and checking tests know that students frequently suggest methods and devices for solving problems of which we teachers never suspected. In addition, mutual help among teachers helps to reveal a variety of interesting problems in the possession of different teachers. This alone is capable of substantially improving the quality of our tests.

Looking for the simplest and/or most interesting solution of a problem or answer to a question teaches students not only how to look for variants of problem solutions but also how to compare them and determine the merits and demerits of each.

This work is a form of creativity and should be conducted regularly. It teaches the students how to find the best variant of solving a problem situation or any creative problem in general, in any sphere of human activity: political, economic, scientific, or military.

The selection of problems, questions, and problem situations to be included in a test should not be based on the diversity of ways in which they can be solved. We have mentioned diversity of methods of solution not because it is absolutely essential or because it should be a guiding principle in determining the content of a test. Diversity of ways of solving problems is desirable, but no more. It offers an opportunity for thoughtful analysis of tests, with the natural active involvement and interest of both strong and weak students.

4.6.16. One convenient method of analyzing a test is to have several students chosen by the teacher, perhaps five or ten, simultaneously solve problems or analyze problem situations on several blackboards. Some of these students should be those who solved their problems during the test, the others those that did not but, by the time of the class analysis, already knew the solutions.

Five or ten solutions written on blackboards are good only when all but one can be concealed by a screen or curtain. Ten solutions written out one after another as they are discussed by the students take up too much time.

4.6.17. Only one problem of the five or ten on the blackboards should be discussed at a time. This should be done at a fast pace, rapidly firing questions at the students so as to involve them all in the work. The discussion of the problem should substantiate every stage in its solution. When the problem has been discussed it should be screened or erased from the blackboard before proceeding to the next one. The students who had solved the problem being discussed earlier should be involved primarily in justifying the solution rather than actually solving it.

4.6.18. What about a problem that no one, or almost no one, had managed to solve? Such problems should be solved by the teacher with the active involvement of the whole class. He should write the solution on the blackboard, asking the class to prompt him as he goes, also explaining and justifying the procedures. He helps the class analyze the problem by dividing it into sequential, partial problems which enable the students to find the overall solution.

4.6.19. When discussing tests you should choose the students to be called to the blackboard at your own discretion, paying little or no attention to the appeals of those students, weak or strong, who appear eager to do the solution in front of the class. Of course, if a student fails to solve a problem you should call another to the blackboard. The thing to avoid, however, is the creation of a privileged caste of students who are frequently called to the blackboard or asked to answer questions because they continually raise their hands or look pleadingly at you. You should call to the blackboard the strong, as well as the weak and average, students.

Dealing with students who keep pleading for attention is not always easy. Such pleading is usually indicative of things we teachers often fail to understand.

If the student pleading to be called to the blackboard is not very strong and the problem is fairly difficult, it is best to have a look at the student's solution before calling him to the blackboard. If his solution is wrong, don't have him solve the problem. Instead, find one he has solved and ask him to do it at the blackboard.

It is often a weak student delighted at having been able to solve one or two problems who pleads to be called to the blackboard. Having him come up to the board of his own free will could display his failure in front of the class and make him the butt of sarcastic jokes. The result will be the ridicule of a person who until then had probably been taught little or nothing. But after years of working on each course under the supervision of teachers who may be experienced or inexperienced, but are always well-disposed towards the students and who are continuously taught, a once illiterate and helpless student—who had pleaded to come to the blackboard to show off what could have been his very first achievement, at least in his eyes—can grow up to become an energetic and knowledgeable specialist, honest and bubbling with life, a proud and equal member of human society.

4.6.20. It is highly desirable to select the students to be called to the blackboard in advance, while the teacher corrects the test. The selection is simple enough: Choose those students who solve the problem during the test flawlessly. This helps encourage the students who need it to have faith in themselves and their forces.

When you know your class and every student for several years you can judge, when checking problem solutions, the extent to which the mistakes they make are fortuitous in some cases, typical in others, and inexplicable in yet others.

As a rule, incorrectly solved problems should not be done on the blackboard. However, if many students make a common mistake you should analyze it on the blackboard. Sometimes you may call on one of the students who made the mistake. There is nothing humiliating for him in this, provided you explain to the class that most students made it and it is necessary to analyze its causes. It is a good idea to call to the blackboard one of those students whose work effort seems to have slackened lately. A talk with such a student at the blackboard involving the whole class can serve as a signal that you haven't forgotten him and have no intention of forgetting him in the future.

Many, if not most, of the weaker students are usually quiet and inconspicuous. They have developed the firm conviction that they are forgotten and no one cares about them. It is the teacher's job to constantly show them that they are wrong—not in words and homilies, but in deeds, work, and exactingness toward them and himself.

4.6.21. As mentioned before, the problems solved on the blackboard should be analyzed successively. All the students should be gradually and consistently conditioned to the idea of working together with the teacher on the same item. Therein lies the basic meaning of a group of students being taught by one teacher. All forms of work of the students with each other should be left, as much as possible, to the students after classes. The simultaneous work of teacher and class on the same question is a characteristic feature of the lesson. There may be exceptions, such as when the students are given the opportunity to work during class independently without the teacher. But this is done only to be immediately followed up by an analysis of that work to pinpoint its merits and demerits and the ways of consolidating the former and eliminating the latter.

The teacher comes to the classroom to teach the students actively, purposefully, and selflessly, not to observe their independent floundering, which may be hilarious and even to some degree useful, but which has no place at an instructive lesson. Nothing the students can do out of class without the teacher should be done in class. During the lesson the teacher should work together with the students only on those things that they cannot do without him.

4.6.22. When analyzing a problem on the blackboard, avoid asking the traditional question "Is everything clear?" It should never be asked. Students rarely respond to it. Teachers ask it frequently, year after year, for their own peace of mind, but not to establish whether the students have really understood or failed to understand a question. Moreover, both the teacher and the students know this. This question and others like it—"Any questions?" "Do you understand?"—are not just totally useless; they are very harmful to a teaching and educating academic process. Students virtually never react to such questions, even when they are completely in the dark.

We will repeat this over and over again: To ask the teacher a question means to engage in a discussion of it with him. Not many students are capable of this. Students are afraid of revealing ignorance of things they may be supposed to know. They don't venture to discuss a subject they don't understand. It's too big a risk. Educators of all ranks should take note of this. Very few students who really know the subject ever ask the teacher questions. The rest ignore his offer to ask questions. This offer has become empty, phony, and totally meaningless; it creates an appearance that the students' knowledges are up to par and is therefore extremely harmful at all levels of education, including graduate school. It is a fig leaf with which we attempt to cover the ignorance, absence of activity, incompetence, fallacy, and phoniness of the so-called educational system. We use the question to falsely reassure, or pretend to reassure, ourselves and others. Recall the tone in which we ask the question—it is the tone of a person confident that it is, to say the least, stupid to ask such trivialities. Recall when we ask the question—when we are erasing the blackboard to deny the students the possibility of returning to the discussion of a question which we find difficult and unpleasant. We are either afraid of it or simply want to avoid a long and boring answer. Gradually, but surely and consistently, we create an appearance of well-being in class, a class which is actually dominated by ignorance and insincerity, a class in which all the students have long since ceased to respond to the question—just as no one responds to the daily, "How are you today?"

More and more frequently the teacher encounters eyes smoldering with anger and hate for intuitively felt falsehood. He calmly shifts his glance and peers into the distance before dutifully proceeding to the next stage of his work, which has been so thoughtlessly placed on his weak shoulders by a society that has no concern for it.

It is the teacher's duty to constantly confront his students with questions. He must think over and prepare in advance questions of the type: Why can this be done? Why is it done? What alternative variants are there? What are their relative merits? What will happen if we change the conditions thus? Why have these data been introduced into the problem? How do they affect the solution process?—and so on, and so forth.

Naturally, only a highly knowledgeable teacher can handle such work.

All this is not to mean that questions like, "Is anything unclear?" or "Who has any suggestions?" should never be asked. We should not, however, rely solely on them, which is just the case in our country. Sole reliance on such questions is tantamount to turning the academic process into a monstrous farce and a triumph of insincerity, inaction, and cruelty, with respect to our educators and our children.

We repeat again: If students refuse to ask questions even after being sincerely encouraged to do so, this is not indicative of anything at all. It means either all the students have understood everything and are even beginning to assimilate that knowledge—which is virtually impossible; or no one has understood anything and they are all discouraged—which is much more probable; or some have understood, some

284

have not, some have partially understood, and some have misunderstood—which is usually the case at every lesson. Despite this—and that is the point—every student should come away from the lesson not only with a complete understanding of everything that was going on, but also with having already assimilated 70 or 80 percent of it.

4.6.23. We are analyzing a lesson variant in which, say, the solutions of ten problems from a test are written simultaneously by students on the blackboard. The teacher must select the students beforehand (when preparing the lesson) with an eye on presenting the best solutions suggested by all the students, though not necessarily. The students called to the board to present sample solutions should include strong, average, and weak students. This is not hard to achieve since every test has both difficult and simple problems.

When analyzing a test, the problems written on the blackboard should follow the sequence in which the study material needed to solve them was presented during the course. This is not always possible because the most interesting and useful problems are those whose solutions require methods, concepts, and ideas from different sections of the course. Such problems are frequently the most difficult ones, which is why they should be among the last problems used to analyze the test.

4.6.24. The teacher asks questions on different stages of the problem solution and also discusses possible variants of the solution of the whole problem or the individual stages. It is absolutely essential to ask questions of the following type: "Why does the problem statement include this comment, this fact, this information?" "What will happen if it is replaced by other information, namely. . . ?" "Why has this step been made in the solution?" "Can it be omitted or simplified?" and so on.

When a test is analyzed this way no one is bored—neither the strong students nor the weak, neither those who solved the analyzed problem nor those who failed. Questions asked by the teacher are extremely important for the development of the intellectual, creative, and cognitive abilities of all the students. If the teacher doesn't do this work when analyzing a test, virtually none of the students will ever think about such questions.

4.6.25. Work in class on tests after they have been given can and should take different forms. It should, as far as possible, not be repetitive. We are sure that teachers will not simply mimic us. Every teacher can develop his own, inimitable style of work with students. He will develop the forms of that work and the methods that prove best both for him and his students. However, it is essential that teaching and learning activity and any innovations that may be introduced into the classical teaching-learning process be discussed. They must be discussed, observed, studied, and evaluated by the teachers and administrators from one's own and other educational establishments.

4.6.26. While several students are writing the solutions of problems from the test on the blackboard, the teacher works with the rest on one of the problems from the analyzed test. In this case he must make sure that the students at the blackboard have all solved that problem correctly during the test. Such a beginning makes it possible to start the lesson at once with the teacher's own analysis of the test, and thereby set the right pace and atmosphere for what is bound to be a difficult and intense lesson.

4.6.27. As mentioned before, it is all right to have several students at the blackboard simultaneously, writing several solutions of test problems. After that, the entire class can be asked to check all the solutions on the blackboard, compare them with their own solutions, and ask the teacher as many questions as they like. When this is over it is the teacher's time to ask questions, such as "Why?" "What for?" "What if this or that is changed in the statement or solution?", and so on. This form of test analysis, like the variant of discussing all the problems one by one, again goes to show that it is, at the very least, naive to rely on academic feedback based solely on questions asked by the students. Students are incapable of independently performing all the stages of analysis and synthesis leading to the solution of a problem. They solve many problems semi-intuitively. There is nothing wrong with that. However, only the stronger students are concerned with justifying a solution and every step in it. The weaker students do not immediately realize either the need for such justification or its nature. The same is true of alternate solutions, simpler and more refined solutions, and the variation of the data in problem statements and the consequences of such variations.

4.6.28. It is our contention that even the strong students are incapable of doing all this work without help and guidance from the teacher. If anyone assumes that tests in classes are analyzed only by strong students and only for the benefit of the weak students, he is gravely mistaken. Test analyses suggest new variants of solutions, their comparative value, and their justification. These are things the students cannot do themselves, neither the weak nor the strong. It is another thing to say that the strong students are strong precisely because they often—though not always—do this work better. However, not to teach either the strong or the weak on that basis is one of the tragic qualities of our educational system.

After analyzing the first problem we proceed on to each one successively. Each analyzed problem is erased from the blackboard or blocked with a screen, all for the same purpose: The teacher and all the students should work, as far as is possible, simultaneously on the same problem or problem situation. This is a basic method of mass education. There is nothing that can replace or substitute for simultaneous work of all the students on the same question, but it can and must be supplemented.

4.6.29. While some students are writing solutions on the blackboard the others can be offered an entirely new problem, i.e., one which was not in the test. It should not be too simple. Ideally the solution should reveal to the students the cause or causes of the most frequent error on the test. The problem should also be capable of a quick solution so as not to distract the class from the main purpose of the lesson: analysis of the test. The problem is analyzed immediately after all the students have written the test problems on the blackboards and covered them with screens. Questions should be addressed mainly to those students who were not busy at the blackboard and were given the supplementary problem. The solution of this problem should be written out by the teacher himself in a place reserved for this on the blackboard. It should be done rapidly to leave more time to analyze the test.

If the test has more problems than can be written in class simultaneously on all the blackboards, the procedure should be repeated, each time very thoroughly, carefully, and without haste. Then there will be no need to rely on consultations, which no one ever attends.

4.6.30. One of the variants of work devoted to analyzing tests is for the teacher to require the students to resubmit the same tests with solutions of all the problems that had not been solved or had been poorly solved. Such assignments should, however, be given sparingly, because they tend to shift the brunt of the teaching-learning process to the students' shoulders.

In this connection we would like to warn educators that in a new class this process of assigning for homework exercises that were not completed during a test may have to be repeated several times for the same test. This is because many of the students may not be able to do these assignments even in the calmer atmosphere of home, where help and assistance may be received from different quarters. This should be mentioned to the students: They can get any help from any source they can for this work. Otherwise we will be asking too much of them. Avoidance of such situations—i.e., requiring things a student cannot be expected to do—is an extremely important prerequisite for a well-organized academic process.

If, after several attempts by many students, some of the exercises from the test still remain unsolved, this means that they should not have been included on the test in the first place. Apparently, dear educators, you were not able to give the students all they needed to be up to the mark you require. You should thoroughly analyze your own recent work and that of the students. You should also seek the help and advice of a more experienced teacher or administrator. It is a good idea to invite them to attend one or several of your lessons so as to get an objective answer to a very serious question: Have you been making some pedagogical mistakes resulting in inadequate training of your students, even according to your own standards? You may have gone on to a new question before the students had adequately understood or digested the previous one. Or maybe you have been committing pedagogical errors when presenting theoretical materials and exercises in class and in homework. If assignments are too small or too simple, even for the weak students, or two big and difficult, even for the strong ones, the academic process will inevitably collapse—nor may this take all that much time.

If you gave a test that proved too difficult for the students, and this became apparent only when you started checking it, there may be no point in even marking the students' papers. The best thing to do is, at the very next lesson, solve frontally with the class all the problems of the test; or perhaps you could solve all the problems, reproduce the solutions, and hand them out to the students together with the test, explaining that you had somewhat overestimated the students' capabilities. This, however, should not discourage them because after a while they will make up for it. This should also be done in the case of some home assignments.

4.6.31. It is impossible to list, still less analyze, all the variants of lessons devoted to analyzing tests. They are truly innumerable. We cited just a few with the sole purpose of offering some examples of such lessons without claiming any universal application. We hope that they can prove useful, at least to some degree, to schoolteachers and college instructors. We do not doubt that with time the department faculties in every educational establishment will develop many more diversified and interesting lessons. We are currently speaking of lessons at which the teacher performs one of his most important and most difficult pedagogical duties: teaching all the students and analyzing the work they have done independently.

Let us briefly examine several more variants of a teacher's work with a class during analysis of tests.

If only two or three problems of the test presented difficulties and the rest were not interesting enough to be discussed specifically, you should successively analyze only the most difficult problems. In this case you shouldn't call on anyone for help. The very fact that there is a student at the blackboard and the teacher is working with him breeds a sense of comfort in the others. It involuntarily but invariably reduces their attention and the intensity of work. Now you should work at the blackboard yourself. You ask several questions, the answers to which cover the whole solution process of the problem. You should, as before, ask questions of the type, "Why is this fact given in the statement of the problem?" "Where is it utilized in the solution?" "Why and for what purpose do we carry out the next step of the solution?" "How can the problem be solved differently, using a different method?" "What would change in the solution if the statement of the problem contained different data instead of the given ones, for instance. . . ?", and so on.

Discussion of only some of the most interesting and difficult problems of a test during a lesson is one of the most effective and widespread variants of such work at all stages of instruction. It requires less time during the lesson and greater independence of the students.

Whatever form of discussing tests you employ, you should, as mentioned before, require all the students to hand in complete and detailed solutions of all the problems they failed to solve or in which they made mistakes during the test.

Be brave, dear teachers, be brave and don't despair. Some students will continue to make mistakes, even in those problems that you thoroughly discussed in class. Usually this happens when the class is new. This situation, which may horrify the nonteacher, will continue, not for a week or two, but for several months. It all depends on the level of training you inherited with the class and how seriously the students have appreciated your unswerving determination to teach them all. Don't be surprised and don't despair. With some students you will have to repeat such procedures several times with the same test. This doesn't mean that the students are retarded or uneducated or incapable of doing such work. They simply have never been taught that it is their duty to do everything the teacher requires. Obviously, we are speaking of requirements they are capable of coping with.

4.6.32. Most teachers wisely forbear from analyzing tests and independent student assignments because the lesson develops into a protest, a rebellion of the students against everyone and everything. The students work themselves into a rage; the teachers, too. The lessons turn into a series of events unworthy of a civilized person. The consequences vary widely according to the personality of the teacher, the degree of his ignorance and aggressiveness, the makeup of the class, and the degree of its ignorance and aggressiveness.

When the academic process reaches such a stage of disintegration it is virtually impossible to ever set it right. Any positive result is possible only if the new teacher is extremely talented and devoted to his profession and to children. Furthermore, the students must not yet have become implacable enemies of the school, the college, and all those people who are, in their opinion, the cause of all their troubles. Children are convinced that education has been made a torment by their enemies and tormentors, i.e., the teachers, who have turned their childhood and youth, their present and future, into an endless state of stagnation, groveling, humiliation, falsehood, and deceit. They enter life without a future, if they don't opt—under the direct influence of our educational system—for what they see as a future of heroism, romance, hope, accomplishment, glory, devoted friendship, and mutual assistance: the life of a professional criminal.

4.7. THE TEACHER'S ABILITY TO CONDUCT A LESSON

4.7.1. The success of a lesson depends on how well the teacher prepares for it, how well the students do their homework in preparation for it, and on the work done by the teacher and the students during the previous lessons. Especially important is work conceived by the teacher and performed by the students for the specific purpose of assuring the lesson's success.

The success of a lesson also depends on the inherent capabilities of the teacher and the students; on their erudition and general culture; on the level of the knowledges, skills, and habits and intellectual, creative, and cognitive abilities of the teacher and the students; on the mood of the teacher and the students on the day of the lesson. A lesson also depends on the teacher's unswering will to achieve success in pursuance of its main objective, the feasibility of that objective, and on many, many, other things pertaining to the lesson which we still don't know but which we will strive to know for as long as the world exists.

The process of cognition of the lesson is infinite. Some ideas will be found to be erroneous and will be dropped; others will gradually become obsolete and be either updated and improved or rejected. The lesson has never been, and never will be, governed by universal laws suitable for all lessons, regardless of time, the educational system, the level attained by human society, the level of development of the nation, or the level of development of the social sciences in general and educational science, in particular. All this is doubtlessly so, but there are also eternal and absolute truths regarding the lesson. At least, that is how we see it.

One such truth of tremendous importance for the success of the eternally living lesson is the great talent of active teaching. The teacher must be capable of acting in accordance with what he knows about the class as a whole and each student in particular, what he wishes to achieve at the lesson, and the feasibility of that objective today. This objective must be evaluated neither yesterday nor tomorrow, but today, given the teacher's own state and that of his pupils—passive, active, apathetic, aggressive, kind, tolerant, calm, irritated, angry, enraged, or depressed—which can decisively affect the lesson. No single person is capable of foreseeing everything in every detail and without mistake, in advance and outside of the classroom, even if he has worked with the class for several years. However, a teacher can and should sense and evaluate all this as soon as he enters the classroom, or at least after the first few words uttered by himself or any of the students.

After sensing and evaluating, if only approximately, what he will have to deal with, the teacher must make an immediate decision, fateful for the whole lesson. He must decide whether to commence and continue the lesson as he had conceived and repeatedly analyzed it, or to get off to an unanticipated start differing in part or in whole from his original plans.

4.7.2. We would like to repeat one of the reasons why we are so insistent in declaring the need for many-year courses conducted by the same teacher with the same class, i.e., with the same student body. It is that the better the teacher knows his class, its capabilities, and requirements, the closer the lesson he prepares will correspond to the class for

290

which it is designed. A class, however, can never be entered twice, just as it is impossible to enter the same river twice.

Even more importantly, extended work with the same body of students offers the possibility of conducting an effective and instructive lesson even if it is impromptu. This happens when the prepared lesson cannot be conducted efficiently because the class rejects it for some reason or other. The class has fun while the teacher struggles at the blackboard to clarify questions that, on this day, the students happen to be totally indifferent to. If the teacher fails to spot this at the very outset of the lesson and forges ahead, or if he immediately takes offense and starts to lecture the class, the academic process will suffer a grave blow. Relations between the class and the teacher may suffer or disappear altogether.

Another scenario is also possible: upon receiving an assignment to independently think over the statement and conditions of some problem and suggest a plan for solving it, the students start poring over the statement with remarkable zeal and diligence. However, within a few minutes it becomes apparent that the class has no intention of working.

After working with a class for many years the teacher gains intimate knowledge of the lesson in that class. He learns to understand and predict the state of the class, both in advance and during the first few minutes of the lesson. He is therefore able to conduct the lesson successfully, even if he wrongly predicted the state the class would be in when he was preparing for it.

In other words, any educator can acquire firm skills and habits needed to conduct a lesson successfully if he has had the time needed to study the class. It takes a year or more to get to know a class of thirty or forty students. Those who have spent much time conducting many-year courses know this only too well.

The nation's educational system has confronted its teachers with numerous insoluble problems, one of which is how to successfully teach unfamiliar students. It takes a genius of education to accomplish this. In any nation there may be no more than a dozen such teachers.

Finding themselves in a totally hopeless situation, educators don't even consider a successful academic process. They have no idea what it is. That is why our children are also confronted with one of an infinite multitude of insoluble problems: how to independently and successfully acquire knowledges, skills, and habits in the sciences they are studying. Only a handful of highly talented children are capable of this.

4.7.3. One can offer countless recipes, injunctions, and suggestions about what a teacher should do, depending on the state of the class and the purpose and content of the lesson. They are all useless, however, if the teacher has insufficiently mastered the great science of conducting a lesson.

In our profession everything is important. Still, we would like to dwell on certain essential traits with which an effective teacher and a useful lesson should be endowed.

291

The Lesson and the Teacher are closely interrelated. A lesson cannot be created without a competent teacher. Moreover, there must also be students capable of professionally reacting to the teacher; to his actions during the lesson; to his words, expression, gestures, and tone of voice; to his thoughts and ideas. The teacher brings all this into the classroom and must attempt to create something absolutely unique, out of this world, and forever new and inimitable: the Lesson. He must create it that day and hour.

From the moment the teacher walks into the classroom there is not a moment to be wasted: he must immediately breathe life into the lesson—otherwise it will die before ever seeing the light of day. It can't be created at once, in one instant. Therein lies our tragedy, because students refuse to pay in advance before they get the lesson. They refuse to wait until the lesson makes its appearance. Therefore, the teacher must quickly introduce something new, interesting, or promising. The light of the future lesson must illumine the classroom as soon as the teacher enters it. From the very first moments there should be not two but three entities in the classroom: the teacher, the students, and the lesson. All three are instantaneously bound together, each controlling and helping the other.

4.7.4. A teacher without interests or education, denied competent help in school and in college, who is in a hurry to wind up that sacred thing he just began to create, i.e., the lesson, dooms everything living and sacred for the school and college. He murders lesson after lesson, student after student. He is joined by others. All together they doom all that is great and sacred, without which an educational establishment inevitably turns into a house of the dead, filled and eternally replenished with deceased lessons, deceased students, and deceased teachers.

Long before he starts the lesson the teacher should be inspired and imbued with the will and resolve to triumph over all forces that could keep him from pooling his efforts with professional students to create a new shrine, a new lesson. The teacher's will and resolve should be etched on his face as he enters the classroom. This can happen only if he has thoroughly prepared for the lesson. That makes it his creation. He will relinquish it to no one. Together with his students he will make it living, cheerful, and instructive.

The teacher will not waver in the face of bellicose ignorance or misbehavior. He has nothing to fear, because he has prepared for the lesson.

4.7.5. Today we originate lessons that are buried alive by people who were never taught how to create them, like people are taught to create automobiles, watches, earth satellites, and everything else.

More often than not the teacher doesn't even attempt to join with the students in creating a living, omnipotent lesson because he has no idea what that is. It is a creation that is sometimes merry, always businesslike and concerned, sometimes very interesting, and always and invariably instructive and educating—for better or for worse. It is all in the hands of the lesson and the hands of the teacher.

4.7.6. If there are only two elements in the classroom—the teacher and the students or the students and a substitute for the lesson, some assignment given by the teacher who then ended his mission—the triad is dead. The lesson is dead. If this happens regularly, the children either cry or laugh, unhappy and humiliated, deprived of all that they came to the school and the classroom for—to be students of the teacher and the lesson. Children do not suspect and are incapable of understanding or appreciating the trouble they are in, the fate that lies in store, the number of the best years of their lives they will spend suffering in cruel, school dungeons where they will be tormented by equally tormented teachers. Our unfortunate children don't realize how much of their lives they will waste in hopeless attempts to learn something and acquire something, how many of them will foresake everything and end up in a world of dangerous people rejected by society. So innocent and naive today, tomorrow they will be predatory, bloodthirsty thieves and avenging killers. Some may be capable and talented people, but they will take their revenge on society, perhaps not even realizing it themselves, for their ravaged and trampled life, for years of humiliation and useless, deadening work.

4.7.7. At the lesson every student must more or less clearly formulate for himself or hear from the teacher: What is happening now, at this moment? Perhaps the teacher is summing up the preceding lesson to make the current one, as far as is possible, a natural sequel of the previous one; perhaps the class is now working on an assignment needed to expand upon the current lesson; perhaps the teacher has launched a discussion with the class as a prelude to the introduction of new material, or as a means of reproducing previously studied material needed to expand subsequent stages of the lesson, et cetera. When the teacher clearly formulates the assignment for each subsequent stage of the lesson, together with a definition of that stage, this organizes the lesson and gives it purpose. It immediately involves the whole class in the work on the new stage of the lesson, without long and boring declarations or soliloquies by the teacher. It demonstrates the educator's unswerving will and resolve to conduct each stage of the lesson effectively, with the participation of all the students, and to conclude it to the benefit of all the students so as to similarly tackle the next stage—and, thus, step by step, to the end of the lesson.

The teacher should fairly frequently ask the class questions such as: What are we about to do? How will we do it? What is the purpose of this work? Similar questions should also be asked at the end of each stage of the lesson and the lesson as a whole: What have we just done? How have we done it? Why did we do this work, i.e., for what purpose? And, finally, a question that should be asked at the end of *every* lesson: What new things did you understand and assimilate at the lesson?

4.7.8. It is especially important to draw the students' attention to the stage of the lesson most directly linked with the independent work they will be doing at home. As a rule, giving the home assignment should be more than merely listing the numbers of the exercises in the textbook. The teacher must discuss some of the exercises of the home assignment that may be too difficult and will almost certainly not be solved without preliminary discussion in class. It is also necessary to take up questions essential for subsequent work in class, which should therefore be done at home with special thoroughness. For example, anticipating that at the next lesson the topic will be $\int_{-\infty}^{+\infty} \frac{dx}{x^2 + 1}$, the home assignment for that lesson should include exercises reviewing the properties and requiring the drawing of graphs of the functions $y = \tan x$ and $y = \text{arc tan } x$. Otherwise, not only will the students remain totally passive during the next lesson, but they will also fail to understand the concluding stage in the solution of the problem. The teacher will then be forced to go through this stage without involving the students, hurrying and irritated, simply because they have forgotten, or never knew, the properties of the function $y = \text{arc tan } x$. The graph of the function $y = \frac{1}{x^2 + 1}$ can also be included in the home assignment for the lesson, or it can even be discussed while giving the home assignment, if the class's background training is lacking.

LETTER FIVE

HOW TO CREATE A NEW STUDENT

Out of twenty countries, our eighth-grade students ranked the 10th, 8th, 12th, and 16th and 18th for arithmetic, statistics, algebra, and geometry and measurements respectively.
Out of fifteen countries, our twelfth-grade students ranked the 10th, 14th and five times the 12th for precalculus courses and calculus.
        —Second International Mathematics
        Study Summary Report for the United States
        Stipes Publishing Co.: Champaign, Illinois, 1985.

5.1. THE TEACHER TAKES A NEW CLASS

5.1.1. In a new class, the teacher should commence supplementary lessons with those students who need them before any irreversible complications set in. Initially the supplementary work should involve preparation for upcoming lessons and class or home assignments. This will help those students to get involved at an early stage in productive work at the lesson and at home, otherwise the distance between them and the other students will continue to grow. It is essential to pace this work and its intensity at as high a rate as possible, and it should be continued as long as necessary to get all the students actively involved in the class's work.

This takes a tremendous amount of hard work on the part of both the teacher and the students, an effort hardly short of cleaning Augean stables. However, it will pay off within several months or, more often, in a year or so. It all depends on the extent to which the weaker students have fallen behind and on the level of the knowledges, skills, and habits and intellectual, creative, and cognitive abilities of the rest of the class.

5.1.2. All more or less experienced educators are aware of one widespread failing of our students: they never check their work; they don't know how important it is, and even if they do, they don't know how to do it. Time and again, after doing a test or some other independent assignment, a student will, with a triumphant look and happy smile, turn in his work long before the end of the lesson. The next day he discovers with sincere horror and amazement that he has made mistakes in virtually all the exercises.

If the teacher has a new class, he shouldn't punish his students with assignments and tests of even median difficulty without first teaching them the great skill of self-verification. This skill requires titanic and very lengthy efforts on the part of the teacher and the students, and it isn't so easy to learn how to do it. It is totally unrelated to the students' abilities or even the quality of their training throughout their preceding years of schooling. The absence of this skill justly horrifies and discourages both teachers and students.

297

5.1.3. In a new class, the teacher should spare no effort to avoid total student antipathy bred by the fact that when a student makes a mistake the teacher finds it and then punishes the pupil for it. "I studied the material, why do you think I don't know it?"—This is a classic situation even with a good class and a good, perhaps even very good, teacher. If there are too many such statements, accompanied by hostile looks (if not words), it is necessary to beat a hasty retreat. For a while it is best to lower all requirements, without informing the students of this. At the same time they must be told how to prepare the theoretical portion of an assignment at home: read it aloud, striving to comprehend what is read; recapitulate out loud and review the main points without looking into the textbook. At the same time, the teacher should reveal himself, showing how well he can explain the solution of a difficult problem in class. He should then include a similar problem in the home assignment. The teacher shows how well he can explain new theoretical material, prove new propositions, and introduce new concepts, and how interestingly he can pose questions so that it isn't hard—in fact, it is even interesting—to answer them. For the time being he gives small home assignments, which require a minimal degree of independence on the part of the students. He checks them every time, collecting them all, but thoroughly going through only as many as he can—five to seven at this stage, not fewer.

Dear teachers, don't be afraid of grading your students with As and Bs for their assignments. Give them simple tests similar to the class and home assignments, containing a minimal degree of novelty. Continue this subtle game until the hostile looks filled with despair, contempt, or helplessness disappear. The children aren't to blame for the fact that, until you came, no one had ever taught them correctly, that teachers had only pretended to teach them. Gradually and inexorably raise your demands. Easy assignments generate lack of respect for both the subject and the teacher. Give more and more assignments of increasing difficulty, both in and out of class. Check them frequently. Thus, in several months or, more often, a year or so, you will manage to establish an educating and edifying teaching-learning process in the class.

5.1.4. The most terrible situation arises when your new students are unable to distinguish between what is correct and what is wrong. They keep insisting that they are right even after you have thoroughly explained their mistakes, the correct solution, and the right answer. Who among us has not seen hostile, distrustful looks even after a lengthy and detailed answer to a student's question? You must be brave in such classes. At every lesson you should explain the home assignment you are giving. Do this in a much more thorough manner than you have been used to or have seen others do it.

A teacher must combine courage with good training in the field he teaches, otherwise he may not understand what the student doesn't understand. Instead of answering a question, he answers what he *thinks* was asked. That is when he heads for trouble. Nothing and no one can save such a teacher from the class's implacable hostility—a very common scene in our schools today. No one and nothing can save the teacher, except for regularly conducted mini-researches in combination with his utmost efforts in the field he is teaching.

5.1.5. Experienced teachers should see it as their duty to help their new colleagues prepare for lessons. They should discuss their lesson plans and notes and help anticipate the questions that may be asked in class and the answers to them. Obviously, it's impossible to anticipate all questions, but most can be, especially if the lesson is so prepared that they are asked. Day after day, month after month, the teacher should increase his demands both on himself and his students, but in the case of the students he should also follow their reactions attentively. If a majority of the class doesn't or can't understand the teacher, the only thing to do—we repeat this again and again—is to reduce his demands on the class and increase them on himself, thoroughly think out all stages of the forthcoming lesson, and engage in endless mini-researches. Without this sort of effort, either the teacher will be forced to abandon the class, or the class will abandon him. Both happen quite frequently in our country. The main trouble, however, is not that this occurs, but that our educators view this with remarkable equanimity. Our task, they seem to say, is to teach; whether the students understand us and gain anything from our lessons is no concern of ours—it's the students' personal affair. This cruel and essentially helpless point of view is common in virtually all our educational establishments.

5.1.6. Teaching students how to work independently, both in and out of class, is one of the elementary professional duties of the educator. Don't wait for the first test in a new class. Tell the students that when preparing the oral portion of a home assignment, they should first slowly and attentively read the assigned material, starting with review material and only later going over to newly studied matter. When they go over to the new material they should strive to comprehend all the definitions, the meaning of all new concepts and their relationships to formerly introduced concepts, and the proofs of new propositions. During review reading the student should identify and note for himself the theoretical material to be memorized, because comprehension alone is not enough to master new information.

The teacher should not just list the sections in the textbook included in the home assignment. He should give the students precise instructions regarding what to do with those sections, and how to do it: what they should merely comprehend without memorizing and what to memorize so as to be able to reproduce and use it in specific assignments. We discussed this in greater detail in the letters devoted to the teacher and the lesson.

5.1.7. Most students, unfortunately, don't know the difference between understanding and knowledge; we mentioned this incidentally before. This is a terrible and profound tragedy. They say, "I read, I understood, I know," as if this is all one and the same thing. That is why

299

they are unable to use new concepts and propositions when doing exercises, or at least most of them.

We do not mean to say that memorizing new definitions and propositions assures success in a written assignment. We do wish to say, however, that ignorance of factual material, ignorance of definitions and propositions, makes it impossible for the student to do the written part of the assignment at all.

These are banal truths which, however, we feel constrained to emphasize most forcefully. We do this because our educational establishments put our students in a hopeless situation. They fail to orient them on elementary comprehension and subsequent memorization of factual material.

5.1.8. When we rid both students and teachers of the extremely harmful and dangerous system of daily classes in the same subject, the teacher will finally be able to devote himself to fostering an essential skill in his students: the skill of efficiently arranging one's time when doing home assignments. If there are only two lessons a week in one subject, and if that subject is difficult, the student will prepare the same assignment three times a week. In another subject, which he finds easier, he may devote just twenty minutes, and only once a week, to an assignment. Another student may find it best to prepare the same assignment twice a week on two different days. Obviously, endless variants of individualizing the teaching-and-learning process are possible in a format of many-year courses. The children will create those variants themselves, depending on their abilities and requirements, as well as with the help of their continuously learning teachers.

5.2. THE SEARCH AND RESEARCH CHARACTER OF LEARNING

5.2.1. The weaker the class and the younger the students, the more time should be given them before they are required to introduce innovative elements in their work on class and home assignments. Nevertheless, no matter how weak the class, such elements must be present to one degree or another in every lesson and every home assignment, otherwise the level of intellectual, creative, and cognitive abilities will remain stationary, which will lead to the total collapse of the teaching-learning and educating process.

In this country, we educators have applied this essential requirement in our own way. We have reduced the whole teaching, learning, and educating process to the independent work of students, forgetting that, as a rule, they cannot be fully independent during the lesson, otherwise there would be no need for either lessons or teachers. Those educators who see their sole duty in giving home and class assignments should think of this especially carefully. They prefer to disregard the fact that the lesson is a form of instruction quite distinct from independent student work. With the active, professional supervision of an educator, the lesson—and only the lesson—provides the students with an opportunity for intensive, cognitive activity not available in self-education. It is promoted by ways and means, incorporated in the lesson plan, which students studying on their own are incapable of exercising, regardless of the quality and structure of the textbook and study aids. They include:

(1) emotional and instructive dialogue-debates between the teacher and the students;
(2) frontal work with all students in which each suggests his own variant of the next stage in solving a problem in the broadest sense of the word, providing the opportunity to jointly solve problems beyond the capabilities of any student working independently;
(3) dialogue-debates among the students on the next step in analyzing a problem situation, both prior to commencing it and after it is completed;
(4) discussions of the newly studied theoretical material, organized and supervised by the teacher;
(5) discussions devoted to summarizing and structuralizing the studied material during the concluding stage of a specific topic or course;
(6) linking the studied material with material in other fields of learning;
(7) development of the students' oral and written speech;
(8) optimization of the teaching-learning process by the teacher with the help of an optimal—from the point of view of the educational results—blending of the students' work in and out of class;
(9) the teacher's exposition of the basic concepts and ideas of the science on which the study subject is based;
(10) organization by the teacher of a continuous process of consolidating the students' knowledges, skills, and habits—to different degrees for different students, but to some degree for all—in conditions of generated and utilized feedback;
(11) teacher supervision of the development of the students' intellectual, creative, and cognitive abilities with the help of feedback between teacher and students;
(12) generation by the teacher of continuous emotional and intellectual intensity in the class by posing and jointly resolving problems and problem situations, which makes the lesson a successful quest and effective investigation, interesting and exciting to students of all ages, just as any victory is interesting and exciting.

Obviously, before scoring any new victory the students have to master the sum total of knowledges, skills, and habits needed for the successful quests and investigations leading up to that victory. They must also acquire the intellectual, creative, and cognitive abilities sufficient for achieving it.

5.2.2. A teaching, learning, and educating process must display

301

probing and investigative characteristics at all stages regardless of the age or level of development of the students. As they build up their reserve of knowledges, skills, and habits and advance their intellectual, creative, and cognitive abilities—acquired in the process of naive, primitive imitations of quest and investigation during the early stages of education—virtually every lesson can and should become a genuine quest and investigation. It all depends on the teacher, the quality of mini-researches organized by the school management, the quality of supervision of the teacher's work, and the help he gets from a special staff of supervisers and educational administrators specially trained for this.

5.3. TEACHING THE STUDENT HOW TO WORK WITH BOOKS AND THE COURSE

5.3.1. Upon receiving a new class the teacher should not start out by imposing rigid and cruel demands on the students with respect to the theoretical material to be studied. We must be as careful and humane with regard to the students in this as in requirements for doing exercises. Some students come into a new class with the ability to work with a book without anybody's help; others have never done this and have no intention to, because they don't know, or even understand, what it is.

5.3.2. When instructing a new class the teacher should not be in too much of a hurry to assign theoretical material to be studied at home. The reason is that many students will not cope with this work. The result will be a silent but very definite agreement between the teacher and the students that independent assignments can be left undone: many students have been forced into conducting such an experiment with a new teacher, with no ill effects.

The teacher should build up the degree of student independence in studying theoretical questions at home as carefully and gradually as during work with exercises. The theoretical material to be studied at home should be thoroughly analyzed in class: in question-and-answer form, when necessary and possible, or in a monologue or lecture by the teacher, which should always be kept as short as is practicable. In the senior classes the role of lectures in the teaching-learning process should increase so as to teach the students how to listen to and understand another person's speech, a scientific narrative which may not always be easy. We have already spoken of this.

In the system of mini-researches, teachers should be very patiently and thoroughly taught how to work with students during the lesson to the degree necessary and sufficient to assure their successful work at home with the textbook, so as to make such work accessible and interesting.

5.3.3. When teaching students to work with books it is very useful to diversify the methods of gradually involving them in independent and successful activity. Let us offer a few examples.

In class, the teacher asks all the students to read a short (subsequently it will become longer and longer) and possibly complete passage. After they have read it two or three times and digested it, the teacher asks a series of prepared questions, the answers to which cover the basic message of the excerpt.

It is important to warn the students in advance that they should be prepared to immediately answer questions on the section being studied. If this is not done, some students, who lack the habit of active participation in the lesson and prefer to leave all the work for home, will not take part in the work because, in class, they find it too difficult. There are quite a few such children and adults. They may be good students and should not be reprimanded for their inability to work in class. The teacher must reckon with this and not be exceedingly and unjustly demanding when circumstances are objectively favorable for some students and unfavorable for others. Nevertheless, it is necessary to carefully, with understanding of student shortcomings, and consistently strive to overcome them, but without any display of cruelty.

After the students have answered the series of questions posed by the teacher, who deliberately omitted two or three very important questions, he should try to get the students to formulate those unasked questions themselves and then find the answers to them.

Such work should be carried out at the beginning of every course with every new group of students, for as long as the students continue to have difficulty with it. Otherwise we will have committed yet another, and certainly not the last, cruelty by pitting the students against a book and course they are, as yet, incapable of studying.

A new passage is assigned for homework and the students write down the questions they will have to answer at the next lesson.

But this is not all—far from it.

The students should be taught how to independently identify and evaluate the basic contents and fundamental, key questions of the studied course. Initially this work is done in class, and after a while it is included in home assignments. The students should be taught to independently formulate questions in such a way as to gradually learn to formulate only such questions the answers to which exhaust the basic contents of the studied section of the course. They should also be able to answer them. Only after such work on class and home assignments can one go on to the next stage in students' work on the course, giving them both home and class assignments to be done completely independently. However, if the students encounter a situation that is as yet beyond their independent comprehension and learning capability, they should occasionally be helped to formulate some questions, or a series of questions, and the answers to them.

Obviously, with two- or three-month courses such work with the class is impossible. It may sometimes require many months to prevent the studying of a course from becoming a cruel and humiliating experience for the students, resulting in insulting and humiliating attitudes toward a teacher who is unable on his own, without mini-researches, to extricate the class or himself from the quagmire.

5.3.4. Such work on new material should cautiously be filled with blank spots and omissions of some details, or even concepts and their properties and qualities not essential for the current lesson, but which will be required at the next or subsequent lessons. When discussing with the students new material assigned for studying at home, it should be explained that sections of the textbook contain material not dealt with at the lesson deliberately, so as to see how the students will cope with it independently. At the next lesson, the entire material should be thoroughly discussed with the class, praising the students even in cases when, in an ordinary situation, there might have been no need for praise, i.e., when the new material has been thoroughly discussed in class and is being analyzed at the following lesson.

By gradually and carefully increasing the number of blank spots in each theory assignment, as well as the size of each of those spots and the difficulty of the material assigned for home study, the teacher achieves one of the main objectives facing educational establishments. We have in mind teaching students how to work independently with books, a skill that is currently regarded in our educational establishments neither as an objective nor as a result of the educational process, but as a means, virtually at all stages of instruction. Students are totally demolished by difficult and incomprehensible home assignments containing mainly, if not completely, new theoretical material lying beyond their grasp.

5.3.5. The resultant destruction of the educational process is aggravated by two or three dozen exercises given for a single home assignment and covering all exercises from the current section. Very soon the students stop doing their home assignments altogether because they are totally incapable of completing them. They begin to skip lessons because more and more of the material and exercises are totally incomprehensible. In college the number of students attending classes declines precipitously: sometimes all that remain are a few unfortunate beings who follow their teacher with feigned or sincere attention and even affection. After all, the course must be finished.

We should never stop teaching how to work with books, teaching students the great skill of self-learning. The difficulty of courses and textbooks naturally increases with each new academic year, and if the students' cognitive abilities remain at a constant level, it gets harder and harder for them to independently study new, difficult courses and do the required exercises.

Our educators of all levels and ages should refrain from turning school and college courses into courses dominated by an appearance of self-teaching and self-learning. They are duty bound, with the help of more experienced and knowledgeable educators, administrators, and specially trained supervisers—while working in a system of mini-researches—to combine teaching with self-teaching and education with self-education of both the students and themselves. Thus they will gradually enhance the level of the students' cognitive abilities and the degree of their independence and activity in class and home assignments, including assignments requiring the study of theoretical material.

5.4. THE STUDENT'S PREPARATION FOR THE COMING LESSON

5.4.1. Most students should prepare the same home assignment at least twice. Mass studies reveal the effectiveness of this, specifically (1) on the day it is given, when it is easy to recall all the details of the just-finished lesson, and (2) on the day preceding the next lesson, so as to have time to not only understand but also memorize the new material. Of course, such work will become possible only when daily classes in the same subject disappear like a nightmare, like the saddest epoch in the American educational tragedy.

The teacher must keep close track of student activity at every lesson, making sure that every student understands the theoretical material and does all his exercises, in class and at home, thereby preparing him for the next lesson and preventing him from losing touch with the studied course, losing confidence in it, and falling behind in his theoretical studies or exercises. All this is a professional duty, a purely professional commitment—nothing more. It is difficult—it is fantastically difficult—especially during the first few months of work with a new class. However, if the school or college has many-year courses, this extremely difficult stage in the work of both teacher and students can be avoided. Still, we will have to continue for many years to bravely combat student ignorance and the inability of some students, and sometimes whole classes, to prepare successfully for an upcoming lesson, to work diligently and spare no effort, because they have already been corrupted and spoiled by earlier self-learning and do-nothingness.

5.4.2. To help the weaker students, the teacher must work patiently and courageously with them, both in and out of class, to prepare them for the next lesson and prevent or overcome their aversion to the course and their failure to understand it. He must train all the students to regularly and diligently carry out all class and home assignments, theoretical as well as applied. He must involve all the students, the strong as well as the weak, in class debates, constantly and conscientiously raising their level of development, as well as his own. He must make every lesson an event for himself and the students, a holiday prepared in the system of mini-researches.

The teacher must also pay close attention to the strong students. He must regularly supervise their work, aiming for development of intellectual, creative, and cognitive abilities, both in and out of class, and using materials going beyond the course work required of all the students. Thus, day after day, week after week, month after month, every

305

educator can set up a successful teaching-learning and educating process in any class.

5.4.3. During the first years of building up the new educational system, there will be quite a few exceptions—but with each passing year the new system will gain in strength. The number of teachers, classes, and students unable to prepare for each lesson will rapidly decline.

Extensive many-year courses with a constant student body and the same educator—in school as well as during the first years in college—will, by virtue of their very existence, impose high demands on the way the students and the teacher prepare for each lesson, because the quality of many years of work will depend on every lesson. Within the system of mini-researches, lessons will become controllable and highly instructive for all the children, the strong as well as the weak.

We repeat: Every new lesson must be thoroughly prepared to yield tangible results for the educator and the students, results that they can use successfully for many years. By bringing the joy of success, this use will help cultivate students' minds and emotions, their wills, their desire and ability to acquire knowledge independently. It will bring the joy of creative work and happiness to tens of millions of our children and teachers, now condemned to a state of hopeless struggle, helplessness, apathy, and depression.

5.5. INDEPENDENT WORK IN THE PROCESS OF CREATING A PROFESSIONAL STUDENT

5.5.1. One of the prime components of the diversified process of creating a professional student, even more important than tests, is feedback between educator and students based on assignment material for independent work out of class. Of great importance in this connection are discussions on home assignments, led by the teacher and involving all the students of the class. They can help eliminate one of the current failings of almost all school and college students: getting down to work only two or three days before an upcoming test.

5.5.2. The teacher must be taught, with the help of mini-researches, how to work simultaneously with the class as a whole and each student in particular. In the course of discussions he should ask questions that require each student to define concepts, establish the connections between them, and clearly and succinctly justify each step of the assignment. He should also discuss possible variants of doing exercises and justifying them, as well as optimal variants and possible variants of exercises similar in form and content.

5.5.3. In lieu of a discussion the teacher should regularly require the students to present brief but meaningful written answers to different types of questions. This should occupy not more than ten minutes of the lesson, in order to leave sufficient time for instruction. Seven to ten

306

minutes is sufficient for a surprise quiz. Surprise quizzes are necessary to encourage the students to always prepare their assignments for every lesson.

5.5.4. The teacher must require all the students to do their home assignments, although, as mentioned earlier, only some need be collected for checking. From time to time, however, it is necessary to collect all assignments, though again checking only some, while noting whether the rest have been completed or not. Such and similar forms of feedback should be implemented regularly and unswervingly in all subjects; otherwise, the educational process will turn into a farce. The students will soon learn neither to trust their teacher, nor respect him, because he devoted insufficient professional attention to them. No pedagogical innovations can help here.

If one requires the students to work, one must reciprocate with work—work that nothing can replace: honest work performed in large measure in the form of mini-researches. If all we do is demand—by giving tests that are increasingly less meaningful or ostentatiously difficult and that merely sidetrack the efforts of society from the battle against ignorance—the students will grow increasingly embittered. They instinctively realize that they are being bamboozled and treated to a disgusting spectable called school. Over many years filled with useless activity, anger, and hate on the part of the teacher and on the part of the students, the school and college destroy the society that bred them, nurtures them, and is nurtured by them.

5.5.5. A discussion of the material of a home assignment can be conducted without making notes on the blackboard. This is acceptable when the class is strong enough or the exercise is not cumbersome. Even then the teacher should be sure that those students who, for some reason, did not do that exercise can meaningfully follow the operations, their justification, and the assessment of their expediency. In most cases, however, at least some notes should be made on the blackboard. They can be made by the teacher or one of the students. This way we reduce the risk of leaving part of the class in a state of half-bashful or indifferent lack of comprehension, if not total incomprehension.

Whatever the case may be, all students must be required to answer questions. With each passing lesson there should be more and more questions of the type, "Why?" "What for?" "For what purpose?" "Why not do otherwise, like this or like that; what will it lead to?" "Why does the problem statement say this or that?" "What will happen to the solution, how will it change if we change A to B or C in the statement of the problem?"

5.5.6. When question sessions and discussions are systematic, when they accompany all assignments, the need for very thorough checking of the independent assignments of all students gradually declines. Nevertheless, thorough checking of the work of some may be necessary continuously. We would like to add that the more diversified the forms of feedback, the less the probability that the approaches, methods, and devices of working with the class selected by the teacher will cause a negative reaction on the part of the students and the less the probability of such a reaction appearing and becoming a dangerous foe of the successful process of creating a professional student.

5.5.7. The number of student assignments thoroughly checked by the teacher should depend not only on how busy the teacher happens to be on a given day. It should also depend on the composition of the class and its state as a teaching-learning entity: attentive, diligent, indifferent, sleepy, obstinate, et cetera. It should depend on the number of students requiring special help—generally or over a period of time. Some may have missed several lessons and some may have forgotten to do their homework, or have made a habit of not doing it, having concluded that they have already left all the difficulties of the course behind, et cetera.

There are many more cases of children requiring the teacher's special, individualized attention—occasionally or constantly—than we would like to see; but this is beyond our control.

5.5.8. It is our duty not only to give all students knowledge and intellectual, creative, and cognitive abilities; it is also our duty to give all our children the best level of knowledges and intellectual, creative, and cognitive abilities accessible to them. We must do this always, everywhere, in all educational establishments, with the help of active lessons and independent home- and classwork of high scientific standards. We must do this with the help of mini-researches aimed at continuously upgrading lessons as well as the level of development of every teacher and student.

5.5.9. It is most dangerous to turn independent work into no more than a repetition of what was done in class, into no more than a drill, an endless, thoughtless, mad drill—mad because drill assignments are in most cases deadly dull. All independent student assignments should be as intellectually stimulating as when working with the teacher.

5.5.10. As we have said before, in order to put a new class in shape as quickly as possible, it is necessary to start out with assignments that the students, as well as the teacher, have no qualms about coping with. Furthermore, initially the assignments should be very small so that they can be checked thoroughly and the students will be unable to tell themselves that they are too long and there isn't enough time to do them.

The exercises in independent assignments should, as a rule, differ from those done together with the teacher. Some should be easier, some more difficult. The latter, i.e., the more difficult ones, should initially be discussed in one form or another in class. The teacher should ask several questions, the answers to which would offer a basic idea of how to do an exercise. He should then help to partially do some of the exercises orally, leaving the details to the students. This way, during the first few weeks of work with a new class, the educator should be able to convince the students—not in words but in active, thoroughly thought-out and resolute deeds—that independent assignments are a natural continuation of the latest lesson and a prelude to the next one.

308

5.5.11. Independent home assignments should be directly linked with the class lesson: this is fundamental to the educational process. Consistent implementation of this principle is extremely difficult for the teacher, but it is necessary to assure the process's effectiveness.

A lesson given by a teacher in class should be a clearly defined, complete stage of the educational process. As part of that process it should be completed by summarizing and analyzing its results, which should then be used in doing independent home assignments and during subsequent lessons.

5.5.12. As we have said before, it is absolutely essential for the students to perform independent assignments requiring the investigation of results obtained at the lesson and in previously performed assignments. This will gradually create an atmosphere conducive to a successful teaching-learning and educating process. The independent home assignments done by the students within this process should not duplicate class assignments, or vice versa, though they should be connected. They should play a completely independent role, which classroom lessons cannot. We will speak of this in considerable detail in the next section. On the other hand, class lessons, thanks to the presence of a qualified teacher, play a role in the teaching-learning and educating process that home assignments never can.

5.5.13. An instructive and educating teaching-learning process represents an organic unity of class and home education. The relative proportion of each of these forms of study in the teaching-learning process is never constant. It necessarily varies, depending on the age of the students, the current study material and the style of work of the educator, his pedagogical credo, and his pedagogical tastes and convictions.

5.5.14. It takes time and experience for a teacher to learn how to find optimal variants, how best to balance classroom lessons with independent out-of-class studies from the point of view of the effectiveness of learning and the degree of novelty and difficulty for the students. It is absolutely essential to acquire collective experience shared with other teachers in work on mini-researches. Classroom lessons and out-of-class independent work originate, are created, and are perfected in mini-researches. They embody educational skill and educational wisdom: it is the wisdom of an educational research group led by supervisers, educators, and administrators, who may still lack in experience but are sincere people dedicated to our children's upbringing and education, seeking truth and finding it—perhaps not at once, perhaps through a series of mistakes and setbacks. But in a country with millions of school-teachers and college and university professors, truth will triumph. It is here, nearby, around the corner. It has only to be seen and understood. This requires the keen eyes of young, bold, and talented teachers, the wisdom and experience of people who have devoted years to the labor of education; it requires their unity and their joint, tireless efforts.

5.6. SOME ASPECTS OF HOMEWORK

5.6.1. It would be a mistake to assume that homework is no more than a supplement to the lesson, that its sole purpose is to complete what was left undone during the lesson and help the students cope with the next or subsequent ones. Homework has its own specific objectives. It possesses potentialities of its own not found in the lesson, and failure to realize them results in the deterioration and impoverishment of a student's school or college education, which acquires indelible negative features.

5.6.2. One of the characteristic features of homework, which distinguishes it from work in class, is the student's total independence, something which can be achieved in class only with difficulty. Furthermore, homework also requires what we will call the students' organizational independence, something totally impossible in class. The student must commence his home assignment alone, without any direct outside influence from anyone whomsoever. He must independently draw up his work plan. He must decide the sequence in which to do all the day's home assignments and approximately how much time each one will require. He must also decide if he will do some or all of the assignments given for a later date with the idea of returning to them for reworking on the eve of that date.

5.6.3. Unfortunately—we must repeat this again and again—our children are denied this opportunity by daily lessons in the same subject. They turn the teaching-learning and educating process into a mechanical one in which the educator is relegated to the purely technical role of handing out class and home assignments and, later, tests. The tests are of necessity based on only mechanical memorization of the crumbs of scientific information that the students were capable of quickly memorizing and retaining, because daily courses leave no time for teaching or learning. The basic principle of our education is to give a test as soon as possible, before the students can forget all they have learned.

The school and college game is played without even the suggestion of a teaching-learning and educating process and over the shortest possible period of time. It is a national fatal delusion that courses must be short. It is feared that if a two-month course is taught over a year, or an annual course over several years, the students will forget everything: it will be necessary to go back to knowledges, skills, and habits destroyed by time; it will be necessary to prevent their destruction or even, God forbid, restore them; it will be necessary to make sure that the students fully and exhaustively comprehend the basic concepts, ideas, and structures of classical and modern science, because without comprehension, relying only on mechanical memory, those bothersome children won't endure for long. It will be necessary to conduct regular consolidation and revision classes aimed at summing up, structuralizing, and systematizing the students' knowledges, skills, and habits and developing their intellectual, creative, and cognitive abilities in all fields of learning. Without such work, a drawn-out course will soon destroy itself because the students will quickly forget what they did and learned only a few months, if not weeks, ago. They will cease to remember or understand the words of the teacher and the textbook even at the mechanical level. The appearance of education—the pride of our politicians and educators—will give way to unmitigated pedagogical and educational darkness, in which it will be impossible to create even an illusion of a teaching-learning and educating process; this is a prospect that our politicians and educators fear more than anything else.

5.6.4. When a student independently sits down to do his homework—when he does it to the end, and does it every day without guidance or supervision on the part of anybody at all—the credit for this must go first and foremost to the teacher and then, perhaps, to the student, if he has never done this before. It is the result of an ocean of labor put in by the teacher to prepare and conduct lessons, prevent shortfalls in the students' knowledges, and eliminate those that do occur in good time. It is the result of an ocean of labor put by the teacher into participation in mini-researches when going through his courses in college, and later, when working as an educator. It is a measure of the pedagogical achievement or defeat of any educator, more objective than our toy tests and torture tests of 400 or 500 questions, tests devoid of meaning and derogatory to human dignity.

The teacher must devote much time, energy, effort, and attention to the students; he must give his loyalty and sincere, selfless love to them to get them seated behind their desks and involved in work, not only in class, but at home as well, where there is no teacher, no lesson, no school supervisors, but where there are the temptations of television, radio, books, siblings, and the great outdoors, with fun and games, laughter and merriment. Don't rely too much, dear teachers, on nonworking mothers, grandmothers, or grandfathers keeping the TV switched off or the children working. No one but you can save the teaching-learning process from the sure demise toward which it is heading. Supplementary assignments and sessions for lagging students and seminars for the most gifted should be made irreplaceable hallmarks of an educating teaching-learning process; every minute of the lesson and every home assignment should be thoroughly thought out, together with other teachers, supervisors, and administrators, to make them interesting and instructive, capable of stirring the children into activity and eagerness to work; home assignments should be in line with what the children can do, while constantly and invariably building up their degree of novelty as compared with classwork; all home assignments should be discussed in class before they are given and after they are done; the ways and means of establishing student feedback should be varied to the greatest degree possible—these are all things, without which the teaching-learning process cannot exist.

For the teacher's efforts to be successful he must be motivated by a sincere desire to help the students, not to persecute and punish them

311

in response to feedback. Such help can take various forms: frontal checking of several of the most important problems from the latest assignment, with or without blackboard notes; checking home assignments during work with the class on new material, if the assignment was given for that purpose, i.e., to create the opportunity for work on the class assignment; giving a five- to fifteen-minute quiz at the end of the lesson with success in it dependent directly on the quality of the home assignment done for the current lesson; collecting and checking, after every lesson, only three to five home assignments of both weak and strong students, grading them like tests or according to some other principle declared in advance and strictly adhered to by the teacher; checking several assignments, mainly those of weaker students, while collecting the assignments of all the students, and grading the former like a test (fulfillment of the assignment is checked for all, but whose assignments were checked thoroughly and graded is known only to those involved)—and so on, and so forth.

All of the above are completely feasible when the students are given no more home assignments than they can reasonably cope with, for too copious an amount of assignments embitter the students and alienate them from us and the subject.

5.6.5. Elements of novelty in home assignments as compared to classwork are absolutely essential. They should be introduced inexorably, though gradually. It is more dangerous to confront students with insuperable obstacles in their home assignments than in class assignments, because in class the teacher can quickly figure out that he overestimated the students' capabilities and come to their aid. This can't happen at home. Furthermore, at home it's so much easier to abandon work on an assignment than in class, during the lesson. If one home assignment after another proves to be too difficult for the students, they will soon stop doing them altogether. After that it will be very hard, if not impossible, to get the class back to doing home, and even class, assignments, because they are completely interdependent. Our mistakes cost both us and our students much more than their own mistakes.

5.6.6. A few more remarks should be made concerning students' work at home. First of all, a teacher must earn the fulfillment, or even attempted fulfillment, of home assignments by his students: yes, yes, he must earn it by honest, competent work, by his devotion to the students, his love of them and his implacable will to give them knowledges, skills and habits and a level of development of their intellectual, creative, and cognitive abilities in keeping with their age and the studied course. Secondly, the teacher should work with the class on the home assignments, completed or to be completed by the students at every lesson, in one form or another; we described several forms of this work before. Thirdly, whatever the form of work of students with home assignments, it is essential for the teacher to maintain a dignified posture, showing due respect for the students and himself—to refrain from picking on the students, from pursuing and exposing those who have failed to do the assignment—while at the same time in no way reducing unswerving exactingness toward the students and himself. Fourthly, the teacher must hold home assignments in great respect and profoundly understand that they present one of the chief opportunities for the students to learn to study at length on their own and persevere in attaining set goals. Fifthly, home assignments are one of the most important forms of educational work in which the students must decide for themselves whether they have adequately prepared the theoretical material, whether they have done their written assignments completely and correctly, whether they have made mistakes in solving problems—even if the answer is apparently correct—and whether they can justify every step in the solution. Finally, at the present stage in the development of the theory and practice of mass education, home assignments are the principal means of individualizing the teaching-learning process.

5.7. THE DIFFICULTY OF HOME ASSIGNMENTS SHOULD INCREASE STEADILY FROM ONE SECTION TO ANOTHER

5.7.1. As we have said many times before, one of the methods employed in our educational system which gives it mystic traits beyond the comprehension of ordinary people is the fragmentation of the educational process (which is by its nature and intent continuous) into completely isolated, linearly arranged segments. The most graphic manifestation of this trend, destructive to both learners and teachers, is the fragmentation of courses into short mini-courses.

Another manifestation of the highly harmful fragmentation of the educational process is the internal partitioning of initially fragmented courses into isolated, unconnected sections. The cause and effect of this are clear and obvious to all. However, the learners and teachers obviously find themselves in different positions. The learners are driven to frenzy and despair. The teachers are infectiously cheerful. And why shouldn't they be? They discussed addition of fractions with the class, then assigned the students all the exercises and problems of the section at once—no use wasting time—and that's that. It someone didn't understand or doesn't know something, that's all right: there'll be a test and it will set the record straight. Instead, maybe the teacher talked about differentiation of an implicit function and cast a wreath of forty problems on the students' feet; again, everything is fine and the test will show.

Only in primary school and in some elementary schools are problems and other exercises in every section repeated and varied for a while. In all other educational establishments, pedagogical cruelty triumphs over common sense.

5.7.2. To ensure the maximum effectiveness of home assignments they should always and invariably include material from different sections of the course. This is an essential prerequisite of a successful educational process in all educational establishments.

Obviously, when introducing new study material, exercises assuring correct comprehension and assimilation of the newly introduced concepts, ideas, and propositions must be given. But in addition, every home assignment must always also include exercises from the preceding few sections of the course. This should be done at every lesson, thus having exercises from every section completed at home discussed and worked on in class many times.

In each new home assignment the exercises from each section should be made increasingly difficult; the assignments from the new section are initially the simplest. Furthermore, in each section several of the most interesting exercises should be left for reviewing the course, especially if there is no collection of problems, questions, and problem situations covering the whole material of a chapter or course at the end of it.

5.7.3. Exercises and problems occurring in summarizing home assignments and dealing with the material of a whole chapter and the preceding chapters should always include exercises of higher-than-average difficulty. The degree of difficulty should be gradually increased together with the distance from the study material to which the exercises pertain. Initially given only for illustration and developing solving techniques, the exercises are gradually replaced with creative ones, which can no longer be solved with the help of known algorithms and require the high level of intellectual, creative, and cognitive abilities the students are expected to possess by that time.

Such exercises should not depress the students, who should derive joy from them. Such joy, the joy of at least elementary creativity, imbues a person with confidence in himself, in his strength and capabilities. It quenches the brutish instincts, develops feelings of human love and the need to help others, and channels human abilities and energy into creative efforts, not destruction—the destruction of material and spiritual values, the destruction of human destinies and lives.

The teacher must be very, very careful with home assignments containing exercises and problem situations of higher-than-average difficulty, which are creative in character and involve material from several sections of the course. He must also be cautious, wise, humane, and yet consistently exacting. He must regard as his prime professional duty not only teaching his students how to use different, even difficult, algorithms and how to use very useful and effective study aids: he must also teach them to think, to acquire new knowledge independently. He must teach children to independently obtain new results in the process of purposeful reasoning and purposeful, creative activity.

5.7.4. Creative activity must be taught and supervised from the day a child first comes to school to the day he graduates from college or university. This must be done continuously, constantly, tirelessly, devotedly, with inspiration, and creatively. If it wishes to survive, a modern nation must build up an educational system supervised and reproduced

314

by creatively thinking people capable of maintaining a continuous creative process in all children, both those who are more capable and those who are less capable, both the serious-minded as well as the less serious-minded. We teachers have the duty of imbuing our children with capabilities for creative activity as a result of the organization and implementation of a creative educational process, both for the children better prepared at home for work in school and the totally unprepared. We teachers have the duty of adequately preparing them by engineering a process of intensive development of their intellectual and creative abilities.

5.7.5. Current textbooks on subjects containing assignments to be done by students independently, especially in math and science, are so organized as to prevent the students from either overburdening themselves with thinking or developing their creative and cognitive abilities. We are speaking of a legitimized system of arranging problems and other exercises at the end of every section of the textbook, then at the end of each chapter. This system should be eliminated from all our textbooks as quickly as possible, and here is why.

Even when we assign the students problems from several sections simultaneously, and then from the exercises concluding the chapter, we each day needlessly but involuntarily deprive the students of the opportunity of independently carrying out the most important, creative stage in problem solving. We have in mind the choice of ways and means of problem solving, because that is just what the name of a section or chapter tells the students. All that occurs is a drill, i.e., instruction only in techniques, thoughtless toying with new concepts and symbols instead of the development of the students' intellectual, creative, and cognitive abilities. This is one of the causes of the tragic straits of our education: Students wander from one class to another, gradually growing up, but they remain on the same level of intellect and creativity with which they came to us.

New courses exact higher demands on the students, who, however, remain unprepared. This is also largely due to the fact that they have only rarely had to solve problems and problem situations completely on their own because this was all diligently done by the author of the textbook and the teacher following in his wake.

5.7.6. There are, apparently, several ways of preventing the titles of textbook sections and chapters from serving as prompts for the students, suggesting what should be done and how, but one appears to us both simple and convenient.

Suppose a textbook has five chapters and 100 sections, with twenty problems at the end of each section, another fifty at the end of each chapter, and another 100 at the end of the book, for a total of $20 \times 100 + 50 \times 5 + 100 = 2,350$ problems. All these problems should be placed at the end of the book and numbered consecutively, after first being arranged pedagogically correctly. We will show what we mean by this. We can and should require this of the authors of textbooks; conversely,

315

we are in no way obligated to use textbooks that do not meet our requirements.

Here is one version of how an author could work on such a book of five chapters, 100 sections, and 2,350 problems. For the sake of convenience, let us divide the whole material of the book into 100 lessons. To each lesson we assign fifteen to thirty problems, all of them placed only at the end of the book.

For the first lesson, only a few problems will be assigned for work in class and at home, much fewer than for all the other lessons, because the home assignment for each subsequent lesson will also be including problems from preceding sections. (If the course is a continuation or follow-up of previously studied courses and studying it will require reviewing some sections from them, the very first lesson, as well as several subsequent ones, should conclude with home assignments containing material from the previous courses.) Following the second lesson, the home and class assignments should include problems from both sections: most from the second, but several from the first as well. Following the third lesson the assignments will include problems from all three sections, and so on.

The author of the textbook should do all this work: In the teacher's manual he must distribute all 2,350 problems over 100 groups so that each group will include problems from both the new section and preceding sections and chapters. Nowadays it is very hard to persuade college instructors and schoolteachers to do such work with assignments because the problems and other exercises are at the end of the sections and chapters. It may not be easy, even in an atmosphere of active mini-researches involving the best experts and administrators. Besides, teachers are overburdened with work as it is, and they shouldn't be charged with doing more tiresome work; moreover, they cannot always perform successfully or expertly. A well-qualified author can do it for the others. Most importantly, the students will be doing problems independently, without being prompted as to which section or chapter they belong to. This is especially important when studying factorization of polynomials, techniques of integration, convergence and divergence, applications of the derivative and definite integral, solving problems in analytic and Euclidean geometry, and so on.

The educator is by no means obliged to accept the author's help, either completely or in part, and he can assign as many problems of different kinds as he thinks necessary for every lesson. But he should understand that, for example, in Lesson 25, which contains some material from Section 24 and some from Section 25, the author included problems from both sections, say four from Section 24 and six from Section 25. In addition, the author may have included ten problems from previous sections and chapters of the textbook for purposes we have just mentioned.

Of course, the division of the course into 100 lessons does not assume that the course must necessarily consist of 100, and only 100, lessons.

If one teacher covers the book in eighty lessons, while another may require 110, 130, or 200 lessons, the teacher will have to draw up every independent assignment as he sees fit. In such cases, the work done by the author can be used as one of the variants or as the basis for compiling classwork and home assignments covering the material of the whole book. To facilitate the teachers' work, the teacher's manual should indicate the section to which each exercise refers.

With a booklet referring the problems to specific sections and chapters, teachers who can and wish to work on the course without any outside help can ignore the author's assignment of problems to particular lessons.

Many of our troubles will disappear if all the exercises are placed only at the end of the textbook and if, for every lesson, we give exercises not from one section, but from five or ten. Then every lesson will serve not only to introduce new information but also to

(1) prevent the destruction of knowledges with the help of problem solutions and by reviewing theoretical material from preceding sections;

(2) restore destroyed knowledge;

(3) generalize, systematize, and structuralize knowledge assimilated by the students;

(4) develop the intellectual, creative, and cognitive abilities of students;

(5) prepare the students for assimilation of new information and the solution of new classes of problems, sometimes long before they are explicitly introduced to new information.

5.8. THE MAIN TYPES OF HOME ASSIGNMENTS. THE TEACHER'S ABILITY TO ASSESS A STUDENT'S DIFFICULTIES

5.8.1. The main types of home assignments for students are

(1) home assignments that provide students with the opportunity to profoundly comprehend and firmly assimilate all that was presented in class and thoroughly digest the new material so as to be able to continue studying the course at subsequent lessons;

(2) home assignments that include material studied previously—perhaps even in previous years—full and free mastery of which is absolutely essential for conducting the next lesson or series of lessons;

(3) home assignments that include material absolutely essential for the next lesson or series of lessons, which the students had never studied before but which they can study on their own;

(4) home assignments that include (a) material studied at the last few lessons but of higher-than-average difficulty, and (b) problems and problem situations of a creative, generalizing, and systematizing nature;

(5) home assignments that include material from previous years or months of study—depending on the length of the course—enabling the students to solve creative problems and consider problem situations based on past studied material, as well as to grasp the full picture of the fundamental scientific ideas expounded in the course over several years or months: development of the concepts of number, exponent, function, identical transformations, equations and inequalities—on the basis of the material of both algebraic and transcendental functions—the axiomatic method in mathematics, geometric transformations, measurement, et cetera. The teacher cannot give such assignments as frequently as he conducts lessons in the class; rather, they should be given ahead for a week, two weeks, a whole month, or even more;

(6) home assignments that prevent the destruction of the students' knowledges, skills, and habits acquired over the last few years and months;

(7) home assignments that restore knowledges, skills, and habits lost by the students over the last few years and months.

5.8.2. If the teacher is able to organize in his class a teaching-learning and educational process of such quality as to be confident that his students take his subject, in general—and homework, in particular—seriously, he should, in most cases, start the lesson with new material; this should be done energetically, without wasting a moment's time on specifically checking the students' homework. This may entail an element of risk, but then, all teaching entails risk. We take a risk every time we come to a lesson that it may have to be changed or even destroyed for a variety of reasons which we may never even have anticipated. That is why one of the prime objectives of pedagogical education, both in college and after the young teacher starts working in a school or college, is to teach educators to foresee and evaluate, as precisely and objectively as possible, the emotional and professional attitude of every student toward the as yet nonexistent, upcoming lesson and to evaluate the situations that may present the greatest danger for each student and the future lesson as a whole. Such situations can be caused by either the nature of the taught material or the state of the students—not today, but the state they will be in at the *next* lesson. This ability can be developed only as a consequence of extensive work with the same body of students so that the teacher knows the class as a whole as well as each individual student. A lesson can never be successful or instructive if the teacher is unable to predict and anticipate, to some degree of accuracy, every step and every minute of the lesson before conducting it. One cannot prepare a lesson in general, suitable for a class in general. There is no such thing

318

as a class "in general." There are only *specific* classes and students endowed with infinitely different qualities and capabilities. It is for those classes and those students that we prepare our lessons. It is in those classes that we conduct our lessons, created for them specifically, gradually building up the students' knowledges, skills, and habits and fostering their intellectual, creative, and cognitive abilities.

A teacher can anticipate a lesson and the difficulties each student may encounter during it only in a class he has worked with for many years. We have said this before and we say it again. That is how professional students and professional teachers are created. Our college courses lasting a few months and year-long courses in school essentially deprive our educators and our educational system of the possibility of successfully preparing lessons and conducting the teaching-learning process, everywhere and always. Let us prevent this from continuing forever.

5.8.3. After beginning the lesson with the creation of problem situations and setting up a series of problems and exercises, the solutions of which will cover the lesson's contents, the teacher should, as he proceeds, make use of the results obtained by the students in their home assignments. Indeed, this is one of the purposes of those assignments: to systematize the theoretical material and restore the students' ability to solve problems and do exercises essential for the success of the current lesson. In this case, the work of the teacher and the students on home assignments given at the preceding lessons can be woven into the fabric of the lesson and blended organically with the introduction of new information and further elaboration of the course material.

It is also good for the teacher to get the lesson off to an energetic start under his all-embracing guidance, because this immediately gives the lesson purposefulness and a well-paced tempo. Furthermore, even though we introduce elements of innovation in all home assignments, we should sometimes try to eliminate the very fact of explicitly working on previously studied material. It is also important to avoid monotony in lessons—such as invariably starting out with checking home assignments—while unobtrusively dealing with their essence. This is important, despite the inevitable risk to the lesson and the teacher as creator of that lesson, as well as the person who puts it into effect in terms of the taught subject and the taught class.

One more extremely important comment is called for. When the teacher starts the lesson by reviewing the home assignment he will inevitably prompt the students regarding the solution of problems and analysis of problem situations, which will come later in the lesson. This is because at the beginning of the lesson the teacher will formulate information that, as intended by the educational process, should be actualized by the students, as far as possible independently, when solving problems and analyzing problem situations. This in turn will unjustifiably eliminate the main difficulty in solving any problem: the choice of ways, means, and methods of solving it. Considering all this, and depending on the makeup of the class and difficulty of the lesson, the teacher should

319

decide for himself whether to do his prompting. He should decide whether to work on the home assignment at the beginning of the lesson (which will be in large measure based on that assignment) or to weave the material of that assignment into the lesson without accentuating it specifically. Perhaps it would be a good idea to give this preparatory home assignment several lessons in advance of the lesson it is intended for, provided the teacher can expect the students to be able to use it several days later. The teacher may also opt not to give that preparatory assignment at all if, during the lesson, he intends to require all the students to successfully solve problems and analyze situations without the benefit of a special home assignment. However, an educator must have the moral right before his students for such a step. If this is the case, students will not be offended by such exactingness towards themselves; on the contrary, they will be as proud of their teacher as they are of themselves.

5.9. TEACHING STUDENTS HOW TO DO HOME ASSIGNMENTS

5.9.1. We have come to one of the most difficult and most important pedagogical problems: the problem of creating a professional student in the course of teaching him how to do home assignments.

As mentioned before, during the first few days of work with a new class, the teacher should give home assignments containing a minimal element of novelty in comparison with the work done in class. While imposing firm demands on the class from the very outset, the teacher must also be confident that his demands are realistic enough to be met. If they go beyond the students' capabilities—not from the teacher's point of view, but from that of the students, whose training may be very poor—his relations with the class will inevitably and rapidly deteriorate. The students will feel, not without justification, that the new teacher is their enemy, an adversary whom they must resist, because his demands, often insisted upon with righteous indignation, go beyond what they are capable of doing.

The teacher should regularly discuss the students' independent assignments with them: what sequence is best suited to carrying out their various stages, how to verify progress from one stage to another. He should also tell the students how he intends to work at the next lesson on the assignment given for it and what questions he will expect the students to answer. They should write those questions down and be told where to find the answers to them when doing their homework—in the textbook or somewhere else. The students should be asked to formulate the answers to some questions then and there at the lesson, but without writing them down, thus enabling them to go over those answers a second time at home.

320

This kind of work in class—i.e., doing parts of the home assignment—is not only instructive. It fosters in the students a moral commitment to complete work begun in class at home. At the same time, such an approach should not be overworked, for the students should also have a sense of personal responsibility for home assignments.

From time to time the teacher should encourage the students to pool their efforts to draw up a scheme or plan of doing and checking the most difficult exercises. Those students who feel it will be helpful may write the plan down. At the next lesson the teacher must check the home assignment exactly as he promised. Never deviate an iota from your promises, dear educators. There can never be any justification for this.

5.9.2. Do not begrudge the students time to teach them how to do home assignments. That time will pay off handsomely in the course of subsequent work with the class. On the other hand, don't be carried away by another extreme, equally dangerous for both the teacher and the class. It is less apparent in short-term courses, if only because they are so short. We are speaking of excessive concern for class and home assignments, such as when the teacher discusses them in great detail, sometimes even down to explaining how to actually do them, which is totally impermissible. As a consequence, the students are left with nothing to do but the technical aspect of their work. If this stage of work with the students goes on for too long, the class loses interest in the subject, the teacher, and both his class and home assignments. The students get bored with the subject and the teacher, they become sarcastic, and all the teacher's work is undone.

5.9.3. Inexperienced teachers are incapable of coping with such situations. They tend to pander to the students in an attempt to get an instructive and educating teaching-learning process launched, and in their efforts they increasingly do the students' work for them, thereby increasingly harming the students and themselves. Only mini-researches can prevent or halt this dangerous process.

It is very easy to spoil a class. One can, either deliberately or through inexperience, opt for the road of least resistance, the road of removing all obstacles facing the students, making them, as well as their parents, school administrators, and the teacher himself, happy and pleased. In such cases, the course continues to be both interesting and comprehensible—for a while. But very soon the teaching-learning and educating process perishes.

A short course doesn't give the students time to get bored. They have no time to realize that they should be disgusted, not delighted, with such a lively, merry, interesting, easy, short course which draws so quickly to an end. What a pity—no—what a horror that such courses exist! They teach nothing but imitative activity. They may, perhaps, give some knowledges and skills; however, these are short-lived and useless because they are based solely on memory. The teacher ignores the development of his students' intellectual, creative, and cognitive abilities. They finish the course at the same level of potential independence, independent thinking, and action at which they began it.

The kind of courses described above dominate our schools, where they gradually deteriorate into the teacher's open intimidation of his students or the students' intimidation of their teacher. Yet our unprofessional administrators of education are quite pleased with them, although they should arouse professional indignation and a desire to intervene before the students and the teacher get to openly hate and despise each other. Beware of such courses. They doom all that is alive in the educational system.

5.9.4. Systematic mini-researches can forestall or eliminate these and many other forms of the teacher's work with his students which are equally baneful for education, regardless of what the students may think of the course or their educator. In this connection we would like to stress that students' comments about their teacher cannot serve as justification for either reprimanding or praising him. To be sure, students readily discern a teacher's lack of knowledge, his carelessness or professional helplessness, and they readily state their opinion openly and fairly. They are, however, incapable of judging his pedagogical principles or educational work. We must all clearly realize this and not rely too heavily on students' judgments when evaluating an educator's work—especially, be it noted, when their judgment is highly positive.

5.9.5. The previous training and potential independence of students attending school, college, or university remedial courses may be so low as to make it necessary to commence the process of creating professional students from scratch, from the very basic skills and habits of doing home assignments. Our appeal, "You are older, you are adults, you should know how to do home assignments and must be able to do them," is but the helpless cry of a helpless educator or of one who has no desire to teach our children as they are today.

It is necessary and possible to get virtually any class to work, no matter how difficult it might seem. Instead of complaining of difficulties we should strive ceaselessly for every child, for every student, for his knowledge, skills, and habits, for his intellectual, creative, and cognitive abilities, for his fate and happiness, present and future.

When you take over a new class, start working with it selflessly and sincerely. Try to help the whole class and each student. Don't be frightened if at first you feel a wall between yourself and the students. Begin with the most elementary demands, those which they can surely meet, and encourage them to do so. Don't be afraid of setbacks. Don't panic, even if most of the students refuse to follow you. Try not to pay attention to this. Do take note of the slightest achievement of each student. Don't be afraid to praise, but don't be too lavish—otherwise the students may feel happy when you are sad. Start out by requiring the students to do imitative work. After factoring, say, $ab + ac$, ask them to factor $ab - ac$, then $a^2 + ac$, then $ab - b^2$, and so on. This must be done very seriously, without any levity. Include in the home assignment exercises similar to those done in class. At the next lesson thoroughly discuss every home problem or question. After that, collect all or some of the students' notebooks. If you feel that most of the class hasn't done the home assignment, don't collect it, and don't tell the students that you had meant to, as such information could help the students legitimize not doing home assignments. Beware of and avoid this above all. Collect the home assignments of some three to five students who have done them. After a while you can and should, gradually and cautiously, start collecting assignments that may not have been fulfilled; that is, from those students you are not sure have done their assignments. Start grading the home assignments in the students' notebooks and in your register. Start doing this very carefully. Don't grudge good marks, but don't save the bad ones either. Hand out both, keeping an eye on the class to gauge how it takes this. Never give too many poor grades at once. This invariably arouses merriment. The students gradually get used to receiving low grades for quizzes, tests, and independent class and home assignments and they start reacting to them with laughter and genuine merriment. They begin to realize that so many low grades present no danger to anyone precisely because there are so many of them. Gradually identify for yourself a group of the weakest students and work with them tirelessly. Your efforts will be rewarded. Not at once, surely, but in our job nothing happens at once, especially in a positive direction. Win over to your side one student after another; fight for each one, not by means of jokes or flattery, but through honest, devoted effort, through love of all the children, the good and the difficult. Gradually identify a group of the best students. This group, which is your seminar in the subject, should be assembled on a voluntary basis. During seminar sessions encourage students to become your assistants—not as privileged members of the group but as honest and able helpers. Foster their abilities. Encourage their intellect, will, creativity, and independence on the basis of material not included in the syllabus, otherwise you will be creating an aristocracy in the class along with plebeians. Never allow this to happen. It cripples souls, destroys everything upright, human, bright, and noble in the students, and arouses their active protest and hatred of the teacher. Continue to work tirelessly in the system of mini-researches in your classes, as well as in the classes of other teachers. Devote yourself to your work completely, totally, to the end. You can comfort yourself with the knowledge that this isn't forever. The students will appreciate you, some earlier, some later. They will start doing their class and home assignments better and better, and more and more willingly. Love and respect every child and give him all your efforts and knowledge. He will reward you with devotion and appreciation of the subject, yourself, and his work with you.

Such a struggle for the class, for the right to work with it successfully, for the right to require the students to live up to your requirements when doing assignments, can be very difficult and very protracted. Be ready for it. Sometimes it can take months or even years to bring a class up to par. That is why we keep on insisting on the need to have a constant student body in the same teacher's class for several years in school and for a year or more in college, especially in math and science courses and English language and literature.

One-year and sometimes even six-month courses in school and courses of a few months in college are essentially meaningless and frivolous; they deny mini-researches and teacher learning. This is suicidal for the nation and self-destructive for the educational and political systems. It is a breeding ground of irresponsibility and depression among both students and teachers, because neither have the time to achieve any positive results. Sensing and realizing this, neither attempt to do anything useful in school or in college. Everyone looks patiently forward to the end of the course. Anticipation of a quick end is a consolation for both sides, whatever the degree of inaction or pretense of action on the part of both learners and teachers. Those who feverishly attempt to launch something useful (or at least regularly give home assignments) soon abandon the idea. They begin to realize that it is impossible to achieve success, give the students knowledges, skills, and habits, and promote the development of their intellectual, creative, and cognitive abilities before the end of the course. In addition, their colleagues become outraged with such a violation of the universal, unspoken, but scrupulously adhered-to plot. It is a plot of necessity, an unwilling plot, but one dominating all our country's educational establishments: don't teach, and don't allow others to teach, because it is a useless and dangerous undertaking.

5.9.6. Of course, short-term courses are not the only cause of the all-American tragedy. We have spoken of many others. However, let us get back to the question of how to get the students of a new class to complete and perform well on their home assignments.

The students will gradually understand and learn your demands. With the help of mini-researches you will see and understand the shortcomings and achievements of your students and yourself. The students will, without any prompting, soon understand and learn your qualities, your shortcomings, and merits. Cherish all the good they know about you or suspect in you. Strive to get rid of all that is unnecessary and unacceptable in the pedagogical process, which you may hear from your colleagues in the course of mini-researches or from the students themselves. With each passing month and year, the still helpless people—children as well as adults—will begin to sense their forward movement; they will feel the knowledges, skills, and habits they obtain. This is the road to victory. Continue the good work—sometimes better, sometimes a little worse; we aren't gods. But cherish your prestige among the children. Love and teach them, learn yourself, teach other educators, learn from them and your administrators. What begins in a new class as hard, debilitating labor gradually fills you with a feeling of satisfaction for yourself and for others, students as well as teachers. Gradually you will find your work becoming less and less difficult, though it will never become simple or easy. Every educator who teaches and learns in the system of mini-researches has to work; it will never be easy, but it will be creative work, bringing happiness and joy.

Gradually but cautiously increase the difficulty of some exercises—never all—assigned for homework. After a while—you will have to judge when yourself—seek help in mini-researches. When you do this will depend on the makeup of your class, the number of weak and very strong students. From this point on, every home assignment should include at least one, but not more than two or three, very difficult exercises.

5.9.7. We will now discuss one of the main reasons why we regard home assignments as an essential form of work for developing the students' intellectual, creative, and cognitive abilities to a degree unachievable by any lesson or system of lessons. We are speaking of exercises of greater-than-average difficulty, for which one lesson may not be enough.

Of course, any exercise can be started at one lesson and finished at the next. This is not very accommodating for either the teacher or the students, but it need not be necessarily avoided as a matter of principle. In our work we confront more difficult situations when, during one lesson, we have to finish a problem, introduce new material, review, summarize, and systematize old material and then introduce and comment on a home assignment—all within forty or fifty minutes. However, it isn't a good idea to have problem solutions spill over into several lessons on a regular basis. This detracts from the clarity and precision of the educational process. Everything is so made up in this case that the students can't always cope with the following questions: What is going on at the lesson? What should we do? Such a hodge-podge, with frequent alternations of types of work during one lesson, is very dangerous. There is a great show of activity, yet the students leave the lesson unable to answer the question, "What knowledge did I obtain from the lesson today?"

After every lesson, every teacher must be able to answer the question, "What did I accomplish for the class during this lesson?" In fact, he must have that question in mind in advance, when preparing for the lesson. This will enable the students to say what they achieved for themselves at the lesson. Incidentally, such questions should be regularly addressed to students. They are extremely useful for both the students and the teacher. The teacher obtains high-quality feedback within the few minutes assigned at the end of the lesson to a quick discussion of what each student and the class as a whole gained from it.

We should, however, realize that, despite the difficulties which splitting an exercise over two lessons presents for both the teacher and the students, it performs an extremely important instructive and educational function which requires neither additional time nor special efforts on the part of the teacher. We have in mind that the students gradually learn to do things not necessarily at once, at the first go, in just a few minutes; rather, they attack the same problem several times, something most of our students are never required to do.

If the teacher has included the concluding work on a problem begun in class in the home assignment, at the next lesson he should discuss all stages of the solution done in class and at home. Solution of the problem must be completed with the participation of the students who were unable to do it at home. This is followed by a summing up of the solution and consideration of possible variants.

After teaching the students how to solve problems of above-average difficulty in several stages and over several days, we can start giving them such problems regularly. When this level is reached, the bulk of the home assignment, as usual, is given for the next lesson, while one or two exercises are given to be done within a week or two.

Without such work on problems of above-average difficulty, the educational process is dead and artificial. It cannot develop the students' intellectual, creative, and cognitive abilities; instead, it retards them. It lacks the quality of individualizing the students' work, when one student may require an hour to solve problems at home while another may take three days. However good, sincere, and competent the teacher's educational work during the lesson, it must be supplemented by individualization of the teaching-learning process with the help of home assignments.

When such week- or two-week–old assignments are discussed at the lesson, they should not take up too much time. If many students failed to solve the problems, even a whole lesson may not provide enough time to discuss them. In such cases, one can—or, perhaps, should—discuss difficult exercises at remedial sessions.

Remedial lessons should be used to prevent any buildup of ignorance. The teacher should help the weaker students do the most difficult exercises from the latest assignment and work systematically on the material to be studied during upcoming lessons. The weak students should be able to participate actively in the work at all lessons. Therefore, some of the most difficult sections should be gone over with such students twice or even three times, i.e., prior to, during, and after the regular lesson. This is our professional duty. Without such work, conducted regularly with those students who wish to take part in it, as well as with those whom the teacher requires to participate, there can be virtually no teaching-learning in conditions of mass education, however good our teachers, curricula, and textbooks may be.

Unfortunately, this is not the only reason for the absence of mass education. We are attempting to deal with only the most dangerous ones.

5.9.8. Thus, from being reproductive in the junior classes, home assignments evolve—gradually and consistently, month by month, and year by year—becoming more and more difficult and filling up with elements of student independence and creativity. They evolve into a powerful means, the only one of its kind, of individualizing the process of education and developing the intellectual, creative, and cognitive abilities of all students. This can never be achieved by a teaching-learning process which restricts itself to only classroom lessons, in school as well as in college.

5.9.9. Each assignment should be upgraded to the extent that from information accepted by the student at the level of polite concurrence, it develops into an active tool in his hands. This is achieved with the help of a series of exercises which can only be done if the student has successfully fulfilled the assignment and fully understands the procedures involved. Note that we are speaking of an important and effective means of developing a professional student and a professional teacher. It involves evaluation of the quality of fulfillment of the first assignment by evaluating the quality of fulfillment of a second assignment, which could not have been done without successfully coping with the initial one. This work can be carried out frontally during the lesson: the teacher asks the students to explain each new stage in the fulfillment of the new, i.e., verifying, exercise. Each such stage is discussed by the whole class. At the teacher's request, different students point out its pros and cons, or perhaps errors, and they must be required to justify their opinions. Approximately the same pattern is followed during the next stage, and thus until the exercise is done. Depending on its complexity, notes on the blackboard are made either by the teacher, by one of the students, by a succession of students, or they are not made at all. When the bulk of the work has thus been carried out, the students can be offered the opportunity to complete it independently then and there in class. The conclusion should then be verified either orally or with notes on the blackboard, depending on what the teacher feels and sees as he walks about the class, looking into the students' notebooks and talking to some of them (but very softly so as not to bother the others). Sometimes, especially during the first weeks of work with a new class, it is necessary simply to collect the assignments done by the students and grade them like quizzes. It may not even be necessary to collect all the assignments—if the teacher is very busy.

Until such time as the class is convinced—by deeds, not words, because words don't teach anybody anything—that independent work, including homework, is simply an organic element of the lesson, frequent brief quizzes are absolutely essential. The quality shown in doing them will be in direct proportion to the quality of the students' earlier work on their independent assignments. Such quizzes should be conducted regularly for a considerable time, subsequently returning to them occasionally. To prevent the students from forgetting that independent assignments are as important as every other kind of work, it is necessary to grade the quizzes, which should, of course, include both new and reviewed theoretical questions.

We fully realize how difficult this work is for the teacher and the students. It is especially difficult when students come to a teacher without the firm conviction that independently done assignments are an integral part of the teaching-learning process. Every teacher must realize that revitalization of the students' knowledges, turning them from a deadweight into a tool and means of continuing educational and cognitive activity, is one of the fundamental purposes of education.

5.9.10. There are many ways in which the teacher can show new students the close relationship between lessons and home assignments. For example, he can help them solve a difficult problem up to a certain point, after which he asks them to continue on their own.

Such an assignment need not be given toward the end of the lesson. In fact, it shouldn't, because it may leave the students with an unpleasant feeling. They may feel that it is the teacher's fault that they have to do additional work at home, which might not have been assigned had the teacher been better prepared for the lesson. That is why the students should never be required to finish work at home that remained unfinished at the end of a lesson. This is a method a teacher may arrive at spontaneously, without realizing its dangers. It is so easy to opt for this, because it easily removes the problem of completing the lesson clearly and on time. The students, however, don't like this. They may express their protest openly, grumbling to themselves, but so that the teacher can hear, with words like, "Again, 'finish at home' " or, "There's enough homework as it is." In other words, the students perceive such assignments—we repeat this again—not as assignments by the teacher but as work for the teacher, doing what he failed to do in class. That is why if you intend to assign the completion of the problem for homework, you should interrupt work on this problem in class well before the end of the lesson.

The completed solution can be checked at the next lesson by asking several students questions, with or without making notes on the blackboard, depending on the structure and complexity of the problem. The best way of checking is by introducing a new problem directly linked with the one to be checked. Once in a while checking can and should be done by simply collecting the students' notebooks.

Understandably enough, it may not always be possible to collect and check the work of all students. You may check the work of half the class at random, or perhaps a third, or you may simply collect the work of three to five students designated in advance. One thing you should never do, however, is ignore an assignment. The only rare exception can be made if something happens that is totally beyond your control. We repeat the following again and again: Total indifference to independent assignments, either class or home, irritates the class and arouses its protest. The teacher quickly loses prestige in the students' eyes, and it is difficult, if not impossible, to restore it. One by one the students will stop doing assignments. It is extremely difficult to reverse this process.

5.9.11. If independent assignments include new theoretical material and exercises on which no preliminary work has been done in class, the teacher should be extremely careful, at least in two respects. Firstly, this should be the exception rather than the rule. In other words, never place the whole burden of the teaching-learning process on the students, leaving to yourself the task of merely recording their achievements or failures; this is an extremely popular and very commonplace occurrence in our country, which is cruel, inhuman, self-defeating, and detrimental to the nation. Secondly, when getting to know a new class you should select only relatively simple and small exercises for such assignments; otherwise, you may scare away from yourself and your subject students who may be potentially very good but are unable to cope with such work because of lack of experience, inadequate previous training, or simple inability to work completely independently on totally new material.

The great ability to work completely independently on totally new material should be an important result of the teaching-learning process, but by no means should it be a method. This process must be supervised by the teacher in an educational establishment where mini-researches are a form of work of all educators and administrators.

Most of our educators, unfortunately, usually follow quite a different pedagogical strategy. They amazingly and incredibly treat cognitive abilities as something inherent in children. As a consequence, a high level of cognitive abilities, one of the most important and difficult results of the teaching-learning process, is most cruelly and incredibly regarded as one of its means. It is hardly surprising that students and teachers are unhappy, that students rebel and fall into rages for no apparent reason discernible to our educators, politicians, and administrators. Children drop out of courses, schools, and colleges and, driven to utter despair and hopelessness, attack their peers and tormentor-teachers. They do not realize that their teachers are as much the victims of the monstrous process of intellectual and moral destruction of the nation as they themselves are. As they grow up, they spontaneously flock together into groups of people rejected by a society which first tried to destroy them. They have managed to survive, but now they are out to destroy the society which alienated and rejected them through the efforts of teachers who knew not what they were doing.

5.9.12. If a teacher wants his students to take home assignments seriously, he must approach them seriously and competently himself. The teacher can wipe out the positive results of all his efforts if he fails to realize the tremendous importance of home assignments in the teaching-learning process and is unable to make the students do them regularly.

One of the most common mistakes of teachers, which can totally destroy the teaching-learning process, is to give home assignments that are so large that even the most diligent students simply don't have the time to do them. When such assignments are given regularly, the students have no other recourse but to abandon them before they are halfway through. If this goes on for some time, a teacher who expects his students to complete their home assignments places them in an increasingly difficult position. This is especially likely if the quality of feedback involving home assignments is low.

The students will soon start repaying in kind. They will place the teacher in situations that will soon become hopeless. Blank spots will start to appear and dangerously expand in their knowledges, skills, and habits, making them incapable of actively participating in the work organized by the teacher in class. Both sides—the teacher and the students—will become irritated with each other. Very soon, irritation will escalate into open hostility as the teacher demands more and more impossible things. He bases lessons and assignments on the erroneous assumption that all assignments have been done fully and successfully. Education assumes one of the ugly forms in which our country abounds and which has nothing in common with an instructive teaching-learning process. The lesson rapidly deteriorates until it no longer teaches or educates, until it no longer offers knowledge, skills, and habits or develops intellectual, creative, and cognitive abilities. The teacher and students lose all interest in and respect for each other. Instead of a teaching-learning process there is a process of teacher and students sharing the same classroom, with numerous variants of this process.

Another way of turning home assignments from an important and irreplaceable component of the teaching-learning process into a bane is to give assignments too difficult for most of the students, which only a few can do. The teacher does nothing in class to help the students cope with their assignments. If, in addition, he cruelly demands that all the students always do all their assignments, his relations with them will rapidly become hostile. Most students are constrained to resort to different forms of dishonest protection.

We repeat: difficult assignments and very difficult assignments to be done both in class and at home are necessary. But the class must be purposefully and patiently prepared for them. That is what school is all about; it is *not* about forcing children into cruel encounters with assignments they are incapable of doing and which only embitter them, causing despair, loss of self-confidence, and the moral disintegration of the personality. By gradually increasing the difficulty of assignments, while at the same time gradually reducing his own involvement in doing them, the educator fosters in all his students willpower and the desire and ability to overcome difficulties and to gradually and consistently build up their intellectual, creative, and cognitive abilities.

However, preliminary work with the class to ensure the fulfillment of difficult assignments is not always necessary. All students should be given the opportunity to test themselves with easy and difficult assignments, both with and without the teacher's initial help. In the latter case, however, they cannot all be required to cope with an assignment. Instead, at the next lesson the teacher either asks volunteers to do the assignment on the blackboard or he discusses it in detail with the class.

5.9.13. Home assignments that offer an insight into the basic scientific ideas treated in the course can be given only in the final school years. Their main purpose is to systematize and structuralize the material studied over several years, i.e., the material of the whole course. They can be carried out in the form of reports delivered by students in class or at seminars for the strong students, to which all students of the senior grades are invited. The schedules of such reports should be drawn up and the reporters selected in such a way as to give each student several weeks to prepare his report. Reports should be made only by volunteers, and if some topics remain unreported they should be presented by the teacher.

We need not go into the importance of such work. We should, however, note that every report should conclude and sum up the work done by all the students during the home and class assignments that preceded it. For example, one assignment requires the students to review the textbook definitions of the concept of power with an exponent that is a positive whole number other than one, its properties and operations with such powers, with proof of theorems and clear distinction of propositions: definitions, theorems, corollaries. The assignment also includes powers with exponents 1 and 0, to which theorems of powers with exponents other than 1 or 0 also apply. At the next lesson the students review powers with exponents that are negative integers. It is stressed that a^n, where $a \neq 0$ and n is a negative integer, is a common fraction; for example, 2^{-2} should be regarded as simply another way of writing the common fraction $1/4$. Then follow lessons at which the concept of power with positive and negative fractional exponents is developed and generalized. It is specifically noted that only positive numbers and zero can be the base of a power with a positive fractional exponent. The base of a power with a fractional negative exponent can only be a positive number. A power with a fractional exponent is regarded only as an alternative form of writing an expression with radicals, which may sometimes be more convenient for performing an operation. The reporter generalizes and systematizes this material and proves some theorems which were not proved in class. He may schematically introduce the concept of power with an irrational exponent and the concepts of algebraic and transcendental numbers.

The teacher should draw up a schedule of meetings with each reporter so as to prevent the preparations for the report from deteriorating into a one-night effort and make sure that it is conducted gradually, without interfering with the normal educational process in other school subjects.

We offer brief outlines of two reports generalizing some concepts of arithmetic and algebra in the school course of mathematics which can be used by strong students and teachers:

Outline One

The concept of number is impossible without such fundamental arithmetical concepts as equality, sum, and product. On the other hand, those concepts are meaningless without the concept of number. There can be no equality, sum, or product without the concept of number; there can be no concept of number without the concepts of equality, sum, and product. Numbers possess properties which we express in terms of the concepts

331

of their equality, sum, or product. These four concepts cannot be considered separately: they have meaning only in relation to each other. We cannot speak of a fraction as a number until we know how to compare fractions among themselves and with integers, as well as how to add and multiply them. At the same time we are comparing, adding, and multiplying fractions, not something else.

The concepts of number, equality, sum, and product are interdependent; the evolution of number is inseparable from the evolution of the concepts of equality, sum, and product. From the formal logical aspect, the evolution of these concepts is essentially an evolution of the concept of number.

At a certain stage of this evolution, a new type of number is created. The new number, developed as a result of the development of the concepts of equality, sum, and product as applied to the old number, acquires a qualitative individuality in unity with these concepts. The evolution of the concepts of equality, sum, and product as applied to the newly created number leads to a new stage in the development of the concept of number. In the logical sense this process is guided and determined by the principle of permanence, which lies at the root of the development of our arithmetic and the principle of the feasibility of inverse operations. To be sure, arithmetic could be developed on the basis of other principles, but then we would have a different kind of arithmetic than the one we now deal with in school.

Expanded systems of numbers should not contradict the initially developed system. The results we obtain using only numbers of the initial system should not contradict results obtained in the expanded system. To avoid contradictions and a great complication of arithmetic, the expanded system should retain the laws of operations with numbers established with respect to numbers in the initial system. In this process, individual concepts are interconnected and interrelated: we cannot define the equality or sum of complex numbers without defining the equality or sum of real numbers; we cannot define the product of fractions without defining the product of whole numbers, et cetera.

The concepts of equality, sum, and product constitute the arithmetical content of the specific type of number. Numbers are different because they are differently compared, added, and multiplied. The concepts of difference, quotient, power, root, and logarithm differ for different numbers, but they develop and change not independently, not defining new numbers, but under the influence or, rather, as a consequence of development of the four fundamental concepts. If the equality, sum, or product of complex numbers is not defined in the conventional way, the definitions of power, root, difference, or quotient may remain the same, but their content will change. The meaning and content of the fundamental concepts as applied to a specific type of numbers is given by their definitions; the meaning and content of the derivative concepts is given by the unity of their definitions with the content of the fundamental concepts.

Thus, in consistently expanding the concept of number from whole to complex (hypercomplex) numbers one can take the following course: Having whole numbers and showing the laws of operating with them, we introduce each successive type of number by means of definitions. We denote a new number by a symbol, and then define the following: firstly, the fundamental concepts of equality, sum, and product of the new number; secondly, difference, quotient, power, root, and logarithm. The meanings of the concepts in the second collection, as pointed out, depend on the meanings of the fundamental concepts, i.e., the concepts in the first collection, although their definitions coincide in form in all stages of the evolution of the number. In this process of building a field of complex numbers, the fundamental concepts for each new type of number are given in such a way that the fundamental laws of operations remain valid in application to any complex numbers. In other words, the fundamental laws of operations are always valid for all introduced numbers, because we introduce them, or rather, we introduce the four fundamental concepts, in such a way as to preserve those laws.

Outline Two

In the latter nineteenth century, Georg Cantor developed his set theory, which has had a tremendous impact on all contemporary mathematics. Modern algebra studies sets in which certain operations are defined. The idea of the general concept of an operation arises when considering the addition and multiplication of numbers. However, in different branches of mathematics and its applications, operations are frequently carried out not with numbers but with elements of sets of an arbitrary nature. For example, in the composition of forces, any two forces are correlated to a third, called their *resultant*. In other words, the operations need not be conventional operations of addition or multiplication in the arithmetical sense, but rather laws or rules making it possible to establish a correspondence between two elements, a and b, of a given set, and a third element, c, of that set.

The concept of field arises as a result of comparing the properties of basic number sets: a set of all rational numbers, a set of all real numbers, and a set of all complex numbers. Two fundamental operations are defined in each of these three number-sets: addition and multiplication, and the basic laws of sum and product are valid. For each operation, within a given set an inverse operation can be performed; there is a unit element—that is, we deal with fields.

Rational numbers, real numbers, and complex numbers can be approached as the subjects of algebraic operations. As the students study algebraic operations and their properties in different number sets, they are introduced into the sphere of the ideas of algebra.

The school course devotes considerable space to algebraic operations. We operate with monomials and polynomials. More often than not, algebraic operations with monomials and polynomials are performed mechanically; sometimes the student forgets that each letter in those operations represents a certain number. However, there is an important positive aspect in such mechanical performance of operations. The letters in an algebraic expression can be interpreted not in terms of numbers but as some other targets of investigation. When solving problems of a geometrical or physical nature, we frequently perform arithmetical operations not with numbers but directly with quantities.

333

Two sets are called isomorphic with respect to a certain operation if a one-to-one correspondence can be established between their elements, such that it extends to the results of the operation. For example, to the sum and product of arbitrary elements of the first set there correspond a sum and product of corresponding elements of the second set. In that case the relationships prevailing in one set can be used to judge the relationships prevailing in the other. Therefore, in algebra, isomorphic fields, rings, and groups are considered to be identical. The corresponding elements of two isomorphic sets possess the same properties with respect to the considered operations. Hence, if one set is substantially easier to review than another, it can serve as a model for the latter. Algebra studies sets to the precision of isomorphism with respect to those operations which are considered in the given theory, specifically, with respect to one operation in group theory, and with respect to two operations in ring and field theory.

The school course in algebra considers the field of rational numbers, the field of real numbers, and the field of complex numbers. These number fields can serve as models of all fields isomorphic with them. For example, the set of all rational numbers and the set of all rational points of a number axis are isomorphic with respect to addition and multiplication, provided the addition and multiplication of points are defined as follows: The sum $A + B$ and product AB of two points, $A(a)$ and $B(b)$, are, respectively, points $C(a + b)$ and $D(ab)$. It is easy to define the property of density for the set of all rational numbers, but the set of all rational points of a number axis is isomorphic with a field of all rational numbers; hence the set of all rational points of a number axis will also possess this property. On the other hand, measurement leads to the conclusion that rational points do not cover all the points of a number line. From this follows the idea of expanding the set of rational numbers so that a number could correspond to any point of the number axis.

To every positive number there can correspond the logarithm of that number. We obtain a one-to-one mapping of the set of positive real numbers onto the set of all real numbers. From the theorem, $\log(ab) = \log a + \log b$, it follows that we have an isomorphic mapping of the group of all real positive numbers with respect to multiplication onto a group of all real numbers with respect to addition. The practical use of this isomorphism is well known.

5.10. ALGORITHMIC PROBLEMS AND THE STUDENT'S CREATIVE ACTIVITY

5.10.1. When a child has learned subtraction, say, (1) $\frac{3}{7}$ out of $\frac{5}{7}$, the problem (2) $1 - \frac{3}{7}$ will be a creative one for him. He must be given the opportunity to solve it independently and to justify the solution. After this problem he should be given the opportunity to independently perform the subtraction operation (3) $6 - \frac{3}{7}$, then (4) $6\frac{5}{7} - \frac{3}{7}$, then (5) $6\frac{5}{7} - 4\frac{3}{7}$, then (6) $1\frac{1}{7} - \frac{3}{7}$, then (7) $6\frac{1}{7} - \frac{3}{7}$, then (8) $6\frac{1}{7} - 2\frac{3}{7}$.

A sufficient number of exercises of the first four types should be solved in class during the first lesson so that all the students, without exception, learn to cope with them without difficulty. This is hard, very hard, because solution of problems of the first four types should be left to the students; i.e., each of the first four examples is written on the blackboard and the children attempt to solve them. They make suggestions and justify them while the teacher allows the class to evaluate every new suggestion. Of all the suggestions made for each example, the best is chosen.

However, dear educators, don't be overly optimistic. Today colleges abound in people who write $5/7 - 2/3 = 3/4$, and they do this after finishing high school and attending remedial courses in which we place so much hope, instead of putting the teaching-learning process together in our schools.

After solving two or three examples of each of the first four types, we proceed to the next stage of class work: we give the students all four types of examples simultaneously, not in the order we initially gave them but, say, (3), (4), (2), (1)—obviously, with new numbers and with large numbers. Everyone knows that large numbers should not be used when introducing new operations and concepts because they tend to distract the students from the content of the assignment, making it hard for them to understand what it's all about. However, this doesn't mean that large numbers should always be avoided. They are necessary in life, as well as in other sections of the course. They are also essential for consolidating sprouting skills and barely glimmering habits.

Depending on the composition and level of training of the class, on how the students solved the four examples with large numbers in the new order, and on how they explained and loudly and clearly justified their solutions, the first four problems can be repeated during the same first lesson in the order (3), (2), (1), (4). This should again be done with clear and loud justifications, and blackboard notes written alternately by the teacher (with student participation) and by the students themselves. Alternating work at the blackboard between the students and the teacher should be done in all classes. On the one hand, this introduces at least a semblance of diversity into the lesson. On the other, the students learn to use the equal sign correctly, which present-day college students can't do and are incapable of comprehending.

If there is time left at the lesson, a word problem can be solved, using the operations discussed during the lesson. This, again, should be done with the greatest independence of the students and with the supervision of the teacher, who asks questions, draws all the students into the discussion, sums up the process, and requires the class to explain the process and give clear answers.

The home assignment for the next lesson should include all problems, types (1) through (4), with large numbers and word problems, or (1)–(5), or (1)–(6), all depending on the composition of the class. Examples of types (5) and (6), if they are included in the home assignment, can first be discussed orally in class, without permitting the students to take any notes, or they can be simply assigned for homework together with examples (1)–(4) without any preliminary work on them in class—if you know the class well enough to require the students to independently do problems that are still creative for them. The students will accept this without protest because they are used to such requirements and know how to handle them.

In any case, work on home assignments with problems of types (1)–(4), (1)–(5), or (1)–(6), should be resumed at the second lesson.

5.10.2. When problems (1)–(4), or (1)–(5), or (1)–(6) are given for homework, problems of types (7) and (8) should not be introduced at the second lesson or in the homework assigned for the third lesson. It is, however, necessary to get the students to solve problems (1)–(6) in any order and to give word problems, problems such as (9) $\frac{5}{7} + (1 - \frac{3}{7})$; (10) $\frac{5}{7} - (1 - \frac{3}{7})$; (11) $(1\frac{1}{7} - \frac{3}{7}) - \frac{4}{7}$; (12) $(1\frac{1}{7} - \frac{3}{7}) + \frac{4}{7}$, et cetera.

Depending upon how well the students are prepared, they can be kept on problems (1)–(6) and (9)–(12) for a longer time, both in school and remedial courses in college.

Problems (7) and (8) should be introduced gradually, only after you are sure that the students have no difficulty solving all problems of types (1)–(6) and (9)–(12), in class and at home.

Problems (7) and (8) are, at this stage, creative ones for the students, since they do not as yet know the solution algorithms. The students should use the knowledge obtained previously to find the correct solutions.

5.10.3. Never assign all creative problems for homework on the assumption that at home the children will have more time to think them over and cope with the assignment. You can assign some of them, occasionally in the junior classes, more frequently in the senior ones. But in any case, i.e., whether those creative assignments were for home or class, you should leave time at the lesson to justify, formulate, and verify the results.

Of course, it is tempting to have creative problems solved out of class because we are always short of time and hurrying to get ahead. However, this is extremely dangerous, especially for young teachers and instructors of remedial courses in colleges who are overly optimistic and later wonder incredulously why half the class comes to the finish line with no knowledges whatsoever.

5.10.4. Problems (7) $6\frac{1}{7} - \frac{3}{7}$, and (8) $6\frac{1}{7} - 2\frac{3}{7}$, can be given at a lesson simultaneously, at once, and not in sequence. The students should be given time to think them over and then comment on what the problems have in common and how they differ. After this they should think about how to reduce the new problems to the solution of known problems, specifically, (7) $6\frac{1}{7} - \frac{3}{7} = 5 + 1\frac{1}{7} - \frac{3}{7} = 5 + (1\frac{1}{7} - \frac{3}{7})$ $= 5 + (\frac{8}{7} - \frac{3}{7}) = 5 + \frac{5}{7} = 5\frac{5}{7}$; (8) $6\frac{1}{7} - 2\frac{3}{7} = 6\frac{1}{7} - (2 + \frac{3}{7})$ $= 6\frac{1}{7} - 2 - \frac{3}{7} = 4\frac{1}{7} - \frac{3}{7}$, as was in (7).

5.10.5. The students can and should be given most algorithmic

336

problems before formulating the algorithm, thereby fostering their creativity. The problems will remain creative for the students until the algorithm or rule is introduced; but if the algorithm is introduced on the basis of solved problems by the students themselves, this is practically a research project. In this sense, all identical transformations of algebraic and transcendental expressions and the solutions of all equations and inequalities can and should be used to encourage the students' intellectual and creative efforts. Teachers can be taught how to organize such education only in a system of mini-researches.

The teacher and the students must justify each step, discuss its expedience, argue, present proofs, draw conclusions, correct mistakes, and look for the truly optimal variant: this is what contributes to the development of the students' knowledges, skills, and habits and intellectual, creative, and cognitive abilities, every day, at every lesson.

During the next five to ten lessons, in every home assignment we should give, along with new material, problems of types (9)–(12), but now based on the material of all problems of types (1) through (8). Once in a while, one or two such problems should be analyzed in detail in class.

Lessons and home assignments provide both the students and the teacher with a continuous flow of feedback involving the teaching-learning process of the class as a whole and each student in particular. However, this occurs only when home and class assignments blend organically into a unified, instructive teaching-learning process, mutually complementing and qualifying each other.

5.10.6. Involving children in a creative process, in which the problem solutions are found through creative reasoning rather than with the help of a cut-and-dried algorithm, should be continuous, extending through all subjects and years in school. This is the only way to rear creative persons, not by any special educational devices or homilies. Proud and self-confident, they will be grateful to society for the joy of creative life. They will be grateful for the joy and happiness that they have been given and that they have won in the process of long, hard, creative work, in the course and as a result of a teaching, learning, and educating process. This process should be supervised and directed by professional educators and professional administrators.

To effectively teach students how to do creative problems, it is necessary, especially during the initial stages, to discuss and draw up plans for solving them. This process should never end, despite any difficulties, otherwise learning will deteriorate into imitation. The students should pool their efforts to draw up the exercise plans, perhaps through frontal work with the teacher. Those who wish to can write the plan down so as to have a guideline for doing an assignment which would otherwise be too difficult for them.

As the class progresses, work on such plans should gradually decline from writing them down to oral discussion. With time, the discussions, too, will be reduced to hints, but they are not eliminated altogether.

From time to time, more difficult problems and other assignments can be introduced with suggestions or hints about how to do them. They may come from the teacher or from some of the students. During the lesson, the class should be given time to think the problem over and find ways of solving it. If none of the students can offer a solution plan or basic guideline, this should be done by the teacher or not at all—the teacher can leave its discussion for the next lesson.

Without solving creative problems with the gradual, steady involvement of the students, the studied course turns into a more or less dull drill. If drills dominate in teaching, they destroy the students' intellectual, creative, and cognitive abilities. Nevertheless, drills have been and remain a very important component of the teaching-learning process, something which our educators also seem to have forgotten.

5.10.7. In order to teach the students how to solve new creative problems, the teacher should sometimes initially solve one or more less difficult problems with them. These problems should be included in a difficult creative problem assigned later on as one or several stages in its solution. Of course, the teacher should not let the class know of this. Depending on the class's training, such auxiliary problems should be introduced either shortly before the solution of a new creative problem or well in advance. The number of auxiliary problems also depends upon the quality of the student body and what the teacher can expect of them.

5.10.8. Some students may not require such forms of instruction: in fact, there could be quite a few such students, though over the last twenty years their numbers have been declining. They can solve all problems given to the class independently without any help at all. Such students should be given the opportunity not to participate in the class discussion of creative problems, leaving them to solve other creative problems. They should also be encouraged to participate actively in seminars and olympiads and to solve additional problems and exercises taken from professional books and journals.

The first thing a teacher must do is give the students a list of books in his subject for independent work, organize a seminar for gifted students, and organize the solution of problems of olympiad difficulty in class and at home, with preliminary and subsequent work on them in class. This work should be accompanied by a gradual reduction in the degree of teacher involvement in the solution of such problems, obviously to the extent that this is made possible by the class's training, level of development, and rate of learning of the skills of solving problems of greater-than-average difficulty.

5.10.9. It is extremely important to get the students to realize that creative problems may require several attempts to solve them, at different times of the day and on different days. To this end it is useful to supplement regular assignments given after each lesson to all students with assignments consisting of creative problems and spanning a week or two so that the students can have plenty of time to work on them.

338

Students attending seminars, where most problems are creative, should also be given assignments a week or two in advance so as to give them more time to work on them. Only in this manner can children be taught successful creative work.

5.11. REVIEWING PREVIOUSLY STUDIED MATERIAL

5.11.1. Work by both the student and the teacher on assignments that include reviewing previously studied material is extremely difficult and important. All class- and homework should, as a rule, include review. In practice, this means combining two assignments—not always related to one another—into one, merging two lessons—which may not always be related—into one.

The very fact of merging two different types of activity is indicative of the difficulty of such work. However, a teaching-learning process that is not thus organized over several years—in the same subject, by the same teacher, with the same group of students—can never be successful. This is especially true of mathematics and science, because the study of these subjects, more than of any other, should result in developing not just knowledges and skills, but a system of structurized knowledges and skills; it should result not just in habits, but in a system of firm and perfect habits. It should also promote a stable process of development of intellectual, creative, and cognitive abilities through every year of education. Only on the basis of these systems and abilities, developed over many years of intense and devoted efforts, is it possible to build an edifice of classical and modern sciences, at first in school and subsequently in college and graduate school.

5.11.2. When discussing assignments involving new material, the teacher may sometimes restrict himself to listing the exercises the students should do at home—if similar ones were done fairly successfully in class—as well as to the sections of the theoretical course which were discussed at the lesson. The measure of the teacher's responsibility increases greatly when he assigns for homework exercises and theories studied earlier and which have to be reviewed. This is because the assignment is superficially familiar to the students and represents a variant of apparent knowledge, which it is much harder to transform into genuine knowledge than even outright ignorance.

If the teacher hopes to implant genuine knowledge in his students, he must see to it that every lesson is accompanied by a review of previously studied material, both in class and at home. Not a single lesson should be conducted, nor a home assignment given, in school or in college, without carefully preparing a set of exercises on previously studied material, discussing those exercises before and after they are done, and analyzing and discussing earlier-studied theoretical material. The best way to systematize, generalize, and structuralize the students' knowledges is to review previously studied material. The only way to prevent the destruction of students' knowledges, skills, and habits, at all stages of education, is to review them thoroughly and regularly.

In the portion of a home assignment that includes review, the teacher should discuss the most important concepts, ideas, and structures to which the students should give special attention. Without such help, and without feedback organized by the teacher, the review can be useless. Some exercises that include the reviewed material should be done in class before and after the students are required to do such exercises at home. Reviewed key theoretical questions should sometimes be first discussed in class and then assigned for homework. The sequence can also be reversed; it all depends on the difficulty of the material and the amount of time that has passed since the students first studied it. But whether the reviewed material is difficult or simple, whether it was studied recently or long ago, whether the review exercises are difficult or simple, and whether they were previously done recently or long ago, it is as senseless, cruel, and useless to leave all the review work to the students themselves as it is to abandon them without the teacher's help and supervision in any other form of the teaching-learning process—in class or at home.

When a review is not relevant to the new material each lesson should be broken down into two parts: 1) review of the previously studied material; 2) study of new information and acquisition of new knowledges, skills, and habits.

Review, systematically conducted in class and in the system of home assignments, possesses a logic of development which follows the logic of development of the studied science, rather than the order imposed by the curriculum. It is subordinate more to the basic ideas and structures of the science than to the sequence in which those ideas are taught: development of the concept of number; development of the concept of exponent; development of the concept of identical transformations of algebraic and transcendental expressions; development of the concepts of equation, inequality, and structure; development in the school course of the ideas and concepts of calculus; development of the ideas and concepts of analytical geometry, geometric transformations, and measurement of lengths, areas, volumes. Such review, especially in the upper grades, sums up and structuralizes the students' knowledges, skills, and habits as related to the logic of the science to which they belong, and thanks to which the students gain an idea of the sciences represented in the school course. Thanks to this, knowledges, skills, and habits undergo not only, and not so much, a revival as a rebirth. They are generalized, systematized, and structuralized in accordance with the system of science, not of school subjects in which the development of the system of science is inevitably placed on the back burner, mainly for educational considerations, as well as for considerations of the students' utilization of knowledges in adjoining sciences and in practical activity.

5.12. ON THE WORK OF WEAK AND STRONG STUDENTS

5.12.1. Never concentrate solely on the weaker students—those who have difficulty mastering the subject, or have missed lessons for different reasons, or get no attention at home—but nor should you forget them. Supplementary classes and supplementary, sometimes individualized, home assignments for them change the whole situation: not at once, nor in a week or two, but slowly and truly. Children who had once lagged undergo a remarkable change. They even undertake difficult creative tasks that they are as yet incapable of solving. See to it that this doesn't happen too often. Failure after extensive tutorial work can discourage a child, who can lose faith in the teacher and in himself. You should try to shield children from such failures for as long as possible, while at the same time gradually driving home the idea that achievements are inevitably accompanied by failures.

During supplementary classes for weak students it is a good idea to go over the things to be done at subsequent lessons—not exactly, perhaps, but in a fairly close manner to what they will be doing in class within the next few days.

We can and should give children from disadvantaged families the things they failed to acquire in the family. By establishing one or two prekindergarten grades we could prevent the influx of weak students into schools. Even so, we will have to upgrade material studied earlier and work on new material with those students who, for years, are unable to keep up with the rest of the class. This work is a must for all teachers and those children whom the teachers designate as requiring such supplementary work. This work is also a must for children who miss classes because of sickness and those who suddenly stop doing their homework because something is the matter with them or with their families, something we may not know and never get to know. Groups for such work should include no more than five or ten people.

All teachers and administrators must fight for every student, for every child, during all the long years at school, abandoning none. Children are very sensitive to sincere and to hypocritical teaching. In the former case, they are grateful to us and strive to study; in the latter, they go looking for sincerity where they think they can find it: in the world of criminals.

Through special invitation, regular and supplementary classes can be attended or viewed on videotape by parents or elder relatives, who will to some extent learn what education is all about and what to do at home to help the child. Supplementary classes can also be entrusted to teacher trainees, but only under the supervision of a schoolteacher or college instructor.

341

This must go on day after day, year after year, without interruption, teaching the children sincerely and patiently, without giving them time to be corrupted. College can never make up for what the school fails to do.

Supplementary classes and auxiliary home assignments give teachers the opportunity to overcome shortfalls in students' knowledges, skills, and habits which have accumulated over past years. They also provide the opportunity of instilling study habits in the weaker students and upgrading their intellectual, creative, and cognitive abilities to the level needed to continue acquiring an education.

Special seminar classes with strong students, together with special systematic assignments, should contain high-level theoretical material and assignments, the difficulty of which should not be built up gradually. The students themselves should be able to determine the degree of difficulty of an exercise and the ways of solving it. In most cases, these classes should not be in any way associated with the material currently being studied in class. They will keep the stronger students in a state of creative tension and successful creative activity.

The composition of the groups for supplementary lessons at below-the-average class level and of the seminars conducted at higher-than-average level may change fairly frequently. Students may move from one group to another, and there should be nothing surprising in this. Students who missed school because of illness will go over from the higher level to the group for weaker students. Capable students who, for various reasons, have blank spots in their knowledges, skills, and habits may quickly fill these gaps in the group for weaker students and move up to the seminar, where work is conducted on a higher level than in class, and be among the foremost there.

The level of our students' knowledges, skills, and habits and intellectual, creative, and cognitive abilities depends on us alone. It can't and shouldn't be the *same* for all students, but it can and should be the *highest possible* for every student. Only then will the students be able to develop their intellectual, creative, and cognitive abilities at the fastest possible rate, which, however, may vary from one student to another. This is only natural and is nothing to worry about. All the students will have a certain minimal level of training which enables them to successfully continue their education. Those with exceptional abilities can ascend to the heights of education they can and wish to achieve.

We would like to make a few more remarks concerning supplementary classes with weaker students. If a school has a course that differs from the one studied by a weak student only in the greater amount of time devoted to it in class, the student should be advised to attend that class. Such advice should be given extremely tactfully and cautiously. A student may have a much higher opinion of himself than does his teacher. He may feel offended and discouraged, causing him to lose confidence in himself. However, you must talk to him sincerely, with tact and understanding, suggesting that he should either transfer to another group or attend special classes. You should tell him that there is nothing shameful in attending special supplementary classes: at this point, there is nothing wrong with it. Tell the student that you're simply advising him to attend these lessons; if he doesn't like them, he needn't continue. If the student rejects both the other course and the supplementary classes, you should work with him very attentively and tactfully, not gloating over his mistakes and shaking your head as if to say, "I told you!" Perhaps the very fact of such a talk with the teacher will induce him to take the trivial road of simply studying the subject more attentively and diligently. This may well keep him abreast of the class and make him grateful to you for a useful talk. However, if the student begins to lag behind the class and senses this himself, you should talk to him again, more insistently and perhaps in the presence of his parents and/or a school administrator. Now you can tell him that it is absolutely essential for him to attend supplementary classes or transfer to a group in which the work is done at a slower pace. If you don't do this, your student will begin by daily accumulating vague ideas about some theoretical topics and their practical applications, followed subsequently by total incomprehension of both.

Teachers of all educational establishments must consider it their primary duty to keep students from falling behind the work of a study group. This is easier for both the teacher and the students than later investing a tremendous effort to bring a student up to the state when he can work at the class's pace successfully, and restoring his lost faith in his strength and capabilities.

It goes without saying that two- or three-month courses in college and one-year courses in school virtually deny us the possibility of preventing and overcoming student failure. Such courses are nurseries of failure and ignorance; they are an effective means of destroying the educational system.

Many teachers have stronger students regularly coach the lagging ones. Usually one good pupil begins to help a student who needs help. This is either begun spontaneously, out of friendship, or at the tactful but insistent request of the teacher and the lagging student. This form of help should never be rejected, either in school or in college. Such work is extremely useful to both students—the helped and the helper. The helping student consolidates his knowledges, skills, and habits. He learns to voice his thoughts clearly, something he not always manages in class, or manages but rarely. Classes are large, there is a catastrophic amount of material in each course, and the teacher rushes ahead, leaving behind not only weak students but strong ones as well.

5.12.2. As a consequence of work on home assignments and their unity with classwork, as a consequence of conducting regular supplementary classes with the weaker students on the basic material of the course, the teacher is able to conduct an active teaching-learning process involving both the weak and the strong students. In the course of this process, the once weak students will catch up with and pass stronger students—not all of them, but the less brilliant of them. There is nothing wrong with that. All it means is a victory for the educator and the students.

Students who were formerly strong—not because of talent or ability, but through industriousness and diligence—will inevitably move back to the places they deserve. Formerly weak students—not all, but the talented and gifted—will acquire knowledges, skills, and habits and a standard of intellectual, creative, and cognitive abilities, enabling them to occupy the place they deserve in class as well as in life.

We can and should employ all the means at our disposal to prevent an explicit distribution of places in a class. The most trusted method is absolute evenhandedness with regard to all students; patient and courageous equanimity and imperturbability in the face of the most foolish answers to the most interesting questions; asking the same questions of all the students, but looking for the answers of those who need the most work. Weak students require attention to encourage confidence in themselves, in their forces, and in the strength and devotion of their educator, who strives to raise them to the light of intelligence, to the joy and happiness of creative cognition. The stronger students require preservation of the state of active learning and preservation and development of their quest for active cognition, for the happiness of creative work.

5.12.3. Unfortunately, there are countless methods of murdering the teaching-learning process and tens of millions of our students, both weak and strong, together with it. One such method is the monstrous requirement, which is *a priori* unfulfillable and *a priori* cruel for all: forcing children to prepare for two, three, or even more tests at once. The tests are all held on the same day, with brief intervals between them, or with no intervals at all.

Who suggested such an insane idea to the creators of our pedagogical archipelago? What guided or guides them to needlessly place children in a totally hopeless situation?

Obviously, if the tests are worthless it doesn't really matter if there are one, two, three, or more a day. However, there are also tests that *are* worth something.

Such a testing system is incredible, insane, and extremely cruel. How much time must a child spend preparing simultaneously for two or three tests in different subjects? How much pain and bitterness accumulates in his heart during those long hours and days filled with work on two or three courses at once? What do we achieve by such punishment, dear educators and school and college administrators? Do we want to show how exacting and implacable we can be? That we are inexorable in our demands, and therefore children, mothers, and fathers will respect and value us? Come, come, that is not the way to win the sympathy and respect of children and parents. This requires endless effort, patience, and skill; it requires mini-researches and many, many other things. We must love children selflessly and serve them selflessly, while demanding reciprocity. To achieve this, it is necessary—every day, at every lesson—to

344

give them knowledges, skills, and habits and develop, consolidate, and constantly upgrade the level of their intellectual, creative, and cognitive abilities. This is very, very difficult. It is even harder to learn this ability. Moreover, no one has ever taught, or ever intends to teach, this most difficult and most necessary ability. We have never learned this and have no intention of learning it. This failure on our part is out of naiveté, cruelty, inability, unwillingness, or all these reasons together or any combination of them.

Many of our educators will certainly not see all of this as applying to them; therefore, they will not take offense. Most other educators will probably see this as referring to them, but, nevertheless, they will not take offense, either. We feel sure of this because the truth, the true causes of the disintegration of our education and the optimal variants of building it up, must be set forth as clearly and concisely as possible. Now is no time for taking offense. Verbosity and false humaneness can sink the whole problem of building up the educational system in an ocean of long-winded, pseudoscientific, florid gobbledygook. It is a time-worn, but still effective, device. It makes it possible to hold the nation's children in darkness and ignorance in the name of false slogans.

Not only three tests a day are inhuman and cruel. Three tests a week—or better, even two—are the maximum that can be given in schools and undergraduate school, at the cost of some administrative effort. The schedule of tests, coordinated among all educators and advisors, should be prepared in advance and made known to the students. There may well be exceptions due to circumstances. We are speaking of the number of tests that can be given to a student in one week.

Department heads and school and college administrators should be held personally accountable for overloading students with tests and home assignments. No one, save for administrators, can cope with such very difficult work, either in school or in college. It is difficult and tiring, as is everything in the educational system that would claim success: it is difficult and tiring to double and triple the time devoted in all schools and colleges to courses in math and science; it is difficult and tiring to prepare a good lesson; it is difficult and tiring to conduct mini-researches in all educational establishments so as to prevent the teaching-learning process from deteriorating and destroying everything living and creative in our children, and instead having it mold critically and creatively thinking people, worthy members of a worthy society.

5.12.4. Under the system of many-year school courses in the same subject, it becomes possible for the teacher to give special summer assignments to students who reveal gaps in knowledge during the academic year and/or display a remarkable ability to forget everything. Such students must be kept in touch with the subject they had difficulty with during the summer vacation, otherwise they will be quite helpless when they return to school. Some will abandon the course or drop out of school.

The assignments should cover the main theoretical and practical questions and problems from one or two previous years that are essential for studying the course during the next year. They should require three to five hours of work per week throughout the summer. In the fall, the students return the assignments to the teacher, who reviews them, superficially or thoroughly, depending on the student, and returns them within the first month of the new academic year.

LETTER SIX

Teacher Trap in the Names of Holmes and Carnegie

The vast bulk of the writing on professional education assumes that education is already a profession . . . rarely is education referred to as anything but a profession . . . I have done my best to avoid uncritical comparisons and superficial analogies between education and other occupations . . . Comparing education to "the professions" implies that education is not a profession. . . .

> —Myron Lieberman, Ph.D. *Education as a Profession.* Prentice-Hall, Inc.: Englewood Cliffs, N.J. 1956. pp. vii, viii, ix.

How to teach mathematics [at undergraduate school]. *You can't. Neither can you teach swimming, basketball, or how to ride a bicycle. The student either learns by doing, or he doesn't learn at all. You can only help by introducing material at a proper pace, checking his progress regularly, and judging his degree of mastery.* Undergraduate Committee Minutes. [*Mathematics majors] (i) have very bad writing habits; (ii) do not know calculus; (iii) do not know graphing; (iv) are extremely weak in inequalities; (v) have lack of any intellectual experience.*

> —Department of Mathematics of a research university, a charter member of The Holmes Group. 1985, 1986.

6.1. MORE ON A NEW TEACHER FOR THIS COUNTRY

6.1.1. In the teaching profession, unlike that of an accountant, veterinarian, lawyer or doctor, it is not only the levels of knowledge, skills and expertise at which teachers commence their professional careers that count, nor only the levels of their mental, creative and cognitive abilities. What is really important is how all those qualities were acquired and what educational ideas and principles were fostered and acquired in the process. Moreover, and more importantly, it is extremely important what humanitarian qualities were acquired and what moral principles were fostered as a result of that process. It is so important because those are the principles and ideas, the pedagogical and humanitarian philosophies and moral standards that teachers bring into the schools. And those are the philosophies and moral standards which they will be instilling in our children as they teach and educate them. For better or for worse, regardless of the teacher's will, those principles, ideas, philosophies and moral standards will inevitably become ingrained traits of our children, traits of the nation. This is something to which the Holmes and Carnegie groups fail to pay attention.

6.1.2. Teacher preparation colleges should, from the very outset, avoid forcing their students to take courses that are cruel and, therefore, extremely harmful to them and to their own future students. Yet such courses predominate today in American undergraduate schools. They are beyond the students' comprehension, insurmountably difficult, jejune and illogical. They are crammed with fantastic amounts of illiterate, unscientific, indigestible material that is included for no apparent reason. The time allotted for studying them is incredibly limited. These courses foster a sense of insecurity and fear in students, forcing them to learn by rote, without the slightest comprehension. They breed despair and anger, nervous breakdowns, drug addiction and drinking, and they arouse protest. The courses are taught by graduate students or professors preoccupied with their own affairs and studies, not with teaching. They provide neither knowledge, skills nor habits, they discourage the development of the intellectual, creative and cognitive abilities of both

349

those who dreamed of becoming teachers and those who couldn't care less. Moreover and more dangerously, they are the embodiment of militant antipedagogy. They discourage people from considering education as a profession and discourage a loving attitude in those who do decide to become teachers. Because of those courses undergraduate schools lose more than half of their contingent of intending school teachers. The few survivors get great examples of cruelty and uselessness in the teaching-learning process and of total indifference to the fate of students. All of which they naturally transfer, with youthful energy and gusto, to the schools. In this way they copy not only their former helpless, hapless schoolteachers, made so by colleges and universities; they also copy indifferent people forced into the role of college instructors. They come to the school cruel and callous, indifferent to their students' fate, with no faith in teaching, destroyed by the pretense of teaching.

6.1.3. The fundamental operating principle of American teacher education colleges today should be the following: The teaching-learning process in undergraduate courses in the academic subjects which the teacher will be teaching in school should not be conducted in the form of conventional mini-research projects involving only the faculty. Such mini-research projects are discussed in detail in Letter Two of this book, specifically in 2.1.6 and 2.10. The process should take the form of mini-research involving the most active participation of the students, i.e., of prospective teachers.

This new kind of mini-research will do more than just offer students, for the first time in their lives, the opportunity to witness a genuinely humane, didactically kind, accessible and instructive teaching-learning process of a kind they have never before seen or heard, much less taken part in. Through their own experience, guided by the college professors, they will grasp all the details of that process, its spirit, methods and techniques, its form, content and technology. They will realize its value, significance and importance for their future students, because they will have realized its value, significance and importance for themselves.

This will happen not only thanks to college professors and mini-research projects. It will happen because in the years ahead, for as long as the nation feels it is necessary, colleges will have to teach thoroughly prospective teachers simple things which they should have been taught, but never were, at school: instead of testing them.

Today there is still no one to teach our children these things at school. Nor will there be anyone until America teaches its present and future teachers what teaching is all about and how it should be done. The duty of teaching all this to present and future teachers—instead of embittering and testing them—lies with teacher education colleges. Only they can do this. And they must do it constantly so as to fill our schools with educated and capable teachers, so that schools may develop and maintain a stable, effective, active, humane and didactically kind educational process accessible to all students.

350

6.1.4. As an instructor in his academic subject, the professor at a teacher education college must thoroughly and patiently discuss and assess the pedagogical value of his work with the prospective teachers. He and his colleagues will thoughtfully, humanely, and with didactic kindness teach prospective teachers more than just the basics of their academic subjects. Their job description will, thus, include not only the duty of consistently and patiently explaining to the prospective teachers the concepts, ideas and structures of the academic subjects they will be teaching in school, taken in their interrelationships, correlationships and development. They will also be duty bound, together with the prospective teachers, to thoughtfully, humanely and patiently analyze, demonstrate and optimize pedagogical ideas, techniques and methods, pedagogical philosophy and technology. They will do this intentionally and incidentally, overtly and covertly, explicitly and implicitly.

In other words, the professor at a teacher education college must professionally, i.e., in a pedagogically knowledgeable, kindly, patient, humane, benign, thorough, diligent, sincere and, once again, patient fashion, teach our prospective teachers the subjects they will be teaching at school, together with the technology of teaching. Then and only then will teachers teach our school children in a knowledgeable, kindly, patient, humane, benign, thorough, diligent, sincere, and once again, patient fashion. If the Holmes and Carnegie groups had not disregarded these elementary truths of teacher education, these elementary truths of teacher training, they would not have launched their anti-educational revolution in this country, to the drumbeat of loud calls for professional teachers.

6.1.5. The idea that the teacher must supervise and guide the teaching-learning process, as well as the concepts of pedagogical kindness and technology of education are alien to our school, and teacher education colleges are to blame for this.

In college courses in academic subjects the professors should have taught you, dear teachers, that student learning should be supervised in an active, kindly and humane fashion, or the children may wander off in wrong directions, pursuing false goals. This can embitter and alienate them from their studies and from school. It can destroy their mindset and moral integrity, forcing them out into the street, into a world of crime.

Every day, at every lesson, prospective teachers must see and understand how their own teacher—the college professor—strives in a thorough, sincere, and kindly fashion to have them all correctly understand and comprehend what they had learned at the previous lesson. The professor should start the lesson by explaining that this is absolutely essential. It is essential because any lesson is of value only to the extent that it has proved to be useful to all the students. It can be useful if only because, together with the preceding lessons, it made the current lesson possible with the active, creative involvement of all the students. If the

351

preceding lesson failed to give all the students, at the very least, the knowledge and skills needed to perform the home assignment—one within the students' powers but requiring a degree of creative effort—it should be reviewed in some form or other or repeated in its entirety.

In other words, prospective teachers must understand that there is no sense in conducting a lesson without a thoughtful and thorough discussion of the oral and written sections of the accompanying home assignment. On their own the students are unable to judge how correctly and successfully they have digested the contents of the previous lesson. They are unable to judge how correctly and successfully they have done their homework. The teacher and only the teacher should give them kindly, courageous and selfless help; the teacher and only the teacher can and must give the students courageous and selfless help in understanding what part of the assignment they did right or almost right, and what they did wrong. As a rule, the home assignment should be based on the topic of the previous lesson and other relevant material.

In addition, the professor has given them an assignment which includes the material of several previous lessons not related to the last one, but absolutely essential for the current one. The professor must thoroughly and thoughtfully explain to his students—prospective teachers—that a lesson can be conducted successfully only when the students are prepared for it, both by all their previous work in the course and by successful fulfillment of home assignments designed specifically for the lesson and to be understood and assimilated by all the students. Here, too, the students themselves are unable to judge of the extent to which they are prepared for the lesson in this respect, i.e., with respect to reviewing and recalling the material needed for successfully conducting that lesson. This is the teacher's job, not the student's. It is a job for a professional teacher with thorough professional training and a thorough professional education.

The professor at the teacher education college performs the very minimum of his professional duties when he begins each lesson by ascertaining, and then impressing on his students, that they have all correctly understood and assimilated the material of the previous lesson. He must ascertain and then impress on them that they have recalled everything necessary to understand and assimilate the material of the current lesson. He must show them that they were able to do their latest home assignment correctly and to respond to all his questions because they were able to draw upon the previous lessons. He must explain that he prepared his questions in advance so as to ensure that the students' responses to them would reveal the degree and depth to which they had understood all the previously covered material that they need in order to successfully master the new material of the current lesson.

If the instructor finds that the students' comprehension is insufficient for work on the current lesson, he has two alternatives. If he thinks it feasible, he should attempt, then and there to upgrade the students' knowledge to a level adequate for the lesson's success. Or he should abandon the original lesson plan. In the latter case the lesson should be postponed until such time as it can benefit rather than harm the students. Things that benefit the students include: actively discussing the lesson under the teacher's guidance; overcoming reasonable difficulties in the course of the lesson; acquiring new knowledge and skills (in the course and as a result of overcoming such difficulties) that the students can identify and, together with the teacher, regard in a positive light; upgrading previously acquired knowledge, skills, and expertise under the active guidance of the teacher. Things that can make a lesson harmful include: student indifference; the absence of any difficulties or, on the contrary, the presence of insurmountable difficulties that make students fear both the course and the teacher; a lesson that leaves the student with a sense of its futility and uselessness; the absence of any results that give the student a feeling of satisfaction, of joy or of gratitude to the teacher for his efforts in preparing and presenting the lesson.

6.1.6. Day after day, lesson after lesson, the professor at the teacher education college must show the prospective teacher how to acquire yet another great pedagogical skill: the skill of commanding constant student attention during lessons by involving them in active mental effort. He must tell them how he manages to prevent them from acquiring an incomplete, partial and/or distorted comprehension of new concepts, ideas and structures, and what he personally does to achieve that goal. He must call their attention to the fact that most students are incapable of avoiding such incomplete comprehension on their own and the teacher must constantly help them. He must show the prospective teachers, by word and by deed, that one of the educator's professional duties is to develop a technology for each lesson, such that the basic concepts, ideas and structures of the academic subject under study—every new element of knowledge—is made up of elements of the student's personal intellectual and/or sensory experience.

6.1.7. During classes and when discussing those classes with their professors in mini-research sessions, our prospective teachers must also master the technology of summarizing and expanding in a humane and pedagogically kind fashion the knowledge that the students have previously acquired. They will master the technology of introducing new operations during the lesson by means of a natural, logical expansion and development of old operations with which the students are already familiar. They will understand and master how an educator should gently identify and courageously and thoroughly fill in the gaps in students' knowledge, skills and habits during all stages of the lesson and all stages of the educational process. This is the teacher's job, not the student's, as many of us conveniently believe. It entails hard, exhausting, but noble and rewarding work.

6.1.8. Another of the teacher's prime duties is to strive constantly to get full, exhaustive responses from the students, coupled with substantiating statements, both oral and written. For many, many years students are incapable of judging the quality of their answers on their own. To avoid the many years of painstaking work needed to improve student statements, the creators of American education have simply banned teachers from listening to those statements: that is easier for both parties. And to prevent their inquisitive, bothersome charges from pestering them with their discoveries, schools try to get rid of them as frequently as possible. Every year in school and every two or three months in college the hapless and helpless students are transferred from one course to another before they have had time to comprehend, assimilate or master anything.

6.1.9. The professors at teacher-education schools must teach prospective teachers not only how to get knowledgeable substantiating statements from their students. They must teach the prospective teachers how to stand up for their own opinions and how to teach students to stand up for theirs.

6.1.10. Technology of education also includes: the ability to teach students how to express themselves clearly, both orally and in writing; the ability to draw students into discussions, encouraging them to cite examples and counterexamples; the ability to teach the students to reason logically and succinctly and to fully justify their actions.

6.1.11. In the course of mini-research projects in teacher education colleges prospective teachers must also gradually master the difficult technology of correcting student mistakes and at the same time explaining how to avoid them. They must be taught how to prevent new mistakes and how to teach students to evaluate and monitor their own progress.

6.1.12. The job description of every professor at a teacher education college should require that he do more than check the result of a student's exercise, or even the results of every stage of an exercise. The important thing is to thoroughly study the whole process that the student follows in doing the exercise. What's more, schoolteachers must be taught (by their own experience in teacher education college, among other things) how to bring out the reasoning behind a specific process; how to get a student to explain why he took a certain path and not another; what prompted him to begin an exercise this way and not some other; the pros and cons of different methods; what thoughts guided the student—including prospective teachers—in proceeding from one stage of the exercise to another, etc., etc.

6.1.13. The job descriptions of professors at teacher education colleges and of schoolteachers should also include the following tasks: When giving students assignments, both oral and written, in-class and home, the teacher should highlight and identify their most difficult and dangerous pitfalls. He can sometimes discuss these pitfalls in class or have relevant portions of the assignment done in class, either analyzing them in detail or leaving such analysis to be done by the students on their own. In any case, this work should be carried out in such a way as to leave the assignment both sufficiently difficult and within the student's grasp, provided he devotes the requisite time, effort and diligence.

6.1.14. It should be noted that we are not speaking of merging two courses, such as math and mathematics education, physics and physics education, etc. We are speaking of instruction in math, physics and other academic courses for prospective teachers, quite apart from their instruction in methods courses. What we have in mind is the kind of teaching that is done at teacher education colleges in the courses most closely associated with school courses—teaching in such a way as to make the philosophy and technology of the educational process clear to both the teacher and the taught. Ultimately, both philosophy and technology must be explicitly formulated. This can be achieved during discussion of lessons before and/or after they are conducted. The discussion should involve both the professor and the prospective teachers. It may or may not involve other college professors, but in any case it must take the form of a mini-research project of which we have spoken at length and in detail before (2.1.6; 2.10).

As far as we know, nothing like this is being done anywhere in the world. As far as we know, nothing like it is being done because there is no need for it anywhere in the world. As far as we know, there is no need for it anywhere in the world, because nowhere in the world does the absence of an educational process in schools and colleges spew forth such masses of totally ignorant people as in these United States. In the coming decades the nation will have to produce teachers not by resorting to upgraded and crueler testing systems, as proposed by the Holmes and Carnegie groups, but by introducing better and more humane systems of educating them. It must provide these teachers—taught by college and university professors and administrators, for there is no one else to do this—with educated, humane, benign and educationally knowledgeable supervisor-administratiors, who have also been taught by colleges and universities. These administrators should deal solely with the school's academic affairs. Other people should be responsible for managerial, financial and all other duties. These supervisor-administrators must organize regular mini-research projects by the schoolteachers (2.1.6; 2.10; 3.14–3.21; Letter Four, Letter Five).

6.1.15. What do the Holmes and Carnegie groups suggest? Failing to see how teacher education colleges can be made effective enough to train knowledgeable professional teachers, they would close them down. Teacher training would be transferred to the teachers themselves and to schools, which to date have no professional teachers and nowhere to acquire them. In other words, every school should become a teacher education institution, while teacher education colleges should be closed down: Neither more nor less!

Having failed to learn anything in undergraduate school, the graduating major in arts and sciences must learn everything during the summer. But what was he doing for four years, if we want to deprive him of his summer in order to bring him up to par? Wasn't four years enough to teach him what we hope to cram into him in two or three summer months? Couldn't we have selected would-be teachers from among the undergraduate students at an earlier date and started training them in our profession in undergraduate school?

"Many writers specify a long period of formal training, meaning by this a period of training in educational institutions, as one of the characteristics of a profession. . . . Actually, formal training *is* typical of the professions."*

Why do the medical schools begin abandoning the 4 + 4 formula and converting to the 2 + 5 formula? Because they want hands-on experience in their professional school for five years rather than only three or four. How many years do we intend to devote to our professional school? Zero? Yes, zero. We tried four years, but were unable to offer the nation anything worthwhile. Fewer and fewer people choose to be teachers, and those who do acquire nothing in college and are fleeing from the schools. So now the supervisors of teacher education and public education in general have decided to step aside, telling teachers: Go study, become teachers, then come to us to take your examinations. We'll test you, you can be sure of that. We'll set up a National Board, upgrade the system! That all this will only embitter you more and offer nothing in return is of no consequence. You'll do likewise and treat your students to tests instead of an education. That's how it's done in this country.

6.1.16. We are also going to develop "sound examinations to better screen individuals entering teaching."† Only the testing we suggest will contrast sharply with the testing of the Holmes and Carnegie groups.

The thing is that to train a prospective teacher it doesn't really matter how much he or she remembers after graduating from the noneducating school we ourselves have created. It isn't so important whether we can immediately punish those whom we ourselves have failed to teach anything for 12 years. The important thing is whether our teacher education colleges will be able to offer humane, instructive, extensive, thoroughly taught courses that will use humane methods—without cruelty and without endless tests—to teach prospective teachers, who in turn will be humane towards children. Only those students whom we are unable to teach successfully will be considered as having failed our test, and we will punish them by gradually forcing them out of the college. The fault will be ours, but they will be punished. We will continue to teach the rest humanely and thoroughly, using accessible courses, with minimal testing and maximal use of the teaching-learning process, setting demands that we can reasonably expect them to meet. We will spare no effort to make fine teachers of them, for it is in our own best interests

*Myron Lieberman, Ph.D. *Education as a Profession.* Prentice-Hall, Inc.: Englewood Cliffs, N. J. 1956. p. 6.

†*Tomorrow's Teachers: A Report of The Holmes Group.* The Holmes Group, Inc.: East Lansing, Michigan, 1986, p. viii.

to have those teachers put through high school people who can later be taught successfully in college. We will spare no effort to continue to teach those teachers in school, with minimal testing and maximal use of the teaching-learning process and mini-research projects. It will be primarily in our own interests for them to put through school people capable of continuing their education at least with the help of the country's best professors—those at teacher education colleges—and with the help of our most accessible courses, taught by professors of the highest caliber.

6.1.17. If the professors at teacher education colleges still fail in teaching the prospective teachers, they will know that they have only themselves to blame.

They will understand that if students continue to avoid teacher education colleges, it will mean that school teachers remain pathetic and unhappy and that our children don't want to be like them; in other words, as we have said before, everything must be done to improve the teachers' lives. But if teacher training institutions continue to get people whom they are unable to make into teachers, this will mean that: (1) Either teachers are not all that unhappy, but something prevents them from working well, which is why schools graduate ignorant people, i.e., it is necessary to help the schools, and only teacher education colleges can help them, no one else. (2) Or the schools are graduating quite adequately trained people, but teacher education colleges haven't learned yet how to make teachers of them.

Thus, the circle will close: teacher education colleges will continuously improve the educational system and in the process improve themselves. The nation will acquire a self-reproducing, self-improving, humane, benign structure which will turn out better and better teachers who are themselves both humane and benign. Theses teachers will draw students to teacher education colleges who will become humane, benign teachers in love with the educational process. These teachers will teach our children successfully—in a humane and benign fashion, with minimal testing and maximal use of the educational process.

6.1.18. The Holmes and Carnegie groups are not only making a show of wanting to get the educational system to work with the help of ideas which they do not dare apply in order to make their own undergraduate school system work. They are guided by monstrous, incredible demagogy: proclaiming the establishment of an educational system with the help of nonexistent products and nonexistent results. Their initial product is the nonfunctioning system of undergraduate education that they supervise. They obsessively propose to make teachers out of arts and sciences majors. Even by their own admission, today's undergraduate school produces totally ignorant majors.*

Incredible? Yes.

How should one view this: as a desire to attract attention, or a sign of despair? Oh, no, much worse. It is one more cold-blooded attempt

*_Tomorrow's Teachers_ . . . , pp. 5, 16, 48, 49.

to lay the blame for the failed system of public education on its victims, the teachers. It is the terrible death agony of that socially dangerous structure called the educational system. This agony is even more irrational, paradoxical, illogical, inconsistent and dangerous for society than the structure itself. It is even more cruel, mortally dangerous and destructive with respect to students, teachers, and the nation.

6.1.19. This brings us to a question of extremely great importance: where are students to get the extra hours needed to study courses in academic subjects at teacher education colleges? As we said earlier, we intend to organize these studies in the form of mini-research projects, with the active involvement of the prospective teachers. They will be people who cannot imagine themselves outside the teaching profession, who wish to devote all their lives to children, who cannot live without the school. They will be our supermoms and superdads, not "high-caliber" self-seekers.

To answer this question we would like to set forth another basic organizing principle of the new American teacher education colleges, in addition to the principle of conducting mini-research projects with the active involvement of prospective teachers. These principles will distinguish them fundamentally from any undergraduate school in this country.

We envisage an increase in the total number of contact hours for prospective teachers to 3,000, i.e., approximately a 50-percent increase, because we must give them an extra 1,000 contact hours in academic subjects. The purpose of such an increase in contact hours is not to increase their total study load in undergraduate school. Quite the contrary.

6.1.20. Today we turn out ignorant teachers mainly because, instead of teaching them more during contact hours, we force them to do a lot of work—a lot of unsuccessful work—on their own. Given the current level of high school graduates, this has led to a breakdown in the entire educational system, because the future teachers are unable to cope with the current volume of independent work and the current content of the study material. They either drop out of college (up to 50 percent) or they finish college ignorant and embittered, believing neither in teaching nor in education (the other 50 percent).

6.1.21. The reason why we would increase the number of contact hours in academic subjects by 1,000 is not to make teachers out of "high-caliber" self-seekers who will turn schools into crematories of human souls, hearts and morals. We need the extra 1,000 hours in academic subjects so that people who love children, who fervently aspire to become teachers but have gained nothing from their schooling will be able to devote their lives to children—to their education and upbringing. We want them to have the opportunity to acquire a genuine college education. We want to make this a real opportunity, not a fiction.

We will fill the teacher education colleges with the best professors—educators in their own right, regardless of the number of publications to their credit. We will use 50–100% higher salaries to recruit such professors from all our universities. We will also make today's best schoolteachers regular faculty members, even if they don't have Ph.D.'s. We will do this because without brilliant schoolteachers on the faculty of teacher education colleges we shall never be able to make them true teaching institutions of genuine benefit to our prospective teachers.

6.1.22. The 50-percent increase in the total number of contact hours in teacher education colleges should be done within the four-year framework. It is essential that the tuition costs for our prospective teachers, our supermoms and superdads, should not be increased. In fact, they might be reduced 20–25% for applicants to all teacher education colleges currently having trouble meeting enrollment targets. That is what the nation should spend money on if it seriously intends to teach its children, instead of throwing them into the street, at the mercy of wolf packs of alienated people. That is what it should spend money on if it genuinely means to recognize "the central role teachers play in the quality of education."* The attempt by the Holmes and Carnegie groups to use tests to ensure that prospective teachers are educated, humane, loving, caring and qualified is cruel and useless.

6.1.23. We will make the 3,000-hour educational process in teacher education colleges creative, instructive and active. Based on mini-research projects, it will offer the prospective teachers profound and durable knowledge in their field. It will offer them the development of intellectual, creative and cognitive abilities fostered by active methods of instruction and consistent development of the content of the academic subjects being studied—their basic concepts, ideas and structures. It will offer them fine graphic examples and lessons in pedagogical technology and teaching techniques. It will also offer them research classes and conference classes. It will offer them mini-research projects in which teacher education professors who are first-rate educators will involve them in developing lessons that are models of creative teaching. But for this, teacher education colleges need one more fundamental feature: study periods that are two hours long, not one. The advantages of longer periods were discussed in Letter Three, section 3.14.3.

6.1.24. An educational process in teacher education colleges, in which each period is a two-hour conference, will be accessible to the supermoms and superdads graduating from today's schools with an ardent desire to become teachers. They, not callous self-seekers, are the ones whom we will convert into millions of educated, humane, kind, responsive, patient, caring, capable, conscientious, industrious people in love with their profession. They will be incapable of imagining life outside the school—life without our children, without constant concern for them. Such an educational process will also be increasingly fruitful for

*A Nation Prepared: Teachers for the 21st Century. The Report of the Task Force on Teaching as a Profession. Carnegie Forum on Education and the Economy, 1986, p. 6.

359

our best professors, who will be able to interact more effectively with the help of two-hour mini-research periods.

Both the prospective teachers and their professors will soon understand that a true educational process in teacher education colleges is not possible without the active, dedicated involvement of the professors, including yesterday's brilliant schoolteachers. Today the nation entrusts all of them with the unprecedented mission of creating four or five million educated, upright teachers dedicated to children and to the country. If teacher education colleges fail to justify the nation's hope in the very near future it faces an imminent demise.

6.1.25. If we want to teach teachers we must teach them. The time has come to stop testing our teachers and children and start teaching them. That is why we intend initially to increase only slightly the number of courses for students of teacher education colleges. We need the extra **1,000 hours to convert most of the prospective teachers' work in aca-**demic subjects from cruel and useless independent studies into humane, instructive, accessible contact hours. This is essential for the nation until schools start turning out people far more educated than they are today, people with successful independent learning skills and habits.

6.1.26. A student's weekly work load at a teacher education college can comprise either two six-hour and three four-hour courses (4, 6, 4, 6, 4) or three six-hour and two four-hour courses (6, 4, 6, 4, 6).

6.1.27. Our high school graduates will quickly appreciate the transformation of teacher education colleges into humane, instructive education establishments accessible to all. They will no longer enroll in vain hope in today's colleges of arts and sciences, where no one teaches or ever will, and where consistently more than half the students drop out.

6.1.28. No one will teach our children anything in the arts and sciences departments as long as American universities regard the teaching of students as a means of existence rather than as their primary purpose. Their goal is clear and noble: research in the name of science, in the name or scientific advances and the good of the nation. And no one can deny our scholars that great goal. But if our goal is to give our children a modern education in school and in college, then alongside the research departments in fields other than education, there must also be departments engaged in research on education per se (2.12). The establishment of teacher education colleges that produce efficient and humane teachers who are professional in substance as well as in form, will be the nation's first step towards the achievement of that great goal.

6.2. ON A NEW TEACHER AND A NEW SCHOOL IN THE NAMES OF HOLMES AND CARNEGIE

6.2.1. As we have said before, in their efforts to turn out professional teachers the politicians and the administrators of teacher education colleges would again place the whole burden on the shoulders of the teachers themselves. Moreover, they are erecting some new, completely insurmountable obstacles to their goals.

6.2.2. As before, having endured all the torments of brutal school courses and emerged from school virtually ignorant, the prospective teacher must then endure all the torments of brutal undergraduate courses and come out of undergraduate school virtually ignorant, because the work of present day undergraduate schools in American research universities cannot be improved even in fifty years without EdRL and EdRI (2.12). Then, ignorant as ever, the new teacher must overcome even more insurmountable obstacles, in test after test after test, administered by increasingly sophisticated testing boards while teaching concurrently under the supervision of a Lead Teacher.

6.2.3. Lead Teachers are expected to appear miraculously before any other teachers, and to appear in all the nation's schools at once. Otherwise, who will be training teachers tomorrow? These Lead Teachers must apparently appear all at once to replace teacher education colleges, and appear in vast numbers, God knows from where and God knows how: In fact, the woods are expected to appear before the trees have had time to grow. Under the supervision of these hypothetical Lead Teachers, people who have profited little, if at all, from either school or college are expected to become knowledgeable teachers. Should such a Lead Teacher ever appear in a school, he could well be as ignorant as his trainee: We see no way for him to be any more knowledgeable. Moreover, he could also be cruel, opinionated, sadistic, dictatorial, mediocre, stupid, egotistic, and money-hungry, with no understanding of, and no liking for children and teachers—a person who joined the teaching profession to gain power over young teachers.

6.2.4. Such a Lead Teacher will totally embitter young teachers, provided they have not been totally embittered already by all the years of torment, humiliation, absence of teaching, insurmountable courses and endless tests in today's cruel, indifferent schools and even more cruel and indifferent colleges. They will inevitably transmit this bitterness to our children. The number of alienated people, drug addicts, alcoholics, thieves and murderers will increase. Today, a murder is committed in this country every twenty-four minutes, i.e., sixty murders daily.

6.2.5. This embitterment will be taken out even more on slow learners, because they will be keeping schools and teachers from getting bonuses for having few dropouts, regardless of how the teacher trivializes his courses to entertain and entice the children. The slow learners will also prevent the teacher and the school from receiving bonuses for a high student pass-rate, regardless of how factographic the tests—how trivial and geared to mechanical memory—which will be one more cause of the schools's impatience with, and dislike of, children from poor families. Besides, teachers will increasingly despise and dislike these children because every year fewer and fewer of them will be going on to college, and their schools will be losing money and prestige. This will happen because the demands on people entering college are rising, while the educational process is rapidly fading, giving way to research, even in colleges, where it still flickered.

6.2.6. Teachers will also become more embittered towards one another. Some, naturally, will be more adept than others at helping the school get more money. The more adept teachers will hate the less adept ones for dragging the school down. The latter will despise the former for being so adept and for hating them.

Thus, in the drive to get more money, teachers will inevitably build up hatred towards one another and the children.

6.2.7. The atmosphere in school will also become increasingly tense because some young teachers will be better able to please their high-powered Lead Teacher and will become independent before the others. This separation of young teachers into early pleasers and late pleasers (or even non-pleasers) will increase with time as more real people, people of the "highest caliber" and mainly men, join our profession. Men will be very demanding, especially with respect to young female teachers. . . .

6.2.8. This process of transforming the school (which, whether we like it or not, is a prototype and model of our society) into an institution based on hate, envy, anger, deceit and mutual groveling, will be accompanied by a parallel and expanding process of transformation into places of entertainment for the purpose of attracting students. This process will inevitably gather momentum, because schools will have to attract new students by whatever means they possess, just to have as many students as possible, otherwise they will be denied funding.

6.2.9. Thus, our schools, which are a model of the nation and a model and prototype of society—a miniature society—will become increasingly devoid of poetry, romance, dreams, fantasies, lofty thoughts, ideas and morals. They will increasingly become schools to entertain and attract students, schools of cruelty, hate, anger, envy, deceit, schools where the strong humiliate and corrupt the weak.

6.2.10. We have no intention of placing any new demands whatsoever on present or future teachers. We have no intention of placing any new demands on them, because all of them are currently working in cruel and inhumane conditions. They are placed in these conditions by our teacher education colleges and our politicians. Moreover, the politicians and the colleges either do not want to improve those conditions, cannot improve them, or both. And they have suddenly realized that it is not the teachers but they, themselves, who are to blame for the American educational tragedy. So to justify themselves before the nation and appear more active, energetic and professional, the Holmes and Carnegie groups have come up with a mass of hitherto unheard of, totally unrealizable, completely fantastic, cruel and unprofessional demands on our teachers, both present and future. They are not trying to improve the work of teacher education colleges, because that would expose their hundred years of total inertia. For that selfsame reason, they are not really trying to improve the current conditions of children or teachers. They refuse to accept and are inacpable of accepting the fact that without improving those conditions it is impossible to speak seriously of mass teacher training. This is not surprising, because they are unconcerned with mass training of teachers; they are concerned with appearing innocent in the eyes of the nation and history for the catastrophic condition to which they have reduced the educational system, the teachers and the children.

6.2.11. All the Holmes and Carnegie groups offer is some technical assistance of dubious value, not realizing that this assistance will only drive teachers and students father apart. But with desperate ferocity they are erecting ever new barriers in the way of people who want to become teachers. For the task of training knowledgeable teachers—teachers devoted to children—and helping them all their lives (a task that is beyond their powers) they are substituting one that is cruel and detrimental to the nation but that is within their power. It is in their power to deny entry to the teaching profession to those who were born to be teachers,—not accountants or veterinarians—and whom they, the originators of the new anti-educational, antiteacher revolution either cannot or will not train, or both.

6.2.12. Today you, our teachers, are the most unfortunate teachers in the world. All through school no one ever taught you anything. No one ever taught you anything all through teacher education college. Now you are given school classes that from the outset, are unsuitable for a successful educational process. They are unsuitable because politicians and teacher education colleges are afraid of introducing prekindergarten (PK) grades so that later on, in K–12 schools, you will be able to successfully teach more or less homogeneous classes. They have divided K–12 schools into schools spanning only grades K–8, or 6–9, or 10–12, or other combinations. They have done this so that neither students nor teachers would ever get the tempting and natural idea of learning from each other. They have done this so that neither teachers nor students would have the opportunity of associating with each other for thirteen long years; instead, they can happily be rid of one another after a mere three or four years. With an irresponsibility verging on the criminal, they give you five or six lessons a day, fully realizing that no superman or wonder woman is capable of giving more than three full-fledged honest-to-goodness lessons a day. In other words, they have forced schools, which should be havens of happiness and hope, to be dens of falsehood, dishonesty and deceit. They force you to teach courses of incredible scope and content, and of pitiful duration. They loudly dub them math and science courses so that teachers, students and parents are unable to muster the courage to declare aloud that this is a monstrous betrayal of students, teachers and the nation. They cruelly supply you—the teachers—and the students with ignorant, impermissibly difficult textbooks that are ill-suited for a successful teaching-learning process and will not or cannot change anything, even in this respect. They have virtually barred school administrators from helping teachers, because they have failed to teach, and have no intention of teaching, them to give such help. What's more, they force administrators to handle financial affairs, water and gas leaks, and plumbing repairs. They wonder why all those boring, eternally downtrodden, unaccountably unhappy, eternally complaining teachers are always dissatisfied with something, always grumbling. They are surprised that you, whom they themselves never taught anything in college, are for some reason incapable of being proud and independent. Indeed, why shouldn't you be independent of the local authorities? Why shouldn't you finally settle down and start bringing joy and the happiness of cognition and life to yourselves and your students? They not only continue teaching you nothing: they conspire with the local authorities to pay you nothing. But you ungrateful and naive heirs of Socrates, Rousseau, Montaigne, Comenius, Pestalozzi and Diesterweg are still dissatisfied! You are not coming to their teacher education colleges! You are fleeing from schools in horror, abandoning our children! You have gone on strike! Well, for that, they have started closing down teacher education colleges. So if for the last 100 years or so, instead of teaching you anything in those colleges they merely duped you, that is over and done with. You'll no longer be taught or duped, for no one can teach or cares to do so. They'll go on duping you at a higher level, in graduate school. Instead of teacher education colleges, where you managed to glean some crumbs from experts in teaching physics, chemistry or math—for example, how to teach such stupid things as geometry, equations or functions—they'll set up a National Board for Professional Teaching Standards. You'll get a certificate there, like lawyers. Lawyers belong to a profession, after all, so now you, thanks to the Board, will be members of a profession. Lawyers and doctors are trained by the world's best professional lawyers and doctors in professional schools for several thousand hours for three or four years, after completing undergraduate school. But you don't need that. You're clever as it is. You're of a higher caliber than those shysters and quacks. You'll continue to do time in undergraduate school, in arts and sciences departments. No one means to teach you anything there, though they promise to. You will be instructed by those same exhausted TAs, those same professors preoccupied with their research work and publications. And then you'll have a summer preceding the beginning of your work at school, and you'll immediately become educated. A beautiful American summer after undergraduate school. Two long, extended months of hot weather, swimming, walks in the woods, travel: an educator should travel. And you'll quickly learn all you need to know in order to have a mentor, a superteacher over you. You'll have one given to you, although no one knows where to get one. This superperson will work wonders with you. You'll give lessons, too. You'll rake in $15,000 a year, and you'll take test after test after test, because that's what the powers that be want—it's what they can do. What they don't want and can't do is teach you anything. They tried many times, but nothing came of it. Let lawyers and doctors wallow in professional schools for three or four years, that's their business. You won't. You'll just have to make it on your own. You'll make it through the Board, not just any Board, but a National Board, like all respected professionals.

Are you still dissatisfied? Well, here's something else for you to do in school: try hating each other. For that you'll be paid according to how far you've managed to outpace your partner. How many more students you've managed to put through tests. How many more you managed to push into college. How many less you lost on the way, by whatever means, at whatever cost.

Let the tests be worthless, but put the students through them. Let college be a trap for those entering it, but shove them into it. Let your courses become a charade, a show, but keep the children in them. We'll pay you for that. Otherwise the children spill out into the streets, armed with whiskey, drugs, knives and knuckledusters. They will play with these things, they will attack us. You must take those children in hand. Especially those who intend to flunk a test, drop out of school, stay out of college. School is no picnic, and college evidently won't be any better—what criminal ideas! So you have to quickly learn to hate those ideological delinquents and turn them into criminals.

Besides, everyone is sick and tired of those brick schools with glass windows. The teacher stands, the students sit: how awful! Now everything will be different! We'll remake the whole thing! No new layers of paint! Schools will now compete with each other: Those that can lure more students will get more money. Won't it be great for the students and the teachers! One school will have three jazz bands, the other twenty-three! One will have three football teams, the other forty-three! Compete and make money!

6.3. MORE ON A NEW SCHOOL FOR THIS COUNTRY

6.3.1. All the obstacles confronting today's and tomorrow's teachers and administrators are cruelly and inexorably destroying our schools, and they must be eliminated as quickly as possible. Each of these obstacles is so great that it can reduce to naught the greatest efforts of the best teaching staff, say nothing of a single teacher. Without removing all those obstacles at once, down to the very last one, it is irresponsible, demagogic, useless, unprofessional, dishonest, and simply not serious to speak of any improvement in educating either teachers or students.

6.3.2. Every school must have one or even two prekindergarten grades. In other words, we will prepare some children one year for kindergarten, some two, and some not at all. These prekindergarten groups should be open to the children of all families that are unable to prepare their children for today's school. The current practice of taking all children coming into school at different levels of preschool preparation, and mixing and grinding them into a homogeneous mass is cruel to the teachers and to both the better and the worse prepared children. This practice makes the school cruel, useless, and more often than not harmful to students of all levels. The introduction of PK grades will be one of the simplest, most humane and most available ways of overcoming the cruelty and hopelessness of the whole public education system.

6.3.3. Every school should have all grades, from PK to 12. This issue was discussed earlier in Letter Two, sections 2.11.10 and 2.11.11. All elementary, junior high and high schools should be immediately eliminated as administrative and territorial units—though not without some unavoidable exceptions. The teachers and students of these schools' lower and upper grades are artificially isolated from each other. They are deliberately and criminally denied the natural opportunity of learning from each other, of supporting and complementing each other in the complex school organism. This organism is a model of the society that created it, is improving it, and is improving with it.

6.3.4. Low teacher pay is also an important contributor to the sad, enduring process of degradation of the modern American school. It should be increased by 50 to 100 percent.

6.3.5. Another obstacle on the way to building up an effective school system is the incredibly small number of teachers in the country—slightly over two million—and, hence, the incredibly large teacher loads and the huge classes. Such teacher loads are without parallel in the civilized world. Our two competitors, Japan and Russia, which have original, successfully functioning systems of mass, nonelitist education, limit their weekly teacher loads to fifteen and eighteen hours, respectively. But in this country, people claiming to be educators try to make teachers give thirty lessons a week in overcrowded classes. This is cruelty to both teacher and student; it is hopeless where teacher and student are concerned; it is ruinous to teacher, student, and nation alike.

Not even the greatest teacher is capable of conscientiously conducting five or six lessons a day, whatever tests and other punishments he may be threatened with. This should be obvious to anyone who understands what a truly educative lesson is and has ever conducted such a lesson. There are far too few people capable of conducting such lessons in the Holmes and Carnegie groups.

6.3.6. As we proceed to the next barrier to the successful functioning of our schools, we would like to note that this is not just a barrier. It is a wall, a stone wall erected against students and teachers. The name of this wall is math and science courses. After attempting to study these courses, our children—except for a few exceptional, gifted individuals—are left devastated, humiliated, insulted, depressed, and devoid of all faith. There has never been anything as cruel and senseless as these courses in the history of the world. No high caliber teacher is capable of cramming all the ideas and concepts of physics, chemistry, geometry, algebra, biology and calculus into children's heads in the course of one year (2.13). With the help of these courses and of desperate, unfortunate and ill-prepared teachers, the opponents and enemies of mass education deliberately leave millions of our children—those who are unable to cope with such subjects on their own—beyond the pale of contemporary American society and of civilization itself. Can that be their true purpose? It is time we answered this question clearly and frankly.

6.3.7. Had the members of the Holmes and Carnegie groups been less concerned with vindicating themselves in the eyes of the nation and history, they would have first revealed the pitfalls and traps that they have deliberately and insidiously placed in all the paths, corners and intersections of our inhuman educational system. This is not mass education. It is mass deceit. Deceit perpetrated by people to whom the idea of mass education is profoundly abhorrent.

6.3.8. If we really care for our unhappy children and teachers, if we really want to do our utmost to help them, we must immediately increase the time allotted for studying each of those courses three- or four-fold. We must immediately, without waiting for any new demogogic, antidemocratic, fantastic and unnatural revolutions in the teacher-training system, double or treble the number of hours devoted to studying each of those courses in school (2.13).

6.3.9. Gradually, year after year, our schools will be filled with happier teachers who are better taught and do a better job of teaching. They will also be filled with happier and better taught students. These teachers and students will gradually become the creators of, and participants in, an increasingly humane educational process, increasingly accessible and available to both teachers and students. Instead of the unhappy teachers of today's children, each passing day will see happier, kinder, better educated and more cheerful teachers. For the first time in this nation's history, teachers will face difficulties that both they and their students can overcome.

367

This book describes why and how all this should happen. Specifically, thanks to PK grades, student groups will be more homogeneous. Teachers and students from the lower and upper grades will learn from each other. Teachers and administrative supervisors will be involved in mini-research projects. One-year math and science courses with daily classes and illiterate texts (2.12.10) will vanish like a bad dream. They will be replaced with multiyear math and science courses providing in-depth knowledge and comprehension. Teachers will have to conduct no more than 15 classes a week in groups of 25–30 students. They will be able to devote more time to joint lesson preparation, mini-research projects, individual work with stronger and weaker students, to their family and friends, travel, music, art, and literature. Teachers will also have more disposable income to spend.

6.3.10. For the first time in the nation's history, thanks to the simultaneous improvement of teacher education colleges and working conditions in school, teachers will be able to give our children greater happiness and fulfillment in both intellectual and creative work. Our children will increasingly be getting more from you, their teachers, than mere knowledge, skills and habits—more than the development of intellectual, creative and cognitive abilities sufficient to continue their education. They will be getting what every nation must give their children simply to survive: the desire and a genuine opportunity to be like their teachers. They should want and have the practical possibility to become teachers like the ones with whom they spent the best years of their lives and from whom they acquired a lifetime desire to study, work, improve and collaborate with one another in the achievement of common goals. Then and only then will teacher education colleges be flooded with applicants eager to be like you, their fine teachers. There will be so many applicants that we will have to set up a system of screening and testing. It may be a very strict and demanding system, but it will be fair to and honest with our future educators. They will see it not as an effort to get rid of people whom the nation had never tried to teach honestly. They will see this system as a natural and honest effort to select the best of the best school graduates for the noble and highly important job of teaching and educating the nation's children.

The other school graduates, those less successful and less well prepared than the ones we enroll in teacher education colleges, will also have acquired a good, solid, all-round education in school. They will become accountants, veterinarians, lawyers, doctors, engineers, scientists, politicians or businessmen. They will all find their places in life.

6.3.11. The new school will be established with the help of professional teachers trained by the nation in teacher education colleges. Then it will be possible for teacher education colleges to gradually abandon those extremely thorough courses at which prospective teachers will *for the first time* in their lives see examples and learn the principles of developing and the technology of conducting a truly educative teaching-learning process. They can be abandoned, because *for the first time* in their lives people will have acquired all this in school from teachers who, at long last, are happy. There will thus be no need for teacher education colleges to offer such thorough courses a second time around.

6.3.12. As mentioned before, from the very outset, professors in chemistry education, physics education, music education, foreign languages education, etc., will work in close contact with the prospective teachers and with the chemistry, physics, music, foreign language, and other professors. They will attend the latter's classes. In those classes, as well as in discussions with the professors and students—i.e., in the course of mini-research projects—they will clarify and formulate the educational techniques, ideas and methods employed by the various professors, analyze them and unravel the secrets of educational technology. The prospective teachers will gradually become increasingly involved in mini-research projects. These mini-research projects will increasingly take on the features of a research conference. It will be a prototype of the conferences, i.e., the mini-research projects—that the students will take part in during their student teaching and subsequently, after they start teaching in school. Thus, the college professors specializing in academic subjects as well as in education will collaborate closely with one another and with their students, the prospective teachers, in a multiyear process of mastering the technology of education, a process of molding the personality of a professional teacher.

6.3.13. When our teachers start their work in school, they will already know that novel elements should be increased or reduced patiently and consistently in home assignments and tests, while carefully monitoring how the class reacts to them. They will already understand that, along with the usual home assignments and tests that we employ in today's schools and colleges, we should introduce other kinds of home assignments and tests. They should require the student to give a thorough description of the entire process involved in doing an exercise, together with a thorough justification of both the process and its results. The new teachers will be able to look for ways of posing questions that are comprehensible to them and to their students and that require elucidation of both the ideas and concepts in the academic field in question, and the relationships between them. They will have learned the art of properly balancing oral and written presentation in the teaching process; of rephrasing and repeating questions if the class fails to respond to them; of grasping student responses and immediately evaluating their correctness, of comparing different answers to the same question, and of evaluating the depth of answers; they will have mastered the ability to formulate and discuss problem and conflict situations, which is a very important means of fostering creative and criticial thinking ability. Thus, our teachers, first in college, then in school, will gradually, month after month and year after year, master one of the most difficult and essential professional requirements of a modern school teacher: the ability to conduct a discussion with a class, to involve both the strong and the weak students in the discussion, and to quickly formulate questions and react to numerous student answers and counter-questions.

6.3.14. First in college, then in school, our new teachers will also learn how to keep their pupils constantly aware of the real levels of their knowledge, skills and habits. They will learn to do this in such a way that their pupils will be able to assess that level accurately by themselves and, together with the teacher, outline ways of continuously and steadily raising it. They will continuously learn how to keep students from falling behind the progress of the teaching-learning process. They will study the technology of conducting lessons in which the teacher continuously verifies what the pupils know and what they are capable of doing, and on that basis decides what they can learn and will be able to comprehend at the next lesson.

6.3.15. Thus with the knowledge, skills and habits, and the intellectual, creative and cognitive abilities acquired in the teacher education college, our teachers and administrators will be able to contribute effectively to the school mini-research system. Mini-research is not only, and not so much, a continuation of education. It is not only, and not so much, an expansion and upgrading of the knowledge, skills and habits, and the intellectual, creative and cognitive abilities of all school teachers—young and old, experienced and inexperienced—as well as administrators. It is the form, essence and content of school activity. It is a form of the teaching-learning process in which the lesson is the main element. It is an embryonic development of the lesson, its creation and discussion prior to its appearance. It is the development of the lesson in teachers' minds and dreams as applied to a specific class, to specific teachers of that class, and to specific students—the teaching and subsequent discussion of that lesson.

No teacher can, on his own, study, know, understand, respect or love a class, with all its merits and shortcomings. To thoroughly study, truly appreciate and get to love the class and every student in it, to develop and continuously upgrade the strategy and tactics of the educational process in that class, requires the collective effort and wisdom of all teachers. It requires the collective effort and wisdom of teachers working with one another in the form of mini-research projects. It is such joint evaluation, love, collective effort and wisdom of school teachers and administrators that will go into the development and improvement of every lesson, into the development, discussion and improvement of the school's educational process as a whole (2.1.6, 2.10, Letter Three, Letter Four, Letter Five).

6.3.16. Dear teachers, dear scientists, dear politicians, dear representatives of the legislative and executive branches of government: For the educational system to start functioning, for our children to become educated and happy, let us gradually and vigorously introduce pre-kindgarten grades in our schools, while at the same time merging together all small, isolated schools into PK–K–12 schools. Let us also do all we can to reduce the size of clases to 25-30 students, and the teaching load of teachers to 15 lessons a week. We must launch an extensive media campaign to boost teacher pay by 50 to 100 percent. We should increase the length of every math and science course three- or four-fold and at the same time double or treble the number of hours devoted to each course. We must start to strictly monitor the quality of school and college textbooks (2.12.10), making sure that they are literate, understandable, devoid of material lacking scientific merit, offering thorough presentations of basic scientific concepts, ideas and structures. As an interim measure we should gradually reduce the course of study from twelve to ten years in schools experiencing financial difficulties and difficulties hiring qualified teachers, but we should not do this at the expense of the PK grades (Appendix B). We should simultaneously launch mini-research work among teachers of all schools and colleges, charging school principals and vice principals with organizing and supervising it. In addition, all teacher education colleges should offer seminars and courses for school administrators and department heads, so that they can successfully supervise mini-research work. All teacher education colleges should also increase by 1,000 hours the length of the courses in academic subjects that the prospective teachers will be teaching at school. The deans and professors conducting these courses should be required to organize them in the form of mini-research efforts involving all the prospective teachers, as well as the teacher education professors conducting related courses and methods courses. We must supplement all this with continuing education courses for professors who teach math and science in teacher education colleges, at all the country's leading teacher education colleges and universities.

To attract high caliber professors and the country's best school teachers to teacher education colleges we will pay them not less than 150% of the salary they receive today. Gradually, all teacher education colleges will be staffed by professors of the highest caliber. Courses in academic subjects will gradually become more accessible to the prospective teachers and more and more interesting, increasingly preparing them for a successful educational career in school. The prospective teachers will be required to attend mini-research type lessons conducted by the best instructors of college laboratory schools. The college courses will also involve the prospective teachers' work on models of their future school lessons, i.e., on lesson plans (3.6). The best instructors of college laboratory schools and all professors will participate actively in developing these models, as well as improving mini-research work and upgrading their qualifications in a system of continuing education sponsored by all the country's leading universities and teacher education colleges. High caliber professors at teacher education colleges will gain in caliber as they extend their prestige to all spheres of the colleges' pedagogical activities. Teacher education colleges will thus become schools of joy and

371

happiness for their professors and for prospective teachers. As high school graduates learn of these colleges' high pedagogical standards, more and more will seek admission to them. They will find there an educational process that gives them knowledge, skills and habits, develops their intellectual, creative and cognitive abilities, brings the joy of cognition, a humane, instructive, accessible, didactically kind, creative, intellectual, active, intense, vigorous, exciting and interesting process which teaches pedagogical skills and habits, speech, the art of argumentation, defending one's point of view, listening to and understanding others, respecting their opinions, taking them into consideration, and engaging in polemical debate on a high scientific, intellectual, ethical and esthetic level.

6.3.17. We repeat over and over again: The best professors and best teachers scattered all over the country should be urgently brought into our professional schools, i.e., our teacher education colleges, and enlisted in the regular faculty. They should get involved in mini-research efforts to develop courses for prospective teachers. The purpose of the mini-research projects would be: (1) to improve the courses for prospective teachers; (2) To improve the qualifications of professors at teacher education colleges through exchanges of knowledge and work experience between the traditional college professors and the new faculty recruited from among the best school teachers; (3) To improve the qualifications of college graduates by actively involving the prospective teachers in all, or almost all, mini-research work. In other words, we propose to enlist the cream of current school and university faculties in the training of teachers. These educators should be concentrated in teacher education colleges, and they should be induced to come by 50–100% higher salaries for the faculty and, perhaps, for the administrators as well.

6.4 ON THE REAL REASONS FOR THE HOLMES–CARNEGIE MOVE

6.4.1. Why don't the Holmes and Carnegie groups accuse undergraduate school administrators and instructors of the same sins as school teachers?

There is no educational process is secondary school, and within four years half the students drop out. There is no educational process in undergraduate school, and within four years half the students drop out.

The number of students going on from high school to college is rapidly declining. The number of students going on from college to graduate school is rapidly declining.

High school graduates are less and less capable of any useful activity. College graduates are less and less capable of any useful activity.

Crime, suicides, alcohol and drug abuse are increasing rapidly in

372

schools. Crime, suicides, alcohol and drug abuse are increasing rapidly in colleges.

6.4.2. The Holmes and Carnegie groups suggest setting up the public school system as "a system of pay, autonomy, career opportunities" (*Education Week*, Volume V, Number 35, May 21, 1986). We already have such a system. This system is maintained—as proposed by the Holmes and Carnegie groups—only by people of the highest caliber. These people are—as proposed by the Holmes and Carnegie groups—divided into three different categories so as to "make the very best use of a distribution of talent."* This system is headed—as proposed by the Holmes and Carnegie groups—by people of the highest caliber: chairmen, deans, provosts, presidents. This system is called the undergraduate school. This system simply does not work.

6.4.3. Why shouldn't the Holmes and Carnegie groups try to use the same methods to get the undergraduate school to work that they propose for setting up an effective elementary and secondary school? Why don't our deans and provosts try to establish an effective educational process in colleges by paying professors according to student performance, teacher performance and productivity? Why not establish a National Board for Professional Teaching Standards to certify college instructors? Why not install Lead Teachers in colleges to look out for insufficiently energetic professors and "to guide and influence the activity of others?"†

We know why. And they know, too. Because college professors will simply refuse to heed ideas that are a priori destructive for the educational establishment. As for the views of school teachers—they are ignored in this country. Teachers are people of the wrong caliber. Their views, if they dare state them, are ignored. See, for example, Mary Hatwood Futrell's "Statement of Support with Reservations" (*Education Week*, Volume V, Number 35, May 21, 1986, p. 18). See also Letters to the Editor in *U.S. News and World Report*, June 9, 1986, pp. 82, 83.

6.4.4. The Holmes and Carnegie groups are in a remarkable haste to abolish the undergraduate education major. They are striving to do this in research universities above all. Nor is it accidental that they seek support for their insidious plans from the research universities.

First, they themselves represent those universities, so they have influence on them and can count on their support.

Second, research universities, more than other educational establishments in this country, disparage teaching. For that reason they will very readily give up burdensome undergraduate programs, such as the education major, that still shows some spark of pedagogical life.

Third, if undergraduate training at teacher education colleges were eliminated, then teachers would all be products of arts and sciences

*A Nation Prepared . . . , p. 41.

†A Nation Prepared . . . , p. 58.

373

majors. Departments of arts and sciences would increase enrollments accordingly. They would get more money than they have today, more grants, more fame, and consequently, fewer pedagogical responsibilities.

6.4.5. Now much more important questions arise: Why do the Holmes and Carnegie groups want to deprive teachers of the crumbs of pedagogical education offered by teacher education colleges? Why do the Holmes and Carnegie groups want to close down teacher education colleges? Why do they want to turn the school teacher's life into a life of servants and masters? Why do they want to expose teachers to ridicule and contempt, with master-teachers trampling on the elementary human rights of their servant-teachers? Why do they want to set teachers against weak students and against each other? There are many reasons for this. Here are the main ones.

One. They can no longer remain aloof from America's nationwide movement for reform of the educational system. Protests of parents, politicians and public figures against the present-day school are mounting rapidly with each passing year. Enrollment in teacher education colleges is declining precipitously. Alcohol and drug abuse by school and college students is rising rapidly, together with crime, murder and suicides.

Two. By closing down undergraduate schools in teacher education colleges they want to prove that teacher training does not require teacher education colleges, which they would prefer not to manage any longer.

Three. If they were to attempt to improve the work of teacher education colleges, the Holmes and Carnegie groups would have to openly concede their total professional helplessness. It would once again become abundantly clear to the nation that decades have been wasted on totally futile work. Decades of efforts to set up successfully functioning teacher education colleges have produced no results.

Four. In renewed efforts to improve the work of teacher education colleges, they must openly resort to the ideas and practical proposals of others, because they have exhausted all of their own ideas. These new ideas and practical proposals are set forth in *Six Letters to the President of the United States on Educational Reform*. They appear in full in this book. The first five letters were forwarded to organizations and persons, some of whom subsequently became leading members of the then nonexistent Holmes and Carnegie groups:

Dr. Terrel H. Bell, U. S. Department of Education
Dr. Lewis M. Branscomb, Carnegie Corporation of New York
Dr. Edward H. Jennings, The Ohio State University
Dr. Derek Bok, Harvard University
Dr. David P. Gardner, The National Commission on Excellence in Education
Dr. Mortimer J. Adler, The Paideia Group
Dr. John A. Goodlad, A Study of Schooling in the United States

Five. While sharing the ideas set forth in the *Five Letters,* the Holmes and Carnegie groups failed to make use of one of the basic ideas of those letters: the idea of mini-research projects. The *Letters* expound this idea in the context of training and reciprocal training of in-service teachers, student teachers and college instructors. The *Letters* leave to teacher education colleges the simple idea of launching mini-research efforts with the involvement of their professors and the prospective teachers. Obviously, the Holmes and Carnegie groups did not develop this idea.

Six. The fact that the destruction of teacher education colleges and schools will result in the moral, intellectual and physical destruction of several generations of the nation and throw millions of alienated, deprived and criminal people into the streets may be beyond their concern. Or perhaps they don't care, because the consequences of these actions would become apparent only several decades from now, when the Holmes and Carnegie people will no longer be in business.

Seven. The Holmes and Carnegie groups decided to brazenly exploit the successful efforts of American professional schools to find themselves allies and supporters. They needed this to be able to declare to the nation: We politicians and educators are in no way to blame for the disintegration and degradation of the American educational system. On the contrary, we are its saviors. We are saving the nation and its children, just as Abraham Flexner did when, with the help of the Carnegie Foundation, he "transformed medical practice in the United States."*

They prefer not to see that the teaching profession has nothing in common with that of lawyer, doctor, veterinary or accountant from the standpoint of either professional training or professional activity. This profound difference has been given some consideration in this book (2.1.6, 2.10, Letter Four, Letter Five, 6.1, 6.2.4, 6.2.5, 6.3.12, 6.3.15, and elsewhere). We will discuss it at length in our Letter Seven to the President of the USA on Educational Reform, which will appear in a separate publication.

Eight. The Holmes and Carnegie groups have launched this antidemocratic, antipopular campaign not only to place the blame for the disintegration of American education on our teachers, to set them against their students and against each other in the schools, and thereby exonerate and even glorify themselves. They have a different strategic objective: to represent the real destroyers of the American educational system—American research universities—as heroes and saviors of the nation. For over a century they have developed modern science and destroyed the undergraduate school. For this they have earned well-

*A Nation Prepared . . . , p. 7.

375

deserved glory and eternal shame. Now they have decided to use the good names of Holmes and Carnegie to overcome the shame.

Nine. The research universities have undertaken the amputation of undergraduate studies in teacher education colleges for other reasons besides those mentioned here. The thing is that teachers, more than any other undergraduate majors, must bear a lifelong, unmistakable, and as yet indelible stamp of total ignorance. This stamp is forever present for all to see, including those strictest of judges, children. It is a constant reproach to research universities. It is the most vivid proof of the total unviability of the American undergraduate school, which has been sacrificed for the sake of research for NATO, Navy, NASA, etc.

Ten. There is another, deeper reason why the Holmes and Carnegie groups have decided to create the impression, with no grounds whatsoever, that they are capable of creating millions of educated teachers. There is no core of professors of education, no group united by a common principle. There is no core with a vision of the future of pedagogical theory and practice. There is no core with any weight or prominence in society, no core imbued with a sense of its strength and capable of understanding its tasks and the best ways of accomplishing them.

In other words, because of the fragmentation of the educational system—a fragmentation without precedent in the world—schools, colleges and universities have forgotten their common task, which is the instruction and education of American children. They have created an inner world of their own, a world with no concern for students, teachers, lessons, education process or educational results.

APPENDIX A

SOURCE MATERIALS

I. Work in Elementary and Secondary Schools No. 175, No. 30, and No. 585, Moscow, USSR, 1949–1973

1. Prepared and conducted math lessons 8,000
2. Attended and discussed lessons by other teachers 150
3. Participated in meetings of mathematical departments of schools 100
4. Chaired the Department of Mathematics of Elementary and Secondary School No. 30 1961–1968
5. Worked as Senior Scholar in the Mathematics Laboratory, School No. 30 1961–1968

II. Work at Moscow Lenin Pedagogical Institute, USSR, 1954–1973

1. Attended and discussed with students school lessons given by teachers..400
2. Wrote lesson notes with students 1,500
3. Prepared, attended, and discussed lessons with student teachers 2,000
4. Gave lectures on general and mathematical education for prospective elementary and secondary school teachers 1,500
5. Conducted recitations in mathematical education with prospective elementary and secondary school teachers 1,500
6. Supervised graduate work on Ph.D. dissertations 5
7. Participated in meetings of the Department of Mathematical Education 150
8. Designed and developed the system of graduation theses at teacher-education colleges 1961–1968

377

III. Work in the USSR Academy of Pedagogical Sciences, 1949–1973, and in the RSFSR Ministry of Education, 1954–1973

Participated in meetings of the Laboratory of Mathematical Education and in sessions of the Scientific Council 250
Including:
1. Meetings devoted to the compilation and discussion of new elementary and secondary school curricula 100
2. Meetings devoted to the discussion of manuscripts of textbooks for elementary and secondary schools, as well as manuscripts of research monographs by schoolteachers and college professors 150

IV. Work in the USSR with Inservice Teachers, 1949–1973

1. Gave lectures on mathematics and general and mathematical education at teacher-education colleges 400
2. Conducted recitations in mathematics and in general mathematical education at teacher-education colleges 400
3. Gave lectures on general and mathematical education at advanced teacher-training institutes 100
4. Conducted recitations in mathematical education at advanced teacher-training institutes 100

V. Work at The Ohio State University, 1973–1985

1. Gave lectures and conducted recitations in Calculus with Analytical Geometry and in Differential Equations 1,000
2. Conducted lectures and recitations in mathematics for prospective elementary teachers 100
3. Conducted lectures and recitations in elementary mathematics 2,000
4. Took part in seminars for school students and teachers 10

APPENDIX B

ON A TEMPORARY 10-YEAR SCHOOL

We will not be able to start building up a modern system of 12-year schooling at once. We have neither the money, nor the teachers capable of teaching, nor the students capable of learning. We could, of course, disregard this and rush into yet another pedagogical adventure. But this can only lead to a new tragedy for millions of our people.

Extraordinary circumstances require extraordinary methods to control them: the nation must find the courage to suppress its pride and retreat back several years. We must immediately start a process of gradual transition from the 12-year school to a temporary 10-year school with the purpose of using this school to prepare millions of teachers and students, take control of the educational system, and then gradually revert back to the 12-year school.

Today's high-school sophomores, juniors, and seniors will complete their twelve years as before. However, students finishing the ninth grade in the spring of 1986 should be given a choice. Some—the best—can graduate after the eleventh grade, i.e., in the spring of 1988. The others can go on to graduate after the twelfth grade, in the spring of 1989. It will be necessary to exert some pressure on students and perhaps make some temporary adjustments in some legislative acts.

Students finishing the eighth grade in the spring of 1986 will graduate in the spring of 1988, 1989, and 1990. Students finishing the seventh grade in 1986 will graduate in 1989, 1990, and 1991. Those finishing the sixth grade in 1986 will graduate in 1990, and 1991. Those finishing the fifth grade in 1986 will graduate in 1991 and 1992. Those finishing the fourth grade in 1986 will all graduate in 1992. This will complete the establishment of the 10-year school, as presented in Table 2.

Within only two years our long-suffering school will heave a sigh of relief. It will graduate not only its seniors but also some of its juniors. They will go on to colleges, which are currently in ever greater need of freshmen: ". . . a 22 percent decline in the number of U.S. high-school graduates [is] predicted by 1992."*

*Lucia Solarzano, "Colleges Turn Abroad For More Students," *U.S. News and World Report*, March 11, 1985, p. 72.

379

The process of gradual annual reduction of the total number of school students and the consequent increase in the number of college and university students will continue until 1992. Starting with that year the number of college and university students will become relatively stable. This process will continue until such time as we will be in a position to launch the reverse process, i.e., the gradual expansion of the 10-year school into an 11-, and then a 12-year school. We will commence this process only when teachers will be in a position of giving not thirty to thirty-five, but fifteen lessons per week. One cannot speak seriously of a successfully operating school in which teachers are forced to give more than fifteen lessons a week.

Obviously, the transition process from the 12-year school to the 10-year school can be made more gradual, i.e., doing this in more than four years. It can be done in several ways. But we are not sure that other countries around the world will wait patiently while we are extricating ourselves from our troubles. It is more likely that when they see our will and actions aimed at creating a viable educational system, they will surge ahead in all spheres of education of which neither they nor we have any idea today.

Today we actually give our children not twelve years of schooling but only eight or ten. Children simply spend twelve years in school. This is a fact of life with which we must reckon. We will live with the 10-year school for several years, train new teachers, new students, and new administrators. Then we will gradually reintroduce the eleventh grade and see what happens. After several more years, when we feel we have grown stronger, we will gauge our capabilities and go back to the 12-year school.

Students of the senior grades should be told at once that soon their school troubles will come to an end. Otherwise, within the next few years, without math and science teachers, they will physically destroy the miserable remnants of what we call the educational system.

The schools' most active enemies will immediately flee from it, and we will immediately feel better. Even if only those who did not intend to take math and science leave school at once, we will be able to save huge sums for attracting engineers, servicemen, retired teachers, retired servicemen, and retired engineers as teachers, in order to organize K_1 and K_2 and reduce the teachers' load, without which mini-researches and other methods of building up the educational system are impossible.

During the transition years from the 12-year to the 10-year school, we should actively encourage the best students to graduate from the tenth and eleventh grades as quickly as possible. Then teachers will be able to devote more attention to the remaining weaker students.

To conclude our discussion of the question of a temporary 10-year school, we would like to say that we have placed this extremely important question in the Appendix with good reason. The opponents of mass education will try to see in our letters nothing more than the idea of a temporary restructuring of the 12-year school into a 10-year school. They will even forget the need of the reverse process, back from the 10-year school to the 12-year school, of which we speak. They will start to

Table 2

YEARS / GRADES	1987	1988	1989	1990	1991	1992
12						
11	12					
10	11	12				
9	10	11	12			
8	9	10	11	12		
7	8	9	10	11	12	
6	7	8	9	10	11	
5	6	7	8	9	10	11
4	5	6	7	8	9	10
3	4	5	6	7	8	9

combat horrors created by themselves. They will call an absolutely necessary move betrayal of mass education, rejection of the 12-year school, and so on, and so forth. It is our hope and expectation that they won't bother to read the Appendix. And if they do, their excess of energy will have declined somewhat by then.

APPENDIX C

A NATION AT RISK: THE IMPERATIVE FOR EDUCATIONAL REFORM

AN EXCERPT FROM THE REPORT OF THE NATIONAL COMMISSION ON EXCELLENCE IN EDUCATION

The National Commission on Excellence in Education

DAVID P. GARDNER, president, University of Utah, and president-elect, University of California, *chairman*.

YVONNE W. LARSEN, immediate past president, San Diego City School Board, *vice-chairman*.

WILLIAM O. BAKER, former chairman of the board, Bell Telephone Laboratories (Murray Hill, N.J.).

ANNE CAMPBELL, former Nebraska commissioner of education.

EMERAL A. CROSBY, principal, Northern High School (Detroit).

CHARLES A. FOSTER, JR., immediate past president, foundation for Teaching Economics (San Francisco).

NORMAN C. FRANCIS, president, Xavier University of Louisiana.

A. BARTLETT GIAMATTI, president, Yale University.

SHIRLEY GORDON, president, Highline Community College.

ROBERT V. HADERLEIN, Immediate past president, National School Boards Association (Girard, Kan.).

GERALD HOLTON, professor of physics and professor of the history of science, Harvard University.

ANNETTE Y. KIRK, Kirk Associates (Mecosta, Mich.).

MARGARET S. MARSTON, member, Virginia State Board of Education.

ALBERT H. QUIE, former governor of Minnesota.
FRANCISCO D. SANCHEZ, JR., superintendent, Albuquerque public schools.
GLENN T. SEABORG, professor of chemistry and 1951 Nobel Laureate in chemistry, University of California at Berkeley.
JAY SOMMER, national teacher of the year, 1981–82, foreign-language department, New Rochelle High School (New Rochelle, N.Y.).
RICHARD WALLACE, principal, Lutheran High School East (Cleveland Heights, Ohio).

Our nation is at risk. Our once unchallenged preeminence in commerce, industry, science, and technological innovation is being overtaken by competitors throughout the world.

This report is concerned with only one of the many causes and dimensions of the problem, but it is the one that undergirds American prosperity, security, and civility. We report to the American people that while we can take justifiable pride in what our schools and colleges have historically accomplished and contributed to the United States and the well-being of its people, the educational foundations of our society are presently being eroded by a rising tide of mediocrity that threatens our very future as a nation and a people. What was unimaginable a generation ago has begun to occur: others are matching and surpassing our educational attainments.

If an unfriendly foreign power had attempted to impose on America the mediocre educational performance that exists today, we might well have viewed it as an act of war. As it stands, we have allowed this to happen to ourselves. We have even squandered the gains in student achievement made in the wake of the Sputnik challenge. Moreover, we have dismantled essential support systems which helped make those gains possible. We have, in effect, been committing an act of unthinking, unilateral educational disarmament.

Our society and its educational institutions seem to have lost sight of the basic purposes of schooling, and of the high expectations and disciplined effort needed to attain them. This report, the result of eighteen months of study, seeks to generate reform of our educational system in fundamental ways and to renew the nation's commitment to schools and colleges of high quality throughout the length and breadth of our land.

That we have compromised this commitment is, upon reflection, hardly surprising, given the multitude of often conflicting demands we have placed on our nation's schools and colleges. They are routinely called on to provide solutions to personal, social, and political problems that the home and other institutions either will not or cannot resolve. We must understand that these demands on our schools and colleges often exact an educational cost as well as a financial one.

On the occasion of the Commission's first meeting, President Reagan noted the central importance of education in American life when he said: "Certainly there are few areas of American life as important to our society, to our people, and to our families as our schools and colleges." This report, therefore, is as much an open letter to the American people as it is a report to the Secretary of Education. We are confident that the American people, properly informed, will do what is right for their children and for the generations to come.

THE RISK

History is not kind to idlers. The time is long past when America's destiny was assured simply by an abundance of natural resources and inexhaustible human enthusiasm, and by our relative isolation from the malignant problems of older civilizations. The world is indeed one global village. We live among determined, well-educated, and strongly motivated competitors. We compete with them for international standing and markets, not only with products but also with the ideas of our laboratories and neighborhood workshops. America's position in the world may once have been reasonably secure with only a few exceptionally well-trained men and women. It is no longer.

The risk is not only that the Japanese make automobiles more efficiently than Americans and have government subsidies for development and export. It is not just that the South Koreans recently built the world's most efficient steel mill, or that American machine tools, once the pride of the world, are being displaced by German products. It is also that these developments signify a redistribution of trained capability throughout the globe. Knowledge, learning, information, and skilled intelligence are the new raw materials of international commerce and are today spreading throughout the world as vigorously as miracle drugs, synthetic fertilizers, and blue jeans did earlier. If only to keep and improve on the slim competitive edge we still retain in world markets, we must dedicate ourselves to the reform of our educational system for the benefit of all—old and young alike, affluent and poor, majority and minority. Learning is the indispensable investment required for success in the "information age" we are entering.

Our concern, however, goes well beyond matters such as industry and commerce. It also includes the intellectual, moral, and spiritual strengths of our people which knit together the very fabric of our society.

The people of the United States need to know that individuals in our society who do not possess the levels of skill, literacy, and training essential to this new era will be effectively disenfranchised, not simply from the material rewards that accompany competent performance, but also from the chance to participate fully in our national life. A high level of shared education is essential to a free, democratic society and to the fostering of a common culture, especially in a country that prides itself on pluralism and individual freedom.

For our country to function, citizens must be able to reach some common understanding on complex issues, often on short notice and on the basis of conflicting or incomplete evidence. Education helps form these common understandings, a point Thomas Jefferson made long ago in his justly famous dictum: "I know no safe depository of the ultimate powers of the society but the people themselves; and if we think them not enlightened enough to exercise their control with a wholesome discretion, the remedy is not to take it from them but to inform their discretion."

Part of what is at risk is the promise first made on this continent: All, regardless of race or class or economic status, are entitled to a fair chance and to the tools for developing their individual powers of mind and spirit to the utmost. This promise means that all children by virtue of their own efforts, competently guided, can hope to attain the mature and informed judgment needed to secure gainful employment and to manage their own lives, thereby serving not only their own interests but also the progress of society itself.

INDICATORS OF THE RISK

The educational dimensions of the risk before us have been amply documented in testimony received by the Commission. For example:

International comparisons of student achievement, completed a decade ago, reveal that on nineteen academic tests American students were never first or second and, in comparison with other industrialized nations, were last seven times.

Some twenty-three million American adults are functionally illiterate by the simplest tests of everyday reading, writing, and comprehension.

About 13 percent of all seventeen-year-olds in the United States can be considered functionally illiterate. Functional illiteracy among minority youth may run as high as 40 percent.

Average achievement of high-school students on most standardized tests is now lower than twenty-six years ago when Sputnik was launched.

Over half the population of gifted students do not match their tested ability with comparable achievement in school.

The College Board's Scholastic Aptitude Tests demonstrate a virtually unbroken decline from 1963 to 1980. Average verbal scores fell over fifty points and average mathematics scores dropped nearly forty points.

College Board achievement tests also reveal consistent declines in recent years in such subjects as physics and English.

Both the number and proportion of students demonstrating superior achievement on the S.A.T.s (i.e., those with scores of 650 or higher) have also dramatically declined.

Many seventeen-year-olds do not possess the "higher order" intellectual skills we should expect of them. Nearly 40 percent cannot draw inferences from written material; only one-fifth can write a persuasive essay; and only one-third can solve a mathematics problem requiring several steps.

There was a steady decline in science achievement scores of U.S. seventeen-year-olds as measured by national assessments of science in 1969, 1973, and 1977.

Between 1975 and 1980, remedial mathematics courses in public four-year colleges increased by 72 percent and now constitute one-quarter of all mathematics courses taught in those institutions.

Average tested achievement of students graduating from college is also lower.

Business and military leaders complain that they are required to spend millions of dollars on costly remedial education and training programs in such basic skills as reading, writing, spelling, and computation. The Department of the Navy, for example, reported to the Commission that one-quarter of its recent recruits cannot read at the ninth-grade level, the minimum needed simply to understand written safety instructions. Without remedial work they cannot even begin, much less complete, the sophisticated training essential in much of the modern military.

These deficiencies come at a time when the demand for highly skilled workers in new fields is accelerating rapidly. For example:

Computers and computer-controlled equipment are penetrating every aspect of our lives—homes, factories, and offices.

One estimate indicates that by the turn of the century, millions of jobs will involve laser technology and robotics.

Technology is radically transforming a host of other occupations. They include health care, medical science, energy production, food processing, construction, and the building, repair, and maintenance of sophisticated scientific, educational, military, and industrial equipment.

Analysts examining these indicators of student performance and the demands for new skills have made some chilling observations. Educational researcher Paul Hurd concluded at the end of a thorough national survey of student achievement that within the context of the modern scientific revolution, "We are raising a new generation of Americans that is scientifically and technologically illiterate." In a similar vein, John Slaughter, a former director of the National Science Foundation, warned of "a growing chasm between a small scientific and technological elite and a citizenry ill-informed, indeed uninformed, on issues with a science component."

But the problem does not stop there, nor do all observers see it the same way. Some worry that schools may emphasize such rudiments as reading and computation at the expense of other essential skills such as comprehension, analysis, solving problems, and drawing conclusions. Still others are concerned that an over-emphasis on technical and occupational skills will leave little time for studying the arts and humanities

387

that so enrich daily life, help maintain civility, and develop a sense of community. Knowledge of the humanities, they maintain, must be harnessed to science and technology if the latter are to remain creative and humane, just as the humanities need to be informed by science and technology if they are to remain relevant to the human condition. Another analyst, Paul Copperman, has drawn a sobering conclusion. Until now, he has noted, "Each generation of Americans has outstripped its parents in education, in literacy, and in economic attainment. For the first time in the history of our country, the educational skills of one generation will not surpass, will not equal, will not even approach, those of their parents."

It is important, of course, to recognize that the average citizen today is better educated and more knowledgeable than the average citizen of a generation ago—more literate, and exposed to more mathematics, literature, and science. The positive impact of this fact on the well-being of our country and the lives of our people cannot be overstated. Nevertheless, the average graduate of our schools and colleges today is not as well-educated as the average graduate of twenty-five or thirty-five years ago, when a much smaller proportion of our population completed high school and college. The negative impact of this fact likewise cannot be overstated.

HOPE AND FRUSTRATION

Statistics and their interpretation by experts show only the surface dimension of the difficulties we face. Beneath them lies a tension between hope and frustration that characterizes current attitudes about education at every level.

We have heard the voices of high-school and college students, school board members, and teachers; of leaders of industry, minority groups, and higher education; of parents and state officials. We could hear the hope evident in their commitment to quality education and in their descriptions of outstanding programs and schools. We could also hear the intensity of their frustration, a growing impatience with shoddiness in many walks of American life, and the complaint that this shoddiness is too often reflected in our schools and colleges. Their frustration threatens to overwhelm their hope.

What lies behind this emerging national sense of frustration can be described as both a dimming of personal expectations and the fear of losing a shared vision for America.

On the personal level, the student, the parent, and the caring teacher all perceive that a basic promise is not being kept. More and more young people emerge from high school ready neither for college nor for work. This predicament becomes more acute as the knowledge base continues its rapid expansion, the number of traditional job shrinks, and new jobs demand greater sophistication and preparation.

On a broader scale, we sense that this undertone of frustration has significant political implications, for it cuts across ages, generations, races, and political and economic groups. We have come to understand that the public will demand that educational and political leaders act forcefully and effectively on these issues. Indeed, such demands have already appeared and could well become a unifying national preoccupation. This unity, however, can be achieved only if we avoid the unproductive tendency of some to search for scapegoats among the victims, such as the beleaguered teachers.

On the positive side is the significant movement by political and educational leaders to search for solutions—so far centering largely on the nearly desperate need for increased support for the teaching of mathematics and science. This movement is but a start on what we believe is a larger and more educationally encompassing need to improve teaching and learning in fields such as English, history, geography, economics, and foreign languages. We believe this movement must be broadened and directed toward reform and excellence throughout education.*

*The complete text of The Report is published in *The Chronicle of Higher Education*, May 4, 1983.

389

APPENDIX D

EDUCATION AND EXCELLENCE: THE TIME IS NOW

A SPEECH TO THE CITY CLUB OF CLEVELAND, APRIL 26, 1985

Edward H. Jennings, President, The Ohio State University

Good afternoon. I am pleased to be with you today and to have this opportunity to address what is perhaps the most important issue in higher education: how do we provide for society—and, in particular, for Ohio—the very best in higher education? That is the appropriate task of those of us who represent the nation's colleges and universities, and for those of us who, as citizens, recognize the immeasurable value of higher education.

The fundamental requirement for an environment of excellence in higher education is a recognition of what it is that defines the value of a university. All of us in this room can recognize value. We know that our human resources—creative, capable, decisive people—are society's most valuable asset, and that the development of those precious resources is fundamental to a university's mission.

And yet, in considering the value of higher education, the first aspect that often comes to mind is the practical, economic value. Higher education is indeed a major "industry" in America.

The annual outlay for higher education operations in 1984 was seventy billion dollars—a figure comparable to that of the automobile or communications industry. Half of America's basic research and scholarship is conducted at universities. Half of the nation's productivity growth has come from increases in individuals' skills and knowledge—which are generated in our colleges and universities.

It is time that we in Ohio begin to better understand the needs of our higher education resource base in the context of the major industry we represent, and as the magnet to attract even more economic growth that we could become.

But it also is important to remember that the value of education transcends its economic dimensions. We need to recognize that the fundamental benefits from supporting universities are not in keeping ahead of the international business competition; not in maintaining a strong defense; and not in preparing individual students for their first jobs.

Such reasons for support of universities are popular and valid ones. I have myself certainly been—and I still am—a major proponent of support for public higher education as a positive factor in economic progress for Ohio.

But these results, which are indeed important, still come about as by-products of higher education's fundamental reason for being. That is: the pursuit of knowledge and understanding; and, at the core of the enterprise, promoting excellence. The most significant value of higher education is not its apparent practical value, but its inherent value as a vehicle for teaching critical thinking, communication skills, and—perhaps most important for the future—adaptability.

As leaders of business, the members of this audience expect young people to learn as they progress in their careers. We expect them to improve with the seasoning born of experience—from applying specific knowledge, and by trial and error that draws upon a larger arena. Advancement comes from understanding and learning from these experiences. And education's greatest value lies in the intensive college experience of learning to learn.

A college degree must be returned to its proper place as a by-product—one that signifies achievement of a goal, but which is not, in itself, the goal being pursued. That is a fundamental distinction between a college education and a college degree.

The goal of a college education is not to become technically proficient, but rather to become well-educated; to gain a love of learning for its own sake and a capacity to analyze any issue as it comes along; to place issues in a larger context, and identify connections with other fields; to express one's thinking clearly, if not eloquently; and to develop the capacity and motivation to go beyond easy, short-term answers.

Education at the higher levels must have as its primary goal the instilling of critical judgment. And the way to create the capacity to make sound judgments is to show a person again and again what is first-rate—until anything inferior simply ceases to attract.

That is the challenge of quality that we must meet throughout the university—because our institutional example of quality is a vital part of the educational process, in and of itself. We must ensure that the pursuit of excellence clearly defines the context of all our decisions and recommit ourselves to the essential core of what a university education means.

Effective decision-makers must be able to evaluate and selectively weigh complex and often technical information, which requires specific knowledge. But they also must be able to place that information in a larger, long-term context. To quote an academic colleague, John Kemeny, the former president of Dartmouth College, "The last decision must always be a value judgment."

It is exposure to the liberal arts that provides the foundation upon which we base these value judgments and serves as the great preserver of human culture. It is one very important source of the global understanding that is increasingly vital for world trade, for the preservation and functioning of our democratic system of government, and for continued development in all societies. The liberal arts are indeed an eminently practical field of study.

A decline in our capacity to make value judgments and to analyze, innovate, create, and communicate, will condemn us all to a meager existence as it impoverishes our cultural and civic life, and will deny us the quality of life we have the capacity to create for tomorrow. In this context, the values at the heart of a university's traditional mission become even more important—not only in the liberal arts, but in the sciences and the professions as well.

In addition, a university environment for basic research and scholarship—the "ivory tower" that fosters thinking, experimenting, testing, and risk-taking without any immediate, discernible application—has provided the most significant discoveries upon which our lives and our society have progressed. It is important that universities continue to provide that environment through their traditional mission of nurturing creativity and the taking of visionary risks.

That, I believe, is the fundamental source of the dichotomy between the "ivory tower" of education and the "real world." In the "real world," the emphasis is on creating a positive return on investments within a short period of time. In a university, our focus is inherently a long-term one. Thus we have greater flexibility to invest time in taking chances so that the "real world" can benefit from our successes—and learn from our failures.

This "ivory tower," then, is not a term about which universities need to be defensive. It has provided an enormously positive force for progress throughout world history. Our society very much needs people with long-term vision to pursue and expand the frontiers of knowledge. These "impractical dreamers" are the very ones who initiated work on computing machines and electronic miniaturization just a few decades ago.

Our recognition of the intrinsic value of both university education and the broader academic environment is increasingly important in our rapidly changing society. Our future rests in large part on the access of young people to college and graduate education.

As John F. Kennedy once said, "This country reserves its highest honors for only one kind of aristocracy—that which the Founding Fathers called 'an aristocracy of achievement, arising out of a democracy of opportunity.' " I might add that our Founding Mothers would have agreed if, in those days, anyone had bothered to ask them.

In the early days of industrialization, Ohio had the human resources and the natural resources to become a leader of industrial progress. Today, human resources are by far the more important. The quality of human resources is directly tied to the quality and availability of higher education. We need to keep a clear focus on our key resource for the future—new ideas. And the only way to achieve that is to have an environment of quality in higher education.

Yet today, Ohio undervalues higher education and limits opportunities for its young people. Ohioans are far less likely than the average American to pursue a higher education. Ohio ranks low—thirty-ninth in the nation—in the number of high-school graduates continuing on to college.

That is a poor record indeed on which to present Ohio to the nation as a promising location for business. It means our human resources are not being developed to their fullest potential.

Part of the explanation for that poor showing is the traditionally high levels of tuition our public colleges and universities ask our students to pay. In 1983–84, Ohio had the third-highest average tuition levels in the nation per 100 dollars of state appropriations.

Statistics on a national level confirm the relationship between tuition costs and college-going rates. States spending more on public higher education attract proportionally more students into public higher education. Furthermore, initial studies have shown that unemployment rates are lower in states where higher education spending is greater. Ohio could do more to improve its national rank on both indicators.

We have advocated that the share of college costs paid by students through their tuition, be returned to the historic one-third level that marks the tradition of public higher education. But in Ohio, that share had climbed as high as 47 percent in 1982–83 and currently stands at 40 percent.

In the Executive and House Budgets for 1985–87, promising attention was paid to tuition levels. The governor has proposed, and the House has supported, a two-year program of increases to the Instructional Subsidy that would bring the students' share to 36 percent by the second year of the biennium.

This represents the first real increase in the Instructional Subsidy since 1979. I applaud the governor and the House for their actions. But I believe we can do more in Ohio, and we can do it sooner rather than later.

In my testimony in early March before the Education Subcommittee of the House Finance Committee, I noted that an additional investment over the Executive Budget recommendations of no more than 66 million dollars—just four-tenths of one percent of the state budget—added to the Instructional Subsidy would enable our public colleges and universities to hold tuition at current levels for the next two years and return the student share of costs to 34 percent. The last time a one-third share was seen by Ohio students and their parents was 1979–80.

Immediate action would substantially improve Ohio's national ranking. It would allow for a corresponding increase in the college-going rate. Most importantly, it would send a message to the nation that Ohio is serious about providing a well-educated workforce to meet the challenges of the 1990s and beyond. Given Ohio's historic record of poor support for higher education—which places us forty-seventh in the nation—it is incredible that our colleges and universities have done as well as they have. Despite continued underfunding, higher education in Ohio has built a solid foundation of academic quality upon which to base further progress.

The Ohio State University stands at the center of Ohio's academic excellence as the comprehensive, land-grant university for this state. Ohio State is nationally competitive in teaching, research, and related public service. We are proud of the impressive scope and breadth that we have achieved over our 100 years and more of academic tradition.

As is often the case, our reputation is far better known and respected in the national and international academic community than is commonly recognized here in our home state. I want to take a moment to mention just a few indicators of our excellence.

First, let me describe our student body. Its quality is far higher than our open admissions tradition leads the general public to believe.

Ohio State ranks fourth nationally among all public universities in the number of National Merit and Achievement Scholars on our campuses. Having 400 Merit Scholars means that we have one in every fifty of these academically gifted students. We have 2,500 students enrolled in our highly selective Honors Programs. That number is larger than the size of the entire freshman class at many universities.

Recently, three of our graduate students traveled to Tokyo to receive the world's top computer animation award, which they won in competition against established professionals. Others have collected the nation's highest individual student honors in agricultural economics, electrical engineering, horticulture, and dentistry during this academic year alone.

Second, let me briefly describe the academic programs in which these students enroll. Ohio State consistently has several programs ranked among the top five or ten in the nation. Agricultural economics, black studies, genetics, history, chemistry, several areas of engineering, education, foreign languages, and political science are just a few departments with reputations far beyond their recognition in the State of Ohio.

The Department of Dance at Ohio State, including our Bureau of Dance Notation, is widely acclaimed in the New York dance community as one of the best academic dance programs in the country. We also are

395

home to rare and enormously valuable library collections in areas as distinct as American fiction and medieval religious chronicles. In the sciences, Ohio State has national status as one of only a handful of federally designated Comprehensive Cancer Research Centers.

Third, our faculty—who are the heart and soul of our university—rank among the best. Our chemistry department recently provided one of the National Academy of Sciences' newest Fellows; the following year, that most prestigious body awarded its highest single honor to an Ohio State mathematics professor.

An Ohio State professor of veterinary medicine holds the patent on the new feline leukemia vaccine that became marketable this spring and, along with his colleagues throughout the institution, continues this pioneering work—with all its implications for human cancer research. Our Materials Research Laboratory is at the forefront of discovery in the physical sciences and attracts scholars from around the world to work with our eminent faculty members.

But the maintenance and expansion of these internationally renowned programs here in Ohio will not come cheaply—not at Ohio State, nor in any of the other centers of excellence in Ohio's public universities. The quality at Ohio State was achieved over the course of our history by talented and dedicated faculty members, despite poor levels of state support. We have reached a level of quality of which we can be proud, but which we hope will not become a plateau far lower than we have the potential to achieve.

Today, we stand at a crossroads in the great State of Ohio. With relatively modest investments at the state level, we are ideally positioned to make quantum leaps that will benefit the state immeasurably. The upcoming decision of the General Assembly will determine what path higher education will take and, correspondingly, what the future will hold for Ohio.

The choices are clear: continued levels of inadequate funding and the attendant consequences; or a new commitment to excellence in, and access to, higher education.

An impressive set of initiatives has been proposed for the State of Ohio under the concept of Selective Excellence. But because of the proposed tax cuts, the Board of Regents' Selective Excellence funding recommendations were reduced in both the Executive Budget and the House version.

We are still waiting to learn what will happen to these Excellence programs—and to our fundamental support through the Instructional Subsidy—in the Ohio Senate, where tax cuts totalling almost one billion dollars more than the House recommendations are proposed.

The Research and Technology Challenge is a crucial Selective Excellence program. It provides strong incentives through state matching dollars to encourage Ohio's universities to seek a larger share of competitive federal funding for research and scholarship. Relatively small investments will leverage substantial achievements in attracting new funding into Ohio and in expanding research activity throughout the state.

The 1 percent excellence supplements for each institution in the Academic Challenge Incentives target the selective nurturing of key quality centers across the state. The Productivity Improvement programs being fostered for the community and technical colleges are equally significant for creating a climate of opportunity.

Indeed, the combined strength of all these Selective Excellence initiatives—including the Eminent Scholars recruitment effort and the Program Excellence Awards for undergraduate teaching—represents Ohio's best opportunity for long-term success in building the finest possible statewide environment for higher education.

I have been told that what is being cut is only "new" programs, not higher education *per se*. That response only reinforces my point. Ohio's problems can in many aspects be traced to year after year of underfunding of public higher education. That is why these educational excellence funds are new. But the way to escape the problems of the past—and the present—is not by clinging to traditional patterns of spending. What is new, is exactly what is needed to ensure accessibility and excellence.

Much has been said in Ohio about the need to invest in a brighter future and the importance of higher education to that goal. Much has been said in Ohio about our commitment to excellence in our public colleges and universities, because we have recognized that many of the jobs of the future are for those who are educated, and that those jobs will be created as a result of the research now under way in universities.

General Motors has clearly stated that the location of the Saturn plant is dependent on proximity to a major university—meaning to a university-trained workforce and the opportunities for research and development that a university provides. And we have heard of the disillusionment recently expressed by Bobby Ray Inman.

Mr. Inman chose Texas for his Microelectronics and Computer Technology Corporation because of what he believed to be that state's unyielding commitment to higher education. Today, he is angered at recent proposals by the Texas legislature to cut university funding. He calls this at best unsettling and at worst disaster. For his high-technology firm, he considers no other factor more important than a quality higher-education environment.

We need to establish a reputation in Ohio for excellence in higher education. A clear opportunity to gain ground in comparison to other states is upon us in Ohio today. This year, we finally have an emphasis on excellence in the education budget proposals—a new direction which has the potential to fuel substantial progress.

The focus is on enhancing every institution's best research programs; matching non-state funds to increase our capacity to attract even more dollars; and targeting new monies for the two-year schools to respond to specific business training needs. We in the higher education community are being required to set priorities, and we are doing exactly that.

But I would call upon the members of the Ohio General Assembly to direct the same attention to priority-setting in the current tax cutting competition. In determining the size and the timing of the tax cut, our elected public officials need to seriously consider priorities as they affect the general welfare of the state—not only now, but for the long-term future.

There is no doubt that tax reductions can be made this year. But the level of the cuts needs to be considered in the context of the vital revenue needs of higher education. Ensuring adequate—and stable—funding of important programs should come first. Only then will it be appropriate to look at increasing the total size of the reductions in tax revenues that will be available to the state.

Historically, Ohio has been a relatively low tax state. And despite recent increases, Ohio still ranks near the bottom, at thirty-ninth among all the states in taxes as a percent of total income.

We certainly recognize that while Ohio is financially better-off today than it has been for some time, the overall budget remains tight. We know that our support can grow only within realistic limits. But it should be emphasized that the Selective Excellence areas represent the very programs that would allow higher education to seek out and draw into Ohio new funds from other sources.

I am concerned that the State of Ohio is about to throw away a watershed opportunity to engender excellence throughout its public higher education community. As an alternative, let me lay out a simple and realistic three-part budgetary agenda of support for higher education during the next biennium:

- One: Fund the Instructional Subsidy by sixty-six million dollars above the current recommendation. This investment would enhance accessibility and return the students' share of costs to one-third in the coming biennium.
- Two: Restore funding of the five Selective Excellence areas with an additional 25.7 million dollars for the biennium. This would provide full support for each aspect of the program at the level recommended in the Executive Budget.

The total cost for immediate action on both Steps One and Two would be 91.7 million dollars over the biennium, beyond the budget bill passed by the House. A total of less than 5 dollars per-person, per-year, would both restore funding to the Selective Excellence initiatives for higher education and allow our public colleges and universities to hold tuition costs at current levels for the next two years. Relatively small amounts of funding can leverage substantial leaps forward in expanding excellence and generating economic progress.

- Finally, Three: A budget adopted in a timely fashion. Unlike proposals One and Two, this action does not cost the state any money at all.

I have heard disturbing rumors about the possibility of an interim budget. I hear that the uncertainty of a temporary budget might be allowed to continue for as long as two, three, and even six months.

We have lived with interim budgets in the past, and that was understandable in difficult economic times. But there can be no excuse for an interim budget in relatively good economic times. Stability is a vital ingredient of our ability to capitalize on opportunities to enhance quality. An interim budget speaks of instability and uncertainty, and undermines the climate of renewal and optimism that Ohio has the chance to create.

During such times, it becomes impossible for a university to compete. We cannot make commitments to attract top faculty members or to enhance the best academic programs when we do not know what the budget will be. Our own commitment to progress at Ohio State loses credibility in the national recruitment arena when the state fails to back our pursuit of excellence with firm commitments of its own.

The House has completed its budget deliberations in a timely fashion. The Senate is currently hard at work at its own budget hearings. I trust that the rumors about an interim budget will prove to be no more than that—rumors.

I cannot emphasize too much what a critical era this is for higher education in Ohio. If we miss this opportunity to enhance excellence and expand accessibility, future generations will look back and say that 1985 was the year that Ohio chose the wrong path—the path toward mediocrity in higher education and short-sightedness in economic growth.

But if we choose the other path, future generations will look back on the leadership of the state and credit the wisdom and foresight that secured a future of hope, of quality, and of unlimited opportunity for the citizens of Ohio.

We must all work together as concerned citizens—as concerned Ohioans—to be a leader in the current economic transformation with the same energy and resolve that was shown by this state's leadership in the early part of this century. We owe it to ourselves and to future generations to make the decisions that will place higher education, and Ohio, on the proper path once and for all.

The decision is ours. And the time for that decision is today.*

---

*The speech is published in *OSU on Campus*, May 9, 1985.

APPENDIX E

INVOLVEMENT IN LEARNING: REALIZING THE POTENTIAL OF AMERICAN HIGHER EDUCATION

EXCERPTS FROM THE FINAL REPORT OF THE STUDY GROUP ON THE CONDITIONS OF EXCELLENCE IN AMERICAN HIGHER EDUCATION

The Study Group on the Conditions of Excellence in American Higher Education

ALEXANDER W. ASTIN, University of California, Los Angeles.
J. HERMAN BLAKE, Tougaloo College.
HOWARD R. BOWEN, Claremont Graduate School.
ZELDA F. GAMSON, University of Michigan.
HAROLD L. HODGKINSON, Institute for Educational Leadership.
BARBARA LEE, Rutgers University.
KENNETH P. MORTIMER, The Pennsylvania State University, *chairman.*

The strains of rapid expansion, followed by recent years of constricting resources and leveling enrollments, have taken their toll. The realities of student learning, curricular coherence, the quality of facilities, faculty morale, and academic standards no longer measure up to our expectations. These gaps between the ideal and the actual are serious warning signals. They point to both current and potential problems that must be recognized and addressed.

Student Achievement
- One out of eight highly able high school seniors does not choose to attend college.
- Only half of the students who start college with the intention of getting a bachelor's degree actually attain this goal.
- Student performance on 11 of 15 major Subject Area Tests of the Graduate Record Examinations declined between 1964 and 1982. The sharpest declines occurred in subjects requiring high verbal skills.

One cannot blame these trends entirely on the decline in the preparation of entering college students. Part of the problem is what happens to students *after* they matriculate in college. Knowledge about how to improve retention rates and overall student achievement is accessible, but evidently higher education is not using it fully.

One of the principal purposes of our recommendations is to suggest ways in which existing knowlege can be utilized to close the gap between expectations and performance implied by these trends.

Undergraduate Programs and Degrees
- Increasing numbers of undergraduates are majoring in narrow specialties. American colleges, community colleges, and universities now offer more than 1,100 different majors and programs, nearly half of them in occupational fields.
- The proportion of bachelor's degrees awarded in arts and sciences (as opposed to professional and vocational programs) fell from 49 percent in 1971 to 36 percent in 1982. The percentage of arts and sciences (or "general program") degrees awarded by community colleges (the degrees that are most likely to lead to transfer to four-year institutions) declined from 57 percent in 1970 to 37 percent in 1981, with a corresponding rise in occupational degrees.
- Students have abandoned some of the traditional arts and sciences fields in large numbers. Just since 1977, the proportion of entering freshmen intending to major in the physical sciences has declined by 13 percent; in the humanities by 17 percent; in the social sciences by 19 percent; and in the biological sciences by fully 21 percent.
- Accreditation standards for undergraduate professional programs often stand as barriers to the broad understanding we associate with liberal learning. For example, the guidelines of one professional accrediting association confine one-half to two-thirds of a student's baccalaureate program to courses in two areas. Another association prescribes approximately 70 percent of a student's total program and confines that percentage wholly to two subject areas. And according to the standards of yet another association, the bachelor's degree program should involve as much as 80 percent of a student's work in the professional field.

Specialization may be a virtue for some students. But as ever more narrow programs are created, they become isolated from each other, and many students end up with fragmented and limited knowledge. While depth of study in any area has great value, the guidelines laid down by many professional accrediting bodies distort students' expectations and close off their future options. The result is that the college curriculum has become excessively vocational in its orientation, and the bachelor's degree has lost its potential to foster the shared values and knowledge that bind us together as a society.

To a large extent, our recommendations seek to reverse the trends implied by these indicators and to restore liberal education to its central role in undergraduate education.

Faculty
- College and university faculty have lost approximately 20 percent of their purchasing power in the past decade. Furthermore, because of market forces, faculty members in some departments are paid so much more than those in other departments that collegiality has become strained.
- The proportion of faculty who teach part-time increased from 23 percent in 1966 to 41 percent in 1980. The higher the proportion of part-time faculty, the more difficult it becomes to maintain collegiality, to assure continuity in the instructional program, and to preserve coherence in the curriculum.
- The proportion of entering college freshmen intending to pursue careers as college professors dropped from 1.8 percent in 1966 to 0.2 percent in 1982. This 89 percent decline bodes ill for the future of higher education.

Faculty are the core of the academic work force, and their status, morale, collegiality and commitment to their institutions are critical to student learning. When we allow support for such a critical component of the enterprise to erode to the point at which the profession itself has become less attractive to our brightest students, we are compromising the future of higher learning in America. And many of our current faculty feel "stuck" in their careers. They have lost the traditional mobility and vision that motivated so many professors to strive for excellence in teaching and research. . . .

Requirements and Standards
- Fourteen out of 50 state university systems have recently raised their requirements and standards—but only for purposes of admission, not for purposes of graduation. Stiffening admission *requirements* in some areas, such as years of high school study in basic academic disciplines, may well have a beneficial influence on the preparation of entering college freshmen. But imposing higher admission *standards* in other areas—cutoff scores on standardized tests and grade point averages—is an inappropriate response to recommendations for more rigor in subject matter preparation.

403

- Most American colleges and universities award their degrees when students have accumulated a given number of credits distributed among liberal education courses, major requirements, and electives and have achieved a minimum grade point average. Credits are measures of time and performance, but they do not indicate the academic worth of course content. In too many instances, quality control in the assignment of credits to courses is problematic. For example, in some colleges students can earn the same number of credits for taking a course in family food management or automobile ownership as for taking a course in the history of the American city or neuropsychology.
- According to a 1978 survey of 208 colleges and universities that had engaged in institutional self-studies in preparation for accreditation visits, only one in three had either generated or examined data on student learning and growth; only 23 percent had examined students' knowlege in their major fields; and only 14 percent had looked at their students' mental development (e.g., their analytic, synthesizing, and problem-solving capacities). . . .*

*The complete text of the final report is published by the National Institute of Education. U.S. Department of Education. Washington, D.C. 20208. October 1984.

APPENDIX F

INTEGRITY IN THE COLLEGE CURRICULUM

EXCERPTS FROM THE TEXT OF THE REPORT OF THE PROJECT ON REDEFINING THE MEANING AND PURPOSE OF BACCALAUREATE DEGREES

Association of American Colleges Committee

Following are the members of the committee that guided the Association of American Colleges' Project on Redefining the Meaning and Purpose of Baccalaureate Degrees:

ARNOLD B. ARONS, professor emeritus of physics, University of Washington.

ERNEST L. BOYER, president, Carnegie Foundation for the Advancement of Teaching.

DAVID W. BRENEMAN, president, Kalamazoo College.

CARLETON B. CHAPMAN, chairman, department of the history of medicine, Albert Einstein College of Medicine, Yeshiva University.

MARTHA E. CHURCH, president, Hood College.

MARK H. CURTIS, president, Association of American Colleges, *chairman*.

ELIZABETH COLEMAN, professor of literature, New School for Social Research.

HAROLD L. ENARSON, senior adviser, Western Interstate Commission for Higher Education.

PAUL R. GROSS, president, Marine Biological Laboratory.

RICHARD KUHNS, professor of philosophy, Columbia University.

ARTHUR LEVINE, president, Bradford College.

THEODORE D. LOCKWOOD, director, Armand Hammer United World College of the American West.

ROBERT H. McCABE, president, Miami-Dade Community College.

CHARLES MUSCATINE, professor of English, University of California at Berkeley.

LEONARD REISER, professor of physical sciences, Dartmouth College.

GRESHAM RILEY, president, Colorado College.

FREDERICK RUDOLPH, professor emeritus of history, Williams College.

LINDA B. SALAMON, dean, college of arts and sciences, Washington University.

JONATHAN Z. SMITH, professor of humanities, University of Chicago.

The educational failures of the United States are emerging as a major concern of the 1980s. The abundance of reports diagnosing and prescribing for our schools and colleges, the urgency with which they are argued, the evidence that they summon, and the analyses that they offer are persuasive evidence that there is a profound crisis. Even though at first blush it may appear to be an exaggeration to say so, the recent critiques and analyses of American education are as vital to clarifying our condition as were the pamphlets of Tom Paine before the American Revolution and the speeches of Abraham Lincoln on the eve of the Civil War. When our committee was formed in 1982 we feared that our eventual report would be a voice crying in the wilderness. We now know that we have joined a chorus.

Our report addresses the crisis in American education as it is revealed in the decay in the college course of study and in the role of college faculties in creating and nurturing that decay. Although effective remedies will require the dedication and energies and talents of many cooperating individuals and institutions, our own experience as teachers and as students of American higher education leads to one inescapable conclusion: the college professors of the United States, whether they know it or not, have a job on their hands. They will need a great deal of help if they are to perform that job well. But, first, they and the American people must understand the nature of the problem and their shared responsibilities for meeting it. Because the decline of the undergraduate degree is at the heart of the problem, we must come to terms with that reality and develop some understanding of how we arrived where we are.

Evidence of decline and devaluation is everywhere. The business community complains of difficulty in recruiting literate college graduates. Remedial programs, designed to compensate for lack of skill in using the English language, abound in the colleges and in the corporate world. Writing as an undergraduate experience, as an exploration of both communication and style, is widely neglected. College grades have gone up and up, even as Scholastic Aptitude Tests and American College Testing scores have gone down and the pressures on teachers to ease their students' paths to graduate schools have increased. The modest gains in S.A.T. scores in the June 1984 tests suggest a leveling off, but hidden in the statistics are brutal social and economic facts: scores are up dramatically in affluent Connecticut, flat in troubled New Jersey, down in New York City. Foreign language incompetence is now not only a national embarrassment, but in a rapidly changing world it threatens to be an enfeebling disadvantage in the conduct of business and diplomacy. Scientific and technological developments have so outpaced the understanding of science provided by most college programs that we have become a people unable to comprehend the technology that we invent and unable to bring under control our capacity to violate the natural world. . . .

One consequence of the abandonment of structure by the colleges has been the abandonment of structure in the schools. The decline in requirements is contagious, and in the absence of system in national educational arrangements, articulation between secondary and higher education has been allowed to break down. The result is a loss of rigor both in the secondary and in the collegiate course of study. That loss of definition and rigor has encouraged the false notion that there is such a thing as effortless learning, a notion that finds expression in curricular practice and student behavior. As the colleges have lost a firm grasp on their goals and mission, so have the secondary schools.

Another consequence of the accelerating decline of the undergraduate degree is widespread contemporary skepticism about the quality of higher education. There is a public sense that standards are too low, that results are not what they used to be. Why have our colleges and universities turned loose on the elementary and secondary schools thousands of graduates unqualified to teach? Why have regional and specialized accrediting agencies been unsuccessful in arresting the debasement of baccalaureate education? Why have colleges and universities failed to develop systems for evaluating the effectiveness of courses and programs? Why are they so reluctant to employ rigorous examining procedures as their students progress toward their degrees? These are some of the questions that an uneasy public now addresses to those who bear the responsibility for the conduct of American higher education. The questions themselves are further evidence of the decline and devaluation that inspire them. . . .

Central to the troubles and to the solution are the professors, for the development that overwhelmed the old curriculum and changed the entire nature of higher education was the transformation of the professors from teachers concerned with the characters and minds of their students to professionals, scholars with Ph.D. degrees with an allegiance to academic disciplines stronger than their commitment to teaching or to the life of the institutions where they are employed. As appropriate as research is as the focus of energies and resources in the research university, the exclusive concern with research in the training of recipients of the Ph.D. degree—to the neglect of any concern with teaching or with any professional responsibility other than to scholarship—has encouraged college faculties to abandon the sense of corporate responsibility that characterized professors of the pre-professional era.

Adept at looking out for themselves—departmental staffing, student enrollments, courses reflecting narrow scholarly interests, attendance at professional meetings—professors unquestionably offer in their courses exquisite examples of specialized learning. But who looks after the shop? Who takes responsibility, not for the needs of the history or English or biology department, but for the curriculum as a whole? Who thinks about the course of study as it is experienced by students? Who reviews and justifies and rationalizes the academic program for which a college awards the coveted credential: a bachelor's degree?

Here the professors and administrators as well are found wanting. Research and specialization, which are what graduate schools are all about, are not all that undergraduate colleges are about. Responsible research and good teaching are compatible, as every college and university can demonstrate, but in the doctoral programs that have certified successive generations of college teachers the balance has been tipped toward research. That bias has entered the ethos of institutions by virtue of the way that professors have been trained and therefore evaluated. Academic leaders, presidents and deans alike, have on the whole failed to combat the dominance of that bias in the undergraduate college, acquiescing in the accumulation of faculty power residing in departments rather than returning faculties to a sense of commitment to the larger responsibilities of their institutions. While curricular incoherence has many causes, some of them all but intractable, the primary means for achieving coherence are bold administrative leaders and newly responsible professors. . . .

An effective curriculum committee should find itself challenging some of the fundamental assumptions and practices of the academy. It should concern itself with the quality of college and university teaching, on which, after all, the effectiveness of any curriculum depends. In doing so it would have to confront the distorted reward system that makes research a more important factor than teaching or even service on the curriculum committee. The value system of the best and brightest products of research universities puts little emphasis on good teaching, counseling of students, and working with secondary schools and secondary school teachers. While this value system is most evident in the research universities, it permeates all of our four-year institutions, imported as part of the baggage that goes with the Ph.D. degree. Research, not teaching, pays off in enhanced reputation, respect of peers beyond one's own campus, and access to funds. The language of the academy is revealing: professors speak of teaching *loads* and research *opportunities*, never the reverse. . . .

For all of the pervasiveness of the conventional reward system, there is deep disquiet within the academy. Many faculty give only grudging acquiescence to a system that puts the highest premium on research and publication. There is considerable discontent among the professors

408

themselves with the quality of teaching generally; most of them welcome signals of seriousness about teaching and are willing to acknowledge that something important was missing in their graduate school education. For while all of them were prepared to be professional economists or physicists or whatever, none was prepared for the profession of undergraduate teaching, for the ethical standards and levels of performance appropriate to the responsibility of being not only the professor of a subject but a college teacher.

The graduate school model, with its single-minded focus on the preparation for research, serves as the standard by which colleges and universities everywhere judge themselves. In the long run nothing less than the reconstruction of the training of college teachers and a revision of prevailing standards in the recruitment of faculty will liberate the curriculum and the professors themselves from a misguided overemphasis on research and a corresponding neglect of teaching. The enemy of good teaching is not research, but rather the spirit that says that this is the only worthy or legitimate task for faculty members. An emphasis on teaching, moreover, does not require the denigration of research. The finest teachers are often the best researchers. Imparting to students some sense of the wonders, complexities, ambiguities, and uncertainties that accompany the experience of learning and growing can and often should be intimately connected with the dissemination of new knowlege. But teaching comes first. This message must be forcefully delivered by academic leaders responsible for undergraduate education to the research universities that have awarded the Ph.D. degree to generation after generation of potential professors professionally unprepared to teach. . . .

One of the most remarkable and scandalous aspects of American higher education is the absence of traditions, practices, and methods of institutional and social accountability. The spirit of freedom and individual enterprise has supported non-accountability and underwritten a great deal of irresponsibility. . . .

Unfortunately for the development of a responsible profession of college teaching, the academic preparation of the typical faculty member is in a graduate program leading to the Ph.D. degree. The emphasis of the graduate school years is almost exclusively on the development of substantive knowledge and research skills. Any introduction to teaching comes only incidentally through service as a teaching assistant, with only occasional supervision by experienced senior faculty. During the long years of work toward the doctoral degree, the candidate is rarely, if ever, introduced to any of the ingredients that make up the art, the science, and the special responsibilities of teaching. Yet, the major career option for most holders of the Ph.D. degree is full-time teaching in a college or university.

The teaching assistantship is now a device for exploiting graduate students in order to relieve senior faculty from teaching undergraduates. The tradition in higher education is to award the degree and then turn the students loose to become teachers without training in teaching or, equally as ridiculous, to send the students off without degrees, with unfinished research and incomplete dissertations hanging over their heads while they wrestle with the responsibilities of learning how to teach. Only in higher education is it generally assumed that teachers need no preparation, no supervision, no introduction to teaching. Ironically, one of the reasons that universities have shirked their responsibilities to the schools and to their schools of education may be a refusal to take seriously the profession of teaching. If the professional preparation of doctors were as minimal as that of college teachers, the United States would have more funeral directors than lawyers. . . .

The Ph.D. degree is now awarded only on the basis of an evaluation of a candidate's research skills. If teaching in American higher education is to become more effective and responsible, the awarding of the Ph.D. degree should also mean that the candidate has been evaluated as a teacher and not found wanting, and that the formal experience leading to the degree has included appropriate instruction in the responsibilities of the profession.

Programs of assistance and supervision of apprentice teachers, begun in the graduate schools, must continue in the colleges and universities where they gain employment. Institutions of higher education must demonstrate their commitment to teaching at the outset of every new appointment by offering a program which systematically helps the new recruits to improve their teaching styles and their intellectual reach. . . .*

---

*The complete text of the report is published in *The Chronicle of Higher Education,* February 13, 1985.